The Mis
Genesis One

Other titles by Michael L Drake

God is our Rock
The Lord's Supper: A Baptist Perspective
The Covenant Matrix
A King's Bible
By Fear and Fallacy
Māori Culture in a Christian Worldview
The New Māori Myth

Christian Schooling:
The Child Moulders
State Children
The Unequal Yoke
Mathstart
The Wycliffe WORD Programme
In God's World
Schools Need Christ

In preparation:
The Promises God Remembers

The Misted World of Genesis One

by Michael L Drake

Published by

Wycliffe Scholastic

Auckland, New Zealand

The Misted World of Genesis One
Second Edition

Email: mldrake@gmail.com Website: www.michaelldrake.name

Published by Wycliffe Scholastic (An imprint of Wycliffe Christian Schools) 2017, 2020
15A Steeple Rise, Pakuranga, Auckland 2010, New Zealand

American spellings are retained in quotations without correction when supplied by the original. Otherwise genuine English spellings of English are used.

Notations are given as **Footnotes** in the print and pdf editions, and as hyperlinked **Endnotes** in the Kindle edition. References given and works cited – whether in print, in electronic form, or on websites – are not intended to be or imply an endorsement of those works, their content, or their authors.

Second Edition

The First Edition was published in a cumbersome A4 format. Apart from a small number of corrections, mostly typographical, differences in this edition primarily amount to resetting it for a more conventional book format, and revising the Scripture Index to make it more comprehensive. Both indices have also been recalibrating to match the new pagination.

ISBN 978-0-9951339-2-1

[Second Edition in PDF: ISBN 978-0-9951339-3-8]

Previous Editions:

ISBN 978-0-9941495-0-3 [Soft-cover A4]
ISBN 978-0-9941495-1-0 [Kindle e-book]
ISBN 978-0-9941495-2-7 [PDF]

CONTENTS

PART 2: A TRUE MESSAGE

Nothing
God only
God and
Nothing

Six days
Everything
God and
The universe

God unchanged
Nothing changed
to everything
Glorious

Creator

Preface

In July 2013 two distinguished biblical scholars visited Auckland and spoke on Genesis 1. Professor John H. Walton of Wheaton College, and Professor John "Jack" Collins from Covenant Theological Seminary came independently of each other, but in the same month. For as long as I can remember I had believed that Genesis 1 described an event: God's creation of everything out of nothing in six 24-hour days. I had read many volumes on Genesis, and not a few on evolution. I was familiar with the common critical and textual debate, but nothing had shifted my understanding of Genesis.

The visit by Walton and Collins offered an opportunity to examine Genesis 1 from new perspectives, so willing to be persuaded by good data and consistent exegesis, I resolved to consider carefully what they presented. They do not of course teach in isolation. Their work is representative of respected, contemporary, evangelical Old Testament scholarship characterised by an awareness of Ancient Near Eastern (ANE) literature and culture, consideration of genre and other language conventions, an outspoken profession of belief in the inspiration of the Bible by God, and conviction that harmony exists between contemporary scientific models of origins and Genesis 1. Accordingly, I not only listened to them in their Auckland lectures, but read their written works, viewed and listened to video and audio presentations by them in other forums, and read as much commentary on their works as I could manage.

The result has been a clarity I have never before known as to the meaning, message and significance of Genesis 1. I pray that everyone who reads *The Misted World of Genesis One* will enjoy the same assurance as to the reliability of Genesis 1, the same clarity as to how to read it and the rest of the Bible, the same integration of the creation account with the gospel, and the same fellowship with Christ that I have been brought to.

Old Words, New Meanings

Engaging with the work of Walton and Collins necessarily brought me to read other contemporary evangelical views on Genesis. These now compass a spectrum ranging from what is plainly conservative through to what was once considered liberal. Whatever remains of the traditional defining doctrines of an evangelical belief, the plenary inspiration of an infallible Bible that expresses timeless propositional truth in the plain words used is no longer one of them. I share G K Beale's confusion (or is it scepticism?): "I am unsure about what constitutes the definition of evangelical today. So many people of a variety of theological stripes, especially with respect to their stand on the nature of Scripture, take on the name."[1]

Many of those who now identify as "Evangelical" use an evangelical vocabulary to give expression to doctrine, practice and relationships that in previous generations could not have fitted within evangelicalism. Nor would their proponents then have wanted to be so identified! Contributions to this redefinition of evangelicalism have been made from numerous quarters: Modernism and Post-modernism, with their denial of absolutes and redefining of truth; contemporary biblical scholarship with its emphasis on ancient world-views as a shaping dynamic for Scripture; the scientism of the last two centuries with its claims to authority and its commitment to evolution; and a resurgence of sentimental Christian existentialism that displaces doctrine in favour of relationships.[2]

Today, "diverse and even contradictory streams weave in and out of each other under the name *evangelical.*"[3] While some want to reclaim a conservative monopoly on the term "evangelical," and others who appear to have little in common with the evangelicalism of history none-the-less want to be known as Evangelicals, it seems to me that "Evangelicalism" is now irrecoverably eclectic. As a brand it has passed its use-by-date. From a rather different perspective J P Holding appears to have come to the same conclusion: "'Evangelical' is a term I don't disclaim, but I don't give it to myself either. Part of the reason for this is that I'm not clear on what its parameters are."[4]

The "conversation", aiming to pursue a better understanding of the Scriptures, chips away (where it is not hacking away!) at entrenched foundational doctrines of the Bible, at best modifying long-understood meanings of these terms (leaving the impression that tradition has not been totally abandoned), and increasingly redefining them (to the extent that their new meanings are incompatible with tradition). Virtually nothing is untouched: the Bible's plenary inspiration, its verbal inspiration, its infallibility, its inerrancy, its perspicuity, its self-authentication, its sufficiency, its epistemological priority, its transcendence, and its conveying of truth.

The fraternal of scholars redefining evangelicalism find in the expanding knowledge of ancient cultures, languages and literature, tools to be employed in a search for understanding of God's Word as God's Word. Were it not for their view of God's Word as God's Word, many would look very much like the old liberals in disguise. As they question the accuracy and relevance of the biblical text as we have it, as they search for the meaning behind what the text appears to be saying, as they deny that events recorded in the Bible have the same historical accuracy we expect today of factual accounts, as they insist the Bible can only be fully understood in the light of extra-biblical data ministered through experts, and as they propel us to the world-view of myths and cultures clearly alien to the Bible's own witness, what

---

[1] G K Beale, *The Erosion of Inerrancy in Evangelicalism: Responding to New Challenges to Biblical Authority* Good News Publishers/Crossway, Wheaton 2008 p24 Kindle location 349.

[2] Doctrine and relationships need not be antithetical – indeed I would argue that they are inseparable. But I refer here to those who assert relationships can best be developed aside from doctrine.

[3] Michael Horton, "What Are We Celebrating?" in Matthew Barrett (ed) *Reformation Theology: A Systematic Summary* Crossway, Wheaton, 2017, p19

[4] J P Holding & Nick Peters *Defining Inerrancy: Affirming a Defensible Faith for a New Generation* Tekton, (Kindle) 2014, Kindle location 1138

distinguishes them from traditional liberals? The answer is their oft-repeated adherence to the Bible as God's infallible, inspired and trustworthy word. They may indeed they do redefine many of the traditional terms of biblical interpretation (including "infallible," "inspired," and "trustworthy"), but they nonetheless consistently aim to discern a real revelation from the God who speaks by an inspired written word. For them it is not "Has God spoken?", or "Does God speak?" by way of the Bible. For them the questions are the same as for their more conservative fellow Christians: "What has God spoken?", "How has he spoken?", and "How can we know what he is saying?" Yet they answer those questions with concepts of what the Bible is and how it got to be like it is that differ significantly from their conservative brethren.

For John Calvin – and I believe for us – the heart of the issue is the most basic thing that can be said about the Bible: "God is its author."[5] That means that it is reliable and sufficient in itself for understanding what God is saying. It is not subject to the illumination of other wisdom. Similarly, Martin Luther insisted on the perspicuity of the Scriptures, declaring that in them, "nothing whatsoever is left obscure or ambiguous, but all that is in the Scripture is through the Word brought forth into the clearest light and proclaimed to the whole world."[6]

Railing, as only he could, against those who insisted the Bible could not be understood without information from other sources, Luther declared

> The notion that in Scripture some things are recondite and all is not plain was spread by the godless Sophists... who have never yet cited a single item to prove their crazy view; nor can they. And Satan has used these unsubstantial spectres to scare men off reading the sacred text, and to destroy all sense of its value, so as to ensure that his own brand of poisonous philosophy reigns supreme in the church. I certainly grant that many passages in the Scriptures are obscure and hard to elucidate, but that is due, not to the exalted nature of their subject, but to our own linguistic and grammatical ignorance; and it does not in any way prevent our knowing all the contents of Scripture.[7]

Always Plain; Not Always *So* Plain

It has long been recognised that "All things in the Scriptures are not alike plain in themselves, nor alike clear unto all ... but the unlearned, in due use of the ordinary means, may attain unto a sufficient understanding of them."[8] That is, while the Scriptures are plain, not all parts are as plain as others. Some passages need to have the "ordinary means" applied with more labour than others. The meaning of these less plain passages however is not to be found in extra-biblical sources, but, as Calvin and Luther both insist with regard to all of Scripture, in dependence upon the Holy Spirit[9] as Scripture itself is read. By use of "ordinary means" with the help

---

[5] John Calvin *Institutes of the Christian Religion* first published 1536; translated by Henry Beveridge, James Clarke, London, 1962, p71

[6] Martin Luther *The Bondage of the Will* 1525 translated by Packer & Johnston, James Clarke, London, 1957, p74

[7] Luther *The Bondage of the Will*, p71

[8] *Westminster Confession of Faith* I/vii

[9] Calvin *Institutes* p71; Luther *The Bondage of the Will*, p73f

of the Spirit of God, the Bible is not only sufficient, but as it alone is God's Word, it alone explains the Bible.

Nevertheless, in the providence of God there is much today that can be known about God's Word and its world that was not known in earlier ages. So it will not do to reject new directions in biblical scholarship on the grounds that accepting new ideas will force an abandonment of traditional doctrine or confessional agreement. Confessions and traditions are invaluable aids to faith and practice – they are part of the church's heritage that alert us to many an error of commission or omission. Yet they are not Scripture, and if faithful, careful and consistent study of Scripture necessitates modification or even abandonment of tradition, the Bible must rule. After all, much of what Evangelicals hold dear was at one time a radical departure from what was then commonly held to be "good" tradition. While we should not lightly abandon expressions of Christian faith handed down to us by those who wrestled with issues of life and faith and passed them on to us in sacrificial service to Christ, nor should we hang on to them should it become clear the Bible teaches otherwise.

There can be no doubt that modern biblical scholarship, science, linguistics and Ancient Near-Eastern (ANE) studies have enhanced our understanding of God's creation, the history he is unfolding within it, and the context in which the Bible was written. It is commendable to study so as to correctly and unashamedly handle the word of truth.[10] It is also possible to be "always learning and never able to come to a knowledge of the truth."[11] It is not without relevance to the study of Genesis in which myth presently plays such a large part that Paul warned of the danger of devotion "to myths and endless genealogies ... [which] promote controversial speculations rather than advancing God's work—which is by faith."[12]

There undoubtedly is, and always will be, error taught in the name of faithful Christianity. It is not always the revelling deceivers who have insinuated themselves into the church[13] who are responsible for wrong teaching: it can be believers with the best of motives who teach well at times and propagate error at others. Nor is it just that teachers of error can be persuasive, for they can make no impact where people are not predisposed to listen: "the time will come when people will not put up with sound doctrine. Instead, to suit their own desires, they will gather around them a great number of teachers to say what their itching ears want to hear. They will turn their ears away from the truth and turn aside to myths."[14] The "conversation" scratches where there are ears that itch. Both those who teach myths and those willing to follow them are wrong and need correction.

Any of us can err in doctrine and practice – in fact it is no mere possibility but a reality. We can willingly follow error as quickly as we can teach it. Error can be embedded in tradition or novelty, but wherever it festers it needs to be lanced and excised, especially when it leads others astray. Paul confronted Peter as a brother and fellow apostle condemned for hypocrisy, who was subverting the faith of

[10] 2 Timothy 2:15
[11] 2 Timothy 3:7
[12] 1 Timothy 1:4
[13] 1 Peter 2:12-21
[14] 2 Timothy 4:3,4

others, albeit apparently without intent.[15] As J C Ryle pointed out, it is the Apostle who said we should be at peace and in harmony with one another,[16] who nonetheless by his example taught that we should "fear the loss of truth more than the loss of peace."[17]

The Christian commitment to truth as foundational to knowing and serving God inevitably results in differences of understanding and application that are expressed in everything from discussion to functional division. So long as we delight in the priesthood of all believers and the appeal to the individual's conscience – which are themselves foundational to biblical Christianity – we must accord fellow believers liberty to differ while we appeal to the conscience to submit to truth. Difference in understanding cannot be dismissed for the sake of unity, for biblical unity is built on a shared conviction as to what is true. Rather, the pursuit of truth is the building-block of real unity, and we cannot – we must not – be silent when error undermines faith.

Yet framing discussion of biblical truth exclusively in the context of error and correction is not always helpful. Difference discussed in a search for understanding and better practice – our own as well as others' – will not always have the clarity, abrasiveness or significance of confronting Peter's hypocrisy. Accordingly, while we might quote and critique the views and teachings of some whose service to Christ far exceeds our own, our aim need not necessarily be to correct or endorse any man or doctrine, but to seek, through challenge and elucidation, faithfulness and clarity in reading and applying God's word.

Increasing Clarity, Unchanging Message

This book's reflections on contemporary evangelical writing on Genesis is set against this backdrop. Expanded fields of learning have opened up new insights into the world of the Bible and its writing. Yet its meaning and message are unchanged. If we can see with more understanding the idolatrous cultures against which the Bible asserts its message, the message is unchanged even if it is seen in greater relief. If we have a greater understanding of the structure of the universe and the ways in which the components of creation function, the Bible's message is unchanged albeit that message is now illustrated in high-definition clarity. If we have learnt that a right understanding of the Bible brings about a richer relationship with others in the Church, we have learnt nothing but what the Bible has always taught, even if for a while it might have been seen less brightly.

John summarised his aim in writing his gospel with these words: "these [things] are written that you may believe that Jesus is the Messiah, the Son of God, and that by believing you may have life in his name."[18] This wonderfully expresses the concept of the Bible, the written word of God. It is a concept that I believe is the only hermeneutical framework doing justice to the Bible's own claims. The Bible

---

[15] Galatians 2:11-13
[16] Romans 12:16
[17] J C Ryle, *Knots Untied* National Protestant Church Union, London, 1900 (1885) p371
[18] John 20:31

is God's inerrant, inspired word written with words and writers he has chosen so that the words mean what they say and are meant to be understood in the framework of the Bible itself, not through some external filter. As has so often been said, "The Bible is its own best interpreter."

This understanding of the Bible and its interpretation is well expressed in the Chicago Statement on Biblical Inerrancy[19] and the Chicago Statement on Biblical Hermeneutics.[20] Article XIII of the statement on Inerrancy is particularly pertinent to this book: "We deny that it is proper to evaluate Scripture according to standards of truth and error that are alien to its usage or purpose."

For all the apparent clarity of those statements however, not all who subscribe to them interpret them the same way. In fact, some read the *Statements* in much the same way as they read the Bible, attributing meanings to them that do not always reflect the plain meaning of the words as they could be understood without filtering them through particular concepts of truth, historicity and communication. Kevin Vanhoozer, examining how the statement on *Hermeneutics* discusses the way literary form, truth and fact impact on interpretation, comments picturesquely but accurately: "While the [Hermeneutics] Statement does not actually make shipwreck of biblical interpretation, it does incline the good ship Hermeneutics to list rather dangerously ... to the extent that it risks imposing extra biblical categories and standards on biblical narratives."[21] Not all see that as a risk.

Some subscribers maintain that the inspiration and inerrancy of the Scriptures relate to both the words used and their underlying meaning, but that the words used do not convey to a modern reader the same meaning intended when they were first written. In such constructions, only the underlying meaning has relevance for any reader in a different cultural or historical place. In much the same way some subscribers to the *Chicago Statements* agree to their wording while at the same time locating what is called the superficial meaning in a cultural context that is no longer as relevant as the underlying meaning – whatever that might be.

John Walton is one who has emphatically aligned himself with this pattern of subscription. Some months after his New Zealand visit, a new book co-authored by Walton and D Brent Sandy was published. *The Lost World of Scripture; Ancient Literary Culture and Biblical Authority*[22] repeats affirmations Walton has made consistently that he subscribes to the *Chicago Statements*,[23] upholds the inspiration and authority of the Bible as the Word of God,[24] and affirms the inerrancy of the Bible.[25] At the same time however, Walton and Sandy are at pains to explain they

---

[19] http://www.alliancenet.org/partner/Article_Display_Page/0,,PTID307086_CHID750054_CIID2094584,00.html

[20] http://www.alliancenet.org/partner/Article_Display_Page/0,,PTID307086_CHID750054_CIID2095160,01.html

[21] Kevin J. Vanhoozer *Lost in Interpretation? Truth, Scripture and Hermeneutics* in the "Journal of the Evangelical Theological Society" (JETS), Louisville, 48/1 (March 2005) p99

[22] John H Walton and D Brent Sandy *The Lost World of Scripture: Ancient Literary Culture and Biblical Authority* IVP Academic, Downers Grove, 2013

[23] Walton & Sandy *The Lost World of Scripture* p13ff

[24] Walton & Sandy *The Lost World of Scripture* p7

[25] Walton & Sandy *The Lost World of Scripture* p12

are reacting "to the misappropriation of the term *inerrancy*"[26] with the intention of defining inerrancy "to the degree of precision intended by the author ... in the culture and communication developed by the time of its composition."[27] The re-appropriation of inerrancy is worked out by attributing an inspired superficial meaning to the text that would have been understood truly by the authors but not by modern readers who must find the meaning behind the text. It appears that the communication theory they are adopting also applies to the reading of the *Chicago Statements*. They go so far as to argue this applies to the apostolic reading and interpretation of the Old Testament. Their take on inerrancy[28] is that

1. it affirms that the Old Testament prophets were real people, that the text reliably represents what the prophet *and his followers*[29] said, and that through God's inspiration and not the prophet's imagination, the underlying meaning accurately represents God and his plan even if the words do not; and
2. that while what the apostles said cannot be falsified, when they identified fulfilment of Old Testament prophecies they were introducing new meaning unknown to the prophets, and that therefore apostolic commentary on or use of the Old Testament cannot inform our understanding of the Old Testament, and that the plain meaning of what is recorded by the apostles *and their co-authoring communities* cannot convey to us the underlying truth representing God and his plan contained in the OT texts alluded to.

Similarly, John Collins realigns the meaning of "inerrancy" from an inerrant text (which he does not hold to) to an inerrant referent in the text: "The notion of inerrancy, then, aims at explaining why we take a disposition of trust and cooperation when we look for the Bible to speak from God to us."[30] Inerrancy is to be found, argues Collins, in the message if not in the text.

My point here is not to offer an academic evaluation of this shadow-boxing with linguistics, communication theory and concepts of truth.[31] Rather, my point is to highlight the fact that their subscription to the *Chicago Statements*, and their affirmation of commitment to terms such as inspiration, inerrancy and infallibility are not constructed in what has hitherto been considered evangelical among evangelicals and non-evangelicals alike. Far from correcting what they claim is a

---

[26] Walton & Sandy *The Lost World of Scripture* p9 [italics theirs]

[27] Walton & Sandy The Lost World of Scripture p12 (they are quoting David S Dockery Christian Scripture: An Evangelical Perspective on Inspiration, Authority and interpretation B & H, Nashville, 1995, p64

[28] Walton & Sandy See *The Lost World of Scripture* p229 from which this summary is compiled

[29] At this point it is worth also noting they are committed to communal authorship in both Old and New Testaments, stating, for example that "we need a way to include all the authors" of most of Paul's letters. See *The Lost World of Scripture* p238

[30] John Collins "A Historical Adam: Old-Earth Creation View" in Barret & Caneday (eds) *Four Views on the Historical Adam* Zondervan, Grand Rapids, 2013, Kindle location 3046

[31] Albeit I believe they have departed so far from a truly biblical doctrine of the Scriptures that their position differs little in practice from the liberalism evangelicalism has long held to be heretical, even while they uphold other foundational doctrines of evangelicalism such as the divinity and substitutionary atonement of Christ. Statements like this: "They had particular illocutions associated with those locutions that resulted in perlocutions for their immediate audience." [*The Lost World of Scripture* p228] might obscure but cannot completely hide the basic point they are making, that the words of the Bible taken as plainly read cannot be relied upon to determine what God is saying to us.

misappropriation of such things, they are redefining them to mean the opposite of a conventional understanding. Just as we must not, according to them, take the words of the Bible as conveying meaning but instead look for underlying meaning, so it seems we must not take their use of the *Chicago Statement* and the conventional words of evangelical theology as conveying meaning according to the ordinary or plain use of those words, but instead must look for an underlying meaning, one that at times is even the opposite of the plain meaning.

With Words Intended to Have Meaning

It is appropriate therefore that I briefly expand on some of the issues addressed by the *Chicago Statements* that relate to this book. Let me add that it is my intention that the words I use convey the meaning I intend in an unequivocal congruence of superficial and underlying meaning. While explaining the context in which I write, this is not the place to argue in support of this confession; nor do I intend this to be a complete statement of the doctrine of the Bible. Nevertheless, I do want to underscore a number of key issues:

1. The Bible teaches that God is transcendent. He is beyond space and time and creation. Were he not to speak we could not only not know him; we could not know. Yet he has chosen to make himself known to us, his creatures, and to do so through the Bible. Even the knowledge of Jesus – the most perfect "word"[32] – he gives through the written word.
2. The Bible teaches that it has a unity arising from its sole Author, God himself. It is not a collection of disparate books by different authors, but a collection of books by one Author working through many writers. Thus the history, the events, the message and the meaning of each book are part of a unified account of the history, the events, the message and the meaning of the whole Bible.
3. The Bible teaches that the meaning God intended is the meaning given by the writer in the words used by the writer. While it is true that some texts also express a meaning hidden from the original writer,[33] such fuller meaning made clearer in the passage of time and new revelation is never in conflict with the meaning understood by the original writer. God's revelation of himself, of his work and providence, of humanity, and of salvation, is expressed in words and sentences that have intended, objective and discernible meaning. All that is sufficient and necessary to understand the Bible rightly is given in the Bible. Cultural context, for example, can be significant in understanding and applying the message in any particular passage, but such information about that cultural context as is needed is given in the Bible. It is the plain meaning, shaped by the various literary devices employed, and seen in the historical and cultural context that the text itself discloses, read in the setting of the whole of the Bible, that is the

---

[32] Hebrews 1:1-3
[33] Colossian 1:26

meaning God intends to convey to us. "God has something to say and he is very good at saying it."[34]

4. The Bible teaches that God is Sovereign, and that in his sovereignty he has given the language he has had men use in writing his Word; he has created with intention the various motifs, symbols and illustrations he uses; and he has nurtured those he called to be prophets so that they would be fitted to the task. When God asked Moses, "Who gave man his mouth?"[35] he was implying more than that God gives his words to prophets, but that the very thing of using language itself is his gift. God has not stumbled upon images, motifs, metaphors or language, much less upon prophets or cultural context, and seized upon them as the best option he can find through which to communicate. He chose to reveal himself in language he created and developed through prophets and writers he raised up and equipped in cultures of his choice.

True, God approaches us in the language of mortal humanity in the context of a limited creation – but he does so because he has chosen to do so, having made humanity, language and creation to fit the purpose of revealing himself. "Human language should be viewed as a gift of God rather than as a human achievement. God is the first to speak in what would later be considered human words."[36] "Human language is not something commandeered by God despite its weaknesses and unsuitability, but initiated by God as a means of fellowship that remains effectual even on this side of the fall and the Tower of Babel."[37] While it is true that God has adapted his communication to human language, it is also true – and surely a better way of putting it – that God has created and adapted humanity and human language to best suit his purpose in communicating with humans. "Human language is a divinely created means whereby God, from the very beginning, intended to make himself and his ways known."[38]

5. It follows that God is not limited by using humans and their language in communicating with us, but that God communicates with us with exquisite precision and clarity using the language and humans he has shaped to this very purpose. The "problem" of understanding revelation therefore is not in revelation but in our reception of it. There is no need or place for making accommodation for the limits of human writers (whom God has raised, equipped and superintended for this purpose) or conventions of language (which God has nurtured, adapted and transformed for this purpose). So while the reading of God's word requires thoughtful study and the recognition of the conventions, language and context of each passage, the starting point is a faithful submission to the Author and his word.

---

[34] Mark D Thompson, *A Clear and Present Word: The Clarity of Scripture* (New Studies in Biblical Theology 21) Apollos, Nottingham, 2006, p 170

[35] Exodus 4:11

[36] Thompson *A Clear and Present Word* p66

[37] Thompson *A Clear and Present Word* p76

[38] Kevin DeYoung, *Taking God At His Word: Why the Bible Is Knowable, Necessary, and Enough, and What That Means for You and Me* Crossway, Wheaton, 2014 Kindle location 790.

A Lurking Hermeneutical Framework

Lurking behind all this is the inevitable question of hermeneutical framework, in so far as "Hermeneutics explores the conditions and criteria that operate to try to ensure responsible, valid, fruitful, or appropriate interpretation."[39] It is beyond the scope of this book to plumb the depths of this topic. In the first instance I have endeavoured to examine, evaluate and build on the work of others within their own hermeneutical framework: the extent to which they are true to or inconsistent with their own approach has generally established the point being discussed. Nevertheless, I am as others: I do not write from within an hermeneutical vacuum. So let me very briefly push beyond inerrancy to hermeneutics:

1. The Bible is first and foremost God's self-revelation. It is God's word about God. It follows that whatever else it speaks about or to is derivative of that primary function.
2. The *Chicago Statement's* express commitment to an historical-grammatical hermeneutic is sound. That, however, neither excludes recognition of nor conjoint use of a theological hermeneutic. A biblically driven theology[40] is an orderly and dynamic expression of the Bible's teaching within which each passage is considered and to which each passage contributes. Thus interpretation of any passage should inevitably and necessarily be in a theological context, and contribute to the refining of that theology.
3. At the core of the Bible's message, unchanged from the foundation of the world, unfolding in ever clearer detail as book after book was added to the Bible, is the person and work of Jesus.[41] He is the Saviour, needed because of the fall and the fallen, foreshadowed in promise and sacrifice, confirmed in covenant and God's faithfulness throughout history, saving in incarnation and crucifixion, exalted in resurrection and ascension, coming in glory.
4. The primary meaning or message of any particular passage need not be expressly theologically comprehensive. Many Old Testament passages for example have long been understood as messianic or eschatological, and rightly so; but to make every passage overtly so is to distort the Bible. Richard Gaffin's linking of indicative and imperative moods as irreversible but inseparable[42] is extremely helpful. Accordingly, while faithful *application* of any text will be founded in Christ, express reference to Christ, or to any other biblical-theological theme, may be unnecessary or even improperly strained in faithful *interpretation* of many a particular passage.
5. God's plan of redemption – both as to its purpose and process – is unchanged from the beginning, but God has made it clearer as he has

---

[39] Anthony C Thistleton *Hermeneutics: An Introduction* Eerdmans, Cambridge 2009 p4

[40] I am deliberately not distinguishing here between biblical, systematic or historical theology, but taking theology as a whole with this one condition: it is a theology derived from and being shaped by the Bible.

[41] Luke 24:27

[42] Among numerous references: Richard Gaffin *By Faith, Not by Sight* Paternoster, Waynesboro, 2006 pp70ff

spoken to succeeding generations through the course of history.[43] As Scripture interprets Scripture, so later writings throw light on earlier ones, and in particular, the New Testament explains the Old, and is a trustworthy guide to the full meaning of the Old.

6. It should not be inferred on account of this that either the plain meaning of Old Testament passages should be discounted, or that the writers of the Old Testament misunderstood the message they delivered. The New Testament makes clear aspects of the Old not previously seen with such clarity, but it never extinguishes the meaning known with clarity to the original writers. Rather, even as they spoke and wrote, Old Testament prophets knew that what they pronounced also pointed to something greater they understood was there but could not always fully comprehend.[44] They knew they were writing for their immediate audience *and* to an audience in the future.[45] Thus on those occasions when under God's inspiration New Testament writers attribute a meaning to an Old Testament passage that may not be obvious by only reading that Old Testament passage in its original context, the New Testament reveals an aspect of the message that was originally there, was known to be there, but may not then have been fully grasped. That makes New Testament use of and commentary on the Old Testament definitive of the original text and the way in which the Old Testament should be read.
7. The Bible presents a message that is objective: it is true because it is God's declaration of what he knows and chooses to reveal irrespective of man's reception of it or commitment to it. Therefore, any hermeneutic that defines truth or the Bible's message on the basis of the reader's interaction with the text is invalid. As Romans 1 makes clear: when God speaks his message is clear and understood the way God intended; how his hearers/readers receive, respond to, or even pervert that message, does not change the meaning of the message.
8. The Bible insists that the words in which it is written are themselves timelessly unchangeable and the basis for conveying the meaning God intends. The meaning God intends is not an underlying meaning distanced from the words such that the words can be changed from community to community, age to age, without changing the meaning. When Jesus said, "not an iota, not a dot, will pass from the Law"[46] he meant that literally of the iota and the dot as well as metaphorically of even the smallest detail of the Bible. When John wrote, "I warn everyone who hears the words of the prophecy of this book: if anyone adds to them, God will add to him the plagues described in this book, and if anyone takes away from the words of the book of this prophecy, God will take away his share in the tree of life and in the holy city, which are described in this book,"[47] he was writing of the actual words and not merely of their underlying meaning.

---

[43] cf Matthew 13:17 and Hebrews 1:1-3

[44] 1 Peter 1:10-12

[45] 1 Peter 1:12

[46] Matthew 5:18

[47] Revelation 22:18,19

What They All Know

Romans 1 is so foundational for understanding the interface of paganism with God's self-revelation that I found I had to restrain myself from referring to it too frequently in what follows. Romans 1 makes clear that general revelation has made known to all men in all ages what they need to know about God. With particular application to this book, Romans 1 makes clear that "from the foundation of the world" – ie from the beginning recorded in Genesis 1 – all men have seen, understood, and suppressed the truth about God.[48] All idolatry, all pagan religions, and for that matter, all contemporary denial of creation and Creator, have therefore arisen from deliberate choice to suppress God's truth and "worship and serve the creation more than the Creator."

The Bible consciously contrasts its message with and critiques cultures ancient and modern that have perverted the truth. Such similarities as may be discerned between the Bible and ANE texts are not a result of the Bible imitating pagan myths and cosmologies, but are a result of those myths and cosmologies copying and perverting the truth known first as it is subsequently recorded in the Bible:

> In the nature of the case a true cosmology must be a divine revelation. The so-called 'cosmologies' of the various peoples of antiquity are in reality deformations of the originally revealed truth of creation. There is only one genuine cosmology, namely, Genesis one, and this account alone gives reliable information as to the origin of the earth.[49]

Even if ANE texts are older than the text of the Bible, Romans 1 tells us that general revelation ensured that the truth, as recorded in the Bible, was known by the ancient pagans before anything was written in any culture, pagan or biblical. It would be surprising therefore

> not to find some references to those truths in extra-biblical literature. And indeed in ancient Near Eastern myth we do see some kernels of historical truth. However, pagan authors vulgarized or bastardized those truths—they distorted fact by dressing it up with polytheism, magic, violence, and paganism. Fact became myth.[50]

There is no people or culture, ancient or modern, which has not been given by God his revelation of himself as their Creator. Anything that says otherwise has started with the truth of Genesis 1 and adapted it to the particular perversity prevailing in that place at that time. As with almost all perversions, shadows of the truth are retained for credibility such that there will be elements of the Genesis account here and there in ANE myths, fragments "that support rather than deny the historicity of the biblical story."[51]

In the study stimulated by the visit of Walton and Collins, I have not only come to see Genesis 1 in a fresh clarity, but I have also come to see with clarity that Genesis 1 *is* a defining battle in the contemporary war for the integrity, reliability and authority of the Bible. The approach adopted to the reading and interpretation

[48] Romans 1:18-25
[49] E J Young *Studies in Genesis 1* Presbyterian and Reformed, Nutlley (N.J.), 1957 p82 (footnote)
[50] John D Currid *Ancient Egypt and the Old Testament* Baker Books, Grand Rapids, 1997, p. 32
[51] ibid

of Genesis 1 is the default position for reading, interpreting and applying the rest of the Bible. So it is my prayer that those who read *The Misted World of Genesis One* will enjoy a confidence in, and commitment to, the Bible as God's infallible and definitive word given by him in the words he has chosen and imbued with lasting and clear meaning that can be gleaned from within the context of a complete, trustworthy and unified Book.

The Misted World of Genesis One has two quite distinct parts, which, while interlinked can be read separately.

Part 1: ***A True Text*** examines various theories of biblical interpretation that have become popular in post-evangelical biblical studies. These theories have become so influential that they influence Bible teaching across a wide range of respected colleges and churches. Post-evangelicals tend to express an outspoken commitment to traditional evangelical views of the inspiration and interpretation of the Bible, and to seeking the best understanding of that text as God's word. However, they largely reinterpret Genesis in terms of ancient cultures, ancient literature, or ancient myths. The outcome often fits (not always intentionally) evolutionary and scientific constructs. Imagery is also drawn from later biblical text to develop innovative interpretations of Genesis 1. Invariably post-evangelical interpretations tend to set aside the apparent meaning of the biblical text as it is presented, claiming instead to expose some meaning behind the text. Part 1 will appeal particularly to those who have a knowledge of these trends or who want reassurance on how such approaches inform or intrude upon a faithful reading of Genesis 1, but it will also inform readers new to the discussion about influential trends in contemporary Bible teaching that are not always obvious, but are nevertheless influential in churches.

Part 2: ***A True Message*** explains Genesis 1 as it is presented in the biblical text. Originally, I had planned to end *The Misted World of Genesis 1* with chapter 7, but after immersing myself in the clear account of God's glorious creation week that Genesis 1 provides, I did not want to leave readers with nothing but discussion of the largely misleading and misguided distortions of Genesis. It seemed good then to turn to the first chapter of God's word and explore and explain its wonderful words and message. While Part 2 is not without technical discussion (resting as it does on Part 1 for most of the discussion about textual issues), it is primarily expositional and devotional. Those wanting to understand and apply Genesis 1 without plumbing the depths of theological controversy should be able to go straight to Part 2 without reading Part 1.

I am aware that rather than reading the entire book, many might want to turn to it to consider particular issues, answer questions or gain an understanding of part of the biblical text. With that in view, I have endeavoured to ensure each chapter can be read in isolation. That means there will be some repetition of some points in different chapters, but my hope is that this is more help than distraction.

The first edition of this book first went to print as we approached the 500th anniversary of the Reformation. Luther's aim is as suited to Bible reading today as it was when he first wrote that he wanted "Scripture alone to reign, and not to interpret it by my own spirit or the spirit of any man, but I want to understand it by itself and its spirit."[52] In the same way, Philipp Melanchthon's words are as suited to today as they were when first written:

> The merciful Spirit of God has designed that Scripture be understood by all of the faithful with as little difficulty as possible. I beg you, let us not permit divine Scripture to become Egyptian hieroglyphs. The Son of God took upon himself flesh in order that he might not be unknown. And how much more has he willed to be known through the Scriptures which, as a sort of image of himself, he has left to us for a perpetual possession![53]

My aim is that every reader will find here grounds for trusting the text of Genesis 1, and encouragement to engage in faithful Bible reading that results in understanding what is designed by God to be understood by itself and its spirit without difficulty. If what I have written can engender refreshing delight in what God has given us as the first chapter of the Bible (which is the defining foundation for faith), I shall have been blessed.

My thanks go to God who has blessed me so much with an ever richer experience of Christ and delight in his Word and works as I have engaged in researching and writing this book. I pray that it will in some small way return praise and glory to him (Colossians 1:15-18).

While no one else need be called on to justify or explain what is written here (it is my responsibility alone), my thanks go to the many friends and colleagues who have made suggestions and criticism as this book has grown through its first edition and in this revision. Your advice has been consistently encouraging, enlightening and constructive and has contributed significantly through numerous stages of writing. I cannot express too emphatically how much I have appreciated your help, but it seems imprudent to name you in a book you are not responsible for. You know who you are and I hope you know how much I value your fellowship in Christ.

One, however, deserves mention: my special thanks to the ever gracious, patient, loving, clever, gentle, wise, godly and faithful Priscilla Drake, my companion, my helper, and my co-worker in the service of Christ – a gift of God beyond price (Proverbs 31:10-12). This is as true now, if not more so, than when the First Edition was published in 2017.

No substantial changes have been made to the text between the First and Second editions. This Second Edition has been published in a more convenient standard book size (replacing the original A4 edition). While the pagination has changed significantly, the few minor changes made to the text (apart from an additional footnote on page 218) have been mainly typographical or related to managing the changed page layouts. In addition, the Scripture Index has been revised to make it more comprehensive.

Michael L Drake
October 2020

---

[51] quoted by Mark Thompson "Sola Scriptura" p162

[52] Martin Luther, *Assertio omnium articulorum M. Lutheri per bullam Leonis X. novissimam damnatorum* (1520), WA 7:98.40–99.2. quoted by Mark Thompson "Sola Scriptura" in Matthew Barrett (ed) *Reformation Theology*, p154

[53] Philipp Melanchthon, *Epistolas ad Hessum*, *CR* 1:141; *Melanchthon: Selected Writings*,

Introduction: The Misted World of Genesis One

Reading the Bible in Wisdom or Foolishness

"These men ask me to believe they can read between the lines of the old texts; the evidence is their obvious inability to read (in any sense worth discussing) the lines themselves. They claim to see fern-seed and can't see an elephant ten yards away in broad daylight."

~ C S Lewis[54]

Genesis 1 is among the clearest, most comprehensible passages in the entire Bible.

Taken at face value its story-line, its vocabulary, its meaning, are all crystal clear. A child can understand it and comprehend its main message. Not so the wise. Too often they wrap Genesis 1 in mists of so-called wisdom and scholarship that obscure the text and deceive themselves and multitudes of others into thinking that what is plain is not plain.

---

[54] C S Lewis *Fern-seeds and Elephants* 1998 ["Modern Theology and Biblical Criticism," essay read at Westcott House, Cambridge, 11 May 1959 and published under that title in *Christian Reflections* 1981] http://orthodox-web.tripod.com/papers/fern_seed.html

As a result, many readers of Genesis 1 are induced into looking at it as if it is enveloped in spectral mists of clever ambiguity, effluvium of cunningly contorted meaning, and nearly impenetrable miasma of intellectually stunning mystery. Fog-bound readers are told they cannot read without suspending plain understanding and cloning their minds to patterns of interpretation propagated by a priestly caste of mist-guides – commentators and specialists who claim to know better; claim to have textual, cultural or linguistic keys to mysteries they have often manufactured in the first place; and claim to explain why God used a straight-forward text to mean what it does not say. Claiming to be wise, they have exchanged the glory of the Creator for the foolishness of man.[55]

Readers of Genesis are not helped by the fact that the Genesis mists are so pervasive, the dank wafting wisps of doubt and deceit so intrusive, that many good and godly believers, breathing in it too deeply and too long, have themselves become children of the mist. As the breath of men stepping out of a bright room into a cold night forms a vapour to match the mists of the darkness, so these otherwise reliable teachers and writers address Genesis 1 with a roiling vapour of ambiguity and hidden truths from which some, at least, loudly and consciously resile when reading the rest of the Bible.

Various "explanations" of Genesis 1 have drifted in and out of consideration over the centuries, each mist of confusion replacing or merging with the last. Few hang around for long, as the inadequacies of novelty, the inconsistencies of shallow scholarship, or the discovery of new data puff them away. But almost all have one thing in common: an attempt to read Genesis 1 in the murky vapours of the prevailing wisdom of the age, whether that wisdom takes the form of religion, philosophy, science or custom.

Our age is no different: a plain reading of Genesis 1 cannot be conformed to the presently dominant godless evolutionary science, nor to the rapidly emerging[56] pantheistic spiritualism. Yet those who would not for a moment countenance any attempt to conform the virgin birth or the resurrection of Jesus to science or spiritualism appear so mesmerised by the spirit of the age that they attempt exactly that with Genesis 1.

Sadly, staggeringly, what is said of unbelievers who wickedly suppress the truth has become true of believers:

> What may be known about God is plain to them, because God has made it plain to them. For since the creation of the world God's invisible qualities—his eternal power and divine nature—have been clearly seen, being understood from what has been made, so that people are without excuse. Although they claimed to be wise, they became fools and exchanged the glory of the immortal God...[57]

The solution is just as clear, and failure to avail oneself of it just as culpable:

> If any of you think you are wise by the standards of this age, you should become "fools" so that you may become wise. For the wisdom of this world is foolishness

---

[55] cf Romans 1:18 ff

[56] ... and soon to be dominant in a post-scientific era?

[57] Romans 1:18 ff

in God's sight. As it is written: "He catches the wise in their craftiness"; and again, "The Lord knows that the thoughts of the wise are futile."[58]

To Bind Reason or Faith?

This really is the heart of the issue. "Romans 1 is adamant that sinful man suppresses and distorts the revelation of the creation. Any view of the creation that commands a consensus amongst unbelievers must be suspect."[59] This particularly applies to evolutionary science which excludes consideration of any supernatural power engaging with the cosmos in ways contrary to observed nature. "It is true that the heavens declare the glory of God, but the eyes of man's understanding, blinded by sin, do not read the heavens aright... Fallen man must read general revelation in the light of Scripture, else he will go basically astray."[60]

Respected evangelical scholar John Walton, whose reading of Genesis 1 will be explored in detail later, states that he is "willing to bind reason if our faith calls for belief where reason fails."[61] Whatever the intent, the effect of such a statement is to assert that the Bible can only control reason where reason is found faulty. It makes reason, not the Bible, the ultimate authority on truth. There is of course faulty "faith." Faith in reason is one such faulty faith. Christian faith – the faith Walton and evangelicals profess to adhere to – is biblical faith. That is, it is founded in a submission to the Bible as God's infallible, inerrant, authoritative and reliable word.

Biblical faith does not take over where reason fails, but forms the framework by which reason is nurtured and tested. Biblical faith makes all reason subservient, so that reason is shaped by faith, evaluated by faith, confirmed or rejected by faith. The starting point for all thinking is that God is, and that all truth and the only truth is his truth. Reason, properly used, is the attempt, empowered by God's providence, to see and know as God sees and knows. To exclude God, and to exclude faith in God, from the starting point of reason or from the process of reason is to fail in both faith and reason. By definition, reason without biblical faith is not only faulty, it is foolish: "The fool says in his heart, 'There is no God.' They are corrupt, their deeds are vile."[62]

One of the problems in allowing for faith where reason fails is that it hinges on a wrong differentiation between faith and reason. Biblical faith is not a trust in something unreasonable or mystical in contrast to logical reason. Biblical faith is a trust in the Bible as the word of God which can be understood reasonably and reasonably relied upon to interpret experience with consistency that unifies the seen and the unseen worlds. Reason without the Bible is founded in a faith that man without God can work out what is true. It is not that one has faith and the other does not: both are founded in faith. The difference is that a biblical faith trusts the Bible as God's word to be the interpreter of observation and experience which is unified in reasoned dependence upon what the Bible says as absolute truth. Reason without

---

[58] 1 Corinthians 3:18-20
[59] Noel Weeks *The Hermeneutical Problem of Genesis 1-11* in Themelios 4.1 (September 1978) p14
[60] Young *Studies in Genesis 1* pp 53f
[61] John Walton *The Lost World of Genesis One: Ancient Cosmology and the Origins Debate* Inter Varsity Press, Downers Grove, 2009, Kindle location 1600
[62] Psalm 14:1

faith in the Bible trusts reason to be the interpreter of observation and experience which is unified in reasoned dependence upon what reasons says is absolute truth. Biblical faith is not a leap without reason but a reasoned trust in God's word, a trust that when God speaks he is more reliable than we are.

Determining truth by reason without submission to the Scriptures unless reason "fails" is fundamentally flawed, for in such an approach it is reason that determines whether or not reason has failed. If reason is satisfied, even when it conflicts with Scripture, reason rules. It should not be so! The test of reason is the degree to which it agrees with Scripture.

Reason to which biblical faith is subservient denies the supreme authority of Scripture and dethrones God. The Bible is true, not only when reason conforms to the Bible, but also when the Bible and reason are in conflict. The Bible is the truth that must shape reason, and reason is only true when it is shaped by the Bible. "Let God be true, and every man a liar."[63]

Rationalism, Empiricism & Faith

There is an almost unquenchable false optimism with which contemporary culture surrenders to reason and experience (that is, rationalism and empiricism). It is an optimism that invariable minimises faith and often enough scoffs at it, yet it is an optimism that has neither a rational nor empirical foundation. Rationalism and empiricism too are beliefs. What is the gateway to truth? Jason Helopoulos rightly asserts that it is God's revelation:

> Rationalism, not Christianity, believes that reason is *the fundamental* source for knowing and explaining the world. Descartes, the celebrated rationalist philosopher, famously said, "I think, therefore I am." Empiricism is not so different. It stresses experience in the quest for certainty in knowledge. John Lock, the famous empiricist, said, "I experience in order to believe." Both rationalism and empiricism have an overbearing optimism when it comes to reason. The only issue is whether reason is more important than experience or secondary to it. This runaway optimism in reason has no place for revelation. As Christians, we assert that revelation has the primary and principle place.
>
> We do not dismiss reason or experience, but clearly articulate that they are not the gateway to truth. Christianity says, "I believe so that I may understand." Thomas Watson, that ever quotable Puritan, once said, "Where reason can only wade, faith swims." We are a people who have accepted revelation. We believe that God has spoken (John 1) and that what He has spoken is true (Hebrews 6:18). This is our foundation for true and certain knowledge. And this revelation is only accepted by faith, which we only obtain as a gift from God (Eph. 2:20).[64]

Putting it simply, where a plain reading of the Bible, interpreted in its own context and language, is in conflict with anything observed in creation, formulated in philosophy, or embedded in culture, the Bible must be seen as giving the true picture. The infallible biblical text should be used to reshape interpretation of the data compiled by fallible, sinful mankind, not the other way round. More will be

---

[63] Romans 3:4

[64] Jason Helopoulos, http://thegospelcoalition.org/blogs/kevindeyoung/2014/07/31/evangelism-reason-faith/

said in this book about how to read the Bible, how to determine exactly what a text is saying, and how to evaluate the vocabulary and language used in Genesis 1. But it also has to be said here and now that Christians need never be embarrassed by commitment to the miraculous that does not conform to contemporary cosmology, or by reason shaped by the Bible rather than by rejection of God. More of that later too, but for the moment consider this:

> Hear me, you who know what is right, you people who have taken my instruction to heart: Do not fear the reproach of mere mortals or be terrified by their insults. For the moth will eat them up like a garment; the worm will devour them like wool. But my righteousness will last forever, my salvation through all generations.[65]

Embracing Conversations

At the heart of this is what is often called a "conversation" as to the nature of truth, of the Bible, and of the meaning of conventional evangelical vocabulary. "Conversation" and its twin, "dialogue," are code words commonly used to promote heightened corporate spiritual experience that bypasses objective truth. Proponents promote "embracing" others irrespective of beliefs. Yet at the same time they marginalise rather than embrace (and often denigrate) those who are committed to the idea of absolute truth, who engage in discussion to find better expression of truth, and hope on the basis of truth to better know God and promote the better knowledge of God.

By way of example of the equivocal inclusiveness of this conversation, consider this report on divisions in English evangelical Anglicanism:

> Under the guise of reading Scripture more closely or refusing to be bound by traditions of the past, new 'positions' become a rod with which to beat those maintaining the old. The arguments quickly descend from differences of doctrine to the *ad hominem*, where the person holding the doctrine is treated as inferior in ability or imagination ... and in such an atmosphere, godly dialogue becomes impossible.[66]

The various approaches I discuss in this book to revising the way Genesis is read are shifting the source of authority for Christians. Almost every approach requires submission to an expert, instruction in mysteries hidden from a plain reading of the text, or some form of heightened corporate experience. The effect is to shift the source of authority from the Bible read by ordinary people with ordinary skills guided by the Holy Spirit, to the one place where experts, instruction, and corporate experience can all be found: the church.

Unremittingly, albeit probably unwittingly, this revisionism is stripping away from the church one of the Reformation's most valuable gifts: the Bible for every Christian. In its place Christians are being urged to submit to formulae and techniques of teachers inducted into the mysteries of the new Bible-reading; into a sense of the nearness of God supposedly found in community existentialism; and/or into the wisdom of the new priesthood of biblical scholars.

---

[65] Isaiah 51:7,8

[66] John Richardson, "Anglican Update" in *Evangelicals Now* November 2013, vol 26 #10 p5

Constant reference to "scholars" litters writing intended for popular reading, as if reference to "scholars" is sufficient reason for submission to a particular proposition. For example, Peter Enns, although often critical of earlier scholars, and contemporary conservative ones, nevertheless makes frequent appeal to modern scholars who share his perspective with expressions such as "scholars generally" and "it is recognised by scholars" as evidence for his position. Typical is this statement: "Biblical scholars understand the *raqia* to be a solid dome-like structure."[67] There are certainly some biblical scholars who hold this view, but there are many who do not. When, a few lines later, Enns says, "Biblical scholars agree on this understanding of *raqia*" he is being plainly equivocal. His assertion is simply untrue. More to the point, the evidence for this view is dubious, and there is a significant body of evidence for the contrary view.[68] Whether or not "x" means "y" should not be determined by the fact that some experts agree, but by the evidence used or ignored by those experts.

Consider too John Collins' retreat from the perspicuity of the Bible. He contends that "The trick is to discern just how to follow the implications properly. Such discernment is a skill, which is developed through instruction, experience, and correction (that is, through discipleship)."[69] Certainly, the more we read the Bible, and the more carefully we attend to what we are reading, the better we get at understanding it. Yet the idea that there is some special "trick" that can be employed by the crafty, some secret of the conjurer's art that can be practised by the true initiates, some key that can be employed by those who have sufficient discipline to have attained the status of true discipleship, is wrong. It is also dangerous.

The priesthood of all believers and the freedom of every Christian to answer to his own conscience enlightened by the Holy Spirit through a plain reading of the Bible, is being superseded by a return to pre-reformation Church authority over biblical interpretation, and to mysticism in place of Christian experience rooted in biblical truth. Luther's, "Here I stand" has become our, "There we stood."

Where Are the Wise?

In all this there is neither need nor basis for bitterness toward those believers who, trusting in Christ as Saviour and committed to the Bible as God's infallible and inerrant word, read Genesis 1 differently. For all that can be justly said about compromises arising from a desire to minimise conflict between world-views of Bible believers and sceptics, or the intransigence of sectors of the church who despise sensible and thoughtful biblical scholarship, there is no place for attributing any believer's reading of Genesis 1 to any unstated motive apart from a desire to be faithful and careful in reading God's word.[70] Andrew Steinmann's comment sums

---

[67] Peter Enns The Firmament of Genesis 1 is Solid but That's Not the Point Biologos 2010 http://biologos.org/blog/the-firmament-of-genesis-1-is-solid-but-thats-not-the-point

[68] See below p116 "Error! Reference source not found."

[69] Collins Types of Language and Biblical Interpretation 2012 p11

[70] That is not to say, however, that where unsound motives are transparently expressed or inescapably evident, they should not be challenged. It is one thing to examine stated motives; it is another altogether

up the approach of many: "These Evangelical scholars are not seeking to be unfaithful to the Scriptures. They are seeking instead to reconcile Scriptures to the current *Zeitgeist* [intellectual framework of the age] in what they perceive to be a faithful way."[71] As Steinmann goes on to correctly assert, however, "The motivation to accommodate the world often pulls them in directions that leave the Scriptural message distorted in order to make it palatable to broad secular currents in society."

Attempting to reconcile the Scriptures to any age is in error for each age must be reconciled to the Bible; yet such error can arise from well-meaning, albeit mistaken, intention. It does not take much reflection to realise that each believer is not yet perfect, and that the various blind-spots we have, are in some ways like any insights we have. The blind-spots are ours, and the insights are the results of God's sovereignty and grace, so we can boast of neither. Nor can we belittle others on account of differences that depend solely on God's grace and have nothing to do with our supposed wisdom or their imputed dullness.

If we have an insight or strength, it is for the benefit of the body of Christ; and the blind-spots and weaknesses we have (no "if" here!) are compensated for by other believers. Every believer is part of the body of Christ, made up of people like us who have, by God's grace, gifts to share and needs to be met as in one body we serve God. Truth, truly held, need never be abandoned for the sake of a false, sentimental love; but the sacrificial love for other believers that the Bible calls us to will ensure that the truth we hold will be held for the good of the body and the building up of others, not to satisfy our selfishness, pride, or sectarian cause.

And Genesis 1?

> Where is the wise person? Where is the teacher of the law? Where is the philosopher of this age? Has not God made foolish the wisdom of the world? For since in the wisdom of God the world through its wisdom did not know him, God was pleased through the foolishness of what was preached to save those who believe. Jews demand signs and Greeks look for wisdom, but we preach Christ crucified: a stumbling block to Jews and foolishness to Gentiles, but to those whom God has called, both Jews and Greeks, Christ the power of God and the wisdom of God. For the foolishness of God is wiser than human wisdom, and the weakness of God is stronger than human strength.[72]

---

to attribute unstated motives without reasonable cause solely on the basis that what is said "must" imply a particular motive.

[71] Andrew Steinmann, *Lost World of Genesis One: John H. Walton, American Evangelicals and Creation* http://lej.cuchicago.edu/book-reviews/lost-world-of-genesis-one-john-h-walton-american-evangelicals-and-creation/ 2012

[72] 1 Corinthians 1:20-25

The Misted World of Genesis One

Part 1:
A TRUE TEXT
Post-Evangelical Reinterpretations of Genesis 1

"All Scripture is God-breathed and is useful for teaching, rebuking, correcting and training in righteousness, so that the servant of God may be thoroughly equipped for every good work."

~ 2 Timothy 3:16,17

1. Genesis Confused

The Genesis Mists: Reading Genesis 1 in the mist of controversy

"In the beginning, God created the heavens and the earth."

~ Genesis 1:1

The Bible, God's Word, opens with the dramatic creation of the universe in six days. It is an exquisite passage of literature, stunning in its simplicity, mind-bending in its profundity. Written within the unique conventions of ancient Hebrew culture and language shaped by faith revealed and energised by God, this rapidly unfolding story is nonetheless presented within a carefully crafted structure that is ageless. It pictures a diverse yet intimately unified creation vibrantly exhibiting the glory and power of the Creator, and it has one over-arching message: the cosmos is God's.

Despite the clarity of the over-all message however, confusion has dogged the reading of Genesis 1. In the first place there have always been unbelievers. There have always been those who deny that the Bible is the infallible, inspired word of God; those who dispute the imminence of God in creation and providence; those who discard the creation account as myths of an ancient, unsophisticated people. They are wrong. They are not only wrong because of the way they read the Bible and interpret the evidence of creation, and not only because of the erroneous conclusions they come to, but because their starting point of rejecting God makes how they read, the way they view things, and the conclusions they reach inevitably God-rejecting. As E J Young has put it,

> It is perfectly true that if we begin with the assumption that God exists and that the Bible is His Word, we shall wish to be guided in all our study by what the Scripture

> says. It is equally true that if we reject this foundational presupposition of Christianity we shall arrive at results which are hostile to supernatural Christianity. If one begins with the presuppositions of unbelief, he will end with unbelief's conclusions. If at the start we have denied that the Bible is God's Word or if we have, whether consciously or not, modified the claims of the Scriptures, we shall come to a position which is consonant with our starting point. [73]

I make no attempt here to respond directly to their unbelief, albeit there is a proper place to engage unbelievers with the claims of Scripture and the God the Scriptures reveal. Nevertheless, reading Genesis 1 *does* directly address unbelief, and making the message of Genesis 1 clear is a proclamation of the Gospel. God made us, he gives us life.[74] That is the inescapable and reasonable message of the first chapter of the Bible. God declares that it was through his Son, Jesus,[75] that he created, and that it is through Jesus that he sustain all things.[76] Genesis 1, read as it is written, may challenge a different worldview, but what it reveals about creation is reasonable – and more. Because Genesis 1 is the foundation of the good news about Jesus, it points to Christ and as such is "the power of God that brings salvation to everyone who believes."[77] Unbelievers who read Genesis rightly are confronted with God's call to submit to the truth God has revealed, to worship God who has made them, and to believe in Jesus Christ who has made it possible for people he has created to worship and serve their Creator.

There is an Hymn to be Sung

Yet among believers also there has been and continues to be uncertainty, confusion and division. Shared reverence for God as Creator, shared respect for the creation as his workmanship, and a shared commitment to the Bible as a reliable text inspired in its every detail by the Holy Spirit, have not resulted in a shared understanding of what Genesis 1 describes. In fact, it has often been the depth of commitment to those beliefs that has seen discussion on Genesis 1 debated with forceful conviction, a contending for the faith that all too often degenerates into entrenched and bitter ungodliness.

It is not surprising some tire of the debate and begin to question its importance. Is the task of asserting biblical truth to an unbelieving world not enough to engage our energies without debating it among believers? To that the answer must be an emphatic, "No!" for three reasons:

---

[73] E J Young *Thy Word is Truth* Banner of Truth, London, 1963 p187

[74] Acts 17:24-28 "The God who made the world and everything in it is the Lord of heaven and earth and does not live in temples built by human hands. And he is not served by human hands, as if he needed anything. Rather, he himself gives everyone life and breath and everything else. From one man he made all the nations, that they should inhabit the whole earth; and he marked out their appointed times in history and the boundaries of their lands. God did this so that they would seek him and perhaps reach out for him and find him, though he is not far from any one of us. 'For in him we live and move and have our being.'"

[75] John 1:3

[76] Hebrews 1:2,3

[77] Romans 1:16

1. Genesis 1 is God's Word. We can never excuse a trite dismissal of a close and careful study of the Bible because confusion and error surround its interpretation.
2. Understanding Genesis 1 hinges on the way it is read, and that both sets and reflects the way the rest of the Bible is read. The debate about the Bible's first chapter pivots on the method we adopt in reading the whole Bible. We need to know and apply a biblical method of reading God's Word from its very first chapter.
3. The message of Genesis 1 is foundational to the gospel, so if we are going to get the gospel right we need to get Genesis 1 right. Genesis 1 reveals that God is Creator, separate from and sovereign over creation, able to make and do with and change creation as he wills, unbound by anything in creation or any laws of nature. Genesis 1 reveals that God is Creator, and that we are not; we are creatures and upon that creatureliness hangs our absolute duty to serve and worship him; upon that creatureliness hangs the definition of sin and the justice of hell for sinners; upon that creatureliness hangs the one hope of salvation we have: that the Creator has provided a promised Saviour.

The theme-hymn of heaven is this creation hymn: "You are worthy, our Lord and God, to receive glory and honour and power, for you created all things, and by your will they were created and have their being."[78] We too need to sing that hymn, and we need to do so with understanding and conviction.

Event or Process?

At the heart of the enigma is one simple question: Does Genesis 1 describe an event or a process?

Does Genesis tell the story of God creating everything out of nothing into finished existence in a six-day event, or does Genesis 1 describe God making everything in a process of gradual change over an undefined and probably extensive period time? Is creation God miraculously making everything, and bringing to that creation his providential rule; or is creation God miraculously making laws of nature,[79] then superintending them in the universe to bring about that universe by

---

[78] Revelation 4:11

[79] The order God has brought and brings to creation, observed in the reliability and regularity with which things happen, is often alluded to as "Laws of Nature." The existence of such laws is debated by both philosophy and science, yet there is a reliable regularity that science documents through observation and depends upon. For example, what is known as the "Law of gravity" is well known and well used, whether or not it is actually some form of "law." The Bible ascribes the reliability and regularity of creation to God's providence, not to law, although as Abraham Kuyper once observed, the "Laws of Nature" is a term many theologians will "accept, provided we understand thereby, not laws originating *from* Nature, but laws imposed *upon* Nature." [Abraham Kuyper, *Lectures on Calvinism* Cosimo Classics, New York, 2007 (1931) p70 (italics and capitals his)] The problem with a term such as "Laws of Nature" is that it implies both some sort of fixed principle associated with law (to which even God might be expected to conform), and that such so-called laws are somehow embedded in nature so as to function somewhat mechanically without God's direct intervention. The order in creation however is the result of God's imminent, moment by moment sustaining of creation (eg Hebrews 1:3). God does not conform to nature;

natural process? Did God work in creating creation in a different way to the way he works today in sustaining creation?

Was man created from the dust of the earth "in a flash, in the twinkling of an eye," as the dust of the dead will be changed into imperishable living people at the return of Christ?[80] Or does Genesis describe a process by which man emerged by divinely superintended but natural progression from the dust? Did the universe begin, in contrast to the ways by which God ordinarily works in nature, in an eventful way similar to the way in which it will end, rolled up suddenly like a scroll[81] that has been finished with and consumed by fire?[82] The recreation of people from dust, the reduction of the existing universe into nothing, and the creation of a new heavens and a new earth, are all depicted as events unbound by the ordinary processes by which God presently works. Did the universe begin like that too?

At the very heart of the gospel is the resurrection of Jesus: a dead man brought back to life in the most fundamental conflict with the ordinary processes of nature. This miracle is at the apex of account after account of God's miraculous activity in nature, in the history of man, and in the future. The story from creation to new creation is the story of God's miraculous events interspersed with God working in nature with the order and processes he has instituted and sustains; but like the resurrection, creation is miracle unlimited by natural process.

If Genesis describes a process through which God then worked in the cosmos in the same way he now works in the cosmos – whether by direct intervention or by superintending supposed laws embedded in creation – why has creation stopped? How could creation, if it is the necessary natural result of the ordinary processes of nature, not continue while the ordinary processes of nature continue? God stopped creating on the seventh day, yet he continued then as now to uphold that creation by the ordinary workings of his providential running of everything. It follows that something must be different in the way he worked then and the way he works now. It is necessary that in any process of creation that has come to an end, at some point (or at multiple points) God did something that is different from any process that does not result in further creation. At the very least, there has to have been "an intrusion of the supernatural." [83]

Every interpretation of Genesis 1 that treats it as a true account of God's acts must at some point see a disjunction with natural processes. Taking Genesis 1 as a true text necessarily means God worked at some point then (if not at all points then) in a way radically different from the way he now works with his creation.

Genesis 1 inescapably reveals a God of the miraculous who is not constrained by the processes of nature he has made and normally sustains. In particular, Genesis

---

nature conforms to God. There is order and reliable regularity because God constantly acts to provide that order and reliable regularity, and he does so in accord with covenantal promise (eg Genesis 8:22). Kuyper's point is that whatever order there is that is called a law is there because God brings that order to creation, and not because creation itself generates such order. We can depend on what we have come to call laws of nature because God has not left his creation to run itself, but gave and gives order to it.

[80] 1 Corinthians 15:52

[81] cf Isaiah 34:4

[82] 2 Peter 3:10-12

[83] E J Young *In the Beginning: Genesis 1-3 and the Authority of Scripture* The Banner of Truth Trust, Edinburgh 1984 (1976) p44

1 inescapably reveals a God of the miraculous who is not constrained *in his creating* by the processes of nature he has made and normally sustains. Is the miraculous the event of creation itself, or is it God's using the processes we presently observe in nature to create?

The God of Miracles and of Nature

The Bible self-consciously and unashamedly reveals God as a miracle-working God. Christians do not hesitate to assert that God works in ways that do not conform to the order he brings to creation and ordinarily superintends. We unashamedly assert God worked miracles in the Flood, in the Exodus, in the lion's den, in the incarnation and the virgin birth, and in the works of Jesus on earth. We do not hold-back from telling an unbelieving world that God by his mighty power raised Jesus from the grave, despite its obvious incompatibility with science and the way we all observe the universe. The message that everything *will not* go on as it has since the beginning of creation will be scoffed at,[84] but we will continue to proclaim it, just as we will proclaim the truth that everything was not always as it is now.

That God works miracles is of the very substance of the Bible's message, the gospel. Yes, God normally works according to the patterns of nature he instituted and sustains. Yes, we are bound by those patterns and the cosmos functions in obedient accord with those patterns. But not God. He never was, never is, and never will be bound by them. In Genesis 8:22 God clearly covenants to sustain creation according to the natural order he has made, but even as he faithfully keeps that covenant promise he suspends that very order to work miracles as and when he wants. Just as importantly, this verse endorses that such natural patterns exist only so long as the earth endures: when it goes, they go!

Read as it is presented, Genesis 1 unmistakably tells the story of God creating the heavens and the earth, and everything on the earth including mankind, in six ordinarily-timed but extraordinarily-eventful days. The miraculous Creator, not bound by time or space or laws of nature, made everything suddenly, completely. And it was good. It was finished and ready to function as he wanted it to function. That is how the text presents. To read it in any other way we need a reason to replace the plain meaning with something else. Herein lies the working-out of the Genesis 1 enigma: there are numerous reasons advanced as to why Genesis 1 should be read differently. Do they work?

The Way We Read

There is only one legitimate way to read the Bible, "that is to approach it as those who have submitted their entire being to God, who have acknowledged Him as their Lord, and who come to His Word ready to hearken to all it has to say."[85] It is God's word, and it must be read with faith in him and submission to him. Don Carson explains what this means for Christians committed to the authority of the Bible:

---

[84] 2 Peter 3:4

[85] Young *Thy Word is Truth* p190

> I do not know what biblical authority means, nor even what submission to the lordship of Jesus Christ means, if we are unprepared to bend our opinions, values, and mental structures to what the Bible says, to what Jesus teaches. There may be differences of opinion about what the Bible is in fact saying, differences that can sometimes be resolved with humble interaction and much time; but among Christians there should be little excuse for ignoring or avoiding what the Bible has to say...[86]

When we are told, "Without faith it is impossible to please God, because anyone who comes to him must believe that he exists and that he rewards those who earnestly seek him"[87] it is not only saying we must come in faith, but that the aim of our coming is God-ward: it is to please him. The primary aim of reading Genesis 1 must be God's worship. That makes our mastery of Genesis 1 secondary to Genesis 1's mastery of our understanding.

John Walton rightly puts it like this: "God has chosen the agenda of the text, and we must be content with the wisdom of those choices. If we attempt to commandeer the text to address our issues, we distort it in the process."[88] God has chosen the text, its agenda, its meaning, and the issues to which it applies in every age. Commandeer the text, its agenda, its meaning or its application and we distort the text.

The fact that God is Creator is foundational to such an approach:

> If God is the Creator, and man a creature, there is no way in which man can set himself up as a judge of what God has revealed. There is no independent standard which man can drag in by which he can pass judgement upon the 'reasonableness' of God's revelation."[89]

This is one reason why, over the centuries, men have consistently questioned the meaning of Genesis 1. If Genesis 1 can be read in a way that dilutes or denies that God is Creator, man ceases to be (in his own mind, but not in reality) a creature made in God's image to serve God.

The text is commandeered when it is read through an external filter, whether that be a way of looking at the world that is not shaped by the Bible, a presumption as to the message the text is going to bring, or the imposition of issues arising from culture, science or philosophy. The remedy is simple: Take the text to mean what it says unless the text itself demands otherwise. That demand can sometimes be found in the passage being read, or in the book it is taken from, or in other Bible passages – but when that demand comes from outside of the Bible it is an imposter and should be silenced forthwith!

Only a fool would deny that the Bible contains symbols, metaphors and a variety of language techniques that enrich its message and it usefulness. But the Bible itself makes clear where those techniques are being used. If it doesn't, be sure of this one thing – they are not there, and only a fool will find them there.

Real things can also have symbolic meaning, but symbols cannot be symbolic without referring to something real. For example, when in Exodus God commanded

---

[86] D A Carson *Exegetical Fallacies* Baker, Grand Rapids, 1984 p130

[87] Hebrews 11:6

[88] Walton *The Lost World of Genesis One*, Kindle location 169

[89] Young *Thy Word is Truth* p189

the keeping of the Sabbath day, it unquestionably was a real day, but it also had symbolic reference to God's resting ... on the real seventh day of Genesis 1. Without there being a real day in Genesis 1, reference to it would be meaningless and the symbolism of the Sabbath day would be just as meaningless (even though the Sabbath day itself would remain real).

So turning to Genesis 1, we must take it to mean what it says unless there is something in the text to demand otherwise. Words like "create", "made", and "day" have the ordinary sense of *create, made* and *day* unless the text – Genesis 1, Genesis as a whole, or some other passage in the Bible – requires it to mean something else. Therein lies the simplicity and complexity of reading Genesis 1. It is simple to read because what it says has clear ordinary meaning, and there is nothing in the text, in the rest of Genesis, or in any other reference that the Bible makes to Genesis 1, requiring anything other than its ordinary meaning (and, as we will see, every other reference *assumes* the ordinary meaning). The complexity of reading Genesis 1 however arises because all sorts of people add all sorts of filters from outside of the Bible that appear to make Genesis 1 say what it is not plainly saying. Or, to use Walton's term, reading Genesis 1 is simple unless the text is commandeered by some extra-biblical issue being imposed on the text.

No Dependence on the Keepers of Secret Knowledge

There are numerous ways of reading the Bible that mystify meaning. It is not that there are no passages of the Bible that are difficult to understand: some are. But that is no excuse for making passages more difficult to understand by the way they are read. Reputable translators have not attempted to hide the meaning of the text. Consistency of translation in diverse translations throughout the history of the English Bible is a good indicator that the translation is likely to be reliable, and where a text is plain, its plain meaning can be taken as the intended meaning.

Translators have consistently used "day," "created" and "made" in Genesis 1 as the best English words for the original Hebrew. Over the centuries and through a multitude of consultations the translators have written the clearest English they believe can be used. They have not been trying to obscure the meaning as if only those who can access secret knowledge can understand the text. If ever there was a passage that would stimulate a search for "better" translation in the context of contemporary science, culture and criticism, this is it. But "day," "created" and "made" remain.

Yet there continue to be those who insist that some secret knowledge or insight is needed before certain passages can be properly understood. When this is done, Lyndon Drake rightly asserts, a distance is created between readers and the Bible by claiming there is knowledge of the text that "you could never have discovered simply by reading the text. Without meaning to, [those commentators] are saying that the Bible can only be understood through secret knowledge that the translators of the Bible are determined to keep hidden away."[90] As Norman Geisler warns, "if

---

[90] Lyndon Drake, http://arotau.com/2013/01/19/abba-isnt-daddy/ He is discussing a particular error in translating New Testament Greek, but his comment is just as pertinent to Old Testament Hebrew.

the understanding of the laity is contingent on the teaching of experts, then Protestant interpretive experts will have replaced the teaching magisterium of Catholic priests with a kind of teaching magisterium of Protestant scholars."[91]

Understanding must be shaped by the Bible and not by secret knowledge, especially not secrets derived from alien cultures and literature. If Genesis 1 "literally" or "really" means something that it does not plainly mean, that literal or real meaning must be the meaning the Bible itself makes plain, and not "truth" derived from secret knowledge only available from experts informed by inaccessible studies in the cobwebs of lost cultures.

A Question of Words

For those who share a commitment to the Bible as God's utterly reliable word, there is no question that God is the Creator, and the cosmos in its totality is his handiwork. The confusion centres just on three words in Genesis 1: "create," "make/made" and "day." By "create" and "make" or "made" does Genesis 1 mean God made stuff there and then in its more or less finished state, does it describe something else such as a process by which stuff eventually became what it is now, or is it used to describe a change in what God makes the various bits of creation do? By "day" does Genesis 1 mean a 24-hour period (or something close to it), is "day" alluding to some period of extensive time not bounded by the ordinary meaning of "day", or is "day" used to arrange the story of creation without any particular reference to time or "days" at all?

Recently the meaning of "create" has come under fresh review with the contention that it relates neither to instantaneous making of stuff nor to a gradual process of making stuff, but to giving stuff something to do.[92] Where that approach is taken, the word "make/made" is also said to relate to giving material creation some new function rather than making the material creation itself.

Paradoxically, commitment to reinterpreting "create" as giving function to created stuff rather than creating the stuff itself renders unnecessary the popular tendency to reinterpret "day" as a long period of time. So John Walton, having reinterpreted "create" goes on to affirm that the days of Genesis 1 "are seven twenty-four-hour days. This has always been the best reading of the Hebrew text."[93] Leaving, as he does, the entire creative process and the time involved a complete mystery never touched on in Genesis 1, there is no longer any inducement to adapt the "days" of Genesis 1 to mean aeons of time. As Walton explains, "It is evident that the nature of the days takes on a much less significant role than has normally been the case in views that focus on material creation, in that they no longer have any connection to the material age of the earth."[94]

---

[91] Norman Geisler, *Explaining Hermeneutics: A Commentary on the Chicago Statement on Biblical Hermeneutics,* International Council on Biblical Inerrancy, Oakland 1983 [on Article XXIV] http://www.bible-researcher.com/chicago2.html

[92] This is taken up in detail in the next chapter.

[93] Walton *The Lost World* Kindle location 859 (his argument for this is picked up shortly)

[94] ibid

That aside, the text of Genesis 1 seems incredibly transparent in identifying the length of the days. The word "day" is itself plain enough, and if its plain meaning is to be abandoned to some metaphorical sense, there needs to be clear textual demand for that. There isn't. Instead, as the days pass, each is defined as evening and morning. On day three the sun and moon are introduced, not to make but to mark-out the days as they pass. More on this later.[95]

There are other textual issues, as there always are in any close study of the Bible. There is the question of how verses 1 and 2 relate to the rest of the chapter. There is discussion about where the creation narrative ends and transitions into the next part of the unfolding of God's self-revelation. Yet those issues are, when isolated from the core debate, the sorts of issues about which some uncertainty, ambiguity or difference is accepted within a fellowship of those seeking to know the Bible better. Believers commonly explore such issues without heated polemic, seeking for themselves and encouraging each other to come to a richer understanding of God's word and a deeper fellowship with the God who spoke it. Not so the core issues of Genesis 1!

Which Specifics Matter?

It would be a mistake to consider the question of the time involved in the story of Genesis 1 as one of mere academic interest. If we can agree that the Bible plainly teaches that God made everything, does it matter how long he took? If we are submitting to Scripture, it does. There may well be – and probably are – consequential reasons why it is important, but the starting point must be that if God has given us his revelation with obvious particulars, those particulars are important, and we should attend to them, seek to understand them, and make every effort to apply them faithfully. The use of "days" in Genesis 1 is neither accidental nor incidental, but part of a very carefully structured narrative that hinges on the days. God could have inspired the writing of the creation narrative without mentioning "days," and it would have conveyed just as clearly his basic message that the cosmos is God's. But he didn't. For God the "days" have significance, so for us they must have significance.

The answer is the same when we ask, "Does it matter whether 'create' means made there-and-then, superintended process, or given a function?" It is not incidental to God's self-revelation that he is Creator. A right understanding of "create" goes to the very heart of a right understanding of the "Creator." Is God maker, processor or function-manager of the cosmos? Does Genesis 1 portray man as creature, outcome or functionary? How we find answers to those questions, and the answers themselves, define the method by which we read the rest of the Bible and form the framework within which we understand every subsequent reference to God and man. How we understand Genesis 1 is definitive for our understanding of the whole of the Bible. It matters.

If we are to read the Bible consistently, how we read Genesis 1 must fit how we read the rest of the Bible. Genesis 1 is not written in isolation: it is part of Genesis. Genesis is not written in isolation: it is part of the Pentateuch. The Pentateuch is not

---

[95] See *One Day* in Chapter 8

written in isolation: it is part of the Old Testament. The Old Testament is not written in isolation: it is part of the Bible. For all that it is necessary to read the various books of the Bible in their context, an important part of that context is that each part is inspired by God who from the very outset planned to pen, through men, a Bible that was unified in its diversity, transcendent in its cosmology, perspicuous across the generations, and unambiguous in its unchanging but unfolding message.

There is no question that for some the idea that God created everything in six days is just too way-out. It does not fit the cosmos as they know it. It would require a suspension of the laws of nature, or an overturning of the dominant philosophy of the day, or a re-evaluation of the accepted data, or a rethinking of conventional wisdom. There are two things that must said to such sceptics:

1. God can, does, did, and will suspend his normal pattern of providence – what some call the laws of nature – whenever he wishes to work out his purposes. That is what we call a miracle, and God is a miracle-working God.
2. If the Bible text teaches something that is contrary to observation or theory, rules of nature or philosophy, reason or tradition, the Bible wins.

That is not to say the Bible should not be read carefully, and read differently if the text forces a different reading to what has been traditional. If the Bible, read with a proper understanding of the text, removes the "way-out-ness" so that the conflict is removed, so be it. The sceptic's confrontation with the miraculous can be deferred; but it will inevitably arise sooner or later unless every miracle is somehow stripped of the miraculous. But if the removal of confrontation with the miraculous is achieved by reading the Bible, not in the light of its own text, but in the context of extra-biblical information, then the Bible is lost to its readers, not only at that point, but everywhere. For removing the miraculous at one point in which the text demands that it belongs establishes the methodology for removing it at every point. "How are we to believe in a God who can do the unimaginable and forgive our trespasses, conquer our sins, and give us hope in a dark world if we cannot believe that this God created the world out of nothing, gave the virgin a child, and raised his Son on the third day?"[96] As Noel Weeks has written, "It is nonsense to speak of the unique and total authority of Scripture at the same time as we change our interpretation of Scripture to accord with theories drawn from outside Scripture."[97] Glenn Stewart adds, "The whole purpose of Genesis 1, in this regard, is to assert a supernatural beginning. In pagan naturalists *all* nature is inherently magical and 'spiritual', self-creating or being made by material gods."[98]

A Question of Science

A great deal of unnecessary angst is generated by trying to conform the observations, theories and concepts of science to Genesis 1.

The Bible asserts that it is true, and that nothing it teaches is tentative, subject to review, revision or rejection, no matter what observations have been made. That

---

[96] DeYoung, *Taking God At His Word* Kindle location 444
[97] Weeks The Hermeneutical Problem of Genesis 1-11 p12
[98] Glenn Stewart, in correspondence with the author.

is an assertion Christians hold to as a non-negotiable given. Science asserts that everything it observes and postulates is tentative, subject to review, revision and possible rejection. The Bible holds that truth is absolute, although our knowledge of truth may not be complete or fully framed in truth; and that our knowledge of truth is sourced in the revelation of truth by God who truly knows everything. Science asserts its always-tentative truth is sourced in the fallible observations and formulations of people.

It is not that science and the Bible are examining different spheres of knowledge, for they each look at the same cosmos in action, the same handiwork of God. As they look at the same things, the Bible is true and science is tentative: science may describe truly what is truly there, or it may describe it in error, but it can never describe it with the certainty of the Bible. In the formulation of truth, science and the Bible are incompatible unless the observations and descriptions of science are subordinated to the Bible, and efforts to frame them as anything else are futile.

As John Collins says, "If evolutionary theories are opposed to [traditional views of Adam and Eve as our specially created first parents through whom sin and evil came into human experience], then those theories must adapt to accommodate the entire range of evidence."[99] That "range of evidence" includes the definitive evidence of Scripture. If evolutionary theory and Scripture differ, evolutionary theory must change to fit Scripture, not the other way round.

That does not mean that science cannot make valid tentative observations and descriptions of things, whether those are things about which the Bible is silent or not. Nor does it mean that a superficial reading of the Bible should be definitive in science. But it does mean that when the Bible is not silent it is definitive. And it does mean that each and every one of the observations and descriptions of science must be framed in subordination to the overall view of the cosmos given by the Bible.

The Bible is not silent about God being creator of everything: good science will make tentative observations about the cosmos and its functioning, but every observation and formulation of science must be subordinated to biblical truth that God is creator. The Bible is silent about the structure of DNA: good science will make tentative observations about DNA and its functioning, but every one of those observations and formulations of science must be subordinated to biblical truth that God is creator. The observations of science, and the "laws" it formulates can only ever be limited statements based on limited observations. They can never match the clarity and reliability of what God declares from what God knows. "We observe things *now* in time and history as they appear and can be described from *our frame of reference*."[100] Unless they too are inspired by transcendence beyond the universe, they can never be more than that.

What the Bible says about the cosmos is true. What science says about the cosmos is true so far as, and only so far as, it conforms to what the Bible says about the cosmos.

---

[99] C John Collins, *The Evolution of Adam* (book review) http://thegospelcoalition.org/book-reviews/review/the_evolution_of_adam
[100] Glenn Stewart, in correspondence with the author.

God Makes Science Possible

That does not mean that science and the Christian cannot work together. The scientist and the Christian – or the scientist who is a Christian – can explore the cosmos, observe and describe it, and build models (however tentative) that "work." Observations (whether observed by Christians or not) and models formed by science (whether formed by Christians or not) may work to a high degree of consistency. In fact, the Bible reveals a God who is so involved in the orderly operations of the cosmos that the order, the systems, the changes, the patterns, the transformations, the wonder observed and documented by science, can be relied upon as useful approximations of the reality God sustains.

It is not despite God's involvement in the cosmos that science works, but because of it. The observation made today has validity tomorrow because God holds the cosmos in an order that is not subject to random change, spontaneous abrogation, or arbitrary evolution of the laws and patterns of "nature."

Further, the Bible teaches that the making of those scientific observations, the formulation of those scientific theories, and the application of that science to build, explore, shape and make is a result of God's gracious equipping and sustaining even unbelieving human-kind in those very activities. God's providence extends beyond simply keeping the order of creation – it extends to upholding people in thought and activity; thought and activity that could not otherwise be consistently sustained within their fundamentally godless world-and-life view.

A word of caution is warranted: there is a mythology that has been built up around the Bible over the centuries. There is an abundance of "Bible teachings" that the Bible has never taught. As often as not these myths are found in the literature of unbelievers rather than biblical scholars, leading to the construction and demolition of many a straw-man in a way that advances neither science nor faith. But over the centuries Christians too have made the Bible out to be saying what it does not say. Yet the Bible does say clearly much that bears on science, and when it does, it is true. As to origins of the cosmos, the Bible unequivocally teaches that God is the creator of everything and imminently involved in the operation of everything: to that, science must submit.

Neither Genesis 1 nor science demands that we frame our approach to either with explanations of everything. Reality exists whether or not we can explain everything and whether or not our explanations cohere in a universal model. We can, we do, and we must work with incomplete, even faulty, models. It is scientifically valid for scientists to commit to bits of theory and practice that don't perfectly explain other bits, and it is theologically valid for Christians to commit to a view of origins that doesn't explain everything we observe in our fallible, tentative way.

We can be sure that everything does in reality fit because God is the maker and sustainer of reality, even if we can't always describe how it fits. We can be just as sure that when what the Bible teaches does not fit with what we or science has observed, the Bible is right. When we know fully as God knows fully, then we will be able to give a description of observable phenomena that is perfect, that has no conflict with Genesis 1. Until then, a little humility goes a long way.

Since God is Creator, We Are Created

I suspect that the reason evolutionary theory promotes a culture of scepticism in the reading of Genesis 1 lies more in its implications for a creature-Creator relationship than in the challenge of accepting that different "laws of science" and conditions prevailed at the origins of the cosmos from those prevailing today. After all, even evolutionary theory postulates different conditions and different phenomena at various stages of evolution. Many Christians who struggle with the issue of creation in a context where known phenomena and laws must have either been suspended or not yet instigated have no problem with subsequent miracles, such as the parting of the Red Sea or the resurrection of Jesus. These depend just as much on suspension of ordinary phenomena and the "laws of science."

The cultural pressure to deny the miraculous in creation but allow it in other "religious" contexts is illuminating. Contemporary culture allows for individuals, and even communities, to believe in almost anything so long as it does not impinge on others. That is, the wider community allows Christians freedom to believe in the resurrection of Jesus as that affects "them" (the Christians) and not "us" (those who are not Christians). But commitment to creation, however modelled – that is, as event or process – makes people creatures answerable to their Creator. If God made the cosmos, all of us are affected, not just a subculture who can be ignored.

In Athens, Paul founded his call to repentance in creation:

> The God who made the world and everything in it is the Lord of heaven and earth and does not live in temples built by human hands. And he is not served by human hands, as if he needed anything. Rather, he himself gives everyone life and breath and everything else. From one man he made all the nations, that they should inhabit the whole earth; and he marked out their appointed times in history and the boundaries of their lands. God did this so that they would seek him and perhaps reach out for him and find him, though he is not far from any one of us. 'For in him we live and move and have our being.' As some of your own poets have said, 'We are his offspring.' Therefore since we are God's offspring, we should not think that the divine being is like gold or silver or stone—an image made by human design and skill. In the past God overlooked such ignorance, but now he commands all people everywhere to repent. For he has set a day when he will judge the world with justice by the man he has appointed.[101]

Standing in the Areopagus among all its idols and false religion, Paul was speaking to those who had no prior knowledge of God from his word, no prior understanding of the covenant promises or their fulfilment in Christ. But they were people who lived in the created cosmos, and like all people, despite all their attempts to suppress the truth, they were people who had seen and understood the message of creation:

> Since what may be known about God is plain to them, because God has made it plain to them. For since the creation of the world God's invisible qualities—his eternal power and divine nature—have been clearly seen,

[101] Acts 17:24-31

> being understood from what has been made, so that people are without excuse.[102]

Yet the people who see the truth are people caste in the mould of Adam. Though "the heavens declare the glory of God [and] the skies proclaim the work of his hands,"[103] people

> neither glorified him as God nor gave thanks to him, but their thinking became futile and their foolish hearts were darkened. Although they claimed to be wise, they became fools and exchanged the glory of the immortal God for images made to look like a mortal human being and birds and animals and reptiles.[104]

Creation – the cosmos – makes abundantly clear to every person that it is created and that they are created; that it is created by God, and that they are created for God; and that God is by nature God, has eternal power, and will judge each and every one of us. No protest by agnostics, no denial by atheists, no teachings of the wise, and no scoffing by fools, can change the fact that God is creator and judge and that those same agnostics, atheists, wise, and foolish, know this. Those who so devotedly suppress the truth will seize on whatever tools they can find in philosophy and science, cosmology and idolatry, theology and autonomy, mythology and experience, to hide from the truth; but God declares that they have seen the truth and understood it.

It is hardly remarkable that this results in science in which the truth about the cosmos, its origins, and its creator are denied. It is to be expected that the science developed in such a culture of denial expressly denies the activity of God in the cosmos just as it denies the activity of God in its creation. Neither a godless science, nor the godless culture it nurtures and is nurtured by, can be conformed to Genesis 1. Whatever congruency God enables through his providence between what man does and thinks and what God does and knows, we can be thankful for and make use of. Yet we should never expect godless science to be able to explain God and his work, or for man's godless descriptions of a supposedly godless cosmos and its imagined godless origins to conform to God's descriptions of a cosmos that he made, he rules and he sustains.

Scientific Language: Do We Know What We Mean?

One of the silliest statements in this discussion, repeated *ad nauseam*, is that Genesis 1 does not use scientific language. An appropriate response is along the lines of, "Maybe ... so what?" The fallacies here are multiple! It assumes that such language exists and that it has unique usage. In that this statement is never supported by evidence, it depends on the assumption asserted for its acceptance. It does not locate its assertions within any definition of "scientific language," thereby presupposing an undisclosed definition. It implies that "non-scientific language" cannot communicate scientific truth. One could go on, but putting aside the

[102] Romans 1:19,20
[103] Psalm 19:1
[104] Romans 1:21-23

fallacies, it is a silly statement because it is just plain wrong. Genesis 1 is exquisitely scientific, and its language is perfectly suited to scientific precision. Consider:

1. The language used is exactly the sort of language commonly used in science. Compare Genesis 1:1 "In the beginning God created the heavens and the earth" with these examples of what is widely accepted as profoundly scientific: "There is no beginning and no end and ... galaxies continue to form from spontaneously created matter"[105] and, "Multiple universes are created out of nothing."[106] The *language* is identical. There could not be greater conformity of language-use had the authors conspired in a committee to ensure they used the same language in the same way.
2. This is hardly surprising as most of the features commonly ascribed to scientific language[107] are not unique to scientific language. Among these features can be included *structure that presents information in a logical order*, *information is densely packed*, and *there is a focus on things and processes without emotive commentary*. Nevertheless, although they are common to other genre, they tend to be more prominent in language used in scientific writing ... and Genesis 1 is notable for the prominence of these features. In common with scientific language, Genesis 1 presents information in a highly structured and logical order, it is densely packed, and it focuses on things and processes with no emotive commentary at all.[108]
3. One of the most distinguishing features of the language of scientific literature is undoubtedly its use of technical vocabulary. Genesis 1 is filled with scientifically technical vocabulary. True, terms such as "quarks," "peroxisomes" and "entropic" are not used. They are not used because God is not speaking about the intricacies of the cosmos. He is declaring that he created it, and he does so in words that fit exactly.

The terms used to describe what the text is focused on are technical terms used in scientific writing in exactly the same way today: terms such as "light," "seed," "green plants," "water," "animals," and "stars." There is no ambiguity about these terms in Genesis 1, and any theological metaphor that might be developed in later biblical texts (such as for "light") are not only completely lacking in Genesis 1, but depend on the concrete reality of Genesis 1 for the later metaphor to have any meaning at all.

That these terms are commonly used in non-scientific writing does not alter the fact that they have precise scientific reference, and are commonly used in scientific literature with exactly the reference used in Genesis 1. "Create" too, is commonly

---

[105] Stephen Hawking on the Hoyle/Gold "Steady State Theory" reported by Rod Pyle "Stephen Hawking: Big Bang Didn't Need God" Huffington Post, 17/4/ http://www.huffingtonpost.com/2013/04/17/stephen-hawking-big-bang-god_n_3103009.html

[106] Hawking (his own view) ibid

[107] The *New Zealand Council for Educational Research* has a clearly tabulated summary of the common attributes of *Scientific Language* based on the works of Derewianka, Halliday, and Schleppegrell (see http://arb.nzcer.org.nz/supportmaterials/language_of_science.php)

[108] Note that the repeated use of "good" is not such a commentary, but a statement that what had been created was appropriately fitted to the purpose to which it was to be applied.

found in scientific literature (see Hawking's use above as an example) with a meaning, in common with its use in Genesis 1, of being formed or brought into being.[109] In such a context of precise scientific language, there is no reason evident in the text why "day" should not also have a meaning consistent with its ordinary meaning.

4. While there is metaphor used in Genesis 1, that metaphor does not impinge on the clarity of the scientific language or comprehension of the data. It does not diminish the factual accuracy of the scientific data presented. Genesis 1 asserts that the sun rules the day. Fact: the sun shines on the earth in the daytime; metaphor: the sun rules. Those distinctions are easily discernible. In any case, the use of metaphor does not mean "unscientific": many science textbooks use metaphor and simile to explain concepts, but are not thereby declassified as "unscientific."
5. Yet the truly defining feature of scientific language is that it is used to communicate scientific data and meaning. Science has to do with describing what can be observed and how it functions. Modern Western science has the added quality of empiricism: the data, observations and descriptions can be replicated and tested. Empirical science has no way of observing or testing the process of creation, as Hawking himself recognises when he says science can determine "the universe had a beginning" but it can't "say how it began."[110] Yet it can test the descriptions of the cosmos given in Genesis 1, such as that the sun gives light to the earth on a daily basis. At least two of the testable statements made are of particular significance:
    a. Plants and animals regenerate "after their own kind"
    b. Plants birds, fish and (land) animals are to be found located in environments to which they are suited
6. Those statements are significant for two reasons. Firstly, they remain verifiable. They describe observable phenomena that can be and are verified by replicated observation to the present day. There can be few other scientific observations recorded thousands of years ago that survive such scrutiny. Secondly, these two statements *cannot be true for any evolutionary or developmental process of nature.* They are true, of course, when presently examined, but the very process by which the theory of evolutionary/process science postulates as having given rise to them depends upon their not being true at some earlier point which can neither be replicated nor observed. [111]

---

[109] Not always, however, with implication of a "Creator".

[110] Stephen Hawking *The Origin of the Universe* (Undated) http://www.hawking.org.uk/the-origin-of-the-universe.html

[111] Strong argument is made in evolutionary/process theory that predictions of such observable things as fossils, genetic variation, and movement in space and time provide empirical evidence of the postulated process giving rise to observable phenomena. That only holds true if the postulated process could be the *only* explanation for the observable phenomena. Similarly, it is often argued that the observed phenomena that *could* be the result of postulated process have a *probability* of arising from that process, but such probability can only be measured when all the alternative explanations are included in the

Genesis 1 states that from their creation plants and animals regenerate "after their kind" and living organisms are to be found in environments to which they are suited. Genesis 1 checks-out: its data can be tested and its observations replicated; evolutionary/process "science" cannot, for the events upon which it depends for its validity can no longer be observed. Cosmological evolutionary/process science therefore cannot and does not satisfy empirical examination. Genesis 1 is more scientific than the sceptical alternatives can ever be.

The Textbook Distraction

Despite the use of scientific language it can be said that Genesis 1 is not written as a modern science textbook. This is often asserted as if it settles some matter as to the scientific accuracy of Genesis, but as E J Young comments, "Although Genesis does not purport to be a textbook of science, nevertheless, when it touches upon scientific subjects, it is accurate."[112] The concept of a "purely" scientific textbook hinges on a modern misconception that knowledge of the cosmos can be had independently of a theological worldview. The ancients made no such error, so their descriptions of the cosmos were always intimately enmeshed with a view of God's (or "the gods'") involvement: their books of "science" were also books of theology, but no less "scientific" in addressing the cosmos than modern texts.

Framing the reading of Genesis in the context of asking if it is a scientific textbook employs blatant emotional blackmail as well as posing a misleading false dilemma. In an age where "scientific" is used to assert authority and unquestionable truth, the apparent necessity of agreeing that it is not a scientific textbook presupposes concession of a lower level of "truth" in the Genesis text. But science does not have a monopoly on truth. It is entirely possible that the Bible is true even though it is not a science textbook. Noel Weeks identifies the false dilemma posed when the question is asked if Genesis is a science textbook or a religious one:

> Is Scripture a book of religious truths or a textbook of geology? We naturally tend to say it is the former. Yet this question may pose a false dilemma. There is always the possibility that it is a book of religious truths which lays down basic principles which are relevant, even mandatory, for geology. If the question is posed so as to exclude this last alternative, and Kantian philosophy[113] so poses the question, then the basic problem has been solved not by appeal to the explicit teachings of Scripture but by a philosophical presupposition drawn from outside the Scriptures.[114]

Contemporary culture attributes an authority to a science text book that tends to silence mere mortal dissent, as if scientists have become the infallible priests guarding access to cosmic knowledge and dispensing it beneficently to the

---

calculation of probability. What often happens in these arguments is that a probability – however remote – is established, promoted because of presuppositions from remotely probably to *likely*, then read as a *certainty*. This is neither scientific nor rational.

[112] E J Young *An Introduction to the Old Testament* Eerdmans, Grand Rapids, (Revised) 1960 (1949) p49

[113] Weeks *The Hermeneutical Problem of Genesis 1-11* p13: "The basic ideas is a distinction between religious, theological and/or naïve explanations as distinct from scientific, technical ones.... The distinction itself looks suspiciously like Kant's noumena/phenomena distinction."

[114] Weeks The Hermeneutical Problem of Genesis 1-11 p13

grovelling laity. The authority of a science text book lies in its alignment with tentative science, a science dependent upon fallible and partial observation, and its belief in the supposed constancy of the cosmos. The objection that Genesis is not a scientific text book appears at first to provide no help in formulating an interpretive framework for reading Genesis 1. Yet it is the fact that it is not a scientific textbook that makes the Bible so scientifically accurate! If it were a scientific text book, it could only offer tentative information. But because it is God's word and not a scientific textbook, the Bible does what no scientific textbook can do: it gives a true account of everything it addresses.

An even more irrelevant objection is raised by Walton when he says, "Through the entire Bible, there is not a single instance in which God revealed to Israel a science beyond their own culture. No passage offers a scientific perspective that was not common to the Old World science of antiquity."[115] In fact he is wrong on the most fundamental point: the Bible asserts God created everything out of nothing and that mankind, animals, plants, rocks and so on are neither part of God nor of substance contiguous with each other. In contrast, "the Old World science of antiquity" held the direct opposite to be the truth: that everything was contiguous with the gods and had its origins, not in nothing, but in the substance of the gods. The Bible's perspective is plainly not common to "the Old World science of antiquity." *Every* passage of scripture that, like this one, offers a scientific perspective, offers a perspective that is not in the least in common with "the Old World science of antiquity." But right or wrong, the fact that science at any particular point in history is not stated in the terms of later cultures makes no valid point as to the accuracy of the "old" science.

The innuendo in the statements in the same place that the Bible is locked into "the Old World science of antiquity," or "the native ancient cosmic geography" is used by Walton to discourage trust in the world-and-life view of the Bible by emotive association without any demonstrated basis. More importantly it has the implication that because the Bible fails to engage with the science of later generations (or more probably this generation), it cannot be accurate. Actually, the Bible engages emphatically with the science of this generation – the debate on evolution demonstrates that well enough. That it does not engage in *some* of the issues of contemporary science does not invalidate its engagement on the issues it does speak to. The fact that the Bible fails, for example, to discuss the processes of cell division known to us today in no way invalidates the observation that plants reproduced after their own kind. If it did, it would also imply that everything known to us today would be invalid tomorrow, because today we are utterly incapable of science beyond today.

Walton actually makes a point of this: "We are well aware that science is dynamic rather than static. ... What is accepted as true today may not be accepted as true tomorrow. ... Science moves forward as ideas are tested and new ones replace old ones."[116] But even as he does so he introduces yet other fallacies: "So if God aligned revelation with one particular science, it would have been

---

[115] Walton *The Lost World of Genesis One* Kindle location 152
[116] Walton *The Lost World of Genesis One* Kindle location 127

unintelligible to people who lived prior to the time of that science, and would be obsolete to those who lived after that time."[117]

But God is not aligning revelation with science, particular or general, any more than I am aligning myself with science, particular or general, when I say green plants are green. In saying that, I am making a statement that has a truth that stands and is understood with or without a scientific context: artists, cooks, gardeners and small children are all able to understand it. When God speaks, he is stating truth upon which artists, scientists, linguist and philosophers and whoever are able to make commentary, and are free to attempt to conform their framework to it; but God is not attempting to align his knowledge to their puny little worlds. That does not mean that the statements God makes in any particular context are untrue or incomprehensible in any other contexts that don't conform: it simply makes those other contexts wrong.

Ancient is not always Primitive

What Walton actually seems to be driving at is the *language* used, asserting in the same place that God "adopted the language of the culture to communicate in terms they understood."[118] By disparaging the science of the ancients he implies their language cannot be trusted to describe the cosmos in ways that are valid today. It is yet another non sequitur. Walton ignores the fact that the language God used was not that of ancient paganism. Even if it were, his assertion amounts to a denial that old cultures and their languages could make statements in a way that is valid when read by newer cultures. There is a fascinating oscillation in the field of anthropology that alternately idealises the primitive when it suits, then disparages it in the exaltation of modernism when that suits. But such confusion should not be allowed to obscure the fact that something can be valid for ancient and modern alike, and that today we can be informed by the ancients even as we add to their knowledge.

There is however another factor to be taken into account. All that has been said applies to all sorts of literature from all sorts of ages. But the Bible is unique literature: it is revelation. The Bible is God speaking with the intention of being understood then and now. Ancient literature *can* inform modern readers, even though moderns were not in the authors' view; the Bible *does* inform modern readers because we were in the Author's view. God intended that it be read and understood by us. Understanding literary form, and understanding cultural setting, may help form a better picture of the biblical text we read; but understanding that the Bible is revelation is foundational to Bible reading. Walton shapes a view of revelation through the eyes of Ancient Near Eastern (ANE) literature: we should instead shape our view of ANE literature through the eyes of the Bible.

---

[117] ibid

[118] Walton *The Lost World of Genesis One* Kindle location 139

2. Genesis Lost

Mist Weaving: Reading Genesis 1 in the mist of alien cultures

"In the beginning, God created the heavens and the earth."

~ Genesis 1:1

In his book *The Lost World of Genesis One*[119] John Walton argues that Genesis should be read in the context of Ancient Near East (ANE) cultures that surrounded Israel at the time Genesis was written. This is not new, but where it leads is. Warning against the "cultural imperialism" of imposing our contemporary culture on the text, he proposes instead that the Hebrew פרא "*bara*" (create) should be seen to relate to the attribution of function to an already existing material creation, not to the creation of that material form itself.

In Walton's understanding this in its turn inaugurates a cosmic temple in which God will dwell: "After creation, God takes up his rest and rules from his residence" the cosmos/temple.[120] This places God "in the control room from where he runs the cosmos that he set up."[121] The significance of this might not be immediately apparent, but for Walton it lies in this:

---

[119] Walton *The Lost World of Genesis One*. See also John Walton *Genesis 1 As Ancient Cosmology* Eisenbrauns, Winona Lake, 2011 which is a detailed technical treatment of his propositions.
[120] Walton *The Lost World of Genesis One* Kindle location 682
[121] Walton *The Lost World of Genesis One* Kindle location 706

When we thought of Genesis 1 as an account of material origins, creation became an action in the past that is over and done with. God made objects and now the cosmos exists (materially). Viewing Genesis 1 as an account of functional origins offers more opportunity for understanding that God's creative work continues [from his dwelling in the temple/cosmos].[122]

This however raises more issues than it resolves. How does God's "creative work" continue? According to Walton, the creative work of Genesis 1 is God giving stuff that already exists new function; is that still happening? Or is Walton using "create" in a way that is inconsistent with his insistence that it means *function*? If so, how is creating continuing? How does that fit with God's statement that he "rested" from creating of the seventh day?[123] Does it mean he paused, only to take it up again?

Words Mean What Fits

Walton's answer is to redefine "create." Previously he has insisted that it can only mean *attribute function*. He continues to deny that it has its normal meaning of *make*, but to accommodate God's continuing activity in sustaining creation, he redefines "create" to also mean "sustaining functions."

[God] continues to sustain the functions moment by moment ... Creation language is used more in the Bible for God's sustaining work than it is for the original work. ... we reduce the distinction between creating and sustaining ... Genesis 1 puts God in place to perpetuate the functions after they are established in the six days. In this way, day seven, [sic] God taking up his rest in the center of operations of the cosmos, positions him to run it. This continuing activity is not the *same* [his emphasis] as the activity as the six days, but the reason why the six days took place.[124]

At this point Walton's God has become the old theistic "deity" who set it all in motion and now merely superintends the functions of what he once made. His God has been reduced to "no more than an organising principle."[125] Yet that is not the end of his redefining "create."

It is clear from this that the "continuing creative work" of God suggested by Walton should not be mistaken for any evolutionary process that may be supposed to have brought the cosmos to its present state. Walton maintains that the form of the cosmos as we know it existed before Genesis 1, but without its functions. Yet nor is this "continuing creative work" the creative work of Genesis 1 (*giving function*) but a different work of Genesis 1 that was not there in Genesis 1 but is here now and so can be called "creating" even though it does not mean either *making* (which Walton says it can never mean) or *attributing function* (which Walton says it always means).

---

[122] ibid

[123] Walton's concept of God's rest is critical to his thesis and is taken up on page 59

[124] Walton *The Lost World of Genesis One* Kindle location 1152 f

[125] Stewart in correspondence with the author.

Walton goes on to endorse the position of John Stek, whom he quotes,[126] in a very clearly different use of "create" from the usage that forms the foundation of Walton's thesis: "Whatever exists *now* and whatever *will come into existence* in the creaturely realm has been or will have been 'created' by God. He is not only the Creator of the original state of affairs but of all present and future realities."[127]

Although defining "create" as *attributing function* is foundational to his thesis about Genesis 1, defining "create" as *sustaining* and *bringing new things into existence* is foundational to his thesis about the cosmic-temple. Walton rests his case on the simultaneous use of words defined by him in different, mutually exclusive ways. "His concept of 'functional ontology' is vague, and slips around to suit Walton's thesis."[128] It is difficult not to see parallels to another character in a "lost world": "'When I use a word,' Humpty Dumpty said, in a rather scornful tone, 'it means just what I choose it to mean - neither more nor less.'"

And has God really taken up residence in his "control room" in creation to rule, not from his throne in heaven, but from his cosmic temple like a pagan deity? Every biblical reference to God's rule has him seated in heaven, in control from heaven, albeit active in the cosmos. To make the cosmos God's "control room" is to dethrone the God of heaven and demean the God of providence.

There is the real possibility here that Walton's commitment to God ruling from his control room in the cosmos has shaped his interpretation of how the cosmos got be God's control room in the first place. Does he read Genesis 1 to fit with his control room concept, or does the control room concept arise from a faithful reading of Genesis 1?

Walton's Proposals Should be Evaluated

The immediate impact of his proposals is to overthrow the long-held understanding that Genesis 1 describes the creation of a material universe. It is evident that for many this precipitates spontaneous rejection of Walton's proposals without actually examining those proposals. That is unfortunate.

An important point needs to be made here, however: despite the novelty of his ideas and the impact they are intended to have on biblical scholarship, Walton affirms his commitment to a conservative evangelical profession of the inspiration and reliability of the Bible. His stated intent is to uphold the integrity of God's word and to encourage a faithful reading of it.

There is no compelling reason why every Christian should examine every interpretation of the Bible that gains traction in a world that values novelty above faithful exegesis. Convictions that are consistent with the heritage of biblical scholarship passed to us and built on a careful reading of Genesis in fellowship with believers of today are a sound defence against being "carried away by all kinds of

---

[126] Walton gives the reference as John Stek "What Says the Scripture" in *Portraits of Creation* ed. H. J. van Til, Eerdmans, Grand Rapids, 1990, p211

[127] Walton *The Lost World of Genesis One* Kindle location 1163 [his italics]

[128] Peter Leithart "Genesis 1 in Ancient Perspective?" in *First Things First* 20 June 2014 http://www.firstthings.com/blogs/leithart/2014/06/genesis-1-in-ancient-perspective

strange teachings."[129] Yet when a well-respected Bible-teacher of the calibre of Walton advances a new reading of Genesis 1 that he contends is a more faithful reading of the Bible, his proposals should be examined.

It is also evident that there is a body of criticism of Walton that misrepresents what he is saying. That too is unfortunate. It unjustly impugns Walton's scholarship (albeit there may be other justified grounds for critiquing that scholarship), clouds the issues he raises, and makes evaluation and discussion of his ideas more difficult. Nevertheless, neither sympathy nor respect for Walton should dissuade us from the task of examining the Scriptures to see if what Walton says is true (cf Acts 17:11).

Walton presents his argument in a reasoned and persuasive way that progresses from one proposal to the next over eighteen "propositions." He alludes to a range of ANE texts to frame his view of the cultural context in which Genesis was written, and provides detailed analysis of some relevant biblical texts. First impressions are that his conclusions are supported by evidence, and his argument certainly demands careful consideration. Yet closer examination exposes a number of real difficulties. There are significant inconsistencies in the methodology he employs. The presuppositions he uses and upon which much of his argument rests are generally unstated, unjustified and inconsistent with foundational biblical concepts. The significance and meaning he attributes to various ANE texts are often at best debatable. His analysis of the biblical text, and the explanations he gives, are at times not as evident as he asserts.

Cultural Imperialism at Work

Walton rightly rejects the cultural imperialism that would impose our contemporary cultural framework on Genesis. Yet by insisting Genesis be read within a cultural framework shaped by our reading of available ANE texts, it appears that the same error of cultural imperialism is made. Of course, if it were to be demonstrated that Genesis was written within such a cultural framework, it would not be "imperialism" of any sort. But instead of that, as I will show below, Walton merely asserts that the ANE framework is the one through which Genesis is to be read. This is imposing a culture on the text; it is what he calls "cultural imperialism."

To enable such a framework, a picture of ANE culture is constructed that is a synthesis of a relatively few glimpses of little parts of the cultures of a number of nations over a period of hundreds of years. This synthesis is constructed by ignoring both the logic that says such uniformity among different nations over such periods of time is highly unlikely, and the evidence within those texts that such uniformity did not exist.

Over the last 150 years or so, a large number of ANE "texts" have been discovered and translated. Most are fragments; relatively few are complete works. Most are bits of documents recording transactions of daily life, administrative records, and the like; few bear directly on the issues pertinent to the reading of Genesis. They appear to have been composed over a period of more than 1,000 years and originate from more than half a dozen different nations (a conglomerate

[129] Hebrews 13:9

from which Israel is generally excluded), each having its own evolving culture and religion. From this, a single cultural framework is proposed that is foreign to Israel, but within which Israel's literature, it is said, needs to be read. In particular, Walton contends that Israel's view of deity, Israel's use of the word "create", and Israel's concept of the cosmos be defined by that alien synthesis.

This is not unlike attempting to synthesise a single culture from randomly selected fragments of records, bits of correspondence and incomplete works of literature from Continental Europe from 900 AD to 1900 AD, then insisting that a particular text, written by an English community in 900 AD should be read in the context of the fictional monolithic millennial European culture that has been synthesised. In particular, it would require that our reading of that English community's concept of deity, their use of one particular word, and their view of the cosmos in 900 AD, be defined by that modern fictional synthesis of the imagined ancient culture.

The Most Significant ANE Texts Overlooked

For all his endeavours to construct this ANE cultural context, in defining that culture Walton largely ignores the culture expressed in the most complete corpus of ANE texts available to modern scholars. There is a collection of literature from the period in which Genesis was written that contains a number of complete literary works that directly address the issues Walton examines, that self-consciously express a view of deity and the cosmos that radically differs from the other ANE texts, and that Walton presupposes should be interpreted in the light of the other ANE cultures rather than be definitive of the radically distinctive culture they portray. We generally refer to that corpus of literature as the Pentateuch.

Walton's proposals can only have traction through failure to acknowledge that Genesis was written in and for a culture that had radically isolated itself and its world-view (or rather, had been radically isolated by God) from the surrounding pagan cultures. Genesis self-consciously differentiates itself, its message, and the Hebrews to whom it is addressed, from the surrounding cultures of its day. Genesis presents its own cultural context within which ancient and contemporary readers can find the same meaning. Genesis is part of a significant corpus of contemporaneous and subsequent Hebrew literature that presents a consistent and remarkably unchanging view of God and the cosmos. Above all, it reveals God who is both distinct from his creation and different from the idols and gods of Israel's neighbours. Walton gives no compelling reason why readers of Genesis should abandon such a well-defined and differentiated world-and-life-view, such a distinct language, and such radical religious practice, in favour of a synthesis of fragments of the diverse cultures among Israel's pagan neighbours.

Finding Meaning by Accepting an Alien Concept

Postmodernism appears to have had more than a little influence here. The approach of the wider academic community to Genesis is heavily influenced by deconstructionism's assertion that no text can convey the meaning the authors intended. Whether or not this consciously colours Walton's approach, there is a bias of this sort in contemporary critical scholarship that impacts in two ways. Firstly, there is a tendency to accept that the author's meaning is never transparent to a distant audience. Secondly, there is a tendency to accept that texts other than the one under consideration can illuminate the original author's intended meaning better than the author's own words. Those who do not accept constructivism can nevertheless attribute greater doubt about the transparency of the text than fits with the Bible's own testimony. Yet appeal to other ANE texts does nothing to solve that conundrum, for the same level of doubt must be cast on the ability of all ANE texts to convey an author's meaning and accurate cultural information. If the Bible cannot convey to modern readers the meaning the ancient author intended, other ancient texts cannot do any better, especially where many of those texts are not intended to narrate a message of cultural significance to any audience.

Walton concedes that the biblical text does not hold a view of deity that fits the other ANE texts, writing, "It is true that the God of the Bible is far different from the gods of the ancient cultures."[130] So why should we consider Israel to have beliefs about the deity which are not consistent with the biblical text but aligned to Israel's pagan neighbours? His answer, in the absence of any biblical text indicating Israel held such a view, and in the absence of any extra-biblical text that Israel held such a view: "We simply recognize the common conceptual worldview that existed in ancient times. We should therefore not speak of Israel being influenced by that world – they were part of that world."[131]

Why should we "simply recognise" this when the only text available that describes Israel's view of deity explicitly and repeatedly says the opposite? Why should we "simply recognise" this when there is no evidence of a common conceptual worldview apart from a generalised pantheism, and lots of evidence of the opposite? Why speak of either the writer of Genesis or Israel being part of a world they were demonstrably not part of? Why should we "recognise" a world-view in a text for which that world-view is unambiguously alien to the text? In particular, why should we follow Walton as he asserts both that the text of the Bible does not have such a worldview, but that we should read it as if it did?

John Currid identifies three critical reasons why "the common assumption that the Hebrew stories are simplified and purified accounts of Mesopotamian legends is fallacious:"[132]

1. ANE literature becomes more complex, not less, as it builds on earlier works, implying that the simpler Genesis account has not be morphed from earlier ANE literature.
2. ANE myth and epic never develop into historical narrative, which Genesis is plainly presented as.
3. Despite some similarities in ANE myths and Genesis, the differences are so striking and so numerous that Genesis cannot be explained as a text sharing a worldview with other ANE cultures, or as pagan mythology cleansed to conform to a Hebrew perspective – a sort of sanctified myth.

---

[130] Walton *The Lost World of Genesis One* Kindle locations 95-96

[131] Walton *The Lost World of Genesis One* Kindle locations 100-101

[132] Currid *Ancient Egypt* p29

Israel's concept of deity and its literature is unique, free from overt or covert perversions by the perverted religions and literature of its neighbours.

Israel Falsely Accused

That Israel knew something of the idolatry of neighbouring nations and that those nations knew of Israel's uncompromising religion is assumed by Genesis and can be safely inferred from all sorts of sources. It is evident that both Israel and the other nations considered themselves to have opposing rather than congruent religions. It was the fact that Israel did not fit in with Egyptian religion and its culture that caused Pharaoh to fear them, oppress them, enslave them and begin to slaughter their baby boys.[133] And it was just such radically different conceptual worldview (ie "religion") that also meant that as Israel entered the Promised Land, the nations there had to either convert to the true religion given to Israel or be destroyed. As God established his covenant community, there could be no synthesis of paganism with revealed truth.

As evidence of a "common conceptual worldview" Walton asserts that the Bible indicates the "Israelites were continually drawn into the thinking of the cultures around them, whether they were adopting the gods and practices of those around them or whether they were struggling to see their God as distinct."[134] Yet in Genesis no such wandering occurs, much less in any way that would justify reference to Israel "continually" engaging in paganism. Only twice do false gods get a mention in Genesis, and then only in passing: in chapter 31 Rachel steals her father's household gods, and in chapter 35 Jacob tells his household to get rid of any foreign gods they have with them. Whatever the significance of these verses, they do not establish or even hint at a continuous wandering of Israel into a pagan worldview. Examination of Genesis demonstrates Walton's assertion is simply false.

As for the rest of the literature of the same period – the rest of the Pentateuch – that so-called "common conceptual worldview" gets even less credence. In the face of page after page of explicit teaching on the distinctive worldview of the text and the culture in which the text is written that both reject idolatry and cleave to the true God, there are just two references to engagement with idolatry. One is the passing and somewhat obscure reference in Leviticus 17 in which the Israelites are warned to stop prostituting themselves to goat idols (whatever they were). The second is the notorious incident when God was rejected in favour of a golden calf in Exodus. Rather than these evidencing a common view of deity in Israel and other ANE cultures, it dramatically details how Israel could only share a "common view" by rejecting the view given expression in its own text, the Pentateuch.

Genesis is written, as Walton concedes, from an entirely different worldview from the "common conceptual worldview," and records an all-but total abstinence from such a worldview.

---

[133] Exodus 1:8ff

[134] Walton *The Lost World of Genesis One* Kindle locations 96-97

The God of Genesis is Different

True, in later books that do not share an historical or authorial context with Genesis, there are accounts of Israel's repeated turning to the idolatry of that worldview. As the history of Israel unfolds, there is a well-documented tendency of Israel to engage in the idolatry of its neighbours. This Walton claims to be "continuous." While it is a repeated sin, it is hardly "continuous," and is frequently punctuated by periods of faithfulness, many of which were extensive.

In any case, if Israel was *sometimes* un-faithfully idolatrous, it was also sometimes faithful to God, so there were many times when clearly Israel understood God in reference to his self-revelation rather than to paganism. In every instance of Israel's engagement in idolatry, it is reference back to the Pentateuch that forms part of the call to repentance and reform. Neither Israel, nor Moses, nor Genesis shared a worldview with the other ANE cultures.

The Bible's accounts of idolatrous departures from God are pictured as departure from the expression of deity the Bible is giving consistent voice to. Whether or not the people from time to time after Genesis was written shared with pagans their idolatrous concept of deity, the Bible never does. The inclusion of accounts of Israel's sins are used by the later writers to contrast the God the text portrays, and his expectations of worship, with the false gods and their forms of worship.

Far from indicating the text of Genesis views deity with reference to the nations around Israel, the absence of anything of the sort in Genesis, and the later accounts of Israel's immoral forays into paganism, demonstrate that Genesis, as the rest of the Bible, has a distinctly different view of deity. But more to the point, even if subsequent to the writing of the Pentateuch Israel lost the plot, the plot of Genesis unmistakably does not have the commonality with other ANE texts that Walton asserts.

What was the view of deity of the non-Hebraic ANE? Although there was no universal religion, there were a number of common concepts:

There was a plurality of gods

They had origins

They were in continuity with the cosmos and not transcendent

They were of the same substance as mankind and matter

They were in a power struggle for ascendancy over each other

Their powers were limited, and often task-specific

They relied upon and were influenced by magic[135]

They were fickle, malleable and not above deceiving and being deceived

They could be appeased, bribed or persuaded by offerings and gifts

---

[135] The essence of magic is the use of incantations or rituals (mostly known only to a privileged individual or caste) that access the powers of the universe to influence the gods/nature by those impotent to control events directly by their own power (cf God whose speech effects what is spoken).

They operated in a context in which there were no absolutes of right or goodness

They were, in other words, at every point as unlike the God of Genesis as they could be. True, there are some points at which the mythical gods and the God of Genesis are said to have done similar things, such as make things in the cosmos, cause cataclysmic events, and so on. It is clear however that those few points of congruence between the mythical actions of the gods and the revealed works of the God of Israel are points of contrast not similarity. For example, Genesis reveals that God made man from the dirt which he had made out of nothing. That is, God made man of stuff as far removed as it is possible to be from the substance of God who is not of the same stuff as the cosmos. "The dissimilarities are not superfluous but of great magnitude and import."[136] God is not like the gods and does not work like them.

Reconstruction of Hebrew Culture

It is of course more than probable that Moses, having been raised in Pharaoh's court, was very familiar with Egyptian myths, and having spent years in the household of a priest of Midian he may have been familiar with the myths in Jethro's heritage. Yet he rejected Egypt and chose instead to be mistreated with the people of God rather than to enjoy its pleasures.[137] Whatever he knew of false religion, Moses rejected. Without very clear evidence to the contrary – evidence Walton nowhere presents – it cannot be supposed Egypt's myths were a source of influence in Moses' writing of Genesis simply because it is supposed they infused the atmosphere of that day.

While it is likely Moses understood Egypt's myths, it is just as *unlikely* Israel did. Why would they? Socially and culturally they were separated from Egypt and the Egyptians amongst whom their parents had lived. Those who knew anything of Egyptian religion died in the wilderness, leaving a wilderness generation who had no existential knowledge of Egypt. They practiced their own religion, remembered their own heritage, and even while resident in Egypt had been so different they threatened the political and religious domination of the Pharaohs – hence Pharaoh's commitment to genocide and slavery. That is not a context in which Egyptian mythology – much less even more distant myths and cosmologies of other cultures – would shape Israel's religion or influence the writing of Israel's Scriptures.

Nor for that matter is there any evidence that the various ANE cultures had any significant knowledge of each other's religions, myths or cosmologies. What we do know of the various myths indicates they were specific to each community; communities that had no interest in imposing their myths on others or adapting the myths of others to themselves. Even so, had there been a pervasive commonality of myth, and had that mythology and view of deity been the context in which Israel understood deity, it would necessarily have found its way sympathetically and overtly into the text of Genesis. Instead there is only contrast not similarity.

---

[136] John Currid *Against the Gods* Crossway, Wheaton, 2013, Kindle location 670

[137] Hebrews 11:24,25

Walton's claim that "the views of deity in the ancient world served as the context for Israel's understanding of deity … Israel understood its God in reference to what others around them believed" [138] is a fiction. Walton himself says the non-biblical ANE "gods are born and suckled, grow to maturity, contest for satisfaction of appetites and emotions, battle for prestige and power and mastery, indulge in sex, and are subject to failure, defeat, and death."[139] Walton affirms that these gods "make mistakes, misjudgements, and even commit crimes; they can be surprised; so it is clear that they are not to be considered omniscient. They experience uncertainty and confusion, and at times make ill-devised decisions. (They) experienced emotions such as shame and fear."[140]

The assertion that such a view of deity was referential for Israel's understanding of God is simply beyond sensible credibility. "The Hebrew conception of the universe differs radically from the other ancient Near Eastern cosmologies. … it was God's command that Israel repudiate the ways of pagan nations and follow his statutes only."[141]

There can be nothing more dramatically different from the other nations' views of deity than that consistently expressed in Genesis, in its contemporary biblical texts, and in the later biblical texts. "The Old Testament worldview is unique in the ancient Near East, and this is immediately confirmed by its all-pervasive monotheism. It simply does not swallow ancient Near Eastern thought."[142] Walton's argument at this point hinges on a subtle and completely unjustified association of the occasional later practice of Israel and the norms of the text. Behind Walton's thinking is an unstated assumption that Israel, in times the text identifies as failure to know God as he is and has revealed himself, shares the same perspective of deity as the text written to ensure Israel does not share such a view of deity. Any such assumption cannot be logically consistent and is demonstrably false, as the biblical text never accommodates a pagan view of God.

Exegetical Chaos

The absence of idols in Genesis is striking. If the asserted pagan view of deity shared by Genesis and Israel's neighbours really existed, why is Genesis, and especially Genesis 1 and 2 so lacking in both idols themselves and the language of idolatry? All other ANE references to creation, including the only other extant complete ANE creation account, *Enuma Elish*, are utterly idolatrous. They tell of idols who are contiguous with the material world they transmute into being as eminences of themselves. But Genesis, along with the rest of the biblical text, begins with God who is without beginning, who is distinct from the creation which shares nothing of substance with its Creator. Most significantly, in making man he does not make him of the substance of deity but of dirt. Apart from the fact that in both Genesis and *Enuma Elish* the cosmos exists and does so as having come into

---

[138] Walton *The Lost World of Genesis One* Kindle locations 94-96

[139] John Walton *Ancient Near Eastern Thought and the Old Testament* Baker Academic, Grand Rapids, 2006, p103

[140] Walton *Ancient Near Eastern Thought* p104

[141] John Currid *Ancient Egypt* p48f

[142] Currid *Against the Gods* Kindle location 74

existence, Genesis is as different from *Enuma Elish* in concept, narrative and language as it is possible to be.

This highlights the logical and exegetical chaos Walton creates by a series of unstated but critical assumptions even before he begins to argue his case. Here are some of those assumptions:

1. There is "a common conceptual worldview," a common ANE culture spanning half a dozen distinct nations and hundreds of years. *Assessment: In so far as they were all idolatrous, they shared in the worship of "created things more than the Creator."*[143] *Clearly there are commonalities in the practices and the conceptual worldview of idolatry. However, Walton's assumed but unreasoned extension of those basic commonalities to a transcendent culture spanning centuries of shared myths, language, values, politics and science – let alone the cultic particulars that might influence the writing of Genesis – is untenable. Not only is there no evidence for such an improbable thing, such evidence as exists underlines the opposite.*
2. Such a common ANE culture is accessible to us. *Assessment: It is not. The very limited texts we have, give a very incomplete picture of the various ANE cultures, leaving more gaps than filling. There is no Canaanite mythology available, let alone any dealing with creation; there is no Ugaritic text that describes creation; there is no known Hittite creation account; and as we will see below,*[144] *references to creation in Egyptian texts are very brief.*[145]
3. *Enuma Elish* is a definitive point of reference in describing that common ANE culture. *Assessment: In fact it is an isolated text, expressing a novel view of creation inconsistent with early texts from the same cultural heritage.*

Where Are the Gods?

Walton's is not the only approach to the use of ANE religious culture in reading the Bible. For example, John Currid, while emphatically rejecting pagan influence in the writing of the Pentateuch, encourages a reading of the text informed by an understanding of the world in which the events took place. One such is the confrontation between Moses and Pharaoh.[146] He explains much that is not in the biblical text. He illuminates the tense atmosphere that must have prevailed as Moses' staff-turned-serpent consumed the serpents produced by Pharaoh's magicians in failed defence of their god-king crowned with a serpent. For Pharaoh and his henchmen this was a confrontation of one god with another. But not for Moses;[147] not for God; and not for the Bible.

---

[143] Romans 1:25
[144] See below p92
[145] I am indebted to Dr Noel Weeks who has drawn my attention to this in correspondence with me.
[146] Currid *Against the Gods* Kindle location 451ff, and in multiple places in *Ancient Egypt*
[147] Who could not have been ignorant of these facts, but under God's inspiration did not record them.

There are no gaps in the biblical text. We cannot improve on what God has given by filling in supposed gaps in his text. In inspiring the writing of the Bible, God's selection of events, dialogue and detail is not inconsequential: what he has included he has chosen to include, and what he has omitted he has chosen to omit. The details of Pharaoh's world that are not included in the text are not meant to be included as part of its reading. While the study of Pharaoh's world is fascinating and entirely legitimate in furthering an understanding of history and culture, to inject such information into the reading of the biblical text can distort the text and imply that we can improve on the text as given by God. Nothing could be further from the truth.

Is it possible, though, that the writer of Exodus expected his intended readers would have a detailed knowledge of the religion and dynamics of Pharaoh's court? Most unlikely. To begin with, they were the generation raised (and for many, born) in the wilderness. Their life in the wilderness was exclusively focused on the worship of God dwelling in their midst. Even the incident of the golden cow idol while Moses was up the mountain caries no direct reference – explicit or implied – to Egyptian religion.[148] If they had known of such things, the writer of Exodus would likely have drawn attention to the parallels, but he doesn't. The lack of such allusions in the Pentateuch is the second reason why it is unlikely they had a detailed knowledge of an alien religion.

Thirdly, any knowledge the wilderness Hebrews had of Egyptian religion would have had to have been passed to them by their parents – a generation that had grown up in cultural and religious separation from their Egyptian slave-masters even before they entered the religious and cultural isolation of the wilderness. In the unlikely event that such transmission of alien beliefs was widespread, just how much detail would they have actually received? Consider our own generation in this information-rich world where national and cultural boundaries are unprecedentedly porous. How many Christians have more than a faint and superficial knowledge of other religions – Islam, Hindu, Confucian, Shinto, Buddhist? How many even know much about contemporary Judaism? Would the wilderness generation be any different? We are presented with a biblical text that makes no assumptions about readers adding contextual knowledge of distant religions.

How does reading Exodus 7 differ when read with the biblical text on its own, and when read with the insertion of supplementary contextual data? The answer to that lies partly in understanding the nature of Scripture, and partly in recognising the impact of the worldview within which Scripture is read.

When it addresses events, such as those recounted in Exodus 7, the Bible is written with the unmistakable intent of conveying historical events with historical accuracy. Yet it is not a "history" in the sense of attempting to provide all data that could contribute to an understanding of all that happened (if any histories actually do that). Rather, real events are selected and recorded accurately to help the reader

---

[148] Some link the cow to Egyptian cow idolatry – but not the text. Had there been such a link it could hardly have passed without comment in Moses' condemnation of their unfaithfulness to the God who delivered them from Egypt!

understand what God is revealing to his people the way God wants to reveal it. Currid sums up the message of this event with clarity: "Yahweh assaulted the heart of Pharaoh to demonstrate that only the God of the Hebrews is the sovereign of the universe. That Yahweh controlled the heart of Egypt's king is the basic point of the episode related in Exodus 7:8–13."[149] But that is a message that stands out starkly in the biblical text on its own: the extra-biblical information is not needed, and in fact can actually obscure the text.

When extra-biblical data is added to Exodus 7, the entire worldview through which it is read is radically changed; so radically changed that it becomes a different text. Currid's information demonstrates that Pharaoh and his court most likely viewed the confrontation with Moses as a confrontation between deities. That offers a truly fascinating insight into Egyptian culture. But it is omitted from Scripture because it misleads any reading of Exodus 7, for neither God nor his Bible will have anything to do with such a worldview. The worldview of Exodus 7 is one, as Currid recognises, in which only God is pictured as divine, only God is portrayed as determinative, only God is sovereign.

In an extra-biblically informed reading of Exodus 7, there is a contest of power between the Egyptian deities (personified in Pharaoh) and the God of Israel (represented, if not personified, in Moses). But the biblical text entertains not even a whiff of this. The confrontation begins with God saying what he will do. God says that in doing this he will control not only the events but even Pharaoh's heart. God says what the outcome will be. Then God does it. He does it all, and he does it just as he said he would. What's more, although he says that the outcome will include "judgement on all the gods of Egypt,"[150] the confrontation is very clearly a confrontation with Pharaoh the king and there isn't the slightest hint of regarding Pharaoh as anything but a man. This worldview is a core element of the message of Exodus 7, and it is completely warped, if not lost, when extra-biblical data is superimposed on the text.

How that impacts can be seen in the way Currid (and others) tend to read much of the text and many of these events as a polemic against the false gods of ANE paganism. True, there is a polemic against idols, idolatry and false gods in Genesis that runs through the whole Pentateuch: but it is a polemic of non-engagement. This is the case in Exodus 7 just as it is the case in Genesis 1.

Unlike the ANE myths, in Genesis (as in Exodus) there is no confrontation with gods struggling for ascendency, no engagement with spiritual forces. There is no cosmic battle with or between elements of creation, no struggle with the material world that comes into being and life at a word, no contest of power between rulers. Man's creation is not a compromise providing deities with labourers to manage an out-of-control realm, but an instantaneous creation, a mature perfection in God's service and fellowship at a word. God's declarations of what he will do with men are not proposals to be negotiated but fiats as powerful as his word at creation. God speaks, and what he says happens by the power of his word without opposition or hindrance. The elements of creation fit and function at their creation without tension

---

[149] Currid *Ancient Egypt* p103
[150] Exodus 12:12

– in God's evaluation they are truly "good." History unfolds with the same good conformity to God's purposes. Man was the plan from the outset, the ultimate creation in creation made for his dwelling. Pharaoh's judgement was the plan from the outset, not a mere possibility hinging on Pharaoh's choices.[151] The polemic against idolatry in Genesis consists in the stunning simplicity of God demonstrating his greatness in terms of his own being without comparison or conflict, and is expressed in his call to his people to be holy.

When idols and false gods do get a mention in the Bible, it is not in terms of any power or influence they have. That there is to be no idolatry in Israel is not because if idolatry is present in Israel the idols could do anything to Israel – they can't. They have no place in Israel because their presence is offensive to God. They constitute no threat to God, but their presence among the people of his covenant love is evidence of divided hearts that, along with the idols, are an offence to him. Israel is banned from making them or harbouring them, and must throw them out when they are found with them; but no exorcism is needed, and no power has to be overcome in them, as they are mere things. They are sin's gilded excrement to be thrown out as refuse.

Walton rightly warns against a cultural imperialism that imposes an imported paganism onto the biblical text. That can be done just as readily in reading the text in an ANE context as presupposing the writing of the text in such a context.

What Walton Does Not Say

However, something has to be said about what Walton is not saying. As noted above, too many critics misrepresent Walton on several points.

Firstly, Walton is not questioning the authority of the Bible to reliably inform faith. He writes:

> We must not let our interpretations stand in the place of Scripture's authority and thus risk misrepresenting God's revelation. We are willing to bind reason if our faith calls for belief where reason fails. But we are also people who in faith seek learning. What we learn may cause us to reconsider interpretations of Scripture, but need never cause us to question the intrinsic authority or nature of Scripture.[152]

Secondly, Walton is not saying God is not the Creator of the material universe, unequivocally asserting, "Whatever happened, whenever it happened, and however it happened, God did it."[153] In Walton's view, Genesis 1 is not about origins; what exists, exists because at some point not described in Genesis, God made it all. He writes:

> If we conclude that Genesis 1 is not an account of material origins, we are not thereby suggesting that God is not responsible for material origins. I firmly believe that God is fully responsible for material origins, and that, in fact, material origins

[151] Exodus 9:16 with Romans 9:17

[152] Walton *The Lost World of Genesis One* Kindle locations 1607-1610. Nevertheless, as pointed out earlier, by making reason the rule and faith in the Bible secondary, he does effectively undermine the intrinsic authority of Scripture he claims to defend.

[153] Walton *The Lost World of Genesis One* Kindle location 1077

do involve at some point creation [ie "making" not "attributing function"] out of nothing.[154]

Thirdly, Walton does not reduce the days of Genesis 1 to metaphors for extended periods of time, contending that the "reading of the word 'day' (*yom*) as a twenty-four-hour day is accurate."[155] Nevertheless, it is worth noting that in arguing for this view of "day," Walton's methodology, unlike his more contentious assertions, is based on his examination of biblical usage and the Hebrew text without reference to the surrounding cultures or their literature. It is not apparent why he insists reference to extraneous literature is needed for *bara* (create) but not *yom* (day).

Fourthly, Walton does not advocate that there is a gap between verses 1 and 2 of Genesis 1. Noting that by "creation" in Genesis 1 Walton means "assigning function," he explains his view of the relationship of verse 1 with the rest of the chapter by writing:

> The 'beginning' is a way of talking about the seven-day period rather than a point in time prior to the seven days... the first verse does not record a separate act of creation that occurred prior to the seven days – but that in fact the creation that it refers to is recounted in the seven days. This suggests that verse 1 serves as a literary introduction to the rest of the chapter. This suggestion is confirmed by the fact that Genesis 2:1 concludes the seven-day report with the statement that the 'heavens and earth were completed,' indicating that the creation of the heavens and earth was the work of the seven days, not something that preceded them.[156]

Nuanced, Inconsistent or Just Wrong?

When addressing what Walton does not say, it is also appropriate to note that he may intend nuances in his writing that escape the reader – either that, or he is simply inconsistent within his own corpus of writing. I have already referred to the description he gives of pagan ANE gods in his *Ancient Near Eastern Thought and the Old Testament.* In that book he gives extensive descriptions of the ways in which ANE paganism differs from the Bible.[157] Further, Walton also identifies differences between the various ANE cultures.

Yet from such differentiation he synthesises a common culture and world-view – what he calls a "cognitive environment" – within which he asserts the Bible was written and is to be read: "if we do not bring the information from the ancient cognitive environment to bear on the text, we will automatically impose the parameters of our modern worldview, thus risking serious distortion of meaning."[158] This is an elementary logical inconsistency. He argues that the ANE cultures think differently from each other about the world in which they exist, and that the culture from which the Bible comes is different from them all; and that therefore a uniform ANE thinking (that he says doesn't exist) must be brought to

---

[154] Walton *The Lost World of Genesis One* Kindle locations 398-400
[155] Walton *The Lost World of Genesis One* Kindle location 1034
[156] Walton *The Lost World of Genesis One* Kindle locations 408-413
[157] eg the box on p110 "How is Yahweh different from the gods of the ancient Near East?"
[158] Walton *Ancient Near Eastern Thought* p40

bear on the Bible. This is his way of preventing a modern pattern of thinking being imposed on the Bible.

Reading the Bible from an ANE cultural perspective, or reading it from a modern cultural perspective, are not the only alternatives. It is also possible to read the Bible from its own self-confessed cultural perspective. But Walton appears to exhibit a "theological predisposition to distinguish the Hebrew Bible from its [Hebrew] historical matrix"[159] and impose in its place a non-existent uniform ANE matrix. Having demonstrated that a uniform ANE cognitive environment doesn't exist, and that ANE cultures are in any case radically distinct from the biblical one (all the while somehow asserting the opposite!), by "bringing the information of the ancient [alien] cognitive environment to bear on the text" the text is distorted in exactly the same way for which others are rightly criticised by him.

In *Ancient Near Eastern Thought* Walton seeks to apply to the Bible only "information from the ancient cognitive environment" that endorses what the Bible appears to be saying without such a contextual reading.[160] Similarly he rejects any application of paganism that has "negative" connotations for reading the Bible.[161] Not only does this mean a selective application of the ANE texts based on presuppositions as to which outcomes are valid, the implications of this for his approach to Genesis 1 are significant. Since he also claims that Genesis 1 must be read in the context of an ANE "cognitive environment", he implies that the outcome of such a contextual reading does not change the way Genesis 1 is read (otherwise its application would be screened out). Yet it is on the basis of that ANE context that he insists Genesis 1 should not be read in terms of the way it has otherwise been read. Here is a circular argument of the most basic sort: he begs the question!

Whatever ambiguities reside in *The Ancient Near Eastern Thought* however are lost in *The Lost World of Genesis 1*. Although he says that the biblical text is "more important" than ANE literature, because "it is possible for the biblical text to take a different view of ontology than the ancient world,"[162] he nonetheless overwhelms the biblical text with ancient literature. He asserts, "Ancient literature is the key to a proper interpretation of the [Bible]."[163] So, as pointed out earlier, he asserts, contrary to any straight-forward reading of the Bible, "Israel understood its God in reference to what others around them believed"[164] and *bara* means allocate function, not create. He is in error logically and exegetically, and his use of what is understood of ANE culture is in error.

Walton clearly recognises that the Hebrew culture within which Genesis is written, and that the ontology of Genesis 1, are radically different from other ANE cultures. He gives no cogent reason to read Genesis 1 in the light of those cultures. In the next chapter I will examine what happens when he does apply what he deems to be the ANE cognitive environment to Genesis 1, despite such an application being invalid. But thus far, beyond asserting that we should "simply recognise" it

---

[159] Alan Lenzi, "John Walton: Ancient Near Eastern Thought and the Old Testament" [Book Review] *RBL 10/2007* Society of Biblical Literature, 2007, http://www.bookreviews.org/pdf/5831_6156.pdf

[160] See Lenzi for discussion of this

[161] ibid

[162] Walton *The Lost World of Genesis One* Kindle location 48

[163] Walton *The Lost World of Genesis One* Kindle location 186

[164] Walton *The Lost World of Genesis One* Kindle location 96

is so, he gives no sustainable reasons to read Genesis 1 as anything other than a clear and unambiguous account of God creating the cosmos in six days which Walton himself identifies as each of 24 hours' duration.

3. Genesis Haunted

Ghosts of Antiquity: Reading Genesis 1 in the mist of ancient literature

"In the beginning, God created the heavens and the earth."
~ Genesis 1:1

When the disciples saw Jesus walking on the water towards them, they thought he was a ghost.[165] While we have no idea whether or not they believed in ghosts before then, when they saw one, they believed! But they had not seen a ghost. They had seen Jesus whom they knew well. Yet, with a well-formed and thoroughly scientific predisposition to the idea that a man cannot walk on water, when they saw exactly that, they had to find an alternative explanation. The data was clear, but they would not let the data give evidence of reality in a way that did not fit their preconceived reality.

The same thing happened after the resurrection in an incident that is intensely scientific. Jesus appeared to the same disciples. They made an observation (they can see Jesus) and formed an hypothesis (they are seeing a ghost) based on a well-established fact (dead people don't live), which was then tested empirically when Jesus said, "Look at my hands and my feet. It is I myself! Touch me and see; a ghost does not have flesh and bones, as you see I have."[166] Yet looking and touching did not satisfy these sceptics, so he ate some cooked fish as further proof. Even then

165 Mark 6:49
166 Luke 24:39

they did not believe. With all the shared data, the unmistakeable evidence, and prior experience of God being greater than the rules of nature he had made, used, and frequently by-passed, it was not until "He opened their minds so they could understand the Scriptures"[167] that they saw reality as it really was.

The Bible presents a view of reality at odds with the view necessarily used by anyone whose starting point is that there is no God, no Creator, no risen Lord Jesus Christ. Even those who begin with a belief in God as revealed in the Bible can accommodate their view to the prevailing culture in which they live, study, work or witness. The disciples sustained a false view of the risen Jesus through tenacious commitment to the data before them, yet they misunderstood both the data they had and the reality they faced. Without faith in the God of the Bible, reading the Bible necessarily involves distortion of the data and misunderstanding of reality. As for the disciples, so for all who read the Bible: the data alone does not give understanding without the Spirit of God opening our minds.

Luther rightly pointed to a two-fold clarity of the Bible:[168] there is a clarity – he calls it an *external* perspicuity – open to anyone who reads because God's words are plain. But there is also, he argues, an *internal* perspicuity, which is perspicuous only to those who have the Spirit:

> The truth is that nobody who has not the Spirit of God sees a jot of what is in the Scriptures. All men have their hearts darkened, so that, even when they can discuss and quote all that is in Scripture, they do not understand or really know any of it. ... The Spirit is needed for the understanding of all Scripture and every part of Scripture.

When your concept of reality is not real, and what you see does not fit the way you see, you either have to change the way you see or you see ghosts. When anyone brings a pagan concept of reality to reading the Bible, they will see ghosts: they will wrongly describe what they truly see.[169] When anyone brings to the task of reading the Bible a concept of pagan culture shaped by reading pagan literature, they will see ghosts. They will see things that are not there, and they will see what is there in a way that is not there.

When the Bible is read in the shadow of pagan ANE literature, there is a real danger that that shadow obscures the Bible's message rather than illuminating it. The shadow deepens, and with it the obfuscation of the biblical text intensifies. What is said about the data cannot be sustained when the data is examined. Sadly, this happens often in Walton's handling of both the ANE literature and the Bible itself. While not everything Walton says is unsustainable, there are numerous points at which he represents the text in a way that cannot be sustained. Almost any one of these instances on its own would significantly undermine his thesis: taken together they leave little room for a sympathetic entertaining of his re-jigging of Genesis.

---

[167] Luke 24:45

[168] Luther *The Bondage of the Will*, p73f (italics are Luther's)

[169] Of course, "ghosts" are also seen when "reading" the cosmos.

False Dichotomy: Form or Function

Two of Walton's logical inconsistencies are foundational to his thesis:

Firstly, Walton creates a false dichotomy between material form and function. He argues that things can have form (ie physical existence) without function; that Genesis 1 recounts the attribution of function to things that already have form; and that those things may have had form for a long period of time before they were given function. By excluding the logical necessity of a congruence of form and function, or any other alternative, his absolute separation of form and function in creation is a classical false dichotomy. Nevertheless, he argues that such a dichotomy existed in the period Genesis 1 recounts, and that it existed in the mind-set of the writer of Genesis.

There is a significant gap in Walton's argument at this point. His claim is that as the ANE texts separate form and function, so did the writer of Genesis 1, and so must we in reading it. But he never demonstrates that in ANE literature form and function were separated. His claim is that in all ANE literature, form is re-ordered and given different function by the gods, but never made by them. Of course the ANE gods can never make anything because they themselves are integrated with everything: they cannot exist apart from the cosmos, and therefore they cannot be the creators of the cosmos. Their literature cannot address the beginnings of the cosmos because their gods are part of it. But even within that framework, form and function are intimately linked. Function may be changed, but form always has some function or other. There is no dichotomy between them.

Secondly, Walton takes the implication of a state of being arising from the state of material or abstract being described, then insists that only function is described. He argues that what is useless or unproductive is useless and unproductive because it is emptiness or wasteland. He then insists that there is in fact no emptiness or wasteland, only uselessness. His argument is that a state of being useless or unproductive, arose from what is described as a state of being empty or wasteland, then insists that only function is described.

The implication of function (or nonfunction) in this argument is dependent upon the material form or state-of-being that is said to exist or to which there is a likeness. When Walton says, "The contexts in which they occur and the words and phrases used in parallel suggest rather that the word describes that which is nonfunctional, having no purpose and generally unproductive in human terms"[170] he ignores the fact that the description of "that which is nonfunctional" is referenced to the material form of a wasteland, and that without such a referent,[171] the metaphor would be meaningless. In logical terms, his argument goes like this: Since y, therefore x; since x, therefore not y.

---

[170] Walton *The Lost World of Genesis* Kindle locations 445-446

[171] Not only does every metaphor need a meaningful referent, as Noel Weeks points out, "Biblical symbolism relies heavily upon preceding history. ... Genesis 1-3 has no past history upon which to build. It has no store of persons and events to produce images. Its presence in Scripture is the beginning of the

Interestingly, at one point Walton asserts, "Unless something is integrated into a working, ordered system, it does not exist."[172] I tend to agree. It seems likely that everything God made (whenever that happened) had functions. It is hard to conceive of anything existing without it having some sort of function, much less that God would make functionless stuff. Given that everything created has been created to show God's glory, everything has at least that function. But this creates insurmountable difficulties for Walton's thesis:

1. Walton argues that Genesis 1 narrates God taking stuff that already existed and giving it function. Nowhere does Walton attribute pre-existing function to this pre-existing stuff.[173] Walton goes to great lengths to demonstrate that the "formlessness" of Genesis 1:2 means "functionless." Yet, according to Walton, that which does not have function does not exist. It cannot both exist and not exist. If it did not have function until Genesis 1, then it came into existence in Genesis 1. In that case, Genesis 1 may well describe the attributing of function to stuff, but it also necessarily describes the formation of that stuff too. Walton is quite clear on that: "to assign something its functional role ... is to bring it into existence."[174] If Walton is right about "formless" then he cannot be right about creation being the attribution of function; but if he is wrong about "formless" then he still cannot be right about creation for then Genesis 1 describes the bringing into existence of substance. In either case his basic thesis is excluded by his own propositions.
2. Yet in the very next sentence he asserts "something must have physical properties before it exists." This is linguistic conjuring, using the word "existence" with a commonly understood meaning in a way he defines to the exclusion of common understanding, and doing that with what amounts to little more than a passing comment in the fine print. Walton consciously but with restrained admission uses "existence" to describe physical existence that does not exist.
3. Walton insists that the pre-Genesis 1 "earth is described as not yet functioning in an ordered system."[175] Yet in this non-functional, non-ordered period of chaos, everything that will be given function in the six days of Genesis 1 is supposed to have evolved into the form that will be given function. For Walton, this unproductive non-functional period is the locus for the development evolutionary science describes. It is difficult to reconcile Walton's chaos being so functional when he says God has not yet

store from which future Biblical writers will draw." Noel Weeks *The Sufficiency of Scripture* Banner of Truth, Edinburgh, 1988, p104

[172] Walton *The Lost World of Genesis* Kindle location 222

[173] Least there be any misunderstanding, by "pre-existing" I refer to "before Genesis 1" and do not imply that Walton proposes the stuff given function in Genesis 1 has some eternal existence. He doesn't. As already noted he clearly asserts this pre-Genesis stuff has at some point been created *ex nihilo* by God.

[174] Walton *The Lost World of Genesis* Kindle location 222

[175] Walton The Lost World of Genesis Kindle location 453

given it function, or being so systematic in the evolution of everything when he says God has not yet ordered it in a system.[176]

4. Allowing, for the sake of discussion, that the pre-existing stuff had pre-existing function, was that function some sort of holding-pattern function whereby God created a universe with pointless function until he gave it a different, useful function as described in Genesis 1? That would account for God's description of the new function as "good", for it would now be doing something that glorified him and fitted his purposes ... which implies that before then it didn't (ie it was not good). Or was the pre-existing function also good, serving some purpose that in Genesis 1 is ended and replaced? Or perhaps God made the stuff and gave it function at the same time ... perhaps.
5. This highlights the conundrum Walton has created by presupposing a false dichotomy between form and function. Though he starts with that dichotomy, and rests his entire thesis on it, he cannot avoid recognising that form and function go together, and that the dichotomy, as he asserts here contrary to what he has asserted elsewhere, does not in fact exist. There is only one conclusion that makes sense of all this: Genesis 1 describes the creation of a physical cosmos given form and function at the same time.

Creation is Impossible in ANE Pantheism

The pantheism of the ANE cultures ensures that within them there cannot be any real creation *ex nihilo* at any point because deities, matter and mankind are contiguous. The gods, the cosmos, people, plants ... all are of the same substance, so it is impossible to have a beginning from nothing. Lutheran scholar Andrew Steinmann has explained this well:

> There is a reason why the pagan accounts assume that matter is pre-existent: because in pagan thought matter is in some way intimately connected to and even part of the divine. Thus, the sun is not simply an object in the sky that gives light and heat to the earth, the sun is a god. It may be the Aten, the solar disk, and an aspect of the god Ra in Egyptian belief. Or it may be Shamash, the sun god of the Mesopotamians. Dagon is not simply the grain god (Judg 16:23; 1 Sam 5:2-5, 7; 1 Chr 10:10), he animates the grain and is intimately attached to it.[177]

It is hardly surprising then that ANE accounts of or allusions to "creation" refer to *changes* in form or function, and never refer to true creation. Genesis reveals a cosmos made out of nothing by the eternal God who had no beginning. The ancient myths excluded God and told of an eternal cosmos that had no beginning. If they are, as claimed, a guide to Genesis, then Genesis can only reveal a change in function. When Walton predicates Genesis 1 on the ANE conceptual world, the

---

[176] "Apparently, during this 'unproductive' phase of the material cosmos produced all kinds of things - on Walton's view, modern science tells us that generation after generation of dinosaurs existed, and lower forms of life evolves into higher forms of life, some sort of human beings came into existence and lasted long enough for God to assign them as images and rulers over the creation. How can that happen when the world is 'unproductive'? How can that happen when nothing has been assigned a function, and nothing has been ordered into a system?" [Peter Leithart "Genesis 1 in Ancient Perspective?"]

[177] Andrew Steinmann "Lost World of Genesis One: John H. Walton, American Evangelicals and Creation"

exegesis of various uses of "create" in ANE literature is pointless, because his presupposition allows for no other possibility than functional creation and the absence of formative creation.

The clarity with which Genesis insists that God is eternal and that the cosmos is not, that God is distinct from the cosmos, that things within the cosmos are differentiated and not transmutable, and that the cosmos is made while God is not, makes it as impossible for paganism to be the interpretive framework for the Genesis account of creation as it is impossible for paganism to conceive of creation. Genesis belongs to a different conceptual world altogether.

Creating a New Use of ברא *Bara (to create)*

There are some 48 Old Testament occurrences of the word *bara* in its basic forms.[178] Walton charts 34 of these,[179] aiming to show that the objects of *bara* (what is "bara-ed" if you like) "are not easily identified in material terms."[180] He agrees with the virtually universal observation that the subject of bara – the "who is doing *bara*" – is always God. But he contends for a non-traditional understanding of the object of *bara*. Instead, he argues, his chart shows that *bara* predominantly refers to giving things function, not to the material formation of those things.

Walton generously aims to help even those who cannot read Hebrew to understand the Hebrew: "Even someone who does not know Hebrew can double check the data."[181] Despite his significant reference to ANE culture as a context for understanding Genesis, he also insists at this point that, "the meanings of words are established and determined by the ways in which they are used" in the text. This is laudable. The principle that use in the text should be the primary means of determining the meaning of a word is fundamental to sound exegesis. Further, for most readers of the Bible, the most useful Old Testament Hebrew scholarship is that which does not merely give a sound translation of the Hebrew text, but gives evidence that can be understood, even if readers cannot read the Hebrew. Unfortunately, Walton's chart and his discussion of it transparently fails on both counts.

He finds that 38 of the objects of 34 uses of *bara* in his list are things, ten are phenomena and one is a condition. He identifies one (Genesis 2:3) as having no direct object. How he allocates the 38 to their categories is obscure.[182] Examining his list of objects, 28 of the 34 references can be identified as material "things" that are made, and five as abstract things that are made. To nine of these he appends a comment indicating that those things have associated functions, but not one of the objects is a function. 34 are concrete things of material substance, and five are abstract things, but things nonetheless, not functions.

---

[178] 38 in the *qal* stem and 10 in the *niphal* stem.

[179] Walton *The Lost World of Genesis* Kindle location 374

[180] Walton *The Lost World of Genesis* Kindle location 383

[181] Walton *The Lost World of Genesis* Kindle location 335

[182] 38 direct objects can be found in his list as he has set it out if compound objects are differentiated and two references to "people" (Genesis 1:27 and 5:2 in which he substitutes "male and female" for people) are treated as compound objects.

Specifically on the basis of this list, he makes the assertion that the objects of *bara* "are not easily identified in material terms." Since his own list demonstrates exactly the opposite, this assertion is not easily explained in rational terms.

True, *bara* can speak of the creation of abstract things that are thereby not material things, but that does not make them *functions*. For example, he lists in his chart the pure heart of Psalm 52:10, and the darkness and disaster of Isaiah 45:7, which are not functions but things, albeit abstract things. That sometimes *bara* speaks of abstract things and that sometimes *bara* can speak of things that are associated with function, does not mean that the only alternative to the creation of material things is the creation or attribution of function.

Changing the Meaning of תֹּהוּ *Tohu (formless)*

Walton supports his thesis that the Genesis 1 account of creation relates to function not form by reference to *tohu* in Genesis 1:2 which is normally translated "formless." He claims *tohu* does not mean "formless" but "functionless." On this basis he claims that the creative work of God in Genesis 1 is not bringing things into existence but changing already existing form from functionless to having function. He produces another table,[183] this time of 20 occurrences of *tohu*, where he makes comments to justify his contention. He then explains:

> Studying this list, one can see nothing in these contexts that would lead us to believe that *tohu* has anything to do with material form. The contexts in which they occur ... suggests that the word describes that which is nonfunctional. ... A word that had to do with material shape would not serve well in these contexts.[184]

As for his table for *bara*, at a first reading this table also seems persuasive. A quick glance at his table shows an overwhelming reference to function. But examining each reference in its biblical context one discovers, alarmingly, that Walton's analysis tells only part of the story. Function is involved, but not to the exclusion of form. Walton's analysis is not merely inaccurate – it is transparently misleading. Rather than there being "nothing in these contexts that would lead us to believe that *tohu* has anything to do with material form," the opposite is true: there is every reason in these contexts to believe *tohu* is specifically about form as well as function. It appears he finds what he is looking for even though it is not there.

When in Genesis 1:2 the earth is described as formless, it is also true it does not function as God intends it should ultimately function. It does not function that way because it does not have the form needed for such functionality. Had God merely attributed function to the form as it then existed, it would not have thereby become functional. The form of the earth had to change: light is introduced, the sky is separated from the earth, and dry land is formed. The function of the earth does not change: its function was always to provide a place for man to live in and in which to serve God. To begin with, it cannot serve that function because it does not have the right form. As the form is changed, the function is not allocated but fulfilled.

---

[183] Walton *The Lost World of Genesis* Kindle location 435
[184] ibid

Function does depend upon God's "allocation," but it is practically worked out as a consequence of, and necessarily dependent upon, the form God creates.

Yes, to some extent *tohu* "describes that which is non-functional" for although it must have some function it is not yet functioning as God ultimately intends;[185] but what it describes is nonetheless a form. It is not as if the form is potentially functional, needing only the attribution by God of some purpose to make it function. It is in a form that cannot function the way God intends. To become functional as God intends, it needs more than a declaration of its purpose; it needs to be changed so that it functions according to God's purpose.

The question of function *is* at the forefront of Genesis 1:2. Taking Genesis 1:1 to be a declaration of God's creative work beginning with the creation of the heavens and the earth that are then described in Genesis 1:2,[186] the "formlessness" of Genesis 1:2 is not talking about it having no substance (after all, it has just been made), but it not being useful (or in the context, not being ready for the ultimate use God has planned). Hence Robert Alter translates *tohu* as "waste."[187] Walton is right therefore to observe that *tohu* has functional reference. But he makes two errors:

1. Firstly, as already noted, he separates function from form. *Tohu* does not have the meaning of being without any substance at all, but of having substance (or "form," if you like) that does not have the function ultimately planned for it. Form and function are linked and a dichotomy between form and function cannot be validly made.
2. Secondly, he extrapolates the supposed dichotomy between form and function in verse 2 into the following verses, according only the attribution of function to all the creative work that follows. Clearly the Bible does identify function for some of the things created (such as the sun), but equally clearly it attributes no function to many of the other things (such as the great sea-creatures) that are nonetheless created. Changing the earth from *tohu* to *not-tohu* involves some attribution of function, but not only the attribution of function; and even when it does involve the attribution of function, that function is inextricably linked to a change in form or substance.

"While functionality of items in God's creation is often brought to the fore in Gen 1, the text itself does not indicate that all created items are to be understood strictly or even primarily in functional terms."[188]

Charting the Evidence

On the following pages I reproduce Walton's table with my own comments appended. Following Walton, "form" here is taken as material, state-of-being, or

[185] While not functioning as God ultimately intends it to function, it nonetheless has some function at that point – if only as the physical locus for the following creation.

[186] Those who see Genesis 1:2 as a comprehensive way of saying there was nothing there when God started to create will not see this as an issue.

[187] Robert Alter, *The Five Books of Moses* Norton, New York, 2004, p17

[188] Steinmann "Lost World of Genesis One: John H. Walton, American Evangelicals and Creation"

"thing," that may have associated function, in distinction from exclusive functionality. From this it can be seen that in fact in only one of the 20 uses of *tohu* cited, does it have reference to "function" above "form."

Not only does the list establish that *tohu* describes things not functions, it demonstrates the semantic range of the word as describing "things" in a state of emptiness, desolation, uselessness and the like. In Genesis 1:2 it describes the earth as initially formed by God as being formless or unproductive,[189] not simply as functionless. Walton's claim that *tohu* refers to function to the exclusion of form simply cannot be sustained.

Tohu: Form or Function?	
Reference	Description
Deut 32: 10	**Walton**: parallel to the wilderness; described by "howling" **Me:** Place where Jacob was found; this can only be form as Jacob could not be found in a howling function **Primary Reference: Form**
1 Sam 12:21	**Walton:** description of idols who can accomplish nothing **Me:** The idols have a state of uselessness (state-of-being), from which it is adduced they can accomplish nothing (function) **Primary Reference: Form**
Job 6:18	**Walton:** wasteland away from wadis where caravans perish for lack of water **Me:** The place where caravans perish: it is a wasteland because of its form, and it functions to cause caravans to perish because it has the form of a wasteland – having the form of a wasteland it could not function otherwise. **Primary Reference: Form**
Job 12:24	**Walton:** wandering in a trackless waste **Me:** The place where leaders wander **Primary Reference: Form**
Job 26:7	**Walton:** what the north is stretched over **Me:** The place over which God spread the northern skies **Primary Reference: Form**
Psalm 107:40	**Walton:** wandering in a trackless waste **Me:** A metaphor in which nobles are caused to wander in a waste place **Primary Reference: Form**

[189] See below p178 for further discussion.

Tohu: Form or Function?	
Reference	Description
Is 24:10	**Walton:** a tohu settlement is described as desolate **Me:** A ruined place **Primary Reference: Form**
Is 29:21	**Walton:** with tohu they turn aside righteousness (similar to Is 59:4) **Me:** Walton's "with tohu" obscures the use of tohu which is here "[with] false testimony" - an abstract but real thing, not a function **Primary Reference: Form**
Is 34:11	**Walton:** measuring line of tohu and plumb stone of bohu **Me:** The measuring line is a thing (in this case "chaos") **Primary Reference: Form**
Is 40:17	**Walton:** worthlessness of the nations; parallel to "nothingness" and the "end" (?) **Me:** The nations are likened to "nothing" **Primary Reference: Form**
Is 40:23	**Walton:** rulers of the world made as tohu; parallel to "nothingness" **Me:** God brings princes to a state of "nothingness" **Primary Reference: Form**
Is 41:29	**Walton:** images are wind and tohu; parallel to "end" (?) of their deeds **Me:** Images are likened to "nothing" **Primary Reference: Form**
Is 44:9	**Walton:** all who make images are tohu; parallel to without profit **Me:** All who make images are "nothing" **Primary Reference: Form**
Is 45:18	**Walton:** God did not bring it into existence tohu, but in contrast formed it for habitation (intended function) **Me:** Formed for the purpose of habitation **Primary Reference: Function**
Is 45:19	**Walton:** Israelites not instructed to seek God in waste places; parallel to land of darkness **Me:** A place **Primary Reference: Form**

Tohu: Form or Function?	
Reference	Description
Is 49:4	**Walton:** expending one's strength to no purpose (tohu) **Me:** "Purpose" may be implied, but not translated! "Nothing" is the thing gained by expending one's strength **Primary Reference: Form**
Is 59:4	**Walton:** describes relying on empty arguments or worthless words (ie dissembling); parallel to that which is false or worthless **Me:** The arguments are empty things **Primary Reference: Form**
Jer 4:23	**Walton:** description of tohu and bohu light gone, mountains quaking, no people, no birds, fruitful lands waste, towns in ruin **Me:** What can be seen is "nothing": described in the unequivocal context of a material created world that is being transformed into nothingness **Primary Reference: Form**

Walton leaves out two instances of *tohu*:

Reference	Description
Jer 14:14	The "things of nothing" (cf KJV) are "idolatries"/worthless divinations (so the NIV) ie things. **Primary Reference: Form**
Gen 1:2	This, of course, is the passage the whole Walton Synthesis hangs on. Walton says "function" here because a. ANE cultures thought of creation in terms of function (not proved) *and* that is definitive for Genesis (unlikely presupposition) and b. every other OT use of tohu is function (false!) So, form or function? **Primary Reference: Form**

Making "Made" Not Mean "Made"

There is a close relationship between *made* and *created* in Genesis 1, and throughout the Old Testament. Walton recognises that unless *made* also has the meaning of attributing function in the way he claims *create* has, his thesis fails. Even if *create* relates attribution of function, if *made* has its usual meaning of referring to a material process, Genesis 1 gives an account of the making of stuff. He examines this briefly in discussing day four.[190] His argument is easy to follow:

1. The verb *made* covers "a whole range of meaning, not only of 'making' but also of 'doing.'" In other words, *make* can mean "make" or "do." "It does not inherently refer to a material process."
2. *Made* in Genesis 1 covers functional making. "Even in the summary statements in Genesis 2:2-4 the verb covers all the activities of the seven days, many of which clearly involve only doing, not making."
3. *Made* in Genesis 1 therefore always means "doing," which is attributing function not making stuff.

This short argument is remarkably unsatisfactory.

To say that throughout the Bible *made* has lots of meanings, and that in Genesis 1 it sometimes means attributing function, therefore in Genesis 1 it always means attributing function, is plainly fallacious.

Firstly, there is indeed a wide range of meanings for *asah*, as there is for "made" in English. Context then must determine the meaning. In most of the uses of *made* in Genesis 1 and 2, the natural meaning involves bringing into being something material. But allowing, for the sake of discussion, that it *could* have functional meaning, nothing in the text requires this, except where it parallels *create*, and then only if *create* is functional in that paring. Elsewhere there is nothing in the text that requires *made* to mean "attributed function" and everything in the text to induce a rejection of that idea.

Secondly, ignoring (if one can) Walton's assertion that *made* does not refer to "making," the fact that *made* "covers function" (if it does, for this is a presumption of Walton's, not a given) does not require that *made* is exclusively functional.

Thirdly, even if in day four *made* could mean attributing function, there is nothing in the passage that requires such a reading, and a great deal that indicates *made* is given its ordinary meaning. In particular, verses 14 &15 make a very clear distinction between the "letting there be" lights in the sky (ie bringing them into existence/substance) and "letting them have functions." The same two distinctions are made in verse 16 where the sun and moon are made then in verse 17 given function. If verse 17 refers to the sun and moon but not the stars, the *making* of the stars in verse 16 is a parenthesis, with stars not being given a function we are made aware of; but if they are included in the function of verse 17, then they too are given substance first, then function.

Fourthly, despite insisting *made* always means *giving function* in Genesis 1, in a later discussion of the *making* of animals in day six (v25) he assumes, contrary to everything he is arguing here, that *made* has the meaning of formed.[191]

Fifthly, there is overwhelming use of *asah* that can only mean *made* and could not possibly mean *given function*.

Sixthly, the assertion that "many [of the activities] clearly involve doing, not making" is far from clear, and involves a false dichotomy between function and

---

[190] Walton *The Lost World of Genesis One* Kindle location 594

[191] Walton *The Lost World of Genesis One* Kindle location 152

form. That created/made things are given a function does not exclude their being materially created concurrently.

Seventh, in the Bible *made* and *created* are both applied to:

the creation of the sun, moon and stars (Genesis 1:16 *made* & Psalm 148:5 *created*)
man (Genesis 5:1, 6:6-7, 9:6; & Genesis 1:27)
the heavens and the earth (Genesis 2:4 and Genesis 1:1)
all (Genesis 1:31 and Genesis 2:3)

There are two possibilities for this: 1. That different meanings are intended, and are used in contrast such that (following Walton) *created* means given function while (*contra* Walton) *made* means given substance; or 2. They have similar meaning and are interchangeable, and given that *made* cannot, at least in some instances, mean "given function" but can always mean "given substance", both must mean "given substance".[192] Either way, Walton's thesis cannot be sustained in every instance, meaning that in some instances at least Genesis is recounting physical rather than functional creation.

Walton's argument runs thus: *Make* cannot mean "making" (note that this is his way of putting it) because *create*, to which *make* is linked (although it is only linked if *create* means "making"), doesn't mean "making." Or simply put, *make* doesn't mean "making" because it doesn't, even if looks as if it does.

Testing the Proposition

How does this work in practice? What happens with *asah* and *bara* at the beginning of Genesis 5? They are used interchangeably: inserting the Hebrew transliterations into the translation: "When God created (*bara*) mankind, he made (*asah*) them in the likeness of God." If different meanings are intended – that is, in the unlikely event the text is intended to read, "When God gave function to mankind, he made them in the likeness of God" the making is intimately linked to the giving of function.

In fact, the concurrent use of *made* and *create* with their ordinarily very close meaning is a strong textual indicator that not only is the ordinary meaning intended, it is being emphasised. At times Walton implicitly concedes this. Without explanation or comment he flip-flops between applying *made* in its conventional use of "formed" and in its "Waltonian" use of "giving function." I have alluded above to the fact that despite insisting *made* in Genesis 1 means "attributing function" as opposed to "forming things", he is quite at home with the "forming" meaning of *made* used in "So God made the animals." In this case the conventional meaning of *made* contributes to his argument that God does not give details of how things have been formed.[193] It appears that for Walton what is "always" the case

---

[192] This is not to deny the distinction between *bara* which only ever has God as its subject and *asah* for which others than God can be the subject. That distinction is important, but does not relate to determining whether or not either word means the giving of function or substance.
[193] Walton *The Lost World of Genesis One* Kindle location 152

(*made* always means "giving function") is only always the case in conditions that suit Walton's argument.

Unique Translation or Misrepresentation?

Among citations of ANE texts Walton gives to support his contention that *create* means "attribute function" and not "make" is the following statement relating to lines 53-58 in tablet 5 of *Enuma Elish.* According to Walton they describe "Harnessing of the waters of Tiamat for the purpose of providing the basis of agriculture, piling up of dirt, releasing the Tigris and Euphrates, and digging holes to manage the catchwater."[194] To support his statement he adds an end-note reference. He does not quote the lines, but here is how those lines read in their usual translation:

> Putting her head into position he formed thereon the mountains,
>
> Opening the deep which was in flood,
>
> He caused to flow from her eyes the Euphrates and Tigris,
>
> Stopping her nostrils he left . . . [this part of the tablet is unreadable],
>
> He formed at her udder the lofty mountains,
>
> Therein he drilled springs for the wells to carry off the water.[195]

It takes quite a stretch of the imagination for "he formed thereon the mountains ... he formed at her udder the lofty mountains" to be read in the way Walton claims as "piling up dirt." Translation of this passage is not straight forward, especially with part of the text missing. *Something* is placed on Tiamat's head, and "mountains" is a commonly accepted translation. To render that *something* as piles of agricultural dirt requires an expectation of some agricultural function. Even then, it is about stuff not function. Certainly the two rivers are created, but there is nothing of function implied. The "flood" could refer to the flooding that deposited silt on the land, but even then lines 53-57 are expressly descriptive of condition, not of function. In contrast line 58 clearly speaks of function arising from the structuring of substance. Not only is there nothing here of exclusive functionality, there is clearly a focus on the creation of stuff of substance without, for the most part, reference to function.

---

[194] Walton *The Lost World of Genesis One* Kindle location 548

[195] Denis Bratcher *Enuma Elish: "When on High ..."* Christian Resource Institute, 2013, http://www.crivoice.org/enumaelish.html There are various translations of *Enuma Elish* as there are significant gaps and also uncertainty over numerous words. None of the translations of these lines I have seen however differ in any way that would legitimise Walton's interpretation. Bratcher includes this note with his translation: "The version presented here is a combination of several translations but is substantially based on the translation of E. A. Speiser in *Ancient Near Eastern Texts Relating to the Old Testament*, 3rd edition, edited by James Pritchard (Princeton, 1969), with modifications based on various other translations (for example, the translation of L. W. King, *The Seven Tablets of Creation*, London 1902)." Speiser was more cautious, not attempting a full translation. Instead, he noted at the point where Walton confidently presents his translation, "At this point the text is fragmentary. But enough remains to reveal that Marduk continues to create 'marvellous things.' He pokes out Tiamat's eyes, and the Tigris and Euphrates rivers flow from them. He forms mountains out of her breasts. Then he drills holes in them, allowing springs to gush forth. Finally, as a memorial to his conquest of Tiamat, he turns her eleven monsters into statues and places them at the gate of the Apsu. After these events are described, there is a gap in the text. The story then resumes on Tablet VI."

What is particularly disturbing about this is that, unless the reader takes considerable pains to check what *Enuma Elish* really says, he assumes that Walton's reference is definitive when it plainly is not. Worse, the reader who also bothers to check his end-note discovers that Walton is not referring to a different translation from the usual one, nor to some authority for his unique interpretation, but to his own commentary on Genesis.

Walton cannot claim these lines in *Enuma Elish* unequivocally say what he implies they say. His is the only translation that "translates" the gaps in the text to say what he says they say, and that is the only "translation" that supports his argument. If he is reading back into *Enuma Elish* his concept of function-creation (the best construction that can be put on his reasoning at this point), that still involves significant contortions of the text. In the light of considerable scholarship that renders *Enuma Elish* completely differently and in a way that fails to support either Walton's "translation" or the conclusions he alone draws from his "translation," it could appear that he has made it up to suit his thesis. At the very least, such misrepresentation does nothing to justify his argument but it does a great deal to raise questions about his methodology.

4. Genesis Paganised

Spectres of the Fall: Reading Genesis 1 in the mist of myth

"In the beginning, God created the heavens and the earth."

~ Genesis 1:1

The myths of the Ancient Near East are fascinating. Those we know of paint a colourful picture of a world that for all its architecture, engineering, science, political structures, art, commerce and literature, believed it was dependent upon gods who were like men. Those myths reveal variegated cultures with this much in common: the mythical gods, mediated through idols, manipulated through ritual, and manifested in nature, were believed to be intimately entwined with the events of everyday life. People's lives, it was imagined, were shaped by the harmony or conflict of those mythical gods, their aspirations, schemes, plans and whims.

It is one thing to be able to picture and follow the story-line of these myths; it is another to understand the role those myths played in their various cultures, and still another altogether to assert the Bible is influenced by those myths or their cultural context. As more myths have been found and translated, the more influential ANE mythology has become in various schools of biblical criticism. Yet that influence has not always been congruent with the ways in which myth functioned in the various ANE cultures, much less with the Bible's own claim to originality, differentiation from the surrounding cultures, the prophetic foreknowledge of God, and God's inspiration of the biblical text.

The assumption that the Pentateuch was written from within the cultural context of ANE cultures has led to a contemporary focus on ANE myth as a source of the language, the concepts, and even the content of the Bible. Even those who date the writing of the Pentateuch after the Babylonian Captivity tend to find ANE myth as influential, supposing a cultural transformation over hundreds of years in the Hebrews but not in the Babylonians. It used to be that it was only those who were considered (and considered themselves) as "liberal" who saw in ANE myths parallels to the biblical text, and dependence upon ANE myths by the writers of the Bible. Now however, writers who assert a commitment to the inspiration and authority of the Bible can also be found asserting that the cultures and literature of the nations surrounding Israel are definitive in the writing and reading of the Bible.

This position is well put by Peter Enns who asserts that our understanding of the Bible must be

> adjusted in the light of the preponderance of ... literary evidence from the world of the Bible that helps clarify the kind of literature the Bible is— that is, what it means to read it as it was meant to be read. Furthermore, all of this can be done in a way that respects and honors the authority of the Bible. Indeed, reflecting on the nature of Scripture like this is the very expression of honor and respect.[196]

Contemporary evangelical scholars tend to bypass the implications for the doctrine of Scripture when Enns argues that in the light of this literature and evolutionary science, "one can no longer accept" as historical the Genesis accounts of the creation of humanity, of Adam and Eve, and of the fall. Some argue instead that "perhaps ... we have been misreading the Bible," and that Enns' book *The Evolution of Adam* "is an important contribution to the discussion concerning Genesis 1-2."[197]

Yet this accommodation of the Bible to paganism *does* undermine the authority and inspiration of the Bible by constraining God to pagan myths and culture. It *does* distort the message of the Bible by making paganism the context of each book instead of recognising the people-of-God-culture as the cultural context, and recognising the Bible in its completeness as the literary context of each book. The methodology of this accommodation is wrong; so wrong that, irrespective of the consistency of its conclusions with the data presented and the rationale argued, those conclusions must be rejected by anyone consistently claiming submission to the Bible as inspired by God.

Maximising Paganism, Minimising God

Even if ancient paganism is correctly understood – and there is a very large question mark over that – crediting that paganism as shaping the Bible involves both a presupposition that it is so, and a presumption that God's inspiration of the Bible was limited to pagan concepts and literary forms, or constrained by God's inability to find (or inspire!) authors better suited to conveying a non-pagan revelation by God of himself in words he wanted to use.

---

[196] Peter Enns, *The Evolution of Adam, What the Bible Does and Doesn't Say about Human Origins*, Baker Publishing Group, 2012. Kindle location 192

[197] Tremper Longman III on the back cover of *The Evolution of Adam*

Pagan influence on the Bible is only found where it is presupposed: whether asserting ANE cultural interdependence, engaging in form-criticism or applying source-criticism, the assumption is that those approaches are valid. If one begins with the assumption they are valid, one can find parallels between the Bible and ANE culture and myth, and one can find variations of the text that "must" arise from different sources. Yet without those presuppositions, there is nothing in the text that prompts such conclusions. Instead, the Bible presents itself as a unified collection of books that have literary and authorial integrity; books so inspired by God as to be his word; books that can be read and understood by all in every age in reliance on the culture and language of the Bible itself.

The Bible is of course replete with cultural references and idiomatic language: yet the Bible itself makes those references and that language understandable. When David says "The Lord is my shepherd"[198] the context makes clear that a shepherd cares for his sheep, and that God looks after the writer with real benefits, for the text goes on to describe that care in detail of unmistakable benevolence. Before reading these lines a person may never have had such an image of a shepherd, but the image is conveyed clearly by the text. The image and its meaning are not dependent upon extrinsic data. Knowing more about pastoral practices in David's day may increase appreciation of the image, but they do not change the image.

Similarly when Jesus says, "My sheep listen to my voice ... and they follow me,"[199] the text is sufficient to indicate a pastoral practice that will be foreign to most modern readers: sheep that follow their shepherd's voice, rather than being driven by fear of a sheep-dog's bark and mustered by shepherds who could only distinguish one sheep from another by tags pinned through each sheep's ear.[200] Extrinsic data may improve understanding of the basic message of the text, but they will not rightly change it.

Limiting the Bible's inspiration to the natural understanding and intent of its human writers – those used by God to speak and record his word – strips the Bible of its supernatural character, and holds God at arm's length from the text, while inserting paganism into every line. It is an approach rightly challenged by James K A Smith:

> Enns' argument is predicated on the working assumption that the meaning of the Scriptures is tethered to—and determined by—the intent of the human authors. Indeed, in this approach human authors seem to be the only relevant authors when it comes to understanding the Bible. There is literally no mention (that I could find) in which the meaning of the Scriptures is linked to what the divine Author might have intended.[201]

Smith explains that "While Enns affirms the inspiration and authority of Scripture, this sort of hermeneutical approach functionally naturalizes biblical

---

[198] Psalm 23

[199] John 10:27

[200] As a child I enjoyed regular involvement with sheep-farming, but never was there any inclination to miss the distinctive differences between what I knew of shepherding in my culture and that of the Bible.

[201] James K A Smith *Whose Bible? Which Adam?* (Book Review of *The Evolution of Adam)* http://www.colossianforum.org/2012/04/24/book-review-the-evolution-of-adam-what-the-bible-does-and-doesnt-say-about-human-origins/

interpretation,"[202] so that God has no real role to play in writing the Bible to convey *his* message, nor does the rest of the Bible have any place to play in providing a *context* for reading each biblical book. The authors are merely human, the message merely theirs, and the context merely paganism. Even the human authors can be minimised as this approach unfolds, for "behind them is a cultural context that not only conditions but determines 'what Genesis means.'"[203] Exactly how God then speaks with the words of the Bible, and what his message might be, is left to speculation.

Ambiguous Affirmation of Inspiration

For many commentators such as Enns myth is not only "out there" in ANE culture and literature: it is the very stuff of Bible itself. Indeed, "Enns affirms the inspiration and authority of Scripture,"[204] but not in the historical-confessional way in which evangelical Christians have always regarded that statement. Enns' position is identical to that by which liberals of the last century differentiated themselves from Bible-believers. Like those liberals, for Enns the "Adam story," the "flood story" and the "exodus story" (with what Enns calls its "'cosmic battle' theme") are all mythicized history which gives the modern reader no account of actual historical events or figures.[205]

Even in locating the meaning of Scripture in authorial intent, Enns discards any notion that factual accuracy is determined if the authorial intent can be determined. Enns asserts, "What ancient authors intended does not determine historicity," and argues that it is faulty exegesis to "allow the intentions of these ancient authors to shape our own thinking about whether or not [the Bible's] literary figures actually were real people."[206]

Nor is Enns willing to allow the Bible to interpret itself. This is of course consistent with what Smith has drawn attention to (above) in Enns' minimising of any unified inspiration of the whole Bible by God. Enns recognises, for example, that Paul unambiguously regards Adam as a literal, historical, first man, but rejects any notion that Paul's interpretation of Genesis "should be included in our own deliberations over human origins. This is an inexplicably odd use of ancient sources. One can only ponder what would happen if we treated all ancient points of view in this manner."[207] Indeed. If we took the ancient text of the Bible in such a way, we would be obliged to find historical truth in its accounts and definitive commentary in its words. That, let me add lest there be any misunderstanding, is a good thing. It is what the Bible claims for itself.

One can also ponder what an affirmation of the inspiration and authority of the Bible now means. For Enns it is no more than an "evangelical instinct" that "the

---

[202] ibid
[203] ibid
[204] ibid
[205] See Peter Enns *Still in the Weeds on Human Origins* Book Review of C John Collins *Did Adam and Eve Really Exist*) https://perspectivesjournal.org/blog/2011/12/16/still-in-the-weeds-on-human-origins/
[206] ibid
[207] ibid

Bible is ultimately from God and that it is God's gift to the church."[208] Clearly for some post-moderns it does not mean what it used to mean. Whether such affirmations of commitment to the inspiration and authority of the Bible are deliberately ambiguous (as were some of the affirmations demanded in the Elizabethan Settlement[209]) or an outworking of the natural devolution of meaningful language is unclear. What is clear however is that not every commentary on Genesis that comes with an affirmation of the inspiration and authority of Scripture can be taken at face-value.

On the other hand, Enns' position is such a self-conscious commitment, it enables him to helpfully pinpoint the inconsistencies of those who attempt to conflate a conventional understanding of the inspiration of the Bible with other truth-paradigms. Commenting on the attempts of some to find in the Bible an Adam "created" from evolved hominids, he perceptively argues that such a

> type of hybrid "Adam," clearly driven by the need to account for an evolutionary model, is not the Adam of the biblical authors. Ironically, the desire to protect the Adam of scripture leads [those attempting this] to create an Adam that hardly preserves the biblical portrait. Evolution and a historical Adam cannot be merged by positing an Adam so foreign to the biblical consciousness.[210]

Enns throws down a further and very interesting challenge to those of us in the Reformed tradition by asserting, rightly I think, "The Westminster Confession of Faith leaves no room for anything other than a first couple read literally from the pages of Genesis and Paul, and therefore entails a clear rejection of evolutionary theory."[211] From his perspective in which the Bible's stories are myths, and affirmation of the inspiration and authority of the Bible does not mean what the Westminster Confession means, Enns is able to see clearly what should be obvious to all. We do well to be alert to the fact that, on a number of planes, an affirmation of biblical/confessional orthodoxy may not mean actual biblical/confessional orthodoxy.

Overstated Similarities

Much is often made of "similarities" between the Bible and various ancient myths. This, it is argued, means that the Bible adapts the myths to its own story and message, or at least shares a conceptual context. That such similarities exist in any substantial way is much more debatable than is often asserted,[212] but even if the similarities are there, the existence of similarities establishes neither proof nor necessity of inter-dependence of the texts on each other.

---

[208] Enns *Inspiration & Incarnation* Kindle location 74

[209] The *Elizabethan Settlement* was an affirmation of the Protestant nature of the Church of England's doctrine and practice under Queen Elizabeth I in which numerous statements were sufficiently ambiguous as to allow many Anglo-Catholics to publicly affirm them while privately retaining their Catholic convictions.

[210] Enns *Still in the Weeds of Human Origins*

[211] Enns *Still in the Weeds of Human Origins.* Enns' particular reference here is to Collins, but he is alert to the fact that Collins is not alone in this approach.

[212] Currid comments, "In regard to the creation itself, there are major differences, that is, core distinctions between Genesis 1-2 and other ancient Near Eastern accounts." *Against the Gods* Kindle location 694

In a thoroughly comprehensive study of myths and the Bible,[213] John Oswalt gives detailed refutation of the idea of textual inter-dependence, and he does so with substantial evidence. He summarises the difference between pagan myth and the Bible as a contrast between continuity and transcendence.[214] He argues that the predisposition of many scholars to a belief in the common origin of the Bible and ANE texts in fact makes them unwilling to recognise the glaring differences that exist.[215] Be that as it may, the differences are so great that occasional vague similarities cannot justify any claim to textual inter-dependence:

> When we compare the characteristics [of myth] with what we find in the Bible, it becomes clear that on every one of these points the biblical worldview differs—and not merely slightly, but diametrically. ... any straightforward comparison must conclude that beneath any possible surface similarities are radically different ways of thinking about reality.[216]

It is worth quoting him at length in his evaluation of one example of supposed similarity. In one Egyptian myth the god Ptah is described as speaking things into existence, which some maintain is similar to God speaking things into existence in Genesis:

> Two things need to be said in that regard. First, as with monotheism, it is nowhere said in the Bible, nor am I saying, that the Bible is the only place where these ideas ever appeared. That is not what makes the Bible unique. What makes it unique is that it maintains these points of view exclusively and throughout. ... in a pagan worldview it is entirely possible to maintain several contradictory views at once. But for some reason, the Bible does not do that, and it acts as if it is not possible. That one document somewhere once suggests that one way of thinking about origins is through the medium of speech is far from being "the same" as the Bible. Second, it is instructive to see what the Egyptian text actually says. It reads, "His Ennead [the Nine Gods] is before him in (in form of) teeth and lips. That is (the equivalent of) the semen and hand of Atum. Whereas the Ennead of Atum came into being by his semen and his fingers, the Ennead (of Ptah), however, is the teeth and lips in this mouth, which pronounced the name of everything, from which Shu and Tefnut came forth, and which was the fashioner of the Ennead.... He is indeed Ta-tenen, who brought forth the gods, for everything came forth from him ..." (ANET, 5). This is not what is being said in Genesis. In fact it is simply an alternate way of expressing the idea that we exist as an emanation of the divine, something the Bible denies vehemently."[217]

Even if the Bible had significant similarities with ANE myths, *dependence* is but one explanation among several possibilities. There is nothing but the presuppositions of sceptics to support the contention that the Bible was shaped by those myths. But the few similarities that actually do exist are overwhelmed by the differences. Not only does the Bible *not* look as if it is shaped by ANE myths, it looks *so different* that contending for biblical dependence on myth is simply untenable.

---

[213] John N Oswalt *The Bible Among the Myths: Unique Revelation or Just Ancient Literature?* Zondervan, 2009

[214] See his headings for chapters 3 & 4

[215] Oswalt *The Bible Among the Myths* Kindle location 3194

[216] Oswalt *The Bible Among the Myths* Kindle location 897

[217] ibid

Equating the Bible to Functional Myth

Walton however goes beyond merely asserting a pagan influence on the writing of the Bible. He says that the Bible actually functions as myth functions:

> For the Israelites, Genesis 1 offered explanations of their view of origins and operations, in the same way that mythologies served in the rest of the ancient world and that science serves our western cultures. It ... serves the similar function of offering an explanation of origins and how the world operated, not only for Israel, but for people today who put their faith in the Bible.[218]

It appears here that Walton is claiming that Genesis 1 *does* offer an explanation of the origins of the cosmos, even though his main thesis has been to deny that. That, he says in this place, is what the Israelites got from it when it was first written, and what we get from it today. We can agree that Genesis 1 does explain the origins of the cosmos, but it nonetheless *functions* in a radically different way to myth. Genesis functions as a *true* account from God instructing people that God is Creator, that creation has its origins in nothing material but in God's will and words, and that God is distinct from creation. Myths re-enact the received history of the seen and unseen sides of a contiguous material/spiritual existence, with the aim of bringing the participants into harmony with cosmic-bound gods.

Two things are happening here: firstly, Walton is assuming that ancient myths had a function of describing the origins of the cosmos in a sort of modern scientific way, although he elsewhere argues otherwise; and secondly, he is implying that Genesis offers an explanation of origins that is not physically and historically true, but sufficient to satisfy the Hebrews in their day. He is wrong on both counts. As we will see, while a handful of ANE texts have accounts or allusions to creation, the primary function of even those texts was not to instruct people as to the origins of the cosmos, but to facilitate manipulation of deities. And the Bible is no mere ancient myth in which "truth" operates on various conflicting levels; rather, it recounts historical truth that is consistently true at every level in all cultures for all time.

If, at the same time as describing the Bible as a type of literature called myth, science is given the same function as myth (as does Walton here), then science ceases to be something to be engaged in within the world-and-life view of the Bible, but an alternative to it. The choice then becomes science *or* the Bible/myth. But science and the Bible do not serve our culture in the same way. They are not therefore mutually exclusive as myth and science are, or as myth and the Bible are. Science offers a tentative description of what can be observed of the reality that cannot be comprehensively or infallibly observed; the Bible infallibly describes the reality known comprehensively to the Maker and Sustainer of reality so that observers of reality can frame their fallible observations in the context of revealed truth. In likening the Bible to myth that serves the same function then as science does now, Walton effectively dismisses the Bible as having any relevance to inform contemporary understanding or observation of the cosmos.

---

[218] Walton *The Lost World of Genesis One* Kindle location 107

Walton regards myth as a way in which a culture expresses its beliefs, "real description of deep beliefs." Therefore, he argues, "we need not be concerned that the Bible must consequently be understood as just another piece of ancient mythology,"[219] although "not presented as their own ideas, but as revelation from God."[220] We should be deeply concerned however, at the dismissal by Walton, Enns and others of the Bible as myth, and the assertion that God revealed himself in deeply held beliefs that lack historical accuracy. But the Bible views God as revealing himself "precisely through God's actions in events in time and space. … the reality [is] that God acts in history and speaks about history. God does not merely teach general truths about himself."[221]

Is There Truth in Untrue Myths?

The term "myth" is used in radically different ways by different people. We are probably on common ground if we take "myth" as at least referring to traditional stories that help transmit a culture's worldview or values. For some, such stories are true, for others they are fictional with an underlying truth, and for others they are simply faery tales with at best generalised moral themes. The assumption is often made that myths are religious, but that is not only not necessarily so, but in the ANE it was often the case (as will be seen shortly) that myths were used for political or educational reasons without overt religious application.

Turning to myths that are religious, it is clear that most if not all picture a reality that does not have a rational unity, or match observable existence and phenomena in literally true ways. Most evangelicals work within a worldview that assumes a non-contradictory unity. We may not understand all the links, but as God made everything in a consistent unity, it is all ultimately knowable without contradiction. From such a viewpoint anyone using myth, with its *obvious* irrational untruths, is considered to accept that that part of their picture is untrue. To some degree or other rationality is suspended so that truth can be found in what is known to be untrue. That is the only way we can accept that some use myths that cannot be rationally integrated into the universe as they know it. This is the paradigm most commonly adopted by evangelicals when speaking or writing of "myth." But it is a paradigm virtually unknown to cultures where religious myths played a part. It is adopted by many in modern and post-modern "spiritual" movements, including many evangelicals. It is, however, another excellent example of cultural imperialism: since, for us, the stories cannot be true, we impose on myth-cultures a consciousness of the fictional nature of their myths. That in turn is used to justify using their myths as a model for approaching our traditional stories (ie the Bible) as the same genre. Yet traditional religious myth-cultures never, so far as I am aware, used myth that way.

The myth-culture I am most aware of is my own Māori heritage in which, for example, the carvings of ancestors are not representative of the ancestors: they are considered to actually *be* the ancestors. The evangelical/rational response to this is to consider myth-believing Māori either to be conscious of the "untruth" of

---

219 Walton *The Lost World of Genesis One* Kindle location 107

220 Walton *The Lost World of Genesis One* Kindle location 112

221 Weeks *Cosmology in Historical Context* p293 foot

regarding the carvings as literal ancestors, or to be lost in superstition where rational knowledge is at best suspended or at worst abandoned. But that only works for post-modern spiritualism (evangelical or otherwise), and completely misrepresents Māori concepts. As Oswalt points out, "In a pagan worldview it is entirely possible to maintain several contradictory views at once."[222] For myth-believing Māori a number of "facts" are wholly and simultaneously true: their ancestors are dead bodies, their ancestors are their carvings (multiple carvings in multiple locations), their ancestors are physically with them, their ancestors are in the realm of the dead, their ancestors are gods ... and so on.[223] In such a worldview the pieces are not expected to fit together "rationally" for that would be completely *irrational* within such a worldview. Empirical knowledge and rational thought are not suspended in such a worldview: they are held to be simultaneously true with knowledge that cannot be subject to empirical examination or expressed in a single unity. In fact, it cannot be otherwise, for in *any* worldview that denies God his place as creator and sustainer of reality there can be no unity – there must be irreconcilable and irrational contradictions.[224]

For evangelicals therefore to say that myths are "real descriptions of deep beliefs" is to completely miss the point. Firstly, the implication is that because the beliefs are "deeply held," untruth can be employed to convey, explain and justify them. This is nonsense, but it is essential nonsense for those who want the Bible to have God-inspired untrue stories to convey truth, for it appears to give them a cultural context for such a genre (albeit a context of mirage without substance). "Truths" that are conveyed by untruths are not truly true – that is, they are not expressed in God's framework, they are not seen as God sees them. They are by their very nature perversions of truth.

Secondly, and perhaps even more importantly, describing myths as "real descriptions of deep beliefs," implies that myths explain the unseen reality in a way that integrates it into the seen reality. Thus Walton asserts myths "explained" things to pagans and Israelites alike, and that the other literatures of myth (such as the Bible and science) function in the same way: truly or fictionally integrating whatever they address into an empirically rational worldview. Not only do myths necessarily fail at such integration, they inevitably lead to idolatry.

The Bible is not Myth

Idolatry can take a number of forms. Overtly, idols are substituted for God and worshipped as gods.[225] Making desires the centre of our lives is idolatry.[226] So too

---

[222] Oswalt *The Bible Among the Myths* Kindle location 897

[223] The importance of carved idols in such myth should not be minimised: as human in origin and form, as part of nature (being stone or wood), and as divine in that it is the ancestor (now become a god), the carving is the embodiment of humanity, nature and divinity united.

[224] This has significant implications on the social/moral front: a murderer, simultaneously and without contradiction, can be held to have done wrong and be good, the esteemed epitome of family values and a disgrace to the family, worthy of punishment and justly aggrieved by the punishment received, excused if "sorry" and vindicated in retaliation against anyone associated with the victim or the justice system.

[225] Exodus 32 cf Nehemiah 9:18

[226] Colossians 3:5

is using a pagan paradigm in an attempt to truly worship God,[227] which is exactly what is done when myth, known to be or regarded as untrue, is used to worship the God of unimpeachable truth.

The key to this is to realise that for cultures using myths religiously, myths are more than stories of value. For such myth-cultures myths are the means by which "the continuities among the human, natural, and divine realms are expressed and realised ... to ensure the orderly functioning of both nature and human society."[228] The myths engage story-teller and listener, actor and participant, in the divine-natural continuity, harmonising individuals, communities, nature and the gods. To classify myths as a genre of untrue stories conveying truth is completely inadequate, for in cultures where myths function religiously, myths are true stories making true the supposed promises of unity declared by the ultimate idol, nature. Myth "is a particular way of looking at reality ... [in which] there are no fundamental distinctions between the three realms: humanity, nature and the divine."[229] This is not the worldview of the Bible.

Religious myth cannot be isolated from its pantheistic function. It follows that the place of myth in the worldview of the ANE cultures involves much more than using untruth to convey truth. In fact, *it does not involve using untruth to convey truth* at all, because myth was never considered to be untrue. Rather, the common conceptual worldview of the ANE within which Walton would have the Bible written and read is one of unrestrained idolatry. The context of myth is not one of allowing untruth to express truth, but of lies taken as truth harmonising the continuity of a pantheistic universe. The use of myth, whether in ancient cultures or modern biblical theology, is quite simply abominable idolatry.

The purpose of this discussion by Walton arguing that myth conveys "deeply held beliefs" appears to be to legitimise the use of ANE myths to frame a context, a view of the cosmos, through which Genesis 1 can be read. Yet, quite apart from the inadequate concept of myth this involves, a number of things distinguish Genesis from myth, and Walton even pinpoints the primary one without allowing it to make any difference:

1. Genesis 1 is truth revealed by God; ANE myths are not.

To this we can add:

2. For myths to be recognised as descriptions of a culture's beliefs, there must be evidence that they were known and accepted popularly within that culture. The evidence is that ANE myths were of very limited circulation among the small elite who were literate, and even then were of limited use. Not so Genesis which was written for an entire people who knew it intimately. Genesis does not describe the beliefs of Israel; it defines what Israel was to believe.
3. As discussed below, much ANE myth appears to have been primarily concerned with sustaining political order, but where it did have direct religious application the ritual use of myth was intended to influence the

---

[227] Leviticus 10:1,2

[228] Oswalt quoting B S Childs, *Myth and Reality in the Old Testament*, SCM, London, 1960 p27-28 in *The Bible Among the Myths* Kindle location 625

[229] Oswalt *The Bible Among the Myths* Kindle location 636

gods favourably. Not so Genesis, which was never used in ritual and was intended to influence people, not God.

The assumption that ANE myths had a primary role of describing the cosmos may appeal but cannot be sustained. Noel Weeks has shown that, contrary to popular contemporary myth about ANE myths, they were not composed with a common purpose, they were not shared among all ANE cultures, and they did not always have the same function in differing cultures.[230] He demonstrates that there is no evidence of cultic or religious use of Mesopotamian myths, and that they were used to teach advance literary skills to a select élite in much the same way as most cultures teach "people to read and write via the literary classics." Although the Hittites had myths, those myths are noticeable for their absence in their numerous, well-documented rituals. In Syrian Ugarit there is no evidence of the cultic or religious use of the known Baal myths, whereas in Emar the rituals are documented but display "no evidence of dependence upon or allusion to myths." In "Egypt we have abundant evidence of the cultic use of myth but do not find that myth written down in coherent form until late."

Weeks makes an instructive comparison between Mesopotamian and Egyptian myths. The Mesopotamian gods were "powerful but unreasonable, self-centred and capricious." The role of the Mesopotamian kings was to keep those fickle gods on-side. Training the literary, administrative elite through such stories served the purpose of "reinforcing the political system." In contrast, the Egyptian gods were not unreasonably inclined to do their own thing but worked harmoniously with the King, so Egyptian myths describe how good government functions and "reinforce the royal position as competent and caring." Although in both these cases the myths were different, and the political systems in which they were used were different, the purpose for which they were used was the same: to achieve political stability. In neither case was their main purpose the explanation of either the nature or the origins of the cosmos.

Informing or Influencing?

Even if ANE myths had held a common cosmic view and had shared a common religious purpose, that view and that purpose would have been in error: they exclude the one true God and his self-revelation from their presuppositions, from their narrative, and from their use. They have nothing but error with which to inform the reading of Genesis.

Walton is correct in recognising that when ANE myths had a religious or cultic use, they described how present conditions were said to have been brought about. But retelling the myths did more than describe how the present came to be. "Retelling of a [mythical] story secures the effects of the story for the present."[231] Myth-telling was neither the celebration of history nor the sacrifice of reverential worship, but a formula used "to exert a measure of control over the divine and

[230] Noel Weeks *Myth in the Ancient Near East* (paper supplied by Weeks)
[231] Oswalt *The Bible Among the Myths* Kindle location 594-595

nature. But perhaps equally important, this understanding also means that humans can participate in nature and in the divine." [232]

ANE myths are no mere cultural novelties, benign accounts of a world-view. Rather, "Myth is a form of expression, whether literary or oral, whereby the continuities among the human, natural, and divine realms are expressed and actualized. By reinforcing these continuities, it seeks to ensure the orderly functioning of both nature and human society."[233]

In contrast, the Bible "is a rehearsal of the nonrepeatable acts of God in identifiable time and space in concert with human beings. Its purpose is to provoke human choices and behaviour through the medium of memory."[234] Reading myths served the same purpose as having sex with a temple prostitute:[235] by words or actions the deeds of the gods were rehearsed, bringing participants into concert with the gods and nature. Fate left no moral choice and held-out no culpability, but fate could be influenced, the gods persuaded, and a taste of divinity experienced if harmony could be achieved through ritual re-enactment in sex, myth, or both. The Bible, on the other hand, reveals God, reveals his will, and revels the consequence of obedience or rebellion. In reading the Bible, people are informed and given choice. God is not influenced by our reading of the Bible, nor are we harmonised with nature or divinity by reading the Bible: we are informed, and hopefully moved. On the basis of that information we make choices for which we are held accountable. The God of the Bible is in control, but unlike the pagan gods, he is in control in righteousness; and people are not captive to fate – their choices are real and God will faithfully superintend the outcomes to ensure they will always be consistent with those choices.[236]

It is not just that the Bible's view of the cosmos and man's place in it differs on a cosmic scale with ANE mythology; the use to which the Bible text and the ANE texts were to be put were also different on a cosmic scale. It is not just that reading the Bible in the light of ANE myths is inappropriate – it is irrational. Genesis 1 is not, by any stretch of the imagination, the same as ANE myths as defined within ANE cultural understanding and use of myth, or within a contemporary understanding and use of myth. To assert otherwise is to engage in cultural imperialism that contorts both the ancient myths and the Bible.

---

[232] Oswalt *The Bible Among the Myths* Kindle location 665

[233] Oswalt *The Bible Among the Myths* Kindle location 626

[234] Oswalt *The Bible Among the Myths* Kindle location 632

[235] "Plant and animal life are the result of divine copulation, for all things in this world that we know have their origins in sexual behavior. Therefore, the thing to do is to get the god and goddess to have sexual relations. If they do, then the rain will fall into the womb of the earth and fertilize it. How do we do that? By asking them to do so, or trusting them to do so? Far from it! We do it for them through ritual enactment. As the worshiper and the priestess have sex together under the appropriate ritual circumstances, the god and goddess do so as well and the rhythms of nature are maintained." Oswalt *The Bible among the Myths* Kindle locations 712-713

[236] Not forgetting, that is, God's gracious intervention for those he loves to justly overthrow the consequences of sin and save the lost who trust in Christ. That too is part of the information given by the Bible upon which people make choices.

Misleading Myths About Myths

Walton presents an image of a relatively large collection of ANE literature describing that world's concept of creation. Even if the error of interpreting the Bible in the light of such literature is set aside, the literature simply does not exist in the way Walton asserts. The texts we have are at best snapshots of a culture: fragments of cultural expression frozen in a moment of time. It takes only a brief reflection on our own culture to realise that quite a large collection of snapshot-texts could be randomly gathered that would give a distorted picture of the way in which our society lives. It would take a truly vast collection of accurately recorded and clearly translated texts before a definitive picture of a complex culture could be reliably constructed.

Walton is correct to comment that some ANE texts give some information about the various views of creation.[237] Rather than contributing a united view of creation, they tend to compete with each other, and indicate even that different cities within the same national culture held different views. But when he then goes on to list what he calls "fully-fledged creation texts" he creates an impression that cannot be sustained by the facts.

Among those "fully-fledged creation texts" he lists:[238]

The *Egyptian Memphite Theology*. Rather than being a "fully fledged creation text" this is better described as a political mystery drama reciting how the powers of the gods have been controlled and balanced. The *Theology* is carved into stone in a fascinating manner, with lines of text radiating from the centre and at times opposing each other on the stone in a kind of graphical antiphony. Its focus is on the supremacy of the god Ptah and the pantheism by which he is everywhere and in everything. It is difficult to regard the reading of Genesis 1 in the light of this text as satisfactory biblical scholarship. Apart from the creation of the gods as eminences of Ptah, "creation" of the cosmos only gets a brief mention:

> ... concerning Ptah-Tenen: "He gave birth to the gods." From him everything came forth: foods, provisions, divine offerings, all good things. Thus Thoth knew and recorded that he is the mightiest of the gods. Thus Ptah was satisfied after he had made all things and all divine words. He gave birth to the gods, he made the towns, he established the nomes, he placed the gods in their shrines, he settled their offerings, he established their shrines, he made their bodies according to their wishes. Thus the gods entered into their bodies of every kind of wood, of every kind of stone, of every kind of clay, in every kind of thing that grows upon him in which they came to be. Thus all the gods and their kas were gathered to him, content and united with the Lord of the Two Lands.[239]

This is not, by any stretch of the imagination, a "fully fledged creation text."

Papyrus Leiden I 350. This is a portion of a ship's log-book covering ten days of a journey, written in an unusual cursive script, with much of the text missing. It itemises correspondence to and from the ship, and the daily issue of food to

---

[237] Walton *The Lost World of Genesis One* Kindle location 250

[238] Walton *The Lost World of Genesis One* Kindle location 247

[239] Translation of the *Shabaka Stone* lines 58-61 in Wim van den Dungen, *On the Shabaka Stone*, Antwerp, 2003, http://www.maat.sofiatopia.org/shabaka.htm

the crew. On the back is a collection of hymns to the god Amun. Although there is passing reference to Amun making himself and everything else, there is nothing in these hymns that is in any sense an account of creation, let-alone a "fully-fledged creation text." It primarily relates to Amun, who is said to have formed his own primordial egg from which he hatched himself, and secondarily to the gods which he variously "sneezed" or "honked" (as the "Great Honker" himself, no less!) or otherwise brought into existence. Light, land, sky and "what is" all get a mention, but only as reference points to the glory of Amun. Far from revealing who Amun is and how he created, the focus is on the unknowability of Amun and his work, with lines 22-24 of the 4th hymn expressing this clearly: "None of the gods knows His true form, His image is not unfolded in the papyrus rolls, nothing certain is testified about Him."[240]

The fact that a ship's log is recorded on the reverse of these hymns also raises the question as to how reverently the hymns were regarded. It would appear that the ship's officer writing the log did not hold the theology of the hymns in particularly high regard; that in turn raises questions about the cultural significance of the hymns themselves. For ANE scholarship they hold significance because there is little else relevant to this discussion available: but if what is available is only available because it was recycled rubbish, how much significance should be placed on that theology as a representative theology? In any case, there seems very little here to help with understanding Genesis 1. It is not a "fully-fledged creation text."

***Pyramid Texts, Coffin Texts* and *Book of the Dead*.** Although there is passing reference to the existence of things, and the gods themselves being generated from eggs, mounds, spit, and opening flowers, (and transmuting into the shape of other gods), these texts too are primarily concerned with the supremacy of Ptah and relationships between the gods. There is no substantial treatment of creative acts themselves. Why Walton inserts the words "especially from Heliopolis, featuring Atum" after reference to the *Book of the Dead* is unclear. There are over 100 references to Heliopolis in the spells for the after-life that make up the *Book of the Dead* and many allude to Atum, but not a single one to creation. These texts have no significance for the reading of Genesis 1, and are not "fully-fledged creation texts."

Proliferating "Proofs" that Don't Exist

Although he alludes to numerous unnamed texts, the existence of which cannot be confirmed, texts Walton specially references can be examined. But with singular consistency they have nothing to contribute to Walton's synthesis by way of being accounts of creation. After the Egyptian texts he lists:

The *Babylonian Atrahasis*. Commonly called a "creation myth," it is more properly described as a "flood myth" in which the structure rather than the creation of the cosmos is seen in outline as a setting for the gods who fight over relative ascendency and about the laboriousness of their work in the existing

---

[240] Wim van den Dungen, *Amun, the Great God :Hidden, One and Millions.*, Antwerp, v#5, 2015 http://www.maat.sofiatopia.org/amun.htm

cosmos. Their violent bickering and scheming leads to the manufacturing of man to take over their workload. The only creation-type account in it is this making of man from the flesh and blood of a slain god, and by the gods "spitting" into the dirt from which man is born 10 months later.

Various (mostly unspecified) Sumerian, Mesopotamian and Akkadian texts, said by Walton to "contain cosmogonic ... or cosmological statements. ... statements in passing [that] at times contain mythological sections that are cosmogonic. Even genealogical lists of the gods are thought to give hints to the extent that cosmogony can be inferred from theogony."

In other words, if you obfuscate enough you can justify a claim that these are creation texts even though they plainly are not.

"Allusions" said to be found in additional Egyptian texts. Walton asserts that the most important allusions are to be found in the *Instruction of Merikare*. This is comprised of a long list of instructions from a king to his son on how he should rule. Near the end, there is a brief reference to creation. It is indeed an "allusion," but nothing more than that. It is unmistakably expressing a pantheistic continuity that is completely foreign to Genesis 1. Despite some interesting points of comparison, this "most important" allusion falls far short of being a creation text, let alone providing insight on Genesis 1:

> Provide for men, the cattle of God, for He made heaven and earth at their desire [or for their sake]. He suppressed the greed of the waters, He gave the breath of life to their noses, for they are likenesses of Him which issued from His flesh. He shines in the sky for the benefit of their hearts; He has made herbs, cattle and fish to nourish them. ... He makes daylight for the benefit of their hearts, and he sails around in order to see them.[241]
>
> [Capitalisation supplied by the translator.]

No actual creation texts are listed or even implied by Walton. The nearest he can get to a creation text is "hints," vague "allusions" and "passing statements containing cosmogonic reference." From these obscure shadows Walton appears to infer they are "full-fledge creation texts," but that is an inference few others are likely to find persuasive.

Walton concludes this short and unconvincing list with the *Egyptian Papyrus Insinger* which is from the 1st Century AD, although it is supposed to have originated in the 3rd Century BC. This does indeed have some 18 lines recounting creation, but why this is considered an ANE text is not made clear. He appears to argue that it continues the tradition established in ANE literature. If in fact that tradition had been established – and it is certainly not established in his references – that would still add little to his core argument. Why should a document from the 3rd Century BC be definitive for the writing or reading of Genesis 1?

---

[241] Translation by R O Faulkner in William Simpson (ed) *The Literature of Ancient Egypt*, New Haven, 1973, pp190f. (The alternative translation is by M Lichtheim.)

In a 2013 speech in Auckland, Walton bolstered his short list with reference to "thousands of texts"[242] that contained "hints" about the common ANE cosmology he claims influenced the Hebrews. Even if they existed, they would not be evidence of ANE cosmological influence on Genesis – but they don't. True, there are tens of thousands of ANE texts in the form of tablets inscribed in the relevant languages of a wide variety of ANE cultures, including a number of languages completely unknown to biblical scholars until the 20th century. But they shed no light – neither by hint nor allusion – on local ANE cosmologies, let alone a common one. They have enabled linguistic studies to advance considerably, and with most being official records of one sort or another, have helped build pictures of the social and economic organisation of various ANE cultures. But so far as informing a cosmology that influenced Genesis, studies of them have so far proved useless, and reference to them as contributing to such an understanding is spurious.

From all this (or despite all this) Walton summarises what he considers are common concepts of ANE cosmology.[243] Apart from the polytheistic pantheism (he describes that as "The cosmos functioned as an extension of the gods, and the gods functioned within the cosmos"), and that the gods tended to be responsible for particular bits of the cosmos, there is nothing that can be definitively attributed to all ANE cultures on the evidence given. Nor, on the evidence given, is there anything here that should provide a context in which to read Genesis 1.

What is interesting is that Walton's bias towards function in place of form surfaces here so directly. He describes pantheism in terms of function not ontological existence, even though those functions are dependent upon existence. He asserts that the "functional orientation of [the *Egyptian Papyrus Insinger*] is obvious." While many of the "things" said to be created are abstractions such as "sleep", "dreams" and "birth," where concrete things are said to be created, their creation in substance comes before the attribution of function. By way of example, here are the first six lines from the translation he quotes:

> He created light and darkness in which is every creature.
>
> He created the earth, begetting millions, swallowing them up and begetting them again.
>
> He created day, month, and year through the commands of the lord of command.
>
> He created summer and winter through the rising and setting of Sothis.
>
> He created food before those who are alive, the wonder of the fields.
>
> He created the constellations of those that are in the sky, so that those on the earth should learn them.[244]

The remainder of his quotation continues in similar vein. Function is indeed obvious here, but not in place of form. Function here is dependent upon form; *and* form gets its function at the time it is created, not at some later stage.

---

[242] From *Understanding Genesis 1-3: Exploring Two Contrasting Evangelical Perspectives,* 17 July 2013. See http://vimeo.com/75344887 and http://vimeo.com/75344886 [I was in the audience at the time.]

[243] Walton *The Lost World of Genesis One* Kindle location 257f

[244] Walton *The Lost World of Genesis One* Kindle location 286f

Enuma Elish: Does It Deliver?

It transpires that in all this literature listed there is but one creation narrative to which Walton alludes, the Babylonian *Enuma Elish*. That could be because it is the only one that exists. "One of the reasons there has been a tendency to try to link Genesis 1 and *Enuma Elish* is that these two are the only known texts from the Ancient Near East with a detailed account of creation."[245]

It is for this reason that so much weight is placed on *Enuma Elish* by those linking ANE culture to Genesis 1. If *Enuma Elish* is excluded from being representative of an imagined but elusive multi-national ANE culture spanning centuries, there is no text of relevance left that is available to scholars that documents the supposed common ANE cultural context within which Genesis 1 is, it is asserted, to be interpreted. We do know that across the nations and ages grouped in ANE culture, a God-less, Creator-less, polytheistic pantheism prevailed; we can be certain of little else in ANE culture that might have relevance to Genesis 1.

The only relevant relationship possible with such diametrically opposed texts is that one is written to refute the other, since clearly neither could build on the other as a source text. If one is sourced in the other, there would be significant rather than tenuous similarities in the two. If one is a refutation of the other, there would be more than opposing worldviews evident at every single point: there would be some direct allusion or cross-referencing in one or the other of the texts. There are no such points of intersection.

Yet even if Genesis 1 was written with such subtlety that *Enuma Elish* was in view but not evidently so, that it was in view needs to be demonstrated before anything can be adduced from that (supposed) relationship. Not only is there no evidence of such a relationship, as discussed above, Genesis 1 is written from within and for a culture isolated physically, religiously, socially and conceptually from surrounding ANE cultures. Even if Genesis had not been written in that context, at the very least it was written to establish such a context. Even if it did not come out of a radically distinct culture, it inducts Israel into such a culture. Its content, its method, and its message are all different from every other ANE text.

Some have conjured up similarities in structure between Genesis 1 and *Enuma Elish*, but those too fail to establish anything but a passing commonality in arranging ideas in a logical order. There is just as much commonality in structure between *Enuma Elish* and the weather forecast for Auckland showing at the side of my computer screen as I write. In fact, there is quite a lot of structural similarity,[246]

---

[245] Weeks *Correspondence*

[246] In both *Enuma Elish* and the weather forecast there is a deliberate beginning and end, statements are frequently fragmented, there is frequent unlinked disjunction between sections, local idiom and jargon is interspersed with language common to other texts, context is assumed, cosmology is significant but largely unstated, there is clear movement in the text from the skies to the earth, both include storms, both use the techniques of narrative and repetition, at least two words used have the same root, one of the words missing from a broken tablet could be reconstructed as something like "Auckland", both have highly functional implications for the material form, both help explain the environment, the texts themselves reveal no obvious application of the information supplied ... and so on. (In fact, one can pretty well do something like this with any two texts: which should induce a considerable caution in

but it doesn't take post-graduate scholarship to discern that neither is written in dependence upon or in refutation of the other.

Setting aside the dramatically different worldviews, and the extensive difference in details of the two creation accounts, what similarities are there between the two? Despite all the hype, very little. In fact, very little at all! Both describe the creation of some of the same things,[247] but in different order;[248] and both involve naming some of the things created. Hardly anything less could be expected of independent descriptions of the same cosmos coming into being.

Chicken or Egg? Creation or Myth?

Perhaps some can find more similarities between Genesis and ANE texts than I can. Perhaps some can demonstrate a level of interdependence. If such interdependence exists, it depends entirely on which came first, the Genesis story or the ANE stories. Romans 1 solves that for us. The myths arose out of a prior rejection of the knowledge of God.[249]

Enuma Elish begins in a "chaos" (which is sometimes made out to be the same as "formless and void") in which birds fly – except that Genesis 1:2 does not describe a condition of "chaos."[250] There are seven days in the Genesis account and *Enuma Elish* is written on seven tablets; but there is no sectional division in *Enuma Elish* corresponding to the different tablets. At the end of each tablet the writer simply ran out of clay and started a new page, the text flowing on without disjunction or division. Oh, and one word (the Hebrew *tehom* translated "deep" in Genesis) may have the same root as the name of the goddess "Tiamat" in *Enuma Elish*[251]... so? Even more tenuous is the theory that one word, only part of which is visible on a broken tablet, if reconstructed from the fragment in a particular way, is sort of linked to the Hebrew word *Shabbat* in Genesis 2.

There is but one apparent similarity that deserves consideration: both texts recount a division of the waters and are said to thereby share a common cosmology. I will consider that shortly.

With so much at stake in making *Enuma Elish* definitive for ANE and Hebrew cultures, each example of the improbability and inconsistency of linking ANE culture to Genesis 1 is dismissed on the basis of a generalised acceptance of textual-dependence for which actual evidence cannot be adduced. Each failed similarity is set aside by appeal to the unseen "obvious" commonality.

---

using textual comparisons in literary criticism in any field. Finding similarities in two texts, and only two texts, proves nothing except that there are similarities from which nothing can be inferred!)

[247] The creation of light, plants and animals are not included in *Enuma Elish*.

[248] The sun, moon and stars come as soon as the heavens are created in *Enuma Elish*, but two days later in Genesis.

[249] Romans 1:18-24

[250] See the discussion above p98ff and again p217 below.

[251] "In reality, the identification of *tehom* with Tiamat is dubious at best. In addition, there is not even a hint of God having to do battle with the deep, and the deep is certainly not portrayed as a deity in the biblical text. The Hebrew creation account understands the deep as the primal world ocean that God created at the beginning of time." [Currid *Against the Gods* Kindle location 692]

When in 1876 George Smith of the British Museum published the first translation of *Enuma Elish* he was committed to the idea that Genesis was a development of Babylonian cosmology – and that *Enuma Elish* was the key to this. The necessary presupposition was that *Enuma Elish* predated Genesis, an assumption that has predominated for years. However, modern consensus dates *Enuma Elish* much later than Moses, which means that if Genesis was written by Moses, it could not be based on or even be a response to *Enuma Elish*.

Yet dating aside, *Enuma Elish* is not even representative of its own cultural heritage, let alone all ANE cultures over multiple centuries. It is an oddity, albeit a fascinating one. Earlier Babylonian references to creation recount a peaceful setting in which there is no violence among the gods, and one of the leading characters in *Enuma Elish*, Tiamat, was virtually unknown.[252] So far from being representative of Babylonian culture, *Enuma Elish* is clearly an innovation. Nor was it a popular text, read and known by multitudes. Genesis is just such a text, designed to be used in daily life of all the covenant people, but *Enuma Elish* was read once a year by one priest to the idol of Marduk in his temple – probably with no one else listening. Unlike Genesis, which is an instructive text by which people learn what God wants, *Enuma Elish* was used for a ritual re-enactment of Marduk's glory by which the priest endeavoured to gain influence with the god to do what people wanted. There is no evidence that *Enuma Elish* was known at all widely, much less that it reflected popular culture.

Whether or not there is a most unlikely literary link between *Enuma Elish* and Genesis, there is no evidence that *Enuma Elish* represents the common Babylonian culture when Genesis 1 was written, much less that it describes an ANE context in which Genesis must be read.

A Solid Canopy of Heaven – or Not!

One of the most pervasive and persistent myths about ANE myths is that the Hebrews shared a belief with the surrounding cultures in a three-tiered cosmos, with a flat-disk-world supported on pillars in water and covered above by a solid dome or vault. Variations of this theme are found in all sorts of literature from Wikipedia to Walton.

The point usually made is that because of this no one should read Genesis 1 as indicative of the structure of the cosmos. Since we moderns have true scientific knowledge in contrast to the myths, it is argued, why should we regard Genesis as giving any reliable information about the structure or formation of the cosmos? Or as Enns claims, "God transformed the ancient myths so that Israel's story would come to focus on its God, the real one."[253] In other words, the Genesis account retells the ANE myths with a focus on God instead of on the false gods, and cannot therefore offer any valid historical or scientific information.

So if the Genesis account is seen as telling a different story from the ANE myths, it is discounted in favour of the ANE myths that are supposed to be the same sort

---

[252] Weeks *Correspondence*

[253] Peter Enns *Inspiration and Incarnation: Evangelicals and the Problem of the Old Testament* Baker Academic, Grand Rapids, 2005, Kindle location 907

of literature with the same non-literal style. Why can no hint of cosmic structure be found in one sample and detailed cosmic structure in another when each is supposed to have the same degree of literal reference? Irrational prejudice decides ANE myths have reliable authority and Genesis has none.

Or if the Genesis account is seen as telling the same story as the ANE myths with a different focus, it has no useful or reliable information apart from a message about the supremacy of God compared to pagan gods. Even if Genesis does not explicitly describe a solid canopy of heaven, the argument goes, that is what was intended because that is what they believed. Once you accept that false presupposition, you can find hints of a solid canopy in Genesis if you try hard enough.

Many accounts of this cosmic myth are accompanied by variations of the diagram reproduced here:[254]

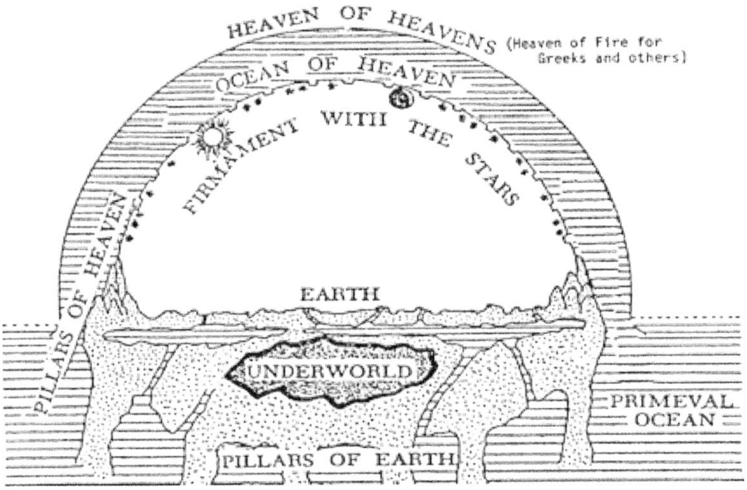

Where does this come from? It all hinges on one map drawn 1,000 years after the ANE period, and selected fragments of ANE documents that invite varied interpretations. To get there, a host of other ANE fragments that give a different picture must be ignored. Noel Weeks has critiqued this approach, showing that there was no uniform Mesopotamian cosmology that could be used to construct this model; that the specifics in various myths (such things as the materials of "heaven", the nature and location of waters, the pillars, and the vault or dome) cannot be consistently represented in a single model; and that unless one adopts particular models of social development (such as a Marxist one) there is no necessity to assume the Hebrews adopted a uniform contemporary model of cosmology even if one had existed.[255]

---

[254] This is copied from Peter Enns Enns http://biologos.org/blog/the-firmament-of-genesis-1-is-solid-but-thats-not-the-point , but can be found in this and similar forms in a multitude of publications.
[255] Noel Weeks, "Cosmology in Historical Context" *Westminster Theological Journal* WTJ68:2 (Fall 2006) pp283ff

In one of the strange quirks of contemporary Old Testament scholarship, a claim can be made for biblical evidence of a Hebrew concept of a solid vaulted sky and associated myths by taking biblical metaphor literally. This stream of scholarship rejects passages presented as history as having any literal meaning, while taking plainly metaphorical passages as having an obscure literality, supporting the presupposition of a Hebrew concept of a solid heavenly vault (and its associated ideas). Thus Heiser finds Job's description of God marking out a boundary between light and darkness[256] as evidence of a solid dome.[257] Similarly, he finds the Psalmist's description of God's "setting the earth on its foundations,"[258] and Jonah's description of sinking "to the roots of the mountains"[259] as evidence that the earth rests on "pillars or sunken foundations."[260] One might have thought that modern geology would agree with Jonah – the roots of the mountains are indeed found at the bottom of the sea – but Heiser's presupposition rules out such an obvious reading, just as it rules out reading metaphor as metaphor. Yet for anyone willing to consider the text in its own light, "The Hebrew conception of the universe as an architectural structure is clearly figurative."[261]

Walton's patronising assertions are typical of the misrepresentation used to discredit the data in Genesis:

> The Israelites ... did not know that the sun was much further away ... than the birds flying in the air. They believed that the sky was material (not vaporous), solid enough to support the residence of deity as well as hold back waters. In these ways, and in many others, they thought about the cosmos in much the same way that anyone in the ancient world thought, and not like anyone thinks today.[262]

Yet he has no basis for attributing these beliefs to the Israelites, nor is there any "same way the ancient world thought" about such things. His "proof" is merely a proposition (he calls it "Proposition 1") for which he adduces no evidence but upon which he builds his arguments for not trusting Genesis as it is written.

We have no idea of the cosmology held by the Israelites before God gave them the true cosmology. Even if they had shared a cosmology with other ANE cultures before God spoke Genesis 1, Genesis 1 does not reveal anything about any such cosmology:

> Whatever that cosmology may have been, we do not know. Had they not been the recipients of special revelation their cosmology probably would have been somewhat similar to that of the Babylonians. There is no reason to believe that their ideas as to the origin of the heavens and the earth would have been more 'advanced' than those of their neighbors. Israel, however, was favored of God in that he gave her a revelation concerning the creation of heaven and earth, and Genesis one is that revelation.[263]

---

[256] Job 26:10
[257] Michael Heiser, *I Dare You Not to Bore Me with the Bible,* Lexham Press, Bellingham, 2014, p3
[258] Psalm 104:5
[259] Jonah 2:6
[260] ibid
[261] Currid, *Ancient Egypt* p 43
[262] Walton *The Lost World of Genesis One* Kindle location 121
[263] Young *Studies in Genesis One* p82

In the chapter discussing *Proposition 1* Walton sets up several false dichotomies that allow for the apparent imputation of a solid-heavens and flat-disk floating earth to Hebrew cosmology. He argues that Genesis 1 does not tell us the earth is spherical or that the stars are suns so it cannot therefore have any valid scientific information. He argues that as the ancients did not distinguish the "natural world" from the realm of God's activity, we cannot expect Genesis to provide information about what we call the "natural world." He repeatedly shifts discussion to ancient literature as "the key to proper interpretation of the text"[264] without demonstrating that his assertion is valid. He dispenses with the fact that Genesis, with its distinctive form, style and content, and written by and for a people in physical, cultural, social and religious separation, and its uniqueness as inspired by God, is in no way similar – let alone identical – literature, by ignoring it.

Even in the ANE literature there is no consistent view of a solid dome, and it strains the text more than a little to find it in the biblical account. Most discussion centres on the meaning of the Hebrew *raqia* translated in the KJV as "firmament" and in most modern versions as "expanse."[265] The basic argument is that because its root has reference to metal that is beaten out and shaped, *raqia* must have the same reference: "The noun *raqia* is derived from the verb that means to beat out or stamp out, as in hammering metal into thin plates (Exodus 39:3). This suggests that the noun form is likewise related to something solid."[266] This is a classic example of the root fallacy.[267] The context in which *raqia* is used is far more significant than its root in determining its meaning: and "solid" just does not fit.

Where Do the Birds Fly?

There is extensive refutation of the idea that *raqia* is a solid dome. Consider G K Beale's discussion, for example:

> Therefore, rather than considered as a completely solid substance the *raqia* is perhaps best thought of as diaphanously spread out and transparent. Thus, "expanse" may be the best translation. The word has this notion in Isaiah 42:5 and 44:24. Even in Exodus 39:3 the verbal form is used for hammering out gold into gold leaf; i.e., the emphasis does not appear to be so much on the substance but on the spreading out of it. Thus, the focus is on the expansive nature in that the *raqia* which Genesis 1:8 defines as "heaven," is spread out from horizon to horizon. If the *raqia* is solid, then how does rain get through it, how do the clouds relate to it, how do the sun, moon, and stars move through it, and how do the birds fly in it (on the latter cf. Gen. 1:20)? There is nothing about the word *raqia* or about the ancient conception of the cosmos that requires the notion of some kind of solid barrier.[268]

Raqia is called "heaven" in Genesis 1:8 and according to Deuteronomy 4:17 it is in that heaven that the birds fly.[269] If *raqia* is solid, the birds are quite exceptional.

---

[264] Walton *The Lost World of Genesis One* Kindle location 182

[265] So the ESV & NIV (2008). In what appears to be an accommodation to the concept of a solid dome however, the NIV (2011) has used the word "vault".

[266] Peter Enns "The Firmament of Genesis 1 is Solid But That's Not the Point"

[267] cf D A Carson *Exegetical Fallacies* pp26ff

[268] Beale The Erosion of Inerrancy in Evangelicalism pp198f Kindle location 4321

[269] cf Weeks "Cosmology" and others

Birds fly in *raqia*, God is enthroned in *raqia*,[270] he sets the stars, planets, sun and moon in *raqia*, [271] the sun, moon and planets move around in *raqia*, and *raqia* is stretched out and spread like a tent or cloud.[272] This is not a picture of a solid dome. The idea that the Hebrews thought the sky was a solid dome is false, and cannot be used to minimise the data given in Genesis one.

Mapping the Mesopotamian World

The map that is supposed to support the myth that the Hebrews and other ANE peoples believed that heaven was a solid dome is the beautiful cuneiform fragment pictured here, dating from about 600 BC now held in the British Museum.[273]

This is a schematic representation of Mesopotamia from a Babylonian perspective. The text gives a number of details that help explain the map. Babylon is in the middle. Various other nations are located in accurate orientation to Babylon. The whole region is surrounded by a salt-water ocean, beyond which are a number of islands or other regions. There is quite a lot that can be learnt about the way the Babylonians who made the map in 600 BC understood their world.

---

[270] Psalm 11:4
[271] Genesis 1:14-18
[272] Isaiah 42:5
[273] http://www.britishmuseum.org/explore/highlights/highlight_objects/me/m/map_of_the_world.aspx reproduced by permission

What does this map tell us about the way ANE peoples, or the ancient Hebrews in particular, viewed their world? Zilch. Nothing. Zero. Unless, that is, you are an Old Testament scholar with a prejudice against a factually reliable Genesis – in which case you can conjure up all sorts of significance from this irrelevant artefact.

An article by Brian Godowa[274] on the Biologos[275] website epitomises this approach. First you age the map, although his making it 200 years older than the date given by other academics still leaves it so far short of ANE culture that it defies credibility to consider it representative of a culture that had long ceased to exist when the map was made as a contemporary map. You then note that it is flat, and imply that means they thought of the world as flat, ignoring the fact that even today maps on flat pages or screens are just as flat as maps on clay tablets. Nobody today would imply users of atlases and sat-navs think the world is flat, so why should that implication be dumped on people who used flat tablets to map their world?

You have what is plainly a schematic map - as schematic as a modern underground rail system map; but you assert it is their representation of real geography, which means they thought of their world as a disk even though the contents of the map indicate a knowledge of Mesopotamia that could not be confined to a disk. You then call the ocean around Mesopotamia a "cosmic ocean", which not only means you are discarding the "real geography" and its real oceans upon which the last assertion was based, but you can now assert that they thus thought of a dome above them holding back the cosmic waters. You ignore the presence of islands on the other side of the ocean, indicating that they did not think this "disk" represented their entire world. You repeat unsustainable assertions (such as *raqia* meaning something solid) and selective bits from pagan myths that are contradicted in other bits of those same myths (such as the pillars of the earth penetrating into waters under the earth).

Next you turn to the Bible a find every metaphor that can be twisted into a description of a physical reality that fits the myth. Finally you accuse everyone who differs with you of taking biblical metaphors too literally (which is what you have just been doing), and conclude "God did not consider it important enough to correct this primitive inaccurate understanding."[276] Poor God! He had to make do with myths, misrepresentations and mistakes. It is just as well we now have experts who can explain what God really did in words we can really understand.

Cynicism is warranted. Even if the cosmology were accurately represented, the equivocal arguments, the irrational inconsistencies, the hermeneutical gymnastics, the misquotations, the selective use of data, and the belittling of God lead to only one conclusion: the whole case that this map represents belief in a solid-domed-heaven above a flat earth floating on pillars in water – and that such a belief can be teleported back hundreds of years – is just rubbish.

---

[274] Brian Godowa *Mesopotamian Cosmic Geography in the Bible* Biologos, (undated) http://biologos.org/uploads/projects/godawa_scholarly_paper_2.pdf

[275] Biologos is an organisation that describes itself as presenting "evolution as God's means of creation, so that the Church may celebrate and the world may see the harmony between science and biblical faith." Its commitment to belief "that God created the universe, the earth, and all life over billions of years" includes belief that God created humans through evolution "in biological continuity with all life on earth." See http://biologos.org/about

[276] Godowa *Mesopotamian Cosmic Geography*

The time between the writing of Genesis and the making of this map is about the same as the time between the signing of Magna Carta with King John in 1215 and the making of the current schematic map of the London Underground. One would be stupid to attempt to determine the nature of the culture and beliefs in King John's day from reading today's map of the London Underground. Is it any less stupid to attribute the beliefs and ideas in this schematic map of Babylon to people just as distant?

The Joshua Option

Having led the people of Israel out of their 40 years in the wilderness into the Promised Land, Joshua put a proposal to them.

> Now fear the LORD and serve him with all faithfulness. Throw away the gods your ancestors worshiped beyond the Euphrates River and in Egypt, and serve the LORD. But if serving the LORD seems undesirable to you, then choose for yourselves this day whom you will serve, whether the gods your ancestors served beyond the Euphrates, or the gods of the Amorites, in whose land you are living. But as for me and my household, we will serve the LORD.[277]

It is evident from this that they knew something of the myths and gods of the surrounding ANE nations, and knew that the God of Abraham, Moses, and Joshua – and his word – was different. There could be no synthesis. It didn't much matter which false myths and gods they followed, or synthesised into their worship of God: any or all meant rejecting and abandoning the true God. The same can be said for us: it doesn't much matter which of the deceitful myths we synthesise into our Bible reading, if we don't throw them away and make the distinctively different God and his distinctively different word exclusive, we are rejecting and abandoning the God of the Bible.

[277] Joshua 24:14,15

5. Genesis Mistaken

Temples of the Mist: Reading Genesis 1 in the mist of temple imagery

"In the beginning, God created the heavens and the earth."

~ Genesis 1:1

According to Walton (and others), the ultimate purpose of the attributing of function to the creation was to make the cosmos a temple for God. This, Walton asserts, is the most important aspect of his approach to Genesis. "The cosmos is being given its functions as God's temple, where he has taken up his residence and from where he runs the cosmos. This world is his headquarters."[278]

Walton claims biblical support for his view that the cosmos is set up to be the temple in which God dwells by quoting Solomon at the dedication of God's temple in Jerusalem, "The heavens, even the highest heavens, cannot contain you."[279] But this says the opposite: rather than the cosmos being the place created for God's dwelling, it cannot contain him; it is expressly excluded from being his residence, even though he is about to presence himself in it.

Walton also refers to Psalm 132 where God is said to rest in Zion as his dwelling place.[280] There is indeed a link made here to God's dwelling in Zion and the Jerusalem temple. Although this is the only passage Walton cites in which there is

---

278 Walton *The Lost World of Genesis One* Kindle locations 1551-1552
279 Walton *The Lost World of Genesis One* Kindle location 794 quoting 1 Kings 8:27
280 Walton *The Lost World of Genesis One* Kindle location 682

such a direct link, it cannot be dismissed on the grounds that there is no other explicit reference. I will return to Psalm 132 after looking at the biblical concept of God's temple,[281] but it is sufficient for the moment to note that even if God's temple shares with pagan temples the idea of it being a place for God's rest and rule, that does not establish that the cosmos of Genesis 1 is a temple.

Walton's main argument for what he calls *the cosmic temple inauguration view*[282] however is the pagan temple concept of deity resting in a temple. This is, he says, "the interpretive key from the ancient Near East"[283] that enables a true understanding of Genesis 1. A much more dominant and universally consistent interpretive key however is that the gods *were* the universe. If we want to understand pagan concept of their world, the key is not found in the temples in which the gods temporarily rested, but in the cosmos that was the gods.

Walton is not alone in viewing the cosmos as a temple in which God dwells. Before looking more closely at Walton's ideas, it will be helpful to look at the work of G K Beale[284], with which Walton interacts.[285] That discussion will then be anchored in looking at the Bible's concept of God's temple. With that in place, I will return to an examination of Walton's *cosmic temple inauguration view*.

Correctly Handling the Word of Truth

Before going there however, the question has to be asked, "Is this important? Does it really make a difference if creation was formed as a temple for God?" It is easy to spend a great deal of time on little things and ignore weightier matters.[286] Every point of biblical interpretation has its place, yet is this among the more important issues of today? I would suggest five reasons for answering, "Yes."

Firstly, we are bound to apply ourselves to rightly understanding God's word, correctly handling the word of truth.[287] Jesus did not criticise the Pharisees for paying attention to the "mint, dill and cumin..." but for neglecting the "more important matters of the law." They should, he said, "have practised the latter without neglecting the former."[288] Whether or not the purpose of creation is a great or little matter, faithfulness to God, respect for his word and a commitment to worship as he wants to be worshiped means we must be sure what the Bible is teaching. That being said however, the purpose for which God made the cosmos,

---

[281] See below p146

[282] Walton *The Lost World of Genesis One* Kindle location 1547

[283] Walton *The Lost World of Genesis One* Kindle location 706

[284] Particularly G K Beale *The Temple and the Church's Mission: A Biblical Theology of the Dwelling Place of God* IVP Academic, Downers Grove, 2004

[285] Walton lists Beale's *The Temple and the Church's Mission* as a resource for "technical support" at the end of his short Proposition (Chapter) 8. Although he does not quote it directly, Walton's discussion of the biblical evidence (cf the pagan evidence Walton primarily draws upon) for the cosmos as temple closely parallels Beale. Beale, on the other hand, makes frequent specific reference to Walton. At times it appears one depends on the other for affirmation of a point originating with the other, extending their own circular arguments into circular dialogue!

[286] cf Matthew 23:24

[287] 2 Timothy 2:15

[288] Matthew 23:23

the way in which we live in it, and the worship of our Creator, are far weightier matters than how much dill we tithe: they are significant.

Using a Biblical Interpretive Framework

Secondly, the way in which we interpret Genesis 1 is significant for other passages of God's word. Later revelation, especially the New Testament, provides an authoritative interpretive framework for understanding earlier revelation. Thus Genesis 1 is rightly interpreted in the light of the rest of Genesis, in the light of the rest of the Old Testament, and in the light of the New Testament. But the method employed by advocates of a cosmic temple view appears to rest more on reading the imagery and metaphor of later revelation back into Genesis 1, rather than on explicit commentary on Genesis 1 in later texts, or on necessary implications for Genesis 1 in later texts.

We can be sure, for example, that the creation of woman from man in Genesis 2 is as it is described because under the inspiration of God's Spirit Paul refers to that as a basis for the relationship of man and woman to each other, and for their mutual dependence on God.[289] We can be sure that the seventh day of creation is a day because God gives that as the basis for establishing the Sabbath "day."[290]

It is, however, an entirely different thing to say that since plants were carved into the walls of the temple, the existence of plants in Eden makes Eden a temple.[291] There is no commentary within the biblical text – explicit or implicit – that indicates that. Nor is there any necessary implication that since the temple used images of plants that can be found in a garden, gardens must be regarded as temples, or that Eden in particular should be regarded as a temple, especially as the carved plants are never referenced to Eden: they could just as easily be drawn from the pleasant places of the day. Wiseman allows a possible connection with Eden on two "ifs": *if* the carvings are symbolic, and *if* they are symbolic of Eden, they "could represent the Garden of God (Eden)". Nevertheless such carvings were "common decorative motifs found in wide use at this time."[292] The consequence of adopting this method of reading possible references in later texts which rest upon possible but unstated conditions back into Genesis 1 legitimises such an interpretive inversion in every subsequent passage for every "possible" reference. Almost anything is then "possible."

Who Approaches in God's Temple?

Thirdly, God's temple in Israel, imaging as it does the heavenly temple, has significance far beyond its function in the cosmos. It does provide a symbolic mechanism for man's approach to God in worship, but it does far more than that. It pictures to us the glory and grace of God's rule in heaven, and the place of the

---

[289] 1 Corinthians 11:11,12
[290] Exodus 20:11
[291] As Beale argues – see below.
[292] Donald Wiseman *1 & 2 Kings: An Introductory Commentary* IVP, Nottingham, 1993, pp118f

sacrificial work of Christ to redeem and sustain an unlovely people loved, an unholy people made holy, a rebellious people reconciled in peace to their Maker.

Unlike the pagan temples of the surrounding ANE nations, God's temple in Israel symbolised and mediated God's approach to mankind. This Temple is described as God's dwelling place in what might appear to be similar terms to those of other temples. But God comes into his temple in mercy. God's earthly sanctuary holds no idol of himself, but a covenant record kept in a mercy seat. God is holy, and without his initiative sinful mankind has no way of approaching God.

Because God approaches man in the temple, man can approach God. Man approaches God in the temple through sacrifices that temporarily atone for man's sin before a holy and wrathful God – temporarily because the sacrifices of animals can never cover sin.[293] Yet those sacrifices enabled man to approach God because they foreshadowed the perfect sacrifice of Christ, the Son of God, in the heavenly temple[294] which the earthly tabernacle and temple imitated. God initiates fellowship with man through the temple and its repeated and inadequate sacrifices[295] that keep pointing to a greater need, a greater temple, and a greater sacrifice. Despite its glory, despite the presence of God, despite the sacrifices, the temple could not provide for eternal fellowship of man with God. The very weakness of the temple is the means by which God points to God's ultimate solution, a solution that eclipses the temple made by men. God ultimately initiates fellowship with man through the perfect and completed sacrifice of Jesus in a sanctuary not made by men but by God.

Yes, God's temple is a symbolic mechanism for mankind to approach God in worship; but such an approach is only possible because of the temple's greater function of mediating God's approach in mercy to created mankind who, through that mercy can not only worship, but can find peace with the Creator. A right understanding of this is foundational to our relationship with God. It means that any temple in Eden before the fall – if it indeed existed – had a radically different rather than identical function, for in Eden at the beginning there was no need for sin to be set aside, no place for the atoning mercy the later tabernacle and temple symbolised and mediated.

Heaven: In or Out of the Cosmos?

Fourthly, interpreting Scripture by Scripture gives a picture of the cosmos, the garden, the temple, and God, that is dramatically and significantly different from that seen when Scripture is interpreted in the framework of pagan ANE temples. Pagan temples reflected the cosmos and pointed to gods contained in and contiguous with it, and over which they exercised limited, contested power. Even when they spoke of "heaven," the pagan mythologies pictured a place within the cosmos, for the pagan gods and the cosmos were of the same substance, and there was nowhere and no one beyond the cosmos. God's temple reflects heaven beyond the cosmos and points to God who cannot be contained in the cosmos which he has

[293] Hebrews 10:4
[294] Hebrews 9:24
[295] Hebrews 10:3

made out of nothing, with which he shares no substance, and over which he rules absolutely.

Fifthly, the cosmic temple concept relates directly to Walton's interpretation of "create" in Genesis 1 as functional rather than material. If there is no temple in Genesis 1, the attribution of temple functionality becomes meaningless, and Walton's claim that "create" means function becomes (on yet another basis) unsustainable.

What are Temples For?

Pagan temples had a variety of functions, but they can be summed up as places where men approached gods like themselves to induce those gods to do what men wanted, whether that be to conduct the spiritual world harmoniously so that it didn't disrupt life on earth, or to provide for specific needs such as a good harvest, a safe journey, or a victory over an enemy. In contrast, God's temple was a place where a holy and completely "other" God came to unholy, created, fallen but loved mankind with forgiveness, cleansing and empowering grace to make it possible for men to do what God wanted.

We may bring to the reading of the Bible various concepts of "temple," either consciously or unconsciously shaped by our linguistic, historical or theological heritage or studies. But the only concept that is biblically valid is the view of the Bible itself.

Pagan ANE temples had in common features that distort the Bible's concepts at almost every point:

1. Often the god was localised in the temple, even sleeping, being woken and fed there; but even when not resident in the temple but in the cosmos, the temple was a shrine to a god who could not escape the cosmos[296]
2. The temple imitated the cosmos
3. The god was usually made visible by an idol
4. The god shared substance with the cosmos that was shaped by the god and others out of themselves or out of the cosmos
5. The temple was the space in which mankind fearfully groomed the god to fulfil the worshipers' desires
6. Every god had to leave whatever temple he rested in to rule or act because he had to locate in the place of action with the material or force with which he shared substance

In contrast, God's temple in Jerusalem

---

[296] eg E I Banks asserts of the great temple at Ephesus "The temple of Diana was not properly the home of the goddess; it was but a shrine, the chief one, devoted to her service. She lived in Nature; she was everywhere wherever there was life, the mother of all living things." E J Banks in James Orr (ed) *International Standard Bible Encyclopedia* 1951 http://www.biblestudytools.com/encyclopedias/isbe/diana-artemis.html

1. Was a place where God who remained present everywhere within *and beyond* the cosmos made his glory and his presence known
2. Was modelled on the reality in heaven,[297] beyond the cosmos
3. Held no representation of God, but instead contained the written record of the covenant basis for Israel's relationship with God
4. Differentiated mankind and the cosmos from God
5. Was the space where God demonstrated his holiness, and his approach to mankind with an offer of forgiveness and peace so that mankind could lovingly fulfil God's will

As Walton explains, in a pagan temple,

> The gods' needs were not cared for just so that the people would be graced with good harvests. The temple was the control center for order in the cosmos and that order had to be maintained. The deity needed to be cared for so that he/she could focus his/her energies on the important work of holding forces of chaos at bay. The rituals, therefore, served not simply as gifts to the deity or mechanical liturgical words and actions. The rituals provided a means by which humans could play a role in maintaining order in the cosmos. ... Sacrifices played an important role in this system. As the food of the gods, it is arguably the most important provision to sustain their presence, favour, and the smooth operation of the cosmos.[298]

It could not be otherwise for the pagan ANE cultures, for their gods were part of the cosmos, and were essentially just men with greater power. The gods may have conducted many of their affairs in a higher realm within the cosmos than mankind conducted affairs, but they were the same kinds of affairs (in both senses of the word), conducted by entities having the same kinds of functions, needs and failings as men, in a relationship of mutual dependence and constant struggle for power.

What Walton misses here however, is what we must keep coming back to: although the gods were met, fed and lobbied in their temples, they did not and could not rule from their temples. If temples were the control centres of the cosmos, they were only so as places from which the gods would venture to exercise control. The gods had to leave the temples to rule because they were the things ruled. For a god enticed with gifts or rituals in the temple to provide sailors with propitious winds at sea, the god of the wind had to be there blowing because he was the wind. No mere word sent from a temple throne could induce remote grain to ripen: the god and the grain were one, and for it to ripen the god had to be there. In stark and unmistakable contrast, the God of the Bible rules by word and authority from outside of the cosmos of which he is never a part.

Despite the truly cosmic difference between the pagan world and the biblical one, Walton asserts,

> The differences in the ritual details and procedures notwithstanding, the ritual world of Israel shared a common foundation with what is known in the ancient world. Leviticus 16 offers a comparative window into this world as an annual rite where

---

[297] Hebrews 8:5

[298] Walton *Ancient Near Eastern Thought* p130

the sanctity of the sanctuary is ritually returned to its equilibrium to preserve the presence of the deity and order in the cosmos."[299]

This is, quite simply, an unmitigated distortion of Leviticus 16 which actually describes how atonement was to be made between Moses and the people, and God! There is nothing in Leviticus 16 of restoring balance to sanctuary or to the cosmos through ritual, or of "preserving the presence of deity" as if rituals could oblige, induce or deceive God into staying for man's good pleasure! The foundation for Leviticus 16 is the holiness of the Creator who shares nothing of substance with creation, yet in grace comes into it to restore a relationship with his creatures who have no role in persuading him to do anything in the cosmos other than display his glory. His people come to him with submissive petition for unmerited mercy and gracious keeping of the promise God has made. "The sanctuary is the way of access to God's presence in its public worship and sacramental rites that address human guilt."[300] There is no common foundation between the ritual world of Israel and the known ancient world.

A Garden Temple?

Beale's work, which stimulates an exciting rethinking of our life and service on earth as priestly worship in the presence of God, is typical of the work of a number of other modern commentators[301] who expound the idea that the Garden of Eden is a temple.[302] This presently popular view of the Garden of Eden gives credence to Walton's proposal. Yet for all that is of value in Beale's work,[303] it appears Beale's exposition at this point distorts the creation account in Genesis.

Unlike Walton, Beale asserts primary dependence upon biblical evidence.[304] He recognises that any similarities between pagan and biblical culture and practice

---

[299] Walton Ancient Near Eastern Thought p131

[300] Collins *Genesis 1-4* Kindle location 2093

[301] While Beale's work dominates evangelical commentary, and numerous other evangelicals (including John Collins and Tim Keller) interact with him, Jewish commentators [eg Lea Mazor, "The Correlation between the Garden of Eden and the Temple," *Shnaton: An Annual for Biblical and Ancient Near Eastern Studies*, 13, 2002, pp. 5-42; and Lifsa Schachter, "The Garden of Eden as God's First Sanctuary" *The Jewish Bible Quarterly*, Vol 41, No 2, 2013, p73] and Catholic commentators [Dwight Longenecker *The Temple and the Garden of God* http://www.patheos.com/blogs/standingonmyhead/2012/11/the-temple-and-the-garden-of-god.html] are among many who work the same territory.

[302] The primary focus of Beale's *The Temple and the Church's Mission* is, as the publisher's blurb states, "that the Old Testament tabernacle and temples were symbolically designed to point to the end-time reality that God's presence, formerly limited to the Holy of Holies, would be extended throughout the cosmos." I do not take issue with this eschatological perspective, but when he extends that to assert "John's vision in Revelation 21 is best understood as picturing the new heavens and earth as the eschatological temple" it appears to me to be in conflict with the passage (Revelation 21) it claims to explain.

[303] Beale encourages hope and faith, and a largely consistent reading of the Bible's story-line by pointing to the eschatological fulfilment of all temple symbolism, from the tabernacle to the church.

[304] With regard to establishing the Garden of Eden as a proto-type temple, Beale makes his case with 14 points: 13 are specifically biblical, but one appeals to ANE concepts of temples. Despite his preference for biblical evidence however, Beale uses what he calls "Evidence from the ancient cultures surrounding Israel" (p58) and contends "that the significance and symbolism of the temple can be better understood in the context of ancient Near Eastern assumptions" (back cover).

could arise just as much from pagan awareness of the truth and/or imitation of Israel, as from Israel's supposed imitation of paganism:

> The resemblance of pagan temples to Israel's temple probably was due, at least in part, to a refracted and marred understanding of the true conception of the temple that was present from the very beginning. ... As the image of God is not erased but distorted in unbelieving humanity, it is plausible that some of the affinities in ancient pagan beliefs and religious institutions to that of Israel's may be due to the fact that they are garbled, shadowy representations about the being of the biblical God and of his design for his dwelling place. [305]

Beale lists 14 parallels between Eden and Israel's tabernacle/temple as a basis for describing Eden as the first temple. In a subsequent 2005 lecture[306] he focuses on nine of these, each of which is taken to imply that Eden had the same temple-function as the temple because the temple employed symbolism reflecting Eden. This is the most basic form of circular reasoning.

Here are some of Beale's "proofs":

1. The temple was the place where God met with Israel, and Eden was the place where God met with Adam.[307] *This not only reads the temple back into Genesis, but assumes that temple equals God's presence, and that God's presence equals temple. But as Revelation 21 demonstrates, God's presence can be experienced without a temple, and that is the goal of redeeming creation from the fall. Given that the creation of a new heavens and earth portrayed in Revelation 21 involves some sort of restoration or recovery of Eden before the fall, Revelation 21 implies God was present without a temple before the fall.*
2. Adam had to cultivate and keep the garden and the temple priests had to "cultivate and keep" the temple.[308] *This turns the practice in the garden upon which the practice in the temple was to be modelled into the same thing without any textual justification. The temple practice is presented as a metaphor for the original (and ultimate) temple-less worship, but Beale turns the referent for the metaphor into the metaphor itself, leaving the metaphor without a referent (and thereby making it meaningless symbolism).*
3. "The 'tree of life' itself was probably the model for the lampstand placed directly outside the 'Holy of Holies' in Israel's temple."[309] *That this should be regarded "probable" stretches the concept of vague possibility to probability, then to proof! Only on the basis of a presupposition that Eden is a temple can this imaginative probability have any credence, in which case it cannot prove its presupposition; and even then it has little by way of evidence and provides a sound basis for justifiable scepticism.*

---

[305] Gregory K. Beale "Eden, the Temple, and the Church's Mission in the New Creation" in *Journal of Evangelical Theological. Society* 48/1 (March 2005) p29 & p51 http://jbburnett.com/resources/beale_eden-temple-mission.pdf

[306] Beale "Eden, the Temple and the Church's Mission" pp5-31

[307] Beale "Eden, the Temple and the Church's Mission" p7

[308] ibid

[309] Beale "Eden, the Temple and the Church's Mission" p8

4. Israel's temple had "wood carvings which gave it a garden-like atmosphere."[310] *So perhaps the temple used imagery to remind Israel of what was lost in the fall and what was to be sought through temple-sacrifice, or perhaps a "garden-like atmosphere", if such an atmosphere can be generated by carvings on a wooden wall, was simply a pleasant context for worshipping the God who created all plants. But Eden was more than a box with carvings creating a garden-like atmosphere: it was a living garden in a vast, open, sinless world. Again, Beale imposes the latter construct on the earlier passage.*

One of the "proofs" offered by Beale however, requires more than passing comment: "it may even be discernible that there was a sanctuary and a holy place in Eden corresponding roughly to that in Israel's later temple."[311] Even with a presupposition that Eden equals temple, it is extremely hard to discern what Beale claims "may" be discerned. There is not even a hint of this "holy place" in the Genesis account of the Garden of Eden. It cannot be located even by implication. In fact, the opposite is implied: it was as Adam walked without being tied to a specific spot in the garden that God met him, not when he prostrated himself at some sacred place. By no stretch of the imagination does this constitute adequate exegetical proof for what Beale admits generations of earlier commentators may have overlooked (or have never seen because it is not there to be seen!). Too much is imagined, while too little attention is given to what the text actually describes.

Yet Beale's reasoning goes even one step further into the illogical. He writes

> Israel's temple is explicitly called a "temple" for the first time in redemptive history. Never before had God's unique presence with his covenant people been formally called a "temple." We have seen how, nevertheless, the Garden of Eden had essential similarities with Israel's temple, which shows that Israel's temple was a development of the implicit sanctuary in Genesis 2.[312]

Follow this if you can:

Israel's temple is the first thing called a temple in the Bible, which would surely suggest the earlier Eden was not a temple, but Beale takes it to mean the opposite;

God's presence is called a "temple." No it isn't! The temple is called a temple, albeit God presences himself in the temple as he had presenced himself in numerous other contexts;

The Garden of Eden had similarities with the temple. Actually, the temple had similarities with gardens, which in turn had similarities with Eden's garden, but inversion of relationship is essential to Beale's reasoning;

The Temple was a development of the "sanctuary" in the Garden, although no "sanctuary" has been found apart from in Beale's possible/probable/certain imagined sanctuary.

---

310 ibid

311 Beale "Eden, the Temple and the Church's Mission" p9

312 Beale "Eden, the Temple and the Church's Mission" p15

So Eden was a temple. Although not explicit in the statement, what follows in his discussion assumes that is the point this paragraph brings us to – but it doesn't!

God Needs No Cosmic Temple

It is important to understand the distinctive function of God's temple in Israel[313] (and its precursor, the Tabernacle). Beale, Walton and others[314] all proceed in this discussion on the assumption that the primary function of a temple is to provide God with a place to presence himself. Yet the explicit absence of any temple reference before the fall despite the presence of God; the explicit necessity for a tabernacle/temple after the fall to symbolise and facilitate the old-covenant relationship; the explicit complete fulfilment of the temple's mediating priesthood and sacrifice in Christ; the explicit transfer of the temple imagery to the church in the new-covenant relationship; and the explicit exclusion of any temple in the new creation in which God is present, all point to the fact that the temple had a mediating function for sinners. Yes, God presences himself in the temple, but not as a royal-residence or throne room: it is a place where sinners can, through mediation, approach a holy God who has initiated such an approach by approaching them. The concept doesn't belong in the first Eden any more than in the new Eden, for in neither place was/is such a sin-overwhelming/redemptive approach needed or even, in the absence of sin and sinners, possible. That God presences himself in the temple does not imply that the presence of God necessitates a temple.

One has to be delighted with some of the implications Walton draws from his temple view:

> When we adopt the biblical perspective of the cosmic temple, it is no longer possible to look at the world (or space) in secular terms. It is not ours to exploit. We do not have natural resources, we have sacred resources. Obviously this view is far removed from a view that sees nature as divine: As sacred space the cosmos is *his place*. It is therefore not *his person*. The cosmos is his place, and our privileged place in it is his gift to us. The blessing he granted was that he gave us the permission and the ability to subdue and rule. We are stewards ... The cosmic-temple idea recognizes that God is here and that all of this is his. [315]

Yet those implications do not rest on the temple idea: God expressly reveals himself as present in as well as transcendently beyond the cosmos. He expressly reveals the creation as his good handiwork over which he places man as his trusted vice-regent. It is "his place" not because it is a temple but because he has made it and rules it. For the same reason the creation is not "his person." We are stewards of that creation, not because the "cosmic-temple idea recognizes that God is here and that all of this is his," but because the word of God declares that it is so.

In fact, if a "temple" concept can be found in the cosmos before the fall (which I argue it cannot), it can only be found there because God reveals himself as present

---

[313] It may be convenient to call this temple "Israel's Temple" in the context of discussing its distinctiveness from the pagan temples of surrounding nations, but the Scriptures constantly refer to it as the temple bearing God's name: it is God's temple, not Israel's.

[314] See the previous section *A Garden Temple?*

[315] Walton *The Lost World of Genesis One* Kindle location 1386

in and over it. In other words, the temple concept does not lead to an understanding of the cosmos being God's but God's declaration that he is present in the cosmos provides a basis for claiming it is a temple.

Fred Zaspel puts it with appropriate clarity:

> God's dwelling remains in heaven, as the "God of Heaven" kind of expression so commonly reminds us. Occasionally the biblical writers give us a glimpse of this "heavenly temple" (cf. Is. 6; Rev. 7:15; 11:1, 2, 19; 14:15, 17; 16:1, 17). It is equipped with an altar (Rev. 6:9; 8:3, 5; 9:13; 11:1; 14:18; 16:7) and "the ark of his covenant" (Rev. 11:19), and consistently it is described in terms of supreme majesty. God resides in this heavenly temple. It is his palace, the place of his throne (Rev. 7:15, et al), from which he rules over all history, directing all heavenly and earthly things in accordance with his own purpose (e.g., Dan. 4:34-35; Rev. 4-5). The holy dwelling of God is secure in heaven, above all the vicissitudes of time.[316]

For Walton however, the significance of the temple idea lies not only in its implications for worship, but in its justification for translating "create" as "attribute function." There is no need for a cosmic-temple to be freed from a secular perspective to see the cosmos as God's, to see it as a sacred resource to be cared for rather than a natural resource to be exploited. All that is needed is to see that Genesis 1 describes God creating the cosmos as God's cosmos over which God rules with a rule entrusted into the stewardship of Adam and his descendants. Without that view of Genesis 1 however, a cosmic temple is almost a necessary condition for a sacred cosmos.

There is yet another problem: Walton argues that Marduk used his temple as a residence,[317] establishing a precedent of Temple as divine residence. However, Marduk's temple was not a residence for Marduk in the way implied by Walton. It was the place in which Marduk met the gods from above and the gods from below to secure their compliance. Having left their usual place of dwelling they rested, not in their own temple but in Marduk's temple, for their "conference." This was not a place from which he ruled the cosmos, for to rule the gods had to be present in the place in which their rule was being exercised. Their temples provide for an interface between men and gods, but to rule the gods had to get up and go places. Marduk's temple is just such a "place": not where he rested or ruled the cosmos but the place in which he met with and manipulated (ruled) the other gods upon whom his continued influence depended. God never came to his temple in dependence to meet with other gods, much less to secure compliance in the spiritual realm!

Walton clearly expresses the unbiblical function of pagan temples when he explains that they "existed as a fulcrum of mutual dependence. The gods had their needs met through the temple and their image was resident in their midst, and the people had their needs met by the beneficence of the contented deity."[318] God has no needs met in his temple, to which in fact he comes to the needy as mediator of unidirectional grace.

---

316 Fred Zaspel, "The Heavenly Temple" http://www.credomag.com/2013/09/25/the-heavenly-temple-fred-zaspel/ 25 September 2013

317 Walton *Lost World* Kindle location 718-721

318 Walton *Ancient Near Eastern Thought* p128

Where is the Presence of God?

What is meant by reference to "God's Presence"? Obviously, God is omnipresent: always present everywhere. Yet the Bible speaks of a presence of God that is just as clearly different from his "everywhere" presence. With minimal discussion of what this means, temple-garden advocates almost universally build their argument on the idea that God's presence in this special way implies a temple.

There is indeed a relationship between God's presence and temples. God is present in his temple: God's temple means God's presence. But God's presence does not mean a temple. The idea that God's presence necessitates a temple is not only unsustainable, it obscures the function of God's temple (both the physical one Solomon built, and the heavenly one upon which it was modelled), distorts the concept of God's presence with his people, and short-changes our eschatological hope in Christ.

If, as Beale argues, the presence of God in the Garden of Eden makes the garden a temple, then the outside of the garden is also a temple, for the presence of God continued with Adam and his family *after* the expulsion from the garden. Among Cain's complaints to God about his punishment for murder, is that he will be excluded from God's presence[319] which till then he enjoyed even though he was not and never had been in the garden. It is as Cain feared: he is sent at that time from God's presence. If the garden is a temple because God is present, then so is the land in which Adam and the rest of his family resided after the fall, the place of sweat, thorns and pain in which they then lived in God's presence.

If this argument is followed through, the whole cosmos, as Walton argues, must be a temple. But Walton's argument for a cosmic temple depends on Eden being a unique temple within a cosmos that is not the temple. The argument is not sustainable.

Wherever it was that Cain was sent, Cain would be hidden from God's presence. If God is present everywhere and the whole earth should tremble at the presence of God,[320] how could Cain be hidden from God's presence? It is clear that God's presence can be generalised, and that it can have a particular meaning quite distinct from its generalised meaning. Cain feared that being hidden from God's presence would result in two conditions: he would be without rest and he would be without protection. There is of course a presence of God in which he brings judgement: that was the presence of God Cain was experiencing when his punishment was announced. Yet Cain fears something else: he fears he will not know the presence of God as Protector and Saviour.

There is nothing merely mechanical about this, as if rest and protection are natural consequences of God's presence, for as just noted God's presence can bring judgement. God rests and protects his people *because they are his*. His presence in this special way, symbolised in but not limited to the temple, is an expression of his personal love for and faithful commitment to people he knows – and wants to be known as – his special people. Typical of a multitude of declarations by God to this effect is Isaiah 43:1, "But now, this is what the Lord says – he who created you,

---

[319] Genesis 4:14
[320] Psalm 114:7

Jacob, he who formed you, Israel: 'Do not fear, for I have redeemed you; I have summoned you by name; you are mine.'" In other words, the "presence of God" when used in relation to particular people has to do with God being with them to give them rest and protection as a deliberate outworking of his faithful commitment to be their God and to make them his people. This does not exhaust the meaning of "God's presence," but it is a necessary condition. There is more to God's presence than this, but never less: when God presences himself with his people he gives them rest and protection as people of his love.

If the whole cosmos is a temple because God is present, Cain managed to end up in part of the cosmos where God is not present, a part that by definition cannot be "temple" because God is not present with loving rest and protection. God must therefore be "present" and "not-present" as the provider of rest and protection in the same space at the same time for the same people. If by God's presence reference is to God's omnipresence, then of course he is present in the entire cosmos. But for the cosmos to be "temple" God must be more than omnipresent: he must be present as protector and giver of rest. But that is *not* the case in "the land of Nod, east of Eden" where Cain went "from the Lord's presence."[321] So in Nod, God is not present in the way he is present in a temple, yet in the cosmos (of which Nod is most certainly a part) God is said to be present as in a temple. The argument cannot be sustained.

God promised Moses that "My Presence will go with you, and I will give you rest."[322] But the text goes on to imply that God's presence would be the distinguishing thing that marked out his people from "all the other people on the face of the earth." Similarly, God promises to "put my dwelling place among you, and I will not abhor you. I will walk among you and be your God, and you will be my people."[323] Not only is God present without a temple, his rest-giving, protection-giving presence is seen to have another feature: it is something that separates his covenant people from all the others.[324] The temple, when it is built, will have this function too: "In the last days the mountain of the Lord's temple will be established ... All the nations may walk in the name of their gods, but we will walk in the name of the Lord our God for ever and ever."[325] The temple symbolised God's covenant relationship with his people:[326] "As for this temple you are building, if you follow my decrees, observe my laws and keep all my commands and obey them, I will fulfil through you the promise I gave to David your father. And I will live among the Israelites and will not abandon my people Israel."[327]

Prior to his promises to Moses, God had made his presence as Leader and Protector of Israel known by a cloud in the day and a fire at night. Moses, Aaron, the elders, and Jethro ate a meal "in the presence of God" made possible by

[321] Genesis 4:16
[322] Exodus 33:14
[323] Leviticus 26:11,12
[324] Paul will build on this to stress the importance of God's new-covenant people being consciously separated from the idolatrous people around them - see below.
[325] Micah 4:1-5
[326] It also foreshadows and has its fulfilment in the eschatological temple-less dwelling of God in the midst of his redeemed.
[327] 1 Kings 6:12,13

sacrifices.[328] In particular God had made his presence known as he gave the tables of the covenant to Moses. God also made his presence known in the original Tent of Meeting where God's will was made known.[329] All this "presence of God" was without a temple, and at the same time differentiated Israel (as the place where God dwells) from the cosmos which is not God's dwelling, and from people who were not people with whom he was present. God was present savingly with his people in a way that fulfils the promise of a presence that brings rest, a presence of personal relationship. With those at enmity with him, God is also present, but without the intimacy of a personal relationship of grace, in a presence that does not bring rest.

The Goal of the Temple is No Temple

God's temple, when it was finally built more than 400 years after the Exodus,[330] was another place in which God made his presence known. The Tabernacle, and by inference the Temple, were modelled on the heavenly sanctuary in which Christ has presented himself in God's presence as our sacrifice and continues to intercede for us as our mediating High Priest. That sacrifice brought to an end the earthly temple, indicating that it was not the presence of God that was associated with the uniqueness of the temple, but the sacrifices for a sinful people – sacrifices that were essential for the presence of God to be benevolent and not destructive. Thus when John looks for a temple in heaven at the consummation of the church's earthly pilgrimage, *there is none* [331] even though the "dwelling of God is with men."[332] God's presence is "more present" than ever, but there is no temple because the temple related to sacrifice for sin.

Earlier in Revelation however, there is a temple. It is firstly reported as a place in which God's people found security and rest until the New Jerusalem is established. Calling the faithful "pillars in the temple of ... God,"[333] John is clearly using a metaphor. To what does it refer? Never again will they leave their place of victory and security,[334] for they will continue to be cared for as they serve God in unbroken communion[335] until the New Jerusalem comes down out of heaven. Once the perfection of the New Jerusalem has come, there is no longer need for a place of refuge from the trials and tribulations of a world awaiting Christ.

Equally significantly however, are the next set of references in Revelation to the Temple:[336] here is a temple from which terrible judgement is sent out against all who will not honour God's covenant, love his people, or submit to his sovereignty. But again, once Christ returns, there is no more sending out judgement – it is

---

[328] Exodus 18:12

[329] Exodus 33:7 ff Once the Tabernacle was established, it took over the name "Tent of Meeting" indicating the God's presence continued to relate to making known his will.

[330] 1 Kings 6:1 (480 or 440 years depending on the text)

[331] Revelation 21:22

[332] Revelation 21:3

[333] Revelation 3:12

[334] ibid

[335] Revelation 7:15-17 & Isaiah 49:10

[336] Revelation 11-16

finished, and there is no longer need for a temple "that is the tabernacle of the covenant law"[337] from which judgement is sent.

The presence of God then, known in the garden before the fall, known in part and foreshadowed from the banishment to the second coming, and fulfilled in perfection in the eschaton, is about fellowship with God who protects, guides and gives rest. God's temple, on the other hand, and in dramatic distinction from pagan temples, is a place where God's grace and holiness meet a sinful and unholy people mediating his presence to give protection, guidance and rest. God is indeed present in the temple, just as he makes his presence known without a temple: but the temple is necessary for grace to overcome law, sacrifice to meet holiness, and the presence of God to be blessing not curse.

Solomon makes just that point in his prayer of dedication:

> But will God really dwell on earth with humans? The heavens, even the highest heavens, cannot contain you. How much less this temple I have built! Yet, Lord my God, give attention to your servant's prayer and his plea for mercy. Hear the cry and the prayer that your servant is praying in your presence. May your eyes be open toward this temple day and night, this place of which you said you would put your Name there. May you hear the prayer your servant prays toward this place. Hear the supplications of your servant and of your people Israel when they pray toward this place. Hear from heaven, your dwelling place; and when you hear, forgive.[338]

God Rested like a Pagan God? Never!

The concept of a temple as a place where God rests is a key motif in the cosmic-temple idea. As previously noted, Walton is not alone when he asserts, "Deity rests in a temple, and only in a temple."[339] Yet the goddess Inanna's sleep under a poplar tree when she was tired[340] must surely be considered a rest, and it just as surely was not in a temple. There may be other examples, but one is enough to dispel the assertion that deity rests *only* in a temple. Yet this concept shapes Walton's interpretation of the seventh-day rest in Genesis, which for him must be a temple-rest, for that is the only place deity rests. Since it is a temple-rest, it is the sort of rest that "results when a crisis has been resolved or when stability has been achieved, when things have 'settled down'."[341] The idea that the seventh-day rest is of a "settling-down" sort of rest is used by him to confirm the garden in Eden as a temple (assuming rather than demonstrating that God takes his seventh-day rest in the garden-temple). That God rested in the garden-temple is evidence for Walton that the seventh-day rest of Genesis is temple-rest, when God "transitions into a condition of stability."[342]

There is such a mix here of circular reasoning, theological creativity, and exegetical novelty that it almost defies analysis. Pagan deities rested in temples after a crisis. Since pagan deities only rested in a temple, when God rested it must

---

[337] Revelation 15:5
[338] 2 Chronicles 6:18-21
[339] Walton *The Lost World of Genesis One* Kindle location 676
[340] Weeks, correspondence (referring to the story of Inanna and Shakaletuda)
[341] ibid
[342] Walton *The Lost World of Genesis One* Kindle location 688

have been in a temple, and as there was no temple the garden must have been the temple. Since God rested in the garden-temple, a crisis or period of instability must have ended and God entered into a state of post-crisis-stability. Since God was in such a state of rest, and since pagan deities only rested in a temple, God must have been in a temple, but as there was no temple, the garden ....

Although he reasons in this manner, Walton also consistently depends on what he has called his interpretive key,[343] the idea in ANE mythology that "temples were not designed primarily to provide a place for worship. They were designed to be residences for deities."[344] Walton is clear that this is what shapes his interpretation of God's rest, and each step in his reasoning comes back to this idea that paganism is the key to Genesis.

Disregarding God's description in Genesis as a rest "from all his work," (ie not a sleeping rest but a cessation-from-work-rest) Walton defines it instead as "transitioning into stability." That God should transition into anything is not easily fitted into a biblical concept of God, and the idea that the transition should be into a condition of stability – presupposing thereby that before the transition God was in a condition of instability – does not seem to come from the text or fit the text. Nor does it fit the rest of the Bible: "I the Lord do not change."[345]

Walton reads a sort of absolute sense of "rest" into every reference to rest. When the text says God "rests from his work," or when Israel is promised "rest from all your enemies,"[346] "rest," in Walton's conception, is not something by which they are relieved of what had been going on but a condition into which they are inducted irrespective of any reference to their prior condition. Thus for God in Genesis, the rest is about transitioning into a state of "normal rule" and for Israel it is about transitioning into a state of "normal life."[347] So it is that, "In the Old Testament ... rest involves engagement in the normal activities that can be carried out when stability has been achieved"[348] whether that normal activity be the normal activity of deity or man.

That is true in reference to that particular rest: "rest from your enemies." Walton rightly links the "rest" promised in Deuteronomy and Joshua to the Israelites as they enter the Promised Land as a rest that enables them to "go about their lives: planting and harvesting, buying and selling ..."[349] Yet that promise alone is enough to indicate that "normality" was not implied by "rest", for that generation who had never experienced anything of the sort would see nothing "normal" in the promise. The promise presented to them an hope of eschatological proportions. The rest promised was neither normality nor stability but something only just short of "new creation."

When Noah's ark comes to rest on the mountain, it *ceases* to be in the normal floating condition of a boat. When Abraham rests under the tree at Mamre he stops

---

[343] Walton *The Lost World of Genesis One* Kindle location 706
[344] Walton *Ancient Near Eastern Thought* p113
[345] Malachi 3:6
[346] Deuteronomy 12:10
[347] Walton *The Lost World of Genesis One* Kindle location 698
[348] ibid. For a look at the OT concept of "rest" that seems more consistently biblical see Chapter 12 p273.
[349] ibid

his normal activity to be refreshed enough to continue it.[350] That aside, even if "rest" in this context implies "normal," it does not do so in every case. When Israel is instructed to "rest" on the Sabbath Day they were commanded to cease from all their normal work,[351] which meant they *could not* "go about their lives: planting and harvesting, buying and selling."

God Became Stable ~ Really?

This argument hinges on the idea of "stability." It is commonly recognised, and rightly so, that in God's rest he continued to sustain creation. So in his rest he continues to work. But was his rest a rest from (ie stopping) the work of creation (as the Bible says) or achieving stability from instability (as Walton says)?

What exactly does Walton mean by "stability"? We might safely assume he does not mean God became stable after a time in which he was not stable. If he means that the earth became stable (rather than God), was the earth unstable before it brought forth trees? While it brought forth trees? Once the trees were brought forth? And after the six days of transitioning into stability, was it stable while new plants and trees were brought forth in the ordinary process of reproduction?

Walton's core thesis is that the "creation" work of God in Genesis 1 is the attribution of function to things in a previously chaotic or non-functional creation, thus bringing about a rest, a stability previously unknown. Yet God leaves anyone who will read the text in no doubt as to what he means by his seventh-day rest. Genesis 2:1-4 makes it abundantly clear that when God rested, he stopped doing what he had been doing. It is not that he brought an end to chaos, but that he brought an end to his orderly work. Four times we read the task of creation ends, and in three of those times redundancy is used for emphasis. Effectively it can be rendered, "When the task had been finished, he finished the task he had been doing, he stopped doing the task he had been doing, and he blessed that day because he had stopped doing the task he had been doing."[352] Further, there is no mention of anything else: no mention of God taking up residence, no mention of God "templing" in the garden. God created the cosmos, then stopped creating. He rested. On that the text is clear. Of pagan ideas of deity taking up residence in a material location, there is nothing in the text. Nor is there any reason in the entire account to imagine anything else.

Walton does however go on to exegete what he describes as "the most important verses to draw all this information together"[353] in Psalm 132.

---

[350] Genesis 18:4

[351] Exodus 20:10 etc

[352] The NIV may have used "created" in these verses more often than a less dynamic rending of the Hebrew would (cf the NASB) but even the "literalistic" translation of Robert Alter leaves the nature of God's rest unmistakable: "Then the heavens and the earth were completed, and all their array. And God completed on the seventh day the task He had done, and He ceased on the seventh day from all the task he had done. And God blessed the seventh day and hallowed it, for on it He had ceased from all His task that He had created to do." Alter *The Five Books of Moses* p20

[353] Walton *The Lost World of Genesis One* Kindle location 688

God's Rest in Zion is Different

Walton says that Psalm 132 describes the tabernacle/temple

> where his footstool (the ark) is located. ... the text is referring to his dwelling place as his throne room and the place of his rule (because of the footstool). In verse 8 the 'footstool' is paralleled by the ark, and the temple ('dwelling place') is paralleled with 'resting place'. This demonstrates that the temple is the place where he rests.

Once again, at first glance Walton appears to be building a convincing case. Turning to the Psalm however, his exegesis raises more questions than it answers. Contrary to his implication, this Psalm does not appear to be about the temple. While there is parallelism between verses 7 & 8, the parallelism appears more antithetical than synthetic. Further, he appears to miss the main point, that God's dwelling and resting place for David was Jerusalem without a temple.

Although the writer of Chronicles includes a quote from this Psalm in the prayer of Solomon at the dedication of the temple,[354] this Psalm is commonly associated with David's bringing the Ark of Covenant to Jerusalem – a "temple-less" Jerusalem at that. He brings it from the house of Obed-Edom where both it and God have been "resting" in a tent, to Jerusalem and to another tent that is neither Tabernacle nor Temple. Jerusalem, not the temple (for there is no temple there) is God's place of rest, mediation, worship and rule. Every point Walton makes about Psalm 132 he applies to a missing temple in Jerusalem, but the Psalm applies it to Jerusalem without a temple: *it is exactly the opposite of what Walton asserts.*

Yet without a temple in Jerusalem were God rested, ruled and mediated, David still had a temple, for in Psalm 5:7 he declares "in reverence I bow down toward your holy temple." Where was it? He tells us in Psalm 11:4 "The Lord is in his holy temple, the Lord is on his heavenly throne." This, not surprisingly, fits perfectly with Isaiah's reporting God's condemnation of sinful Israel with the words "Heaven is my throne, and the earth is my footstool. Where is the house you will build for me? Where will my resting place be?"[355] So too, Jesus declares heaven to be God's throne, the earth to be God's footstool, and Jerusalem the "city of the Great King."[356]

In verse 8 of Psalm 132 David calls on the Lord to "come to your resting place, you and the ark of your might." As he carries the ark into Jerusalem he prays that God will accompany it: may God and the ark come to rest in Jerusalem (which is quite a fitting image for the ark that has been on quite a journey into Philistia and back). Walton wants to make verse 8 synthetically parallel to verse 7 in which David encourages the people to go with him to God's "dwelling place, (to) worship at his footstool." That is, David wants the people to go with him and the ark into Jerusalem to worship God at the place God has chosen to dwell and rest (to be his resting place and footstool): Jerusalem. Walton however says that the parallelism

---

[354] 2 Chronicles 6:41-42 quotes vv8-10; however, some regard this as a later addition, so in the NIV (2011) the quotation is omitted. Whether or not this is the best way to deal with the text has no impact however on the present discussion.

[355] Isaiah 66:1

[356] Matthew 5:35

between verse 7 & 8 means that the ark is God's footstool. This just does not fit the text. Nowhere is the "mercy seat" – the ark – called God's footstool; at least, nowhere in the Bible[357] is the ark called God's footstool, although Walton makes repeated reference to the idea.

God's People Needed a Temple, God Did Not

God needed no temple. But God's people did!

God had no need of an earthly dwelling in which to rest when he had heaven as his home. He had no "mutual needs" to be met through people, a need Walton has ascribed to the pagan gods.[358] But God's people certainly needed some means of mediation that would bridge the gap between a holy and rightly offended God in heaven and a sinful needy people on earth.

So God came to his people with the Ark, with the Tabernacle, and with the Temple with a redemptive, mediating presence. He would become the means by which a sinful people could approach a holy God, and by which a holy God could fellowship with the people he loved. Here he could be propitiated with sacrifice, and here he would make his grace known. The sacrifices were dramatically different from pagan ritual offerings. The pagans fed and satisfied the needs of the gods with offerings; God's wrath was turned aside by offerings which he never ate – in fact, most became food for the priests rather than God who had no needs to be satisfied.

Walton wants his identification of pagan temple function to be definitive for God's temple: "Worship took place at temples, but temples were not designed primarily to provide a place for worship. They were designed to be residences for deities and, as such, places for the performance of cultic rituals."[359] But God's temple is indeed primarily a place of worship and propitiation, and is not where God resides.

In Solomon's dedication prayer, Walton asserts, "Functions are introduced by the request that God would hear from his temple."[360] But a) Solomon does not ask God to hear from his temple but from Heaven; and b) these so-called "functions" are not functions of the temple, but the cause for Israel to approach God and ask for *forgiveness*. What Walton calls "functions" to be put into operation through the temple, are to Solomon evidence of God's judgement and the stimulus to seek forgiveness – the mediating of which is the true function of the temple. Thus, when he goes on to say, "The ideology of the temple is not noticeably different in Israel than it is in the ancient Near East. The difference is in the God, not in the way the temple functions in relation to God," Walton has completely missed the most fundamental of distinctions and misrepresents Scripture in the most fundamental of ways.

---

[357] A possible exception is 1 Chronicles 28:2 where in some translations it appears David describes his plan for a temple as a place of rest "for the ark … for the footstool" where it could be read as "for the ark … *which is* God's footstool"; the ESV appears to have correctly translated this however as "for the ark … and for the footstool" making the ark and the footstool different things.

[358] See above page 119 [Walton *Ancient Near Eastern Thought* p128]

[359] Walton *Ancient Near Eastern Thought* p113

[360] Walton *Ancient Near Eastern Thought* p129

6. Genesis Misformed

Language of the Mist: Reading Genesis 1 in the mist of distorted literary conventions

"In the beginning, God created the heavens and the earth."

~ Genesis 1:1

I once took a group of 5 and 6 year-olds into a very thick early morning fog. I invited them to explore it. They tasted it, they swirled it, they felt it, and they tried to hold it. They chased it and tried to bottle it. It really was great fun. But when we returned inside they had nothing to show for their experiences. They had seen it, they had been immersed in it, but they came away with nothing of substance. Old Testament scholarship that abandons the study of Scripture for the delights of ephemeral imaginations of men can be like that: chasing after a vapour that gives nothing of lasting substance. It need not be so of course: Old Testament scholarship that immerses itself in the Bible can enrich and expand the knowledge of God and his work in a way that strengthens faith and faithfulness. But there is too a meaningless chasing after the wind[361] in some draughty theological halls.

One of the strengths of contemporary Old Testament studies is the attention given to literary form and style. There was a time when evangelical scholars would avoid too close a literary analysis of biblical text even as they recognised the differences in, for example, 1 Kings, Psalms and Ezekiel. They rightly distanced themselves from the methods of liberal scholars who, denying that the Bible was

---

[361] Ecclesiastes 1:14 etc

God's word, used biblical criticism to tear the Bible apart, turning its history into myth (ironically by "demythologising" it), its authors into multiple personalities or time-warped communities, its authority into out-dated custom, and its message into platitudes of another world by which a sense of the divine might be experienced. Sadly, increasing numbers of evangelical scholars are now adopting variations of such approaches.

Yet the Bible *is* literature and its books have varied literary form which, when rightly recognised, help the reader to understand the text and its message. We can be thankful that attention to the literary form now has a normal place in the study of the Old Testament among conservative exegetes. At the same time however, it is evident that useful attention to literary form and style is in danger of being perverted by excess or subverted by a failure to recognise the unique nature of the Bible as God's word.

When Usefulness Becomes Absurdity

Among the most popular concepts in biblical literary study is that of "genre." Contemporary Old Testament scholarship delights in consideration of genre, but in one of the peculiarities of evangelical Christianity, this useful tool that was once spurned as undermining scriptural integrity has now been adopted to the point of a controlling and distorting addiction. Secular literary criticism has long used genre to usefully distinguish between literature of various sorts. But some Old Testament scholarship has taken the study of genre to silly pedantry.

Genesis is generally recognised as some form of historical narrative. To identify Genesis in this way is to use the literary-critical tool of genre identification in a conventional manner. But in a way that is quite foreign to conventional literary criticism, Old Testament scholarship then microcosmises[362] genre, using the term to isolate chapters from their books (we are told that Genesis 1 is a different genre from Genesis), then doing the same for fragments of text (by telling us that certain sentences or shorter portions of text are a different genre from the chapter in which they are found). It is only a matter of time till someone attributes genre characteristics to individual words. In fact, some discourse-analysis comes very close to this by using individual words as precise markers for genre.

This is a literary and exegetical absurdity, but it has a point. If, for example, Genesis 1 is isolated from the basic historical narrative of the rest of Genesis, the "truth" in Genesis 1 can be isolated from the way the rest of Genesis is read, removing it from a plain reading of historical narrative to something mystical, mythical, metaphorical or analogical.

The fundamental error here however is the attempt to force Genesis into the mould of literary classification that fails to recognise the uniqueness of Scripture. Genre is determined by shared criteria, so the moment Genesis is classified as a particular genre, by definition it is expected to exhibit the common features of that genre. Description can rapidly become prescription. Thus a passage of the Old Testament can be described as a particular genre characterised by (among other things) its use of metaphor. That description however subsequently becomes a

[362] I know it is not a word, but I need some light relief!

prescriptive filter through which the text is interpreted metaphorically even if there is no textual indication of metaphor. This descriptive/prescriptive model is particularly evident in studies of Genesis 1 in which great emphasis is given to formulating a very precise genre description[363] upon which all interpretation subsequently hangs.

Yet biblical literature is God-spoken literature, and while it will have features in common with other literature, its most basic feature is that it is inspired by God. No Bible book should therefore simply be classified as belonging to a genre that does not have divine inspiration as its primary characteristic. As the writing of Peter Enns so clearly demonstrates,[364] when biblical books are first classified in terms of secular genre, "inspiration" is defined in a way that fits those genre. It should be the other way round: the unique nature of biblical books as inspired means any genre classification must begin with inspiration.

Classifying Genesis as historical narrative is, despite its apparent initial usefulness, completely inadequate. Genesis has narrative form, but it is the narrative God tells; it is unmistakably history, but it is the history God made and God tells; it is unmistakably like the other four books of the Pentateuch, and just as unmistakably different from other literature of its day, and other books of the Bible. If it is to be classified as a particular genre, it needs a genre recognising its divine origin, and one that recognises the common features of the Bible in general and the Pentateuch in particular.

Some New Testament scholarship has responded constructively to this sort of challenge in identifying genre. The gospels share numerous features with a variety of contemporary secular literature, but for many scholars none is satisfactory – none comprehends all the unique features of the gospels, much less accounts for their God-inspired nature. This leads some to identify of the genre of the gospels as "gospel,"[365] an approach that may well be a model for Genesis and the other books of the Pentateuch.

E J Young stresses the uniqueness of Genesis 1 arising from its being inspired by God: "Genesis one is a document *sui generis*; its like or equal is not to be found anywhere in the literature of antiquity. And the reason for this is obvious. Genesis one is a divine revelation to man concerning the creation of heaven and earth."[366] In a footnote Young goes so far as to question the idea of attributing *any* genre to Genesis 1, stating, "We cannot properly speak of the literary genre of Genesis one," and listing the reasons why it should be excluded from available genre classifications.

Even in terms of contemporary secular literature of its day, the Pentateuch stands out as different. Recognising both its unique features (despite having some things in common with other literature such as historical narrative) and its divine inspiration, the genre of the Pentateuch, if it must be regarded as having a literary genre, is best identified as "Pentateuch." By doing this, not only is the Pentateuch's literary character recognised and differentiated from other literature, "rules" for that

---

363 In most cases without, it must be said, any other literary work exhibiting exactly the same criteria.

364 This is a basic tenant of his extensive writing on the meaning of "inspiration."

365 See Carson & Moo *An Introduction to the New Testament* Apollos/IVP Leicester 2005 pp114f.

366 Young *Studies in Genesis One* p82

genre – the framework within which it is interpreted – are defined by the five books rather than by external constraints.

... and Absurdity becomes Abuse

Among the more outspoken evangelical advocates of genre shaped by secular paradigms are J P Holding & Nick Peters.[367] Their sometimes vitriolic advocacy of a contextualising hermeneutic claims, "The detailed studies of multiple scholars have demonstrated the genre of the Gospels beyond all reasonable doubt" is Greco-Roman biography.[368] Their unabashed arrogance (that the Gospels are Greco-Roman biography "is not open to discussion"[369]) unfortunately tends to obscure an important point they make (that all biblical translation and interpretation involves some degree of consideration of such things as linguistics, genre, context and language devices), as well as obscuring a significant failure in their work (there is no evaluation of what controls legitimately apply to the use of extra-biblical data).

The last point is particularly significant, for having demonstrated (or rather asserted) that some degree of contextualisation is almost always involved in reading a biblical text, all subsequent discussion assumes that their (often radical) contextualisation is not only legitimate, but the only legitimate approach. They are committed to the inerrancy of Scripture, arguing that if the genre employed makes no claim to historical or factual accuracy (eg if Matthew is employing Midrash) then inerrancy is not compromised by a reading of a text that might appear to a modern reader to have a greater degree of literality than they are prepared to concede. In this they share a problem with OT scholarship that is the focus of this book: while aiming to read Scripture faithfully, the identification of a text with a particular genre becomes absolutely and exhaustively definitive; and inevitably that means a text is read in a non-literal way. They dispute this: "No one has claimed that genre determines meaning ... Rather, it has been claimed that genre fills out and helps explain meaning, along with many other factors."[370] The problem with this however, is that while particular meaning may not be completely determined by genre, for many genre the issue of literalism is such that whatever the meaning, it cannot be what the text says in any plain reading.

Unlike OT scholarship, there is at least a significant extra-biblical corpus of contemporary literature with which to compare the NT text. While that, for NT studies, removes the guess-work that is involved when attempting to align OT texts to the inaccessible non-biblical Hebrew literature of the period, the methodology nonetheless involves an alignment of the NT text (and the religion and culture of the writers of the NT text) with the extra-biblical text and its pagan culture on the basis of extra-biblical criteria with no sustainable biblical indicator that this is either a sufficient or necessary condition.

It is not simply that genre identification is useful: it becomes the hermeneutical framework by which, given a lack of explicit controls, interpreters are free to read almost any biblical text as not literal when it presents as literal. Despite their

---

[367] Holding & Peters *Defining Inerrancy*

[368] Holding & Peters *Defining Inerrancy* Kindle location 859

[369] Holding & Peters *Defining Inerrancy* Kindle location 837

[370] Holding & Peters *Defining Inerrancy* Kindle location 1012

protests to the contrary, this is a redefinition of the doctrine of inerrancy that makes the reading of scripture subject to the mysteries and vagaries of specialised scholarship; that effectively makes the Bible inaccessible to ordinary readers unless mediated by an elite magisterium of biblical scholars. Holding and Peters reinforce this when, for example, they attempt to discredit a host of their opponents on the grounds that they have "absolutely no relevant credentials" that Holding and Peters accept as necessary for a correct identification of the genre, and thereby a correct reading of the Bible.[371]

Why Consider Genre At All?

Does knowing the genre make a difference? It is certainly significant if a reader's concept of the genre of a passage controls the way it is read. That is, genre is critical if a reader believes a particular set of rules applies to the text because it is regarded as a particular genre: that reader will tend to apply the rules even if the text does not appear to conform to the rules. It will also be significant if the writer's concept of genre is controlling. That is, genre is critical if the writer constructs his text to conform to the rules of that genre even if the data or message he wants to include does not easily conform: the integrity of the genre is then more important than the integrity of the content. Yet for most writing and reading neither the writer nor the reader is controlled by genre, albeit genre is part of the framework within which every author writes and every reader reads.

That is true of biblical text too. Some genre are clearly more controlled by the "rules" than others. OT poetry, for example, exhibits much tighter control over the structure of the text than OT narrative, and both are best understood when that distinction is made in reading those texts. Yet, as for non-biblical texts, genre is a tool for writing that is usually more contextual than prescriptive, and a tool for reading that is usually more indicative than descriptive.

Richard Bauckham asserts that for readers of the Bible identifying the genre is "is a matter of considerable importance because it determines the expectations with which readers come to that work and how they are going to read it."[372] As we open a text, whether we see it as poetry, prophecy, parable or history will determine how we approach the text and what sort of information we expect it to convey ... to some extent. Our initial expectations are quickly (and often unconsciously) modified by reading the actual text, such that whether typical of that particular genre or not, we see and understand metaphor, allusion, direct speech, information, opinion and so on as we come across them. It is not only that the text itself is far more definitive of the way it is read than any concept of genre the reader brings to it; it is the text that should determine definition of its genre, rather than genre being something imposed on the text by the period or context in which it is written.

---

[371] Holding & Peters *Defining Inerrancy* Kindle location 301 ff and similarly throughout their book.
[372] Richard Bauckham *The Gospels as History*
http://richardbauckham.co.uk/uploads/Accessible/Gospels.pdf

Bauckham demonstrates the usefulness of genre in reading biblical text in his informative work on the Gospels as history.[373] Identifying eyewitness testimony as a feature of the histories written in the same period as the gospels, and identifying the gospels as histories of that period, he argues that eyewitness testimony should be expected as a feature of the gospels. And it is, as he convincingly demonstrates, thereby reinforcing the historical reliability of the gospel texts.[374]

Bringing readers' attention to the way in which the gospel writers draw on and refer to eyewitness testimony undoubtedly improves comprehension of the gospels. But that could be appreciated without any consideration of genre. Its significance has more to do with the question of the reliability of the text considered in the same way as any other text where the frame of reference excludes primary recognition of God's inspiration and all the rich implications that has for the accuracy of the text and the way it should be read. It goes without saying that those who disagree with Bauckham's classification of the gospels as histories – and they are numerous and advance robust arguments – find the rules he attaches to that genre less relevant to either the writing or reading of the gospels.

Bauckham also demonstrates the opacity of genre studies when he goes on to explain that the gospels as histories also share genre identity with OT Jewish histories (different from the "histories" genre with which he has labelled the gospels till this point), and *bioi* or "lives" similar to but not the same as modern biographies. He also stresses that genre is dynamic, rather than fixed, and is always influenced by other proximate genre. Even though he appears to overlook Luke's own testimony that his gospel is on the one hand deliberately aligned to rhetoric as much as to any other genre, and on another hand is a deliberate mix of genre,[375] he highlights the difficulty in definitively defining a particular text as belonging to a particular genre.

Taking a different approach, Richard Burridge, prefers to begin genre determination of the gospels with *bioi*, classifying them as "a form of Graeco-Roman biography."[376] For Burridge genre determines that the gospels were not written "by committees, about concepts, for communities ... (but) were written by a person, about a person, for other persons."[377] Again though, this could be determined from recognising the way in which God speaks through prophets throughout biblical history, and from reading the gospels themselves (even if the particular author is not clearly identified).

More examples could be given of different critics classifying the same texts with bold assurance in different ways, each then applying rules of interpretation that hang on their favoured genre with the same assurance. With such overwhelming uncertainty as to which particular genre specific texts may belong, overwhelming uncertainty must prevail as to how to apply genre rules to reading the Bible. If a text is classified as a different genre, the way it is read is different. However, both

---

373 ibid (and in numerous other works)

374 In fact it is difficult to see whether Bauckham identifies the gospels as histories because of their appeal to eyewitness testimony, or if he found the eyewitness testimony because he classified the texts as histories.

375 Acts 1:1 cf Luke 1:1-4

376 Richard Burridge *What Are the Gospels? A Comparison with Graeco-Roman Biography* (2nd Ed) Eerdmans, Grand Rapids 2004 (1992) p295

377 ibid

Burridge and Bauckham provide useful insights if their references to genre are regarded as indicative rather than exclusively definitive. As for other biblical authors in other settings, it might reasonably be assumed that the gospel writers wrote in a way that did not make their writing totally odd to contemporary readers. They could share and utilize aspects of contemporary genre (such as appealing to eyewitness as would contemporary history writers, and writing about a particular person as would contemporary *bioi* writers) without conforming rigidly to those patterns. Indeed, within such a framework they could be – and undoubtedly were – innovative, combining or ignoring as well as using conventions, and introducing novelty, in ways that engaged readers and best conveyed their message.

Genre cannot be ignored: poetry is different from letters which are different from histories. But having said that, applying the intricacies and uncertainties of complex genre studies to Bible reading can distort that reading by conforming the text to non-biblical patterns of uninspired literature. The fact that many texts exhibit aspects of multiple genre should alert readers both to the variety of features a text may present and to the inadequacies of pressing the text too precisely into the narrow mould of a particular genre. Genre study does not fulfil its promises, bringing much less to the reading of the Bible than is too often claimed: it is helpful but not essential, and falls far short of "determining the expectations with which readers" read God's word.

Creating False Distinctives

Genre is not the only literary-critical tool used in reading Genesis 1, although it is probably the most common among conservative evangelicals. John Collins includes genre among a number of literary-critical tools to he brings to bear on Genesis 1.[378] He recognises that Genesis is narrative, but classifies Genesis 1 as "exalted prose narrative."[379] He is not the first to use similar terminology although it is not evident that each user of such terms intends the same meaning, and Collins explains he is coining this particular term.[380] Tim Keller[381] is among those who quote E J Young as referring to Genesis 1 as "exalted, semi-poetical language."[382] But Young means something entirely different from what Keller and Collins imply. Immediately following his description of Genesis 1 as "exalted", Young goes on to demonstrate that this "exalted" quality affirms the historical accuracy of Genesis 1, and that it affirms its unity of form with Genesis 2. [383] Young then makes two significant observations: firstly, that the language and structure of Genesis 1-3 means that "the first chapter stands in an intimate relationship with what follows."[384] He regards them as essentially the same sort of text using Hebrew

---

[378] In *Types of Language* for example, he explores and applies a range of concepts in language-communication theory.

[379] Collins *Genesis 1-4* Kindle location 527

[380] Collins *Genesis 1-4* Kindle location 522

[381] Tim Keller *Creation, Evolution and Christian Laypeople* The Biologos Foundation, p2 http://biologos.org/uploads/projects/Keller_white_paper.pdf

[382] Young *Studies in Genesis One* p82

[383] ibid

[384] Young *Studies in Genesis One* p83

phraseology with intentional identity between chapters 1 and 2 – they are the same genre. Secondly, he asserts that the historical reliability of Genesis 1 is such that its historical specificity must not be diluted by science:

> The chapter is thus seen to constitute an integral part of the entire book and is to be regarded as sober history. By this we mean that it recounts what actually transpired. It is reliable and trustworthy, for it is the special revelation of God. If this involves conflicts with what scientists assert, we cannot escape difficulties by denying the historical character of Genesis.[385]

This is explicitly, diametrically, opposed to the way Collins uses "exalted." For Young it means magnificent writing that has complete accuracy and reliability in recording and reporting factual historical data. For Collins it means that while historical narrative (ie *not* Genesis 1) has an intent to record and report factual historical data, exalted prose narrative (ie Genesis 1) does not: "By calling it exalted, we are recognising that when we come to examine the author's truth claims, we must not impose a 'literalistic' hermeneutic on the text."[386] By classifying Genesis 1 as exalted prose narrative, Collins re-writes Genesis 1 as figurative, even though it looks as if it is intended by the author to be literal history.

Presuppositions that Determine Interpretation

Collins provides a great deal of insightful and helpful commentary on the early chapters of Genesis in his *Genesis 1-4: A Linguistic, Literary, and Theological Commentary*. Reading his discussion of the text when considered in the light of the text is particularly rewarding.[387] Yet some of the main points he makes, in particular his advocacy of a non-literal reading of Genesis 1, are frequently dropped into his commentary without any logical connection to the text itself, or to his exposition of that text. In formulating the genre of Genesis 1 as "exalted prose" Collins fails to demonstrate convincingly that Genesis 1 differs from Genesis 2 or other prose narrative passages that are not deemed to be exalted; he fails to demonstrate that it is a genre exemplified in more than this one passage; and he fails to demonstrate why exalted language (if in fact it is "exalted") ceases to be factual. In effect, Collins is using "exalted" where others use "poetic" to distance a text from literalism. It appears he wants Genesis 1 to be read with the hesitations about the literal nature of poetry as commonly viewed, while avoiding reference to poetry

---

[385] ibid

[386] Collins *Genesis 1-4* Kindle 532

[387] For example, much of Chapter 4 of *Genesis 1-4* "Genesis 1:1-2:3: The Creation Week" presents informative and balanced discussion about the text and related issues. Similarly, Chapters 2 & 3 are informative in discussing his eclectic approach to "achieving 'ancient literary competence'" (Kindle location 106) – although a close reading results in less clarity on both how he intends to read a text and how he arrives at that approach. For example, at Kindle location 158 he presents an exclusive dichotomy between origins of the text and how it functions religiously, then opts for his personal communications model which itself is never clearly defined let alone necessitated by the dichotomy he here uses to justify it. In fact, it is basic to his style to justify a point by association rather than by logical necessity or even probability, and as often as not the association is one he simply drops into the discussion rather than one logically developed.

itself, because, quite properly, he recognises the absence in Genesis 1 of the parallelism that is a defining feature of Hebrew poetry.[388]

Lonely Exalted Genesis 1

Making a distinction between Genesis 1 and Genesis 2 is obviously essential for anyone reading Genesis 1 as non-literal but maintaining that the account of Adam and Eve is literal. Yet the difference is much more imagined than real. Both are orderly, carefully structured passages of prose describing in precise terms what happened and what was there. They are linked by theme and by the language of verses 2-5 in chapter 2. Far from being self-evident, the claimed distinction is apparent only after it is made. Declaring one to be literal and the other not, superficial distinctions can be identified but not sustained: they are two chapters of the same account with the same appeal to historical events truly described. If one is "exalted" prose because of its language, so is the other.

Collins does not identify other examples of this "exalted" genre that would confirm Genesis 1 conforms to such a genre. The whole purpose of genre identification is to understand the common conventions of a particular genre that are likely to apply to other texts of the same genre. But here we have a genre of one, something that by the definition of genre cannot exist. Identifying it as a genre of one is a subterfuge by which features "common" to the genre can be attributed to a text with completely artificial licence since there are no common features because there are no common texts.

Notwithstanding all this, if Genesis 1 is nonetheless properly described as "exalted," Collins at no point demonstrates that "exalted" means not true. The term "exalted" has about it an implication of something grand or even glorious. But Collins never uses it this way. Rather he introduces "exalted" as describing the idea that Genesis 1 is not literally factual, then says that since Genesis 1 is "exalted" it cannot be literally factual.[389] Yet if "exalted" has any meaning other than this circular construct of Collins', there is no reason why what is grand or colourful cannot also be factually accurate.

Collins does however include Genesis 1 in a broader genre classification. "Genesis 1-11 is indeed 'historical narrative,' but a particular kind that is known from elsewhere in the ancient world, namely 'prehistory' and 'protohistory.'"[390] His reasons for this classification appear to be the literary similarities of Genesis with other ancient literature classified as protohistory.[391] The impact of this is a perfect example of the descriptive/prescriptive motif discussed above: describing Genesis as protohistory aligns it to other literature that at best has merely an "historical core" (a term to be examined more closely shortly) which then becomes the prescriptive

---

[388] ibid

[389] Collins *Genesis 1-4* Kindle location 529

[390] John Collins, *John Collins Replies to Richard Belcher, Jr* http://www.reformation21.org/blog/2012/02/c-john-collins-replies-to-rich.php along with numerous references in his other writings.

[391] eg *Genesis 1-4* Kindle locations 2718 and 4282

framework through which Genesis must be read, a framework that insists Genesis has an "historical core" found within fictional embellishment.

Calling Genesis 1 protohistory appears to leave it still as "exalted prose narrative," but places it within a broader "pre-proto-historical narrative" genre. He claims that defining its genre however, does not "of itself settle anything"[392] as to how to read the text. Collins opts for the second of four approaches he lists as possible: "The author was talking about what he thought were actual events, using rhetorical and literary techniques to shape the readers' attitudes towards those events."[393] His reason for this is that this "best explains how the Bible and human experience relate to Adam and Eve"[394] thereby making human experience a criterion for interpreting and classifying the text. He also implies that the use of figurative language indicates it is protohistory, which in turn is used by him to identify things in the narrative as figurate or symbolic since they are found in a text classified as protohistory!

Collins contrasts this protohistory with what he calls "'straight' history, with a minimum of figurative language."[395] The import of this rests in Collin's expectation that what some readers might (in his view, mistakenly) take as straight history, he will take as symbolic. While defining Genesis as protohistory may not "settle anything" it certainly prescribes the reading of Genesis in a non-literal framework. This is troubling, as once this approach to Genesis is adopted, the interpretation of each particular passage *must* conform to the requirement that it be symbolic rather than "straight" history.

The justification for claiming Genesis 1 is not straight history is, according to Collins, to be found in Chapter 4 of his *Genesis 1-4*.[396] But in that chapter he discusses the structure of Genesis 1, and on that basis alone, without any reference to the historical or literal reliability of the text, classifies it as "exalted prose narrative." Next he states that "by calling it exalted, we are recognising that when we come to examine the author's truth claims, we must not impose a 'literalistic' hermeneutic on the text."[397] With no prior indication that calling it exalted has anything to do with a literalistic hermeneutic, one might expect some expansion on this newly introduced idea, but no, what follows is a section of comments on the translation of the Hebrew text. Thereafter, any possibility that the text should be taken literally is usually quashed by reference to the genre as exalted.

Illogical Circle of Reciprocal Dependency

Why must we not take Genesis 1 too literally? Because it is exalted prose. Why should we not take exalted prose too literally? Because that's what exalted prose points to. Why is this exalted prose? Because of its structure. Why does the structure

[392] John Collins *Did Adam and Eve Really Exist? Who They Were and Why You Should Care* Crossway, Wheaton, 2011, Kindle Edition, p16

[393] ibid

[394] ibid

[395] ibid

[396] Collins *Genesis 1-4* Kindle location 2827

[397] Collins *Genesis 1-4* Kindle location 532

preclude taking it literally? Because it is exalted prose. But why is it exalted prose? Because it is not meant to be taken literally. Why must we not take it literally? Because it is exalted prose. Why should we not take exalted prose too literally? Because that's what exalted prose points to. And so on ... right through the discussion in at least two books[398] and numerous journal articles and reviews. Collins does discuss a lot of other issues and examine a range of data, but never do these logically intrude upon, contribute to or break the circle of reciprocal dependency that it should be called exalted prose because it is not literal and it is not literal because it is exalted prose.

"Genre" identifies a type of writing into which a number of substantial texts fit,[399] significantly differentiating those texts from others. Historical narrative is writing in which a story is told around events that are portrayed as real events having happened at some point in the past.[400] Fiction, in contrast, is characterised by storytelling with events that may parallel some reality but are not intended to be believed as anything more than made-up stories. Similarly, English poetry is recognised by variations of layout, rhythm and rhyme; Hebrew poetry by its parallelism; and both by intensified imagery.

What identifies a genre can be analysed reasonably straight-forwardly, and we tend to intuitively identify the particular genre we are reading. Given the first pages of a novel and a similar length newspaper article, most of us intuitively read them differently, even if one or both contain passages of technical language, flowery imagery or whatever. Any given genre may contain varied language that neither redefines the genre of the text as a whole nor isolates any passage from the whole.

Genre identifies a significant text or book as having common characteristics with other texts or books that help define an appropriate interpretive framework. Thus it might be possible to classify Genesis as historical narrative because there are other books in the Bible and in other literature that share its basic literary features.[401] But to make one chapter of Genesis a genre of its own, is simply an abuse of the term, not unlike slight-of-hand conjuring that diverts attention so that what is actually being done is not noticed. A genre of one makes no real sense, for the idea of genre is to identify common features of a group of texts that have common interpretive features. By defining Genesis 1 as a genre of exalted prose narrative Collins licenses himself to define illusory distinctions to this one passage with no comparative texts to utilise in confirming appropriate genre principles: he can (and does) make the "genre" what he wants it to be.

---

[398] Collins Genesis 1-4 and Did Adam and Eve Really Exist?

[399] "Genre" is used in a variety of arts to identify a broad type that shares characteristics of such things as form, style, subject and content.

[400] Not everyone regards the events as having happened literally. Enns for example regards much of the Old Testament historical narrative to be fictionalised accounts having an historical referent of some sort. However, in terms of discussion of genre, this definition is sufficient.

[401] Although as already noted, "historical narrative" does not do justice to a book that is best classified as "Pentateuch."

Grammatical Precision, Illusory Features, Invalid Inferences

Collins identifies just four features he claims indicate Genesis 1 is *exalted* prose narrative.[402]

1. It is a highly "patterned" or structured passage.
2. It is "broad stroke in its description" speaking of plants and animals rather than "useful taxonomy."
3. It does not tell us how the earth brought things forth.
4. It uses unusual names ("greater light" and "lesser light") for the sun and moon, and "rhetorically high 'expanse'" for the sky.

It is difficult to give the same weight to these four points as Collins does. There is clearly a degree of repetitive arrangement in Genesis 1, but as Young points out, "the primary interest of the writer was not a schematic classification or arrangement of material ... [which] serves the purpose merely of impressing upon the reader's mind the significance of the content."[403] Much of the rest of Genesis is also highly structured without being deemed by Collins to be "exalted." In any case, and significantly, Genesis 1 is highly structured because it gives an account of a highly structured event: anything less-structured would not do justice to the narrative.

Collins is correct to draw attention to the fact that there is more than literary structure in Genesis 1; there is a pattern. Much has sometimes been made of the idea that the writer is framing the story according to a predetermined literary pattern,[404] but whatever pattern there is, is a pattern embedded in the events before it got to the telling of the story. The events are imposed on the story; there is no evidence that it is a literary pattern imposed on the events.

This is the first story, and although when written there may have been patterns of storytelling that could have been adapted, we have none in the contemporary literature of Palestine indicating a pattern that was being followed. The "pattern" it *follows* is the sequence of events, not a literary structure. But in doing this it also does *establish* a pattern, a pattern of six days work and one day of rest that God will embed in law. The pattern of a seven-day week is evident not because God followed a pattern but because he made one to be followed in subsequent ages. The event unfolded in a week, so the story is told according to the week in which it all unfolded. Genesis 1 is patterned, not because it follows a pattern but because it establishes one.

Of course, if there is a presupposition that what Genesis 1 describes is not an event, then a different explanation has to be found for the structure of the narrative. Presupposing a non-literal view of Genesis 1, the only way the structure of the chapter can be explained is as the author's device to get across some point or other. With such a presupposition, Collins finds in the structure of the narrative a "proof"

---

[402] Collins *Genesis 1-4* Kindle 517
[403] Young *Studies in Genesis One* page 86
[404] See below p138 for more discussion on the "framework hypothesis".

of the presupposition that rendered any other interpretation impossible. This is the most basic of *circulus in probando* (or circular reasoning) fallacies.

Collins objects that Genesis 1 is "exceedingly broad stroke"[405] in its description: but that is because it is describing broad stroke events. True, Genesis does not tell us how the earth brought forth ... or for that matter how Eve brought forth, or how a thousand and one other events in Genesis happened. And why should a text that so clearly describes the creation of things "after their own kind" have to include – as Collins demands – a "useful taxonomy" for it to be considered true? "Useful to what?" one might ask. The very basic taxonomy given – "after its own kind" – is perfectly useful in the context of the text, being fitted to describing a creation in which things were created in distinction from each other; there is no need for the sort of contemporary taxonomy that Collins implies is needed to establish the historical/scientific accuracy of the text. Being "broad stroked" does not make it exalted: the mundane can be described in broad-strokes as readily as the exalted. Identifying it as broad-stroked simply makes it an account in broad-strokes, irrespective of all that is comprehended in such broad-strokes.

Collins objects to "expanse," "greater light" and "lesser light" as being unsuitable to historical/scientifically accurate text. But "expanse" is a perfectly appropriate description of what is subsequently named "sky" (or "heavens" depending on the translation), and if "greater light" and "lesser light" are slightly picturesque terms, do these make what is frankly the incredibly unembellished language of the rest of the chapter "exalted"?

In any case, Collins himself notes later in the same chapter in his *Genesis 1-4* that calling the sun and moon "lights" fits the passage perfectly.[406] He points to the sequence, beginning in verse 14, with God announcing his purpose in creating the sun and moon as being lights to mark out day and night. Hence, as Collins makes clear, it fits perfectly that in verse 16, when God is said to make the sun and moon, they are called "lights."[407] God determines to make the sun and moon to be lights, so when they are made they are called lights. Collins explains that this is perfectly consistent with the ordinary use of language in unfolding this story. For him therefore, just a few pages earlier, to describe naming the sun and moon as "lights" as "unusual" language is at best inconsistent, and certainly gives no basis for calling the language of the passage "exalted".

Collins finds Genesis 1 to be using non-scientific language intended to "inculcate a particular view of God and the world - a view shot through with wonder, delight, and awe at the boundless energy and creativity of God."[408] One

---

405 Collins *Genesis 1-4* Kindle location 523

406 Collins *Genesis 1-4* Kindle location 650

407 It is here that Collins suggests that the Hebrew *asa* (made) might not mean "made" but (cf Walton) "given function." He is commendably transparent in his motive, beginning by explaining that for scholars such as himself there is a difficulty in aligning evolution with the creation of the sun and moon on day four. Among a range of possible solutions is the one he favours, of finding that "made" can sometimes mean something like "gave function to." The only evidence he adduces for this is another commentator who asserts the same thing without reference to any examples. On this tenuous possibility he opts for abandoning the plain meaning of the text in favour of aligning it with evolution – not on the basis of textual analysis but on the grounds that this enables day four to fit an evolutionary framework.

408 Collins *Genesis 1-4* Kindle location 2981

wonders if he is reading the same text! The *language* of awe and wonder is found in creation passages such as Psalm 104 in which God is "clothed with splendour and majesty ... rides on the wings of the wind ... in wisdom made them all." Such language, which overtly calls for an emotive response of wonder, delight and awe is dramatically and comprehensively absent from Genesis 1 which is a simple, precise, systematic account of what God did in those six days. Describing "features of the world around us systematically" is a key feature of scientific language, according to Collins.[409] That surely defines Genesis 1 as "scientific," but elsewhere he holds that the systematic structure of this passage makes it "exalted" and not scientific. The language and structure of the passage is, according to Collins' definitions, "scientific," but his presuppositions rule that out, so he defines the passage quite arbitrarily as "exalted" and not scientific. This is befuddling, but not persuasive.

The *subject matter* of Genesis 1 is undoubtedly exalted but not the language. If anything distinguishes Genesis 1 it is the plainness of the language, with its unemotive simplicity, structure, and specificity that is typical of scientific writing.

Framed

Collins' mention of a literary pattern in the sequence of events of Genesis 1 demands a closer look, not only because of the way Collins uses this idea of a pattern, but also because the idea of a literary framework continues to be a popular construct for the denial of a six-day, orderly creation. The "Framework Hypothesis" itself was developed in the early 20th Century by Professor Arie Noordtzjii. He argued that the six days are presented in two sets of three parallels, indicating the intention of the text is to show man as the crowning glory of creation and not to present details of an orderly creation. Most modern adaptations of the Hypothesis overlook this completely. They tend to pick up on the literary pattern as evidence of a non-literal text but ignore the implications of that construct.

A contemporary of Noordtzjii's, Professor G C Aalders of the Free University of Amsterdam pointed to the basic problem of this approach: "In the text of Genesis itself ... there is not a single allusion to suggest that the days are to be regarded as a form or mere manner of representation."[410] Meredith Kline, one of the most respected evangelical advocates of the Hypothesis summarily disposes of that objection by making the text subject to a presupposition that Genesis cannot be literal. In fact, he goes further and asserts his reason for taking this position is to free scientists from submission to the Bible, explaining that his aim is "to rebut the literalist interpretation of the Genesis creation week ... (so that) ... with respect to both the duration and sequence of events, the scientist is left free of biblical constraints in hypothesizing about cosmic origins."[411] His starting point (ie *not* his conclusion from reading the text) is that the text is not literal, and his aim is to allow

---

409 Collins *Genesis 1-4* Kindle location 2978

410 cf Young *Studies in Genesis 1* p47 – this is Young's translation from the original work in Dutch that I have not been able to confirm from the primary source.

411 Meredith G. Kline, "Space and Time in the Genesis Cosmogony" in *Perspectives on Science and the Christian Faith* 48:1, March 1996, The American Scientific Affiliation, Ipswich, p2ff.

scientists to work independently of God's word (ie without submission to what God has said).

There are a number of variations of this idea of a literary framework in Genesis 1, and while adopting one of those models, Collins rejects the basic Framework Hypothesis championed by Kline. Kline's model – which is basically the most popular model – is that days 4-6 are repetitions of days 1-3. It doesn't take much to see this is a difficult thesis to maintain (with fish swimming in seas not yet created and such like). There is also the assumption that a pattern means non-chronological – something not assumed about the similarly highly structured genealogy in Matthew 1 for example.

Collins rejects Kline's model on the basis that it makes the creation a three day event which clearly doesn't fit much else that is said about the creation, especially those repeated references to the six days leading to a seventh of rest.[412] He sees that the text demands some sort of sequence that matters to the author, but nonetheless sees that in his "judgement ... the highly patterned form of this pericope [is] evidence that the reader is invited to sit lightly on sequence and time lengths."[413] So Collins calls upon us to "sit lightly" on the plain meaning because the text *does not* demand this. Odd really. But that is a consistent outcome of personal judgement determining the meaning of Scripture.

Young resolves the issue by stating the too often overlooked obvious: "The basic reason why Moses used the device of six days was that creation occurred in six days."[414]

The six days of creation, and the pattern repeated through each of those six days, is not merely a literary device, but an account of a pattern God adopted in demonstration of his glory, his power, his independence and his creativity:

> This repetition has four principal theological implications. First, creation was effortless. Elohim spoke and things came into being. The mere verbal fiat that exploded the cosmos into existence displayed Elohim's awesome power. Second, the structure confirms creation ex nihilo, that "by the breath of his mouth" the physical came forth from the void. Third, creation was an expression of God's will; he was the one who called it forth, and he did so freely without any outside compulsion (Rev. 4:11). Finally, the pattern of creation underscores the doctrine of the sovereignty of God: all things are subject to his rule because he made all things (Ps. 24:1–2).[415]

"Scientific Language" is not Always a Science

For decades, another one of the most popular ways of attributing non-literality to Genesis 1 has been by describing it as poetry or at least as using poetic language. Yet there is nothing in the text characteristic of poetry. As already noted, the parallelism of Hebrew poetry is absent; so too is the intensification of imagery achieved by rich description (there is virtually no descriptive language at all!) or

---

[412] Collins *Genesis 1-4* Kindle location 839
[413] Collins *Genesis 1-4* Kindle location 848
[414] Young *Studies in Genesis 1* p82 foot
[415] Currid *Ancient Egypt* p45

abbreviated sentence structure; and there is an almost complete absence of metaphor and simile - the very stuff of poetry.

In fact, as a piece of prose its language – vocabulary and structure – is, apart from the repetition and the numbering of the days, plain to the point of being bland. Even the repetition of "God saw that it was good" dulls rather than enlivens the prose, minimises rather than intensifies the imagery, while stressing the goodness God sees. And the formality with which the sections are marked-off by the numbering of the days has more of a technical than poetic flavour. What lifts the passage beyond the ordinary is not the language, but the topic.

John Collins builds on C S Lewis's *The Language of Religion* [416] to apply Lewis's three types of language to Genesis 1. Lewis identified "ordinary language," "poetic language," and "scientific language" as the basic categories in common use.[417] However, by "scientific" Lewis does not mean what is generally referred to as "scientific language" in the present discussion. Lewis means by "scientific" only that it is not ordinary or poetic. In the context of contemporary debate therefore, "scientific" is probably an unfortunate term by which to describe any language that is identified as being neither ordinary nor poetic: there are many forms of language that are not ordinary, poetic, or scientific. Collins recognises this, noting for example, the existence of legalese and jargon (which Lewis would classify as "scientific language"), as well as noting the impact of different registers,[418] but continues his argument on Lewis's three-fold distinction.

Collins maintains there is little scientific language in the Bible,[419] but if scientific is seen as the alternative to poetic or ordinary (which is what Collins wants us to take from Lewis), then one has to say most of the Bible is scientific! It may not be intended, but the effect of using the highly ambiguous term "scientific language" is to make it appear, without any valid basis in the appeal to language types, that the Bible cannot be expected to give data in a scientific manner. Yet Collins also recognises that it should not be supposed "that the scientific language is more 'literal'" nor "that poetic language is of itself any less referential than ordinary or scientific."

Arguing that there is little scientific language in the Bible while using Lewis's definition of scientific language is both confusing and disastrous: in the end it does nothing to help a reading of Genesis 1. Collins runs with two mutually exclusive definitions of "scientific language"[420] indiscriminatingly oscillating between the two, but it is never made clear which "scientific" makes Genesis 1 not scientific – and by his own assertions that would not make any difference to the literal nature of the text anyway! Collin's discussion appears to undermine any idea that Genesis

---

[416] "The Language of Religion" in C S Lewis *Christian Reflections*, Eerdmans, 1964 pp124ff cited in John Collins *Types of Language and Biblical Interpretation*, [paper distributed by Collins, Auckland, 2013] 2012 pp1ff

[417] Interestingly, the example of ordinary language Lewis gives is more descriptive than Genesis 1: compare Lewis's "It was very cold" with Genesis's "There was light."

[418] Collins *Types of Language* p2

[419] Collins *Types of Language* p4

[420] That is, Lewis's definition that anything that is not ordinary or poetic language is scientific language, and the more common idea that scientific language is language that gives literally reliable scientific data.

1 is scientific – but in reality it fails to address that issue at all, let alone provide a basis for a non-literal reading of the passage.

Poetic Language that Cannot be Found

There is a common misconception as to what constitutes poetic language and poetry that can confuse this discussion. The moment intensified imagery or language devices such as metaphor are encountered, too many cry "Poetry!" with the implication then made by many that truth is thereby obscured.

Norman Geisler exemplifies this error in his commentary on the *Chicago Statement on Biblical Inerrancy*, when he writes, "when the prophet speaks of 'trees clapping their hands' (Isa. 55:12) one could assume a kind of animism unless he (sic) recognized that this is poetry and not prose."[421] Of course he is right to see that animism is not intended and that the trees do not have actual hands. This is plainly a metaphor in which the imagery is not to be taken literally, although equally clearly what the metaphor refers to – that creation itself will somehow render glorious praise to God – is to be taken literally. But that does not make the metaphor poetry. While the passage from which it is taken clearly is poetry, the metaphor itself could as well be found in prose as in poetry. It is not that it is poetry that prevents a literal reading of an animistic kind, but that it is metaphor. In a context where the term "poetry" is so often used to undermine confidence in the Bible, it would seem prudent to exercise care as to what is called poetry.

There is also a common perception, encouraged by many who do not want to read Genesis 1 literally, that if Genesis 1 can be classified as poetry it cannot then be read as literal. But as Collins himself has pointed out, this simply is not so. Even if Genesis 1 is regarded as poetry, that is no reason to treat it as anything but literal. By way of illustration, if my wife should write to me with the famous lines beginning, "My love is like a red, red rose,"[422] I would not be wise to assume that in writing to me in poetry and by using a simile to describe her love, her love is not real. I would do much better to realise that her love is not only literally true, but intensely so!

Although Collins rejects Genesis 1 as poetic, his classification of it as "exalted prose narrative" is applied to dismiss literalism in the same way as some appeal to a wrongly supposed poetic form. He recognises that he is essentially doing the same thing by asserting, "This name [exalted prose narrative] is far better than the term some use, 'poetry.'"[423] Rather than appealing to poetic form (which in any case he recognises would not necessarily remove literal reference) as a basis for dismissing literalism, he quite deliberately uses "exalted prose narrative" in the same way. This appears to be little more than semantic conjuring: calling something "poetry" does not necessarily mean "not-literal," so call it "exalted prose." Classify it as a newly coined genre with which no one is familiar, assert that by definition it is non-literal without showing how it differs from poetry in respect to literalism – and so turn it all into allegory. Or not.

---

[421] Geisler [on Article XIII]
[422] The first line of a traditional Scottish song transcribed by Robert Burns in 1794
[423] Collins *Genesis 1-4* Kindle location 526

Appeals to the supposed poetic nature of Genesis 1 can be finished with at this point. Genesis 1 has none of the attributes of poetry, whether that be specifically Hebrew poetry or poetry in general. Consequently, no interpretation based on an asserted poetic form or content in Genesis 1 can be sustained.

The Mists of Symbolism: Missing or Meaningful?

Considerable confusion swirls around the place of symbolism in Genesis 1. Frequently introduced as a feature of genre, it is objected that the symbolism with which Genesis 1 is said to be imbued precludes or at least inhibits too literal an interpretation of the chapter. Yet, while significant symbolism is *subsequently* attached to many aspects of Genesis 1, there is almost no symbolism at all in the text itself.

Symbolism involves one thing representing another thing (material or abstract). The symbol exists literally, but has reference to more than its own existence in that it also represents something else. In common experience, symbolism can be a matter of interpretation: the Rolls Royce driven by a wealthy man might be taken by some as a symbol of his ostentation and by others as a symbol of his good taste. Yet either way the symbolism only works if there is a real car – a literal Rolls Royce at that.

Symbolism in literature however is used to convey a specific reference. A reader might see or miss the symbolism, but it is never left "open" to random interpretation. John Buchan's classic description of a man in *The Thirty Nine Steps* who "could hood his eyes like a hawk"[424] is meant to alert the reader to the man's villainous character. The reader may or may not pick up the symbolism, but the symbolism itself is not dependent upon the reader's interpretation. A symbol in literature is an object or idea that is part of the story that fits into the story line with a literal meaning, but also has an intended meaning beyond what it means at the literal level. No symbolic meaning replaces or displaces the literal meaning, but rather depends upon it.

Further, symbolism is unidirectional in that while the symbol refers to something that exists independently of the symbol, the thing referred to is never taken as symbolic of the symbol. For example, national flags are recognised universally as being symbols of the nation owning the flag. Both the symbol and the thing symbolised are literal. The real flag however has symbolic reference to the nation that exists independently of the attribution of national symbolism to a bit of coloured cloth. I suspect there are few rational people who would invert the symbolism and claim that the nation is symbolic of the flag. Such irrational inversion of symbolism however is common in – and all-but unique to – Old Testament scholarship.

David and his kingship are symbolic of Jesus and his kingship. For that to work, David has to be a real king whose character and rule become images of the surpassing character and greater rule of the coming Messiah. David is a real king

---

[424] John Buchan *The Thirty-Nine Steps* (London 1915) this edition Chatto & Windus, London 1985 p20 (Buchan confirms this symbolism when some chapters later the character is described again as "Bland and bald-headed and hooded his eyes like a bird.... He sounds a sinister wild-fowl!" p103

who is such a part of the biblical story that the narrative in Kings and Samuel could be complete with the ending of his life and rule. But the promise to David and the way his life and rule are used, indicate that as a symbol, his life and rule illustrate attributes of the life and rule of Jesus. Yet that symbolism can never be reversed: Jesus is never a symbol of David.

The things created in Genesis 1 therefore cannot be *merely* symbols. To be symbols they must be real things, and to have symbolism they must have reference to real things. Each time something is made, something real is made; each time a day is mentioned, some real period of time has transpired. What really is meant, for example, when it is argued, "One way to reconcile what current science says about evolution is to propose that the account of Adam and Eve is symbolic, not literal."?[425] There is the symbolism explained by Paul in 1 Corinthians 15 by which Adam is seen to represent all mankind – but to do that Adam has to be a literal man in the first place. If Adam is not real in Genesis 1, Paul's attribution of symbolism to Adam cannot make sense. Even Peter Enns, who says Paul is writing myth about a myth, admits that Paul writes believing what he writes is not a myth, believing that a real Adam existed as the real first human, and believing that he did what Genesis 3 says he did.[426]

What statements that assert Adam is symbolic, not literal, are really saying is that either the text is a metaphor with no intention of providing an historically accurate account of *any* material creation, or that something that is not an "Adam" is created and for literary purposes the text speaks as if that something has the attributes of mankind. Both arguments are put forward by different scholars, but they cannot be sustained as either faithful to or derived from the literature of Genesis 1 which presents as (at the very least) some sort of historical narrative with no internal attribution of such symbolism.

For light, for example to be symbolic – and it is unquestionably taken as symbolic as Scripture unfolds – it must in fact be real, literal, physical light. That light comes to be a symbol of righteousness and truth (among a multitude of other things) means that whenever the context suggests such symbolism, the attributes of light are applied symbolically. Thus when John says "men loved darkness instead of light"[427] the context makes abundantly clear that the saying is metaphorical and that the "light" in the saying is a symbol for what literal light does: it exposes what is hidden in darkness ("darkness" itself being another symbol within the metaphor). No one in his right mind would take John to be asserting that Jesus came into the world as a physical light, or that a physical light could identify particular actions and attitudes as sin. It is a metaphor we understand because we know what light does when it shines in a dark place. The metaphor depends absolutely on what literal light actually does: it is the attributes of physical light that enables the symbol to work. Thus for any of the things created in Genesis 1 to have symbolic use, they must first be literal, real things.

---

425 Tim Keller *Creation, Evolution and Christian Laypeople*, p2

426 Enns *The Evolution of Adam* p120

427 John 3:19

Symbolism has a Literal Reference

There can be no symbolism if the object or idea is not first present as a literal part of the story. Thus when it is suggested "days" in Genesis 1 are symbols for "aeons of time" what is suggested is not symbolism (for if days *means* aeons of time, the days do not literally exist in the story line) but deceit: a word with a plain meaning is being used to convey a hidden meaning without any reference to a literal part of the story.

In contrast, the seventh day in Exodus is truly symbolic: it is a real day that is given a greater meaning as a symbol referenced back to the real first seventh day in Genesis. Subsequently, the literal Sabbath day of Exodus itself becomes a symbol – as in Hebrews 4 and 5 – for the final rest God has prepared for believers.

It is frequently argued that when in Genesis 2:4 God writes, "In the day God made the heavens and the earth", "day" is used as a symbol – in this case as a symbol of a longer period of time. Thus, it is argued, if in Genesis 2 "day" can mean a period of time longer than 24 hours, it *could* be the same in Genesis 1. Yet whichever way Genesis 2:4 is taken, it cannot support the rendering of "day" in Genesis 1 as symbolic of a long period of time:

1. If Genesis 1:1 is seen as part of the first day ending in Genesis 1:5, and if, as seems most likely, the "day" of Genesis 2:4 is, a reference to that day ending in Genesis 1:5, then Genesis 2:4 is simply referring back to the first day, described in Genesis 1:1–5 as the day God made the heavens, the earth, and light. Genesis 2:4 would be referring to that single day and therefore be making no implication of an extended period of time, and would not be symbolic.
2. If Genesis 1:1 is seen as part of the first day ending in Genesis 1:5, and if Genesis 2:4 is taken to include that day and the following days till the end of day 6, the "extended" day of Genesis 2:4 is synecdoche (a part used to represent the whole), a form of symbolism that depends on the symbol being a part and not somehow being the whole. That is, for the "day" of Genesis 2:4 to represent the six days of creation, it must be an actual "day." As such, Genesis 2:4 only makes sense if the parts it refers to are real ordinary periods of one day. If there is symbolism, it only works if "day" means "day."
3. If Genesis 1:1 is taken as a summary of what follows, with day 1 starting in verse 2, then the day in Genesis 2:4 would indeed refer to a longer period than a 24-hour day – it would be referring to six days. But that too is not symbolism for then there is no 24-hour day in the text of Genesis 2:4 from which a symbolic greater period could be adduced. If the meaning of day in Genesis 2:4 is six days, then it plainly means week without any initial contextual meaning of an ordinary day.[428] There can be no symbolism in Genesis 2:4 if "day" does not in the first place mean "day."

Three aspects of biblical symbolism need to be understood for any approach to Genesis 1 to be consistent with the text. Firstly, symbolism can only be symbolic if it has reference to a reality that can serve also as a symbol. The things created in

---

[428] Which is weird – why would God say day when he means week?

Genesis 1 must be reality, as there is no other reality upon which their supposed symbolism can be referenced. Secondly, for symbolism to be symbolic, the symbolism must be transparent in the text: with the exceptions discussed below, not only is such transparency absent in Genesis 1, the text presents as if there is no symbolism. With two exceptions,[429] finding symbolism there requires a search any gold prospector would be proud of. Thirdly, as the Bible unfolds, it accords symbolism to things that at first carried no symbolic weight. True, in God's plan they would become symbolic as his revelation unfolded, but that symbolism was not at first revealed in the text, and cannot therefore be used as a primary interpretive principle.

Biblical Symbolism Does Not Change the Original Text

No one familiar with the first few verses of John's Gospel can read Genesis 1:3 without an acute awareness of the symbolism that light coming into the world comes to have in the Gospel message. John's reference is clearly to Genesis 1, and just as clearly he refers to the light created at the beginning and uses it in a metaphor for the enlightening, saving, and life-giving person of Jesus coming into the world. Yet that metaphor can only have meaning if the light in Genesis 1 is a real, literal light that has properties able to give sense to Jesus being the metaphorical "light." If the light in Genesis 1 is merely a symbol, likening Jesus to such a light caries none of the meaning conveyed when Jesus is compared to real light and what it does. For the symbolism to have any meaning, the light the metaphor is anchored to must be real. The original reality in Genesis (in this case "light") becomes a symbol in John, having symbolic qualities attributed to it, as God in his providence always intended but did not originally reveal, and had not implied in the original text in Genesis.

John also calls Jesus the "Lamb of God." Again, the symbolism is clear: the lamb is the sacrificial lamb that takes away the sins to the world. But when lambs were created in Genesis 1 they are not symbolic: at that time there was no sin, and sacrifice was not foreshadowed, nor would it have made sense. As the history of redemption unfolds, many of the real things of creation are given symbolic meaning – but that never diminishes the reality of their objective, literal creation in the first place. The animals created in Genesis 1 are not symbols in that text, although many will become symbols as the biblical story unfolds.

Yet Genesis 1 is not entirely lacking in symbolism. The symbolism that does exist is identified clearly in the text as symbolism. That the text clearly identifies symbolism when it occurs is in its turn a very strong indicator that what is not clearly identified in the text as symbolism is not symbolism!

In Genesis 1:16 God gives to the sun and moon the function of "governing" the day and the night. In saying this, God clearly gives to the literal sun and moon that have already been created (verse 15) a function they can only have by way of

[429] The sun and moon symbolising governance, and man symbolising God (see below).

metaphor, for the sun and moon do not literally govern. God makes clear the nature of their governance: they are "signs to mark sacred times, and days and years."[430] They are signs, they are symbols. The sun and moon actually exist as literal sun and moon to which symbolism can be attached. How do we know they are symbols? Because the text directly attributes such symbolism to them.

Then too there is symbolism attached to man. He is created in the image of God (verses 26 & 27). Man is symbolic of God. "Man" is really made, but we know he is also symbolic because the text explicitly says so. And what is he symbolic of? "Something" (speaking reverently in literary terms of God) that is already literally independently existent: God. Again the symbolism is explicit in the text, and is referenced to a literal reality independent of the symbol.

But is not the term "man" itself in Genesis 1:26 & 27 symbolic of "mankind"? Not in the text. There is a tendency in modern translations to render the Hebrew *adam* as "mankind".[431] If in fact this is the best translation, then *adam* is not symbolic of "mankind" for it then *means* "mankind". Robert Alter's commentary gives weight to this translation:

> The term *'adam*, afterward consistently with a definite article, which is used both here and in the second account of the origins of humankind, is a generic term for human beings, not a proper noun. It also does not automatically suggest maleness, especially not without the prefix *ben*, "son of", and so the traditional rendering "man" is misleading, and an exclusively male *'adam* would make nonsense of the last clause of verse 27.[432]

A Literal Adam Makes Possible a Symbolic Adam

However, Alter does not follow this though in his translation as, despite what he has noted, the passage is probably better understood as recording the creation of a man (and subsequently a woman): a literal Adam and Eve. The varied use of the article could be taken as accidental, but only with difficulty since the passage is commonly accepted as being carefully crafted, and the points at which indefinite and definite articles are used make sense of the creation of an individual. The fact that God proposes to make "*a* man," indicating one man, and thereafter speaks of the "*the* man," clearly indicates a specific individual, irrespective of any symbolism attached to that individual. Despite his commentary then, Alter seems to support this in his translation: "And God said, 'Let us make a human' … And God created the human in his image, in the image of God He created him."[433] As Alter points out, the definite article is almost always used: an individual, literal man is very much in view. There can be no question that Adam becomes, in the biblical account, the father of all mankind, and in the Genesis 3 Fall, the representative of all mankind.[434] But he is no mere "symbol" of man or mankind: he is the literal first

---

[430] The glorious symbolism here that enriches the call of man to govern creation will be explored in the final chapter.
[431] cf the 2011 NIV
[432] Alter *The Five Books of Moses* p18f
[433] ibid
[434] 1 Corinthians 15:45ff

man. Equally clearly, in making man "in our image" symbolism is attributed by the text to Adam: he symbolises God. But again, he can only do that if he is an actual man. "Man" in Genesis 1 is a symbol of God and a symbol of mankind, but to be that he must be as the text portrays, a real, literal man.[435]

There is no genre description, no attribution of symbolism, that can extinguish the clear intent of the text of Genesis 1 to portray the creation of real, literal things. Whatever symbolism is attached to those things in Genesis or in later Scripture, they are real things. There is no genre description, no attribution of symbolism, that can extinguish the clear intent of the text of Genesis 1 to portray the passing of days with a literalism that the text demands, and subsequent reference in the Bible to that text depends upon.

Similarity Does Not Imply Dependence

Aside from issues of genre and symbolism, other similarities can be identified between the Bible and earlier pagan literature. John Currid, for example, while rejecting adaptation of myths by the biblical authors,[436] shows that "the biblical author [of Exodus] often employs parallel idiomatic expressions ... Egyptian vocabulary ... (and) Egyptian terms."[437] He sees more than similarity though: "many of the incidents in the book of Exodus ... reflect common plot-motifs in the ancient Near East."[438] Here he finds "echoes" of Egyptian literature.[439] Having the same or similar idioms, vocabulary, terms and story-line however, does not indicate "reflection" or "echoes" of one literary work in another: it simply recognises similarity.

There are similarities between Egyptian literature and the Bible (although as Currid has pointed out, these are minimal[440]). For example, both have accounts of hero-deliverers, which is hardly surprising as a hero-deliver is found in the histories of almost every culture. Most are people: they were born, and their birth stories are invariably invested with portents of the ultimate significance of the child. All children face challenges; invariably those challenges take on epic proportions in the stories of hero-deliverers. Similarities in narratives are found from ancient Africa to ancient America, but they do not prove interdependence. Is it surprising that pagan stories imitate God's true stories? Or that in a world that needs a Saviour, much literature finds one? It is the very stuff of story-telling and cultural identity. Apparent literary "reflections" and "echoes" could be found anywhere, but they do not imply dependence.

True, some literary devices, language and idioms are common to the Bible and Egyptian literature. Is it surprising that Moses should write in a style coloured by

---

[435] This applies in the context of ordinary literature/genre considerations. How much more so when account is taken of the fact that this is God's spoken word.

[436] See pp53ff above

[437] John D Currid, "Exodus," in Miles V Van Pelt (Ed) *A Biblical-Theological Introduction to the Old Testament: The Gospel Promised* Crossway, Wheaton, 2016, p69f

[438] Currid, "Exodus," p74

[439] Currid, "Exodus," p75

[440] See John Currid *Ancient Egypt* p48f

his Egyptian upbringing? Or if, as some argue, the author is not Moses, that such a literate author had some facility in Egyptian literary conventions? This is not dependence upon Egyptian literature but use of conventions with which the author is familiar, in the same way as every writer uses conventions with which he is familiar without necessary reflection or echo of other literature.

For Currid, these similarities are evidence of a dependence by which the author sets out to "subtly criticise Egyptian manners, customs, and beliefs" so as to "disparage Egypt" and mock Egypt's gods.[441] But it is highly unlikely that Egyptians of the period read the Bible and certain that it wasn't written for them. As for the Israel for whom the Pentateuch was written, the likelihood of their having awareness of Egyptian religion or liturgy is obviously minimal.[442] So while readers such as ourselves, with knowledge of Egypt not shared by Israel, can see in the language of the Pentateuch a polemic against Egypt and its gods, it is untenable that such a polemic was intended as an overt context in which the text was to be read, or that the Bible was written with a dependence on pagan literature.

The Pentateuch, as for the whole Bible, is unique literature. Inspired by God, it does not share genre identity or literary influence, motif or message, dependence or connection, cultural context or divine conflicts, with non-biblical literature. It is God's book declaring God's message for God's people in God's context with God's words recorded by God's prophets to be read in God's perspective with God's help for God's glory.

---

[441] Currid, "Exodus," p70

[442] See above

7. Genesis Shrouded

Ministering with Mist: Elusive "truth" in a vapid Genesis 1

"In the beginning, God created the heavens and the earth."

~ Genesis 1:1

For a number of summers when our children were young, Priscilla and I took them away from the city, camping under canvas beside a beach in the countryside. On still, cloudless and moonless nights, with no obscuring city dust or ambient light, the *Milky Way* stretched across the black sky with staggering, sparkling magnificence. A multitude of other stars was always visible too – though thinly spread in comparison. The occasional satellite would pass gracefully through the mix, and usually we could also identify one or two planets. Transfixed by the sight above us one night, one of my sons and I each expressed aloud the sense of wonder that gripped us. I said, "Isn't it wonderful!" and at just the same moment he said, "Isn't God wonderful!" One of us saw things as they truly were.

We had both observed exactly the same thing, but I saw nature in which God was given no conscious place, while he saw a God-centred, God announcing creation. He saw and heard the heavens declaring the glory of God, and the skies proclaiming the work of his hands. "Day after day they pour forth speech; night after night they reveal knowledge. They have no speech, they use no words; no sound is heard from them. Yet their voice goes out into all the earth, their words to the ends of the world."[443]

---

[443] Psalm 19:1-3

That night my son saw and heard what creation is there to show and tell. His observation lead to knowledge. I missed it. I heard nothing in the presence of a thunderous melody. My observation hid the true wonder of God's divine nature. I silenced his voice, I wondered in ignorance. I observed as pagans observe. Because of the very nature of the universe as created, observation is never self-contained. It always involves fitting that observation into a framework either acknowledging or denying the voice of God congruent with every phenomenon. Observation of creation always involves acknowledging or denying God's eternal power and divine nature, because that is what is clearly seen in everything able to be observed.[444]

A Biblical Perspective in Pastoral Ministry

A right understanding of Genesis brings a right understanding of the world we live in. Tim Keller argues that it is one of the tasks of a pastor in teaching Genesis "to be a bridge between the world of scholarship and world of the street and pew."[445] Since biblical scholarship is not easily processed and applied, he says, Pastors are "to help both believers and inquirers to relate science and faith coherently."[446] This rightly places debate about Genesis 1 in a pastoral context, for in one sense it matters little to ordinary Christians on the street and in the pew what academics debate – whether good or evil – if that never filters through to everyday faith and life. How Genesis 1 is used to proclaim God's glory to God's people and to a lost world; how it is used to call the lost to faith and to encourage God's people in faith; and how it is used to equip God's people for life in God's creation, are essential components of a faithful reading of the Bible. So what are the pastoral implications of Genesis 1?

Genesis 1 gives us a world-and-life view that should shape both the mega and micro aspects of personal and corporate life. Everything in the totality of our being and experience is as creatures given form, function, life, location and purpose by our Creator. God is the creator of the universe of which he is not a part and by which he is not bound, and has placed us in that universe with responsibility, opportunity, hope, and perhaps above all, creaturely dependence. Genesis 1 lays the foundation for knowing who God is, who we are, what we are here for, where we can go, how we can get there, and the nature of the relationship God chooses to have with us that enables all that to be known and to happen. "Human beings are made in the image of God, and as his image-bearers we are made to work, to rule, to serve as God's stewards, to be surpassingly God-centred."[447] In other words, Genesis 1 is not merely something that needs to be taught in a pastoral context, it is part of the foundation of pastoral ministry.

It is a mistake to imagine that pastoral responsibility to interpret Genesis 1 is fulfilled if scientists and their students can be satisfied. The conflict between evolution and creation can so dominate thinking that we miss the impact of

---

[444] Romans 1:18-20 (again!)
[445] Keller *Creation, Evolution and Christian Laypeople* p3
[446] ibid
[447] D A Carson *The God Who Is There* Baker, Grand rapids, 2010, p23. Carson's discussion "Some Things about Being Humans" (pp21ff) and "Some Things about How Genesis 1-2 Fit into the Whole Bible and into Our Lives" (pp25f) are exquisitely helpful in developing pastoral use of Genesis 1.

evolutionary idolatry in western life and culture as a whole. Just as easily we can miss the comprehensive significance of Genesis 1 for that same western life and culture. Evolutionary ideology reinforces the search for autonomy in the arts as much as in the sciences. Evolutional paradigms shape man-centeredness in sociology and education as much as in biology. The evolutionary exaltation of change shapes values and expectations in business and politics. The amorality of evolutionary ascendency validates the reshaping of moral standards. Evolution's assurance of progress energises salvific hope in the future with a blind denial of decay, degradation and judgement. And at every point, Genesis 1 cries out, "No! Think again!"

Keller rightly challenges the church to minister Genesis pastorally, in a way that helps scientists and their students manage the tension between their field of service and the revelation the One they serve has given. That tension is not resolved by submitting Scripture to a non-biblical word-and-life view. Nor does a biblical world-and-life view prevent engagement in scientific research or application that has been developed in a contrary world-and-life view. As discussed earlier,[448] Christians can work in science even with a differing world-and-life view.

Scientists – as for people in any other vocation – have the best pastoral care when they are helped to see that the fallen people they work with in a fallen world viewed in fallen distortion have a different perspective; yet at the same time are helped to see – as with people in any other vocation, whether driving a bus or painting a picture or cloning a gene – that their vocation involves doing things with the things of creation in a way that is not dependent upon cosmic origins, much less on any philosophy purporting to account for origins.

Biblical pastoral ministry to all people regardless of vocation or field of academic study involves bringing them to a faithful commitment to a biblical perspective, a compassionate understanding that their unbelieving peers and colleagues have a different perspective, and a pragmatic trust in a Sovereign Creator who is intimately involved in upholding and directing the creation in which and with which they work. A shared perspective is not only unnecessary for practical engagement in research or practical application of scientific knowledge, a shared perspective is impossible for Christians working with non-Christians in their world. We have a different perspective: but we can do the same things with the same stuff and expect the same outcomes. That is really delightful, as such confidence depends on stability and order the Creator has covenanted to sustain, whereas it conflicts with the randomness and expectation of fickle change or immutable fate embedded in every other perspective.

For example, geologists can differentiate between formations and rocks, share empirically formed expectations of how those formations and rocks will behave and what resources they might indicate, without any particular view of God's involvement. They can work on shared outcomes without sharing an identical framework of the age of those rocks and formations. Geneticists can model genetic structures and engineer variations without any shared concept of origins. Astronomers can work on observable conditions and project phenomena without any shared belief in when the past changed from what it was to the constancy we

---

[448] pp18ff

now find. Physicists can work with their various models that fit some conditions and not others without a model that explains everything.

The Bible reveals the universe not only as God's creation, but as something held together by God who makes known to us by his word and the observable creation that he is immanently engaged in that creation. It reveals a creation to which he has covenanted constancy. That means Christians can bring a hope, an expectation of order, an assurance of purpose, a confidence in the legitimacy of discovery and rule, and uninhibited delight to vocations that otherwise hold to such things with remorselessly fragile uncertainty. It is what Christian scientists have been doing for centuries and it remains their high calling to serve others as they serve God in that way now. Rather than inhibiting engagement in the sciences, a world-and-life view founded in a confident, trusting, literal, submissive, consistent and faithful reading of Genesis 1 makes it uniquely possible.

In short, pastoral ministry arising from Genesis 1 begins with the voice of creation: "Worship and serve the Creator rather than the creation; interpret and manage vocation and life according to the words of the Creator rather than the created; find comfort and hope in the Creator rather than in the creation; be motivated and satisfied by the Creator rather than by the creation."

Idolising Creation

We are fallen people living in God's creation among fallen people who see creation in a fallen way. The godless unfailingly idolise creation in one way or another, and because we share their nature (albeit as those being transformed in Christ), and are immersed in their culture (albeit striving to "no longer live as the Gentiles do, in the futility of their thinking"[449]), Christians have a tendency to the same idolatry. We find it so hard to "come out from them and be separate .... [to] touch no unclean thing."[450]

Keller defines an idol as "anything more important to you than God"[451] and in a footnote explains that this means anything that becomes "a centre of value by which other values are judged."[452] There can be no doubt that for many – if not most – in contemporary western culture, evolution is such an idol. The temptation, especially for those in the sciences, but just as really if not so overtly for the rest of us, is to use evolution as the value by which other things are judged. This is exactly what is done when evolution is the centre of value by which Genesis 1 is judged. For example, John Collins brings an evolutionary centre of value to his reading of Genesis 1 when he says, "as a modern who accepts contemporary cosmology as part of my world picture ... let us consider whether the biblical picture fits with a reasonable interpretation of the world around us and with what we know to be true of ourselves."[453] A biblical approach works the other way: a true cosmology is that revealed by the biblical text; what is considered "reasonable" is what conforms to

---

[449] Ephesians 4:17
[450] 2 Corinthians 6:17
[451] Timothy Keller *Counterfeit Gods* Hodder & Stoughton, London, 2009, pxvii
[452] Keller *Counterfeit Gods* p181 quoting Thomas C Oden, *Two Worlds: Notes on the Death of Modernity in America and Russia*, IVP, Downers Grove, 1992, p95
[453] Collins *Genesis 1-4* Kindle location 2928

the biblical picture; the truth of what we know of ourselves is defined by the Bible. A biblical cosmologist would say, "As a Christian who accepts the Bible as defining my world picture ... let us consider whether our interpretation of the world around us and what we think we know of ourselves truly fits the Bible's declaration."

Keller follows Collins in arguing for a non-literal interpretation of Genesis 1 that accommodates evolution. For Keller, genre is a key for the understanding of Genesis 1, and Collins' genre description is a key for identifying the genre of Genesis 1. Keller made his views explicit in a paper entitled *Creation, Evolution, and Christian Laypeople*, presented to the first *Biologos* "Theology of Celebration Workshop" in October 2009. That paper is not only striking for its commitment to a non-literal understanding of Genesis 1 and at the same time to a literal understanding of a first Adam and Eve; it is also striking for the different reasoning he gives for those different commitments. For more than a decade of his New York ministry, Keller taught that Genesis 1 should be classified "poetry" and therefore should not be taken literally.[454] He has since adopted Collins "exalted prose narrative" classification, but with unchanged implications for reading Genesis 1. While rejecting the external filter of ANE mythology, he has nonetheless adopted a genre classification which has been overtly developed by imposing an external "centre of value" of ANE culture and mythology through which Genesis 1 is to be read.

Which Centre of Value has Real Value?

Keller refuses to do this in interpreting Genesis 2-3 however, which he insists can only be read as an account of a literal Adam and Eve. The basis of this insistence is not the genre of Chapter 2-3, much less the influence of myth (which he rejects),[455] but the internal evidence of the Bible. Since the rest of the Bible treats Genesis 2-3 as literal, he convincingly argues, so must we. Here he makes the Bible the centre of value through which he reads Genesis 2-3. That is a basic, consistent application of belief that the Bible is inspired by God and given unity by God.

So why not do the same with Genesis 1, and take it as literal because the rest of the Bible does just that? In *Creation, Evolution, and Christian Laypeople* Keller identifies two further reasons, in addition to Collins' "exalted prose narrative",[456] that indicate Genesis 1 should be classified as some form of non-literal genre:

1. "Perhaps the strongest argument for the view that the author of Genesis 1 did *not* want to be taken literally is a comparison of the order of creative acts in Genesis 1 and Genesis 2." [His italics] *This argument hangs on the presumption that Genesis 2 is another account of the creation first told in*

---

[454] The precise period for this is of little consequence, but from a sermon in 2000 through to his 2008 *The Reason for God* he describes Genesis 1 as poetry. For example: "I think Genesis 1 has the earmarks of poetry and is therefore a 'song' about the wonder and meaning of God's creation." (*The Reason for God* p94). The first example of reference to Collins' "exalted prose narrative" I am aware of his 2009 paper *Creation, Evolution and Christian Laypeople* for BioLogos.

[455] ANE myths, he acknowledges, "did not evolve over time into historical accounts, but rather historical events tended to evolve over time into more mythical stories."

[456] All unattributed quotes and references in the following five paragraphs are from that paper.

Genesis 1. According to Keller these two accounts of creation are incompatible: "You can't read them both as straightforward accounts of historical events."[457] *But as discussed in Chapter 10,*[458] *Young affirms with a detailed examination of the text that "Genesis two is not, nor does it profess to be, a second account of creation. Although it does mention creative acts, it is a sequel to the creation narrative of Genesis one."*[459] *It explains in greater detail what God did in the creation of man on day 6. In fact, one of the strongest arguments for taking Genesis 1 literally if Genesis 2 is taken literally is that they have literary and thematic unity: whatever is true of one is true of the other.*

2. The second reason for calling Genesis 1 exalted prose narrative but not Genesis 2, is of a different sort, even though it is also related to the order of events in each chapter. Keller claims that as "Genesis 1 shows us an order of creation that does not follow a 'natural order' at all," it should therefore not be treated as literal, whereas Genesis 2 is said to follow a natural order and should therefore be read as literal. *He has correctly read Genesis 1 as recording creation in a "non-natural" order. But in doing that, Keller is reading it through a centre of value that presupposes the act of creation has to conform to natural order, completely missing the point! In not following a "natural order" God is making the point that he is not bound by natural order. He makes light without the sun and he makes plants before there is rain. Neither God nor his creative acts conform either to the mythology of the Ancient Near East or the naturalism of contemporary western idolatry. He makes things when he wants, as he wants, the way he wants and sustains them as he determines. When he is ready he makes natural order then upholds it according to covenant promise, yet overthrowing it whenever he wants to work another miracle. The lack of "natural order" in Genesis 1 is one of the main points it is making: God is not, was not, and never will be controlled by nature. He made nature and nothing in his creative act was a necessary natural development. Nothing in God necessitated his creating creation, and nothing in his creation necessitated anything else in creation. The order he created, with its embedded cause and effect relationships sustained by his word, was part of what he created, not a centre of value that controlled what God did or how he made creation function then or afterwards.*

It is helpful to consider in more detail why Keller applies different criteria to reading Genesis 1 and Genesis 2-11. The latter he calls "'high' accounts ... of events that actually happened ... despite the compression, omissions and figurative language" used in Genesis 2-11. He recognises that the literary form of Genesis 1 is of the same sort as Genesis 2-11. Having recognised "compression, omissions

---

[457] That is not necessarily so. For one thing it depends on Genesis 2 recording events in chronological order. Genesis 2 differs dramatically from Genesis 1 in which a chronological order is one of the defining features of that chapter. Such a change in structure suggests, at the very least, that chronological order is not a feature of Chapter 2. There are other factors too that mean that even if the two chapters are read as different accounts of the same six days of creation, they can be read in harmony more easily than in conflict with each other.

[458] For a fuller discussion on the relationship of Genesis 1 & 2 see below p215ff

[459] Young *Studies in Genesis One* p59.

and figurative language" as common genre-markers in both Genesis 1 and Genesis 2-11, why classify them as different genre? Why call Genesis 1 "exalted prose" that cannot be trusted literally, and Genesis 2 "high prose" that can be trusted literally?

Keller not only rejects genre as a centre of value for reading Genesis 2-11, just as he rejects the use of ANE myth as a centre of value for reading it; he goes much further and puts up a very strong case for suggesting that if anything is indicated by the way ANE mythology developed, it leads to the conclusion that Genesis 2-3 is an "account of an historical event that really happened." So what makes the difference?

Keller writes, the "relevant text here is Romans 5:12ff, where Paul speaks of Adam and the fall. … Paul believed that Adam was a real figure." The centre of value for reading Genesis 2-11 as literal, reliable history is the Bible itself. The New Testament regards Adam as a real historical figure, therefore so should we. When Keller takes the rest of the Bible as his centre of value, he reads Genesis as literal history; but when he takes genre as his centre of value, he reads Genesis as not-literal history. Keller declares, "The key for the interpretation is the Bible itself." It is a key he applies to Genesis 2-11 *despite* genre indicators, but it is a key he does not apply to Genesis 1 *because* of genre indicators.

This illustrates a pattern evident in much modern Old Testament scholarship: the useful tool of genre identification often becomes so dominant that it is the default centre of value by which the Bible is read, unless some additional reason can be found to submit to the Bible's own commentary on itself.

World Picture in Conflict with World View

John Collins recognises the significance of a centre of value. He consistently draws attention to "the worldview that Genesis 1-4 (and the Bible as a whole) inculcates [which] centres on God and the grand narrative of creation, covenant, fall, redemption, and eventual consummation."[460] He consistently makes this explicit as he considers Genesis 1-4: "The first aspect of that worldview is God the Creator. In these chapters God introduces himself, telling his people and the rest of mankind the most basic things they need to know."[461] Would that every reader of Genesis 1 would get at least that much from it.

However, Collins also goes to some lengths to make a distinction between the "world view" of the ancient world of the writer of Genesis 1 and what, in coining another new term, he calls "world picture". The latter is said to be, "what one imagines to be the shape of the world and the things in it" whereas "worldview is one's basic religious stance toward the world."[462] World view is "normative, while the world picture need not be."[463] In other words, the world picture may be "true" *in some respects* but not necessarily in every respect. In this construction, a writer engages in a "good faith act of communication," if the point being made depends

[460] Collins *Genesis 1-4* Kindle location 3039
[461] Collins *Genesis 1-4* Kindle location 2730
[462] Collins *Types of Language* p9
[463] ibid

on an allusion to something having "truth value," even if the statement itself is not true, and even if it is known to the writer to be not true. The task of the reader is "draw out just what assumptions underlie a good-faith act of communication" so as to "attend to the actual *message*." [The italics are his.][464]

The distinction between world view and world picture may be more imagined than real. Are people limited to only using a world picture and not their world view? Collins is able to express his world view in great detail despite being "bound" by his culture's limited world picture. Are others not able to do the same? When he says, "an author and his audience share a picture of the world (knowledge, beliefs, values, experiences, language), and communication operates on that picture for various purposes"[465] does that really exclude a congruent framing of the discussion in a world view? In any case, Collins has there included "beliefs" in the world picture that is supposed to be devoid of religion, something said to be what makes world view different from world picture. Collins builds a great deal on a distinction it seems even he is unable to maintain consistently.

However, maintaining a definitive distinction between world view and world picture, whether consistently or inconsistently, is a critical condition for discounting the plain meaning of a biblical text and replacing it with a hidden meaning behind the text. The significance of the distinction is meant to be this: every writer and speaker works within the bounds of their world picture. Their world picture will be limited by their knowledge and the conventions of their culture. Our modern world picture differs in many respects from the world picture of the ANE. If we try to read what they have written in expectation of a common world picture, little communication is likely to take place; or worse, miscommunication will occur. We will never get beyond the details about what is described, and we may even take the inconsequential details as the message. Recognising their different world picture enables us to go beyond the details of the text to consider the greater core truths being communicated. If however a definitive distinction between world view and world picture is more imagined than real, or even if it exists but the lines between them are blurred and people can work with both to some degree at the same time, the method Collins advocates that rests on there being an absolute distinction is of little practical help in reading a text.

An Incarnation?

Describing the Bible as God's word incarnated is presently a popular way of asserting that the Bible is necessarily shaped by the world view prevailing when it was given. Just as Jesus is God's Word incarnated, it is said, the Bible is God's word incarnated. The most basic problem with this analogy is that Jesus *is* God: the Bible *is not* God. The incarnation of Jesus involves God who had always existed becoming flesh which till then he was not, without in any way ceasing to be God. That is the nature of incarnation. The Bible never was God: when it was spoken the words existed for the first time and existed in the form in which they were spoken

---

[464] Collins *Types of Language* p12
[465] Collins *Genesis 1-4* Kindle location 2923

without assuming any other form that they were not before they were formed! Nor for that matter do God's words take flesh. The analogy may have a fuzzy sense of Jesus' incarnation being similar to God speaking, but it is without real ontological congruence. Jesus is called "the Word [of God]"[466] not on account of his incarnation, but on account of his making God known. In fact, *he* is the incarnated word, for he is word before he takes flesh, whereas the spoken word *is not* before it is spoken.[467]

Peter Enns is a leading advocate for the incarnational approach. He describes it in this way:

> Just as Jesus was a human being, the Bible is a book that fully reflects its cultural contexts. Jesus is "God incarnate," both divine and human. Likewise, the Bible is a book that speaks God's word but thoroughly reflects the thoughts, ideas, and worldviews of the human authors. ... An incarnational model helps us to see that we should expect the Bible to bear the marks of the perspectives and worldviews of ancient writers.[468]

Few could take issue with the idea that in a very significant way the Bible is a human book, if by that it is meant, "Each writer has his own habits of mind, vocabulary, outlook and interests. Each book has its own character, and is written according to stylistic conventions ... Each book has its own historical and theological background."[469] But Enns goes much further than that by constraining God's communication to the imperfections of the prophets and the concepts of myth and literary conventions embedded in contemporary pagan worldviews. This results, he asserts, in a biblical text that is "firmly rooted in the worldview of its time."[470] He does this by misrepresenting the nature of incarnation; by misrepresenting the cultural context and worldviews of the prophets; and by misrepresenting the reformed heritage he quotes in support of his claim to orthodoxy.

The incarnational model falls at its first hurdle: "Just as Jesus was a human being, the Bible is a book that fully reflects its cultural contexts." But Jesus *never* fully reflected his cultural context – in fact, over and over again he is to be found confronting it. Nor for that matter is Jesus fallible, working within a pagan worldview, or equivocating on the truth through the literary form of myth. Jesus, instead, brings a conflicting God-centred culture to bear on the fallen world into which he has come. Commenting directly on the analogy of Jesus and the Bible,[471] Packer notes, "If the critics believe that Scripture, as a human book, errs, they ought, by force of their own analogy, to believe also that Christ, as man, sinned."[472] If the Bible is incarnate "just as" Jesus is incarnate, and if as Enns advocates the Bible is

---

[466] John 1 etc

[467] This touches on one of the most important conflicting concepts in this debate: those who want to reduce the inspiration of the Bible to the message behind the words may well conceive of a message that existed before the words were spoken. There can be no doubt that what God said was not new to him! But the words of God are what he speaks when he speaks, and it is these that are inspired and convey the message associated directly with the meaning of those words.

[468] Enns, *Peter Enns on the Incarnational Model of Scripture,* Biologos, 2010, http://biologos.org/blog/pete-enns-on-the-incarnational-model-of-scripture

[469] J I Packer *Fundamentalism and the Word of God* IVF, London, 1963 (1958) p107

[470] Enns *Inspiration and Incarnation* Kindle location 322

[471] Although not using the term "incarnational model"

[472] Packer *Fundamentalism* p83

constrained by man and culture, so Jesus is constrained by man and culture: failure and sin must consequently be attributed to him. Needless to say, the Bible asserts just the opposite: Jesus' divinity controlled his humanity, conforming it to his divinity; and in just the same way God's divinity controlled the words of the prophets to conform those words to his divinity. Warfield's comments on this are helpful:

> As in the case of Our Lord's person, the human nature remains truly human while yet it can never fall into sin or error because it can never act out of relation with the Divine Nature into conjunction with which it has been brought; so in the case of the production of Scripture by the conjoint action of human and Divine factors, the human factors have acted as human factors, and have left their mark on the product as such, and yet cannot have fallen into that error which we say it is human to fall into, because they have not acted apart from the Divine factors, by themselves, but only under their unerring guidance.[473]

Enough has already been said in this book to invalidate the assertion that the worldview, cultural context and literary conventions of the Old Testament prophets were pagan. But Enns' use of earlier scholars in the Reformed tradition to claim the incarnational model is an historically held view is quite misleading. While he quotes them accurately so far as he quotes them, he falsely implies that in speaking of a "human" Bible they share with him the concept of a Bible controlled by less-than-divine human, cultural, worldview and literary limits. For example, he quotes Warfield: "the Scriptures are the joint product of divine and human activities … at once divine and human in every part, every word and every particular,"[474] and Hodge: "the very substance of what they write is evidently for the most part the product of their own mental and spiritual activities."[475] But what he fails to clarify is that (in the same manuscript) Warfield and Hodge clearly assert that far from being constrained by their humanity, the prophets had been prepared and were empowered by God in their speaking and writing God's word to conform to God's divinity:

> Each sacred writer was by God specially formed, endowed, educated, providentially conditioned, and then supplied with knowledge naturally, supernaturally, or spiritually conveyed, so that he, and he alone, could, and freely would, produce his allotted part. Thus God predetermined all the matter and form of the several books largely by the formation and training of the several authors … He [the prophet] is brought into place and set to work at definite providential junctures, the occasion affording him object and motive, giving form to the writing God appoints him to execute. The Bible, moreover, being a work of the Spirit for spiritual ends, each writer was prepared precisely for his part in the work by the personal dealings of the Holy Spirit.[476]

Hodge and Warfield argue that God fitted the prophets to his self-revelation by preparing them, equipping them and empowering them in the task. That is the opposite of God being forced to fit his self-revelation to the worldview, literature,

---

[473] B B Warfield *The Biblical Idea of Inspiration* Kindle Edition 2013 [an extract from *The Inspiration and Authority of the Bible* 1948] Kindle location 479

[474] Peter Enns *Preliminary Observations on an Incarnational Model of Scripture: Its Viability and Usefulness* Biologos, [no date given] www.biologos.org/uploads/projects/enns_scholarly_essay2.pdf

[475] ibid

[476] A A Hodge & B B Warfield "Inspiration" in *The Presbyterian Review 6* (April 1881), pp. 225-60 http://www.bible-researcher.com/warfield4.html

character and culture of the prophet's community. Those upon whom Enns leans for support actually hold a diametrically opposite view to the one Enns is claiming they hold and the one Enns is propagating.

This is the heart of the issue: either God controls the mind and words of the prophets, conforming them and their worldview to himself and his worldview, and conforming their words to his; or the prophets control God conforming him to themselves and their worldview (in most models in fact not *their* worldview but that of the pagans around them) and conforming his word to theirs. The incarnational model so constrains and confines God it might better be called the "incarceration model," for it re-forms God in man's image and imprisons God and his speaking within the fallen cosmos.

"Untruth" the Truth

Collins makes extensive reference to "phenomenological language" in his discussion of world picture. We tend to describe things from the perspective of the observer rather than from an "eye-of-God" perspective. Such descriptions are what are referred to as phenomenological. The ancients wrote in phenomenological terms of the sun moving across the skies, for example; but today we know that the movement is only apparent. In reality the sun does not move across (or around) the earth, only appearing to do so as a result of the earth revolving on its axis. Phenomenological language is used when we speak of the sun moving, of sunset and of sunrise. This is language that describes the phenomenon as we experience or see it, but not as it really is. But this is hardly world picture stuff. After all, despite our present much more informed world picture we continue to speak, even in scientific literature, with phenomenological language. Modern almanacs, produced by scientists who have extensive knowledge of the universe and astronomy, state with precision the times for "sunrise" and "sunset." Phenomenological language is not opposed to truth, it is merely one way of communicating it, with no imputation that the data or description is in any way false.

Yet the use of phenomenological language in Collins' approach depends on the details not being true. He explains, "We do not expect such language to be making strong claims about the inner workings of the things it describes; instead it allows us to refer to real events without getting bogged down in such questions."[477] In the example of a sunrise, this means that a writer's reference to the "sunrise" is concerned with the event of the sun appearing on the horizon and not the mechanics of whether the sun actually rose or became apparent as the earth revolved. But that doesn't alter the fact that at sunrise the sun *does* appear.

Too much can be given away in the rush to minimise "truth claims." When reference to a "sunrise" is made, the sun is real, the time is real, the appearance of the sun is real, and the event is described in words that are utterly unambiguous in their context. I don't think Collins would disagree with that. He begins by making the point that in such a use of phenomenological language detail is not expressed with scientific precision. If that was all that he said, there would be little to debate, just as there would be little implication for the multiple "truth claims" evident in a

---

[477] Collins *Genesis 1-4* Kindle location 2920

plain reading of Genesis 1. But in subsequent discussion, all details evident in a plain reading of a phenomenological text are discredited as if by definition *all* details in phenomenological language lack "truth value." As we have seen, that need not be so.

Hence Genesis 1 is read as a "good-faith act of communication" in which the details are not true but the core message (whatever it might be, for that is a matter of interpretation not comprehension) is true. This assessment is made on the basis that it is phenomenological language, which we know does not describe things truly. Except, we don't know that! It is a basic logical fallacy to assume that since some phenomenological language can lack scientific precision in some details, all details in phenomenological language are imprecise. Associating phenomenological language with imprecision is used as a basis for imputing imprecision to all phenomenological language in subsequent discussion. But phenomenological language is in actuality not much different from any other language conveying a message through details: the details must be precise and true for the message to have true precision.

Take the example of the night my son and I rejoiced in the wonder of a beautifully sparkling night sky. His declaration "Isn't God wonderful!" expressed the core message of creation, but it would have been a vapid theological truth claim had it not been made in the context of the detail of real stars in a real night sky. The truth claims of the big message depended upon the truth claims of the details. The message is not fully comprehended without the details: take those details from the story and the message loses clarity and undermines significance.

Take an example of this approach applied to the Bible. Genesis 1:3, reads "God said, 'Let there be light,' and there was light." I am not convinced this is phenomenological language as it seems to me that in Genesis 1 God is giving us a picture of how he saw what he did, rather than it being a picture painted from the perspective of a person on the earth. However, if it is regarded as phenomenological, which detail is to be discarded as not pertinent to truth claims, and what message is inescapable? "God" belongs. Perhaps "said" is merely idiomatic … but as the whole passage is about stuff happening because God spoke, and because God is revealing himself as God who speaks, it would seem necessary that "said" is a detail that must be retained. "Let there be light" seems more than a passing detail when the creation of light is being reported, and certainly if it is left out the verse really has nothing to say. So it has to stay. Perhaps by light is meant the phenomenon that could be seen by an observer, rather than a scientific definition of "light" … but if there was an event the observer saw *something* and for the passage to make any sense at all it must have had the appearance of light. In any case, if something is "seen" light makes it seen, and since it is about the creation of light, what looked like light probably was light. So "light" stays. Even if it is phenomenological language then, every point of detail is a truth claim of significance.

Inspired Error?

It could be argued that the main point of this is that God is Creator. But suppose for a moment that the details of Genesis 1:3 are not to be relied upon as truth claims.

What if they are not true? Does an erroneous account of a creative act of God that, if it happened, didn't happen the way it is described, help communicate an overarching message that something happened that justifies God being called "Creator"? Or does it convey the message that although God is *seen* as Creator, he didn't *truly* create anything, and therefore cannot be considered to be *truly* Creator? For the overarching point to have any truth claim, the component passages must have valid truth claims. Genesis 1:3 must be true in its detail for the overarching message of Genesis 1 to be true.

All this highlights the significance of detail in a narrative: a narrative hangs on the detail. Far from the "inner workings of things" bogging the reader down, those inner workings – that God spoke, that he made, that it was light he made – are essential to the story and to the message. Phenomenological language or not, the details matter, and to matter they must be true (ie making valid "truth claims" if you will).

There is a tendency to blur the lines between phenomenological language and phenomenological world picture as if phenomenological language use in the past always meant phenomenological world picture, whereas phenomenological language can be used without being tied to a phenomenological world picture. We do it in our modern world all the time. Is there any rational reason why the ancients could not have done so also? Constant association of phenomenological language with an attributed faulty or primitive world picture of the ancients colours our perception of their world picture as if the details reported by the ancients can never be relied upon to be scientific rather than phenomenological.

The direct application of this approach is to declare the details of Genesis 1 as belonging to an untrue world picture.[478] What really matters, it is said, are the truth claims made via the medium of that untrue world picture, the inspired core message being communicated through inspired inadequate words and inspired untrue details. Genesis 1 therefore can tell us that God is the creator, but not the details of what, when and how he created: the days, the order of events, the exalted prose, are all to be considered mere devices to communicate the core truth.

Conforming to this pattern, Collins argues that Genesis was written in the context of world picture that today is known to be incomplete, often inaccurate, and largely observed from a phenomenological perspective. Nevertheless, he argues, the truth being conveyed in Genesis is unaffected by the false world picture through which it is being communicated:

> It may well be that some biblical statements reflect a world picture that we cannot share … But this does not mean that the world picture is part of the message being communicated. Most of these cases are more likely phenomenological language, which we know does not make claims even about the world picture. And a number of them … are simply matters of misinterpretation, which we can now correct.[479]

Here Collins argues that the phenomenological language used *does not* "make claims" about their world picture: that is, it *does not* tell us about the way the world is as they see it. At the same time he argues that the use of phenomenological

---

[478] The writer is usually regarded as probably believing their world picture to be true. However, some argue that writers then were as aware as writers now of the conventions of communication that allow for fictional details used as a medium for conveying core truths.
[479] Collins *Genesis 1-4* Kindle location 2966

language *does* "reflect" their world picture: that is, it *does* tell us about the way the world is as they see it. But that, he argues, is irrelevant information not intended to convey meaning to us. Rather, it is a mechanism by which meaning they did not express can be conveyed to us. Into this mix the concept of the Bible's inspiration is injected: the writers of the Bible are inspired by God to write what is not true, and are inspired to write what is not intended to inform us about the phenomena described, so that God can covey to us a message of truth that is not described by the words used but is somewhere behind the text.

Sifting Truth Value from Truth Claims (and Other Conjuring Tricks)

Collins develops an approach to sifting inspired not-truth from inspired truth in biblical texts by working from the idea that a claim to truth in historical writing does not make it true. Whether or not it is true, for the claim to be valued as truth it must somehow be accepted as true. The ideal is to have the truth claim verified by some means. In his scheme, such verification attributes reliable truth value to truth claims:

> The notion is simple and intuitive: a narrative can be historical in the sense that its author wants us to believe that its events really happened; it makes historical truth claims. But sometimes we say that a narrative is historical if we are confident that its events really did happen: we are focusing on its historical truth value. To move from truth claim to truth value implies that we have some criterion for verifying a claim.[480]

It is clear from this that Collins does not consider that the biblical text being the inspired word of God is a sufficient basis for accepting the claims to truth in a biblical text. That is consistent: if God has inspired not-truth as well as truth in the Bible, some other criterion apart from it being the Bible is needed.[481] He gives at least three.[482]

Before reviewing those however, another one of his frequent reservations needs to be considered. Collins warns that even verifying a truth claim by giving that claim truth value may not give assurance of having a reliable text. A text may be considered truly "historical" if its truth claims are verified, but "Historical is not the same as 'complete in detail'"[483] This is a good, old-fashioned red-herring! The fact that it is not complete in detail does not mean that the detail that is given is not true. What he calls "historical" is by his definition something verified as true. But to then

---

[480] Collins *Genesis 1-4* Kindle location 2784

[481] It is pertinent to note here that Collins is not engaging in a conventional textual critical discussion about whether a particular portion of text belongs in the Bible or not. He accepts that the text belongs in Scripture. The task here is to determine whether the text that belongs has truth value as well as truth claim.

[482] There may be more. Collins can be difficult to follow at times as his writing tends to flit from one idea to another, with ideas inserted here and there without consequences being developed at that time, but with implications that do not necessarily follow inserted into the discussion at a later place. Collins also remorselessly hedges his bets: almost every point made is at some point qualified with uncertainty – the only certainty being that the text cannot be relied upon without external verification.

[483] Collins *Genesis 1-4* Kindle location 2791

say it is not true in that the true detail given is not complete detail is a nonsense. To some degree or other *nothing* is ever complete in every possible detail, but that is not sufficient grounds for declaring all statements to be untrue. Dropping this little red-hearing into the discussion at this point taints the discussion that follows: the innuendo that even historically true statements are not really true will tend to colour every subsequent truth verification.

The first criterion Collins stipulates for verifying a truth claim is to check the reliability of the witnesses (which in the cases of Genesis – discounting God himself – means Moses [484]). Collins takes a rather significant step here, for if a reliable witness is verification of the text, and if (as he maintains) Genesis 1 is not verifiable as true truth, the implication is that Moses is an unreliable witness. He does say we "should consider how good a record the witness has in other stories that we have been able to verify,"[485] but that hardly helps with Moses.

This is quite a big call for Collins to make. Although I do not think he spells it out in so many words,[486] an inescapable implication of his discussion is that Moses is not a reliable witness. That does not necessarily mean Moses should be considered a consciously untruthful writer. Something else that Collins never completely clarifies is whether the authors of biblical not-truth knew that what they were writing was not true, or if they were writing consciously to the pattern of ANE mythical literature,[487] or if they thought they were writing what was true, or in writing phenomenologically they were not concerned with the truth value of what they wrote. Nevertheless, if his witness is not true at one point, can he be verifiably true at any point?

The second criterion for verifying truth value is to "consider how competent readers from the same culture (or at least from a culture that shows continuity with the original audience) have taken the narrative."[488] He recognises that this must include the Old Testament and the New Testament, but throws in (of equal value) "extrabiblical Jewish material." To this he adds "the literary milieu in which these pericopes belong, namely, the Mesopotamian creation and flood stories," and the "myth or 'protohistory,' [of the] the Sumerians and Babylonians."[489]

For Collins, biblical literature is a part of the pagan literary corpus. Elsewhere he refers to "important materials from all the cultures of the ancient Near East, those most directly pertinent to Genesis 1 – 11 come from Mesopotamia ... this overarching pattern from Mesopotamia provides a literary and ideological context into which Genesis 1 – 11 speaks" [490] and gives a similar list of ANE literature to that of Walton discussed above.[491] The importance of locating Genesis in this

---

[484] Collins accepts Moses as the primary author of the Pentateuch
[485] Collins *Genesis 1-4* Kindle location 2792
[486] As I have already alluded to, Collins frequently leaves the implications of something he asserts hanging, although he will subsequently assume a particular implication as if stated and proved.
[487] Writing to the pattern of ANE myth does not in itself solve the truthfulness issue. Moderns of a scientific bent tend to impute to writers and users of myth (both ancient and modern) an awareness that myth is not true: there is no evidence of this and much evidence to the contrary.
[488] Collins *Genesis 1-4* Kindle location 2807 – and for the remaining quotations in this paragraph
[489] ibid
[490] Collins *Four Views on the Historical Adam* Kindle location 2665
[491] See above

corpus of ANE literature is that "no one expected the stories [including Genesis] to be read in a thoroughly literalistic fashion."[492]

By saying it "seems" to follow the conventions of pagan literature "of which it is a part" he does not unequivocally commit his readers to that concept – but he never resiles from it either, building from that point forward as if the supposition is a foundational fact. Objectivity gives place to supposition, which itself follows undisclosed literary conventions and mysteries to be unfolded by the privileged caste inducted into the secret formulae.

Thus if a biblical text agrees with ANE myths, it has truth value; if it doesn't agree with ANE myth it does not have truth value. Let me respond unequivocally: no matter what tricks of communication theory are employed, no matter what sleight of hand insinuates unbelief into the world view or world picture of the writers of the Bible, the Bible does not belong to the literary milieu of pagan perversions of truth, and it is not subject to "verification" by the effluent of Mesopotamian, Sumerian or Babylonian rejection of God.

Deciding for Ourselves what has Truth Value

Collins' third criterion for verifying the truth value of a biblical text brings the whole discussion home to roost: if you agree with it, it is truth; if you don't agree with it, it is not-truth. Before I am drowned out by protest, consider what he says, repeatedly: "But what if we are unsure of how reliable the witness is ... There is a kind of external verification that can help us, namely, the way the story comports with other things we have a right to believe." [493] Putting aside the question as to where this sudden mention of a "right to believe" comes from, what exactly do we have a right to believe? His implication – one that is spelt out emphatically in his practical methodology – is that we have a "right to believe" anything from the scientific, cultural or mythical knowledge we bring to the reading of the Bible. In a purely academic context, this argument is not sustainable, but from the point of historic, evangelical faith, it is reprehensible. I contend that a biblical Christianity has only one right to belief – no, only one obligation to belief – to believe the Bible and what it reveals about God and his work. I reject the possibility, much less the "right", of Christians remaining faithful to God and his word when subjecting the infallible Bible to the test of fallible science, corrupt culture or lying myths.

Another instance in which Collins asserts the dominion of man's mind over Scripture is when he says, "For us to say that the Bible authors assert a certain world picture as being true, we would have to be sure that physical cosmology is part of their communicative purpose. As soon as we see this, we are relieved of quite a few of the supposed primitive elements." [494] Here he is considering not merely whether or not the text conveys truth, but whether or not the biblical authors intended to convey truth. But without resolving that, he implies that a biblical cosmology *does not* give a true cosmology, and that the biblical authors did not intend to convey such a cosmology: the second sentence is necessarily dependent upon that implied

[492] Collins *Four Views on the Historical Adam* Kindle location 2744
[493] Collins *Genesis 1-4* Kindle location 2792
[494] Collins *Genesis 1-4* Kindle location 2950

presupposed answer to his apparently open question. Again the truth value in a text is seen as determined by our ideas, even if our ideas are not what the writer has written.

A third example should make it clear this is typical of Collins and not an aberration. "Being careful with the literary conventions allows us to discern several distinct historical truth claims. Properly considered, these claims about the world and ourselves fit well with honest conclusions from ordinary observation and from the sciences." [495] This consideration, he says, "allows us to discern several distinct historical truth claims"[496] in what otherwise is not reliable truth. On this basis, something the Bible says can be taken as truth if we discern that it fits what we have seen and what the sciences have concluded.

It is not that the truth claims he deduces are not a faithful summary of God's teaching. From Genesis 1-4 for example he deduces a core message that "things work this way because God made them to do so, so that we could enjoy his world; we feel a need for his presence because he made us for that, too, and offers it through the covenant."[497] Few would dispute that this is a core message from the text. Nevertheless, there are three huge problems with this approach. Firstly, the text of the Bible is discarded along with the detail so that we no longer have a reliable Bible expressing truth in plainly understood language; secondly, the deduction he makes could be different from the deduction the next person makes, and there is no objective way to discern that, especially once the detail of the text is discounted; and thirdly, once the method is introduced in one part of the Bible, why is it not applied to all of the Bible?

Consistency demands this method be applied to the whole of the Bible. Yet Collins appears to hold firmly to many historic doctrines of evangelical Christianity that arise from a reading of the text that does not pass the test of his three criteria. Does this mean he is applying his methodology inconsistently? Not at all! For him, reason, observations, and knowledge of ourselves determines which parts of the Bible are truth and which parts are not-truth. Where a plain or literal reading of the text fits his reason, his observation or his knowledge of himself he is perfectly consistent in arriving at a literal reading of the text. Nothing makes this plainer than a passage quoted earlier in this chapter: "Let us consider whether the biblical picture fits with a reasonable interpretation of the world around us and with what we know to be true of ourselves." [498] Collins' theology is perfectly consistent with his methodology: if I agree with it, it is truth; if I don't agree with it, it is not-truth.

Dividing Truth

Collins' distinction between world view and world picture depends on the idea that it is possible to form a view independently of the overall religious framework in which the view is formed. It is not. When Collins asserts that a world picture can be formed that is independent of a religious world view, all that is really asserted is that the true position of that view is that God is not involved in the world being

[495] Collins *Genesis 1-4* Kindle location 2995
[496] ibid
[497] ibid
[498] Collins *Genesis 1-4* Kindle location 2854

viewed. That is not a religiously neutral view. It is expressly religious. What Collins calls the world picture expresses the real world view of the observer/writer irrespective of any claims to the contrary. We can only have a picture of the world that excludes God if we have a view of the world that allows the exclusion of God.

Although Collins illustrates his religious/secular division of view, he never demonstrates how one can have a secular view of the world God rules without distorting the truth. He accepts that a world picture may not agree in literal detail with the reality it pictures – in fact, it appears that Collins believes both that the writer accepts this and that the writer expects his audience to recognise this. But God having been excluded from world picture, the disjunction between what is literally there and the world picture is always at the level of what can be observed rather than between the world picture and God's picture. Anything described without God in the picture is not truly described. Thus, while it at first appears Collins' approach may allow for fallible people to give fallible descriptions of what is really there (thus enabling some sort of search for truth within their partially true statements), what he is really providing for is fallible descriptions of what is not truly there to begin with. That does not look like a good place to search for what is true.

Collins has developed a theory of communication constructed from selected bits of competing language and communication theories.[499] Applying this to reading the Bible, he shapes a worldview utilising a range of presuppositions that are antithetical to a biblical worldview. Without engaging in a detailed discussion of language and communication theories, it is sufficient to note that the theories he adapts depend upon concepts that are debated among theorists themselves, and that are largely inimical to biblical concepts of truth and communication. These include the ideas that there is no absolute truth that can be described objectively, that truth cannot be communicated without it being changed, and that each receptor of a statement alters the actual meaning of the statement.

That latter point appears particularly significant in his discussion of "truth claims" v "truth value." As we have seen he claims that what a text might claim (eg an author's claim to be reporting historical data) does not have value as a statement of truth for the reader unless the reader is persuaded by some means or other that the claim is valid. This appears to hinge on distinguishing truth as an absolute from the "value" it might have to a particular person, and making that value dependent upon that person's perception. Behind the theory from which this concept of "truth" is derived is the denial of absolute truth itself: in this framework the only truth that is true is what is true to the individual according to the individual's own perception

---

[499] "I have developed my literary methodology by combining ideas from text linguistics (sic) and speech act theory, literary criticism (e.g., C. S. Lewis, Mary Louise Pratt, Meir Sternberg, and Phil Long), and Biblical theology (e.g., N. T. Wright, Michael Williams, and Christopher Wright), together with my own reflections as a grammarian and lexicographer (mentored by one of the best, Alan Millard)." John Collins in *Interpreting Adam: An Interview with Jack Collins, Part 1*
http://biologos.org/blog/interpreting-adam-an-interview-with-jack-collins-part-1 .
There is not space here to examine how Collins uses language and communication theory, but any concept taken from a particular theory is valid only so far as it is supported by the presuppositions of that theory and the way in which the selected concept is integrated into the whole. In isolation, any such concept has dubious validity, but when various concepts are taken from incompatible theories, even less confidence can be placed in the concepts being extracted and isolated from their context.

or construction. Even when an individual is made the centre of value, it is difficult to hold that an unperceived value that impacts on a person is valueless. For example, a person may or may not perceive they are a sinner, but that truth has an impact on the person whether perceived or not. The impact may differ in particular ways or in degree according to perception, but it will have truth value for that person regardless.

But when God is made the centre of value – the very least to be expected in a biblical reading of the Bible – the value of truth rests no longer in its perception, but in the creator and sustainer of all truth, perceived or not. Romans 1 (again, and among others) asserts unequivocally that God's "truth claims" are true irrespective of their reception, and most certainly have value for everyone whether the truth is perceived or not, received or not. A biblical communications theory must take account of this.

With the Words God Gave

It is not only with Collins that discussion of language and communication begins to lose touch with reality. Vanhoozer appositely confesses, "I believe that God gives us language to communicate."[500] But his discussion subtly shifts from communication being a use of language to it being exclusively about communication since language "never exists simply to state propositions," then shifts again to the existentialism of language being exclusively "a means by which one person acts in relation to others." He has oozed into unsustainable excess. The first time we meet language in the history of the cosmos is when God speaks to nothing and nothing conforms in giving place to everything. The words spoken correspond exactly to the will of God without any person hearing or responding or giving meaning; instead nothing (at times) and stuff (at others) conforms exactly to the meaning of the words God has spoken. Language can have use and meaning without it acting on anyone.

Vanhoozer makes a strong claim to the reliability of the words of the Bible: "True words communicate what is. Words that purport to communicate what is yet fail to do so are false – unreliable, untrustworthy, perhaps even lies."[501] On one level this appears to deal a fairly logical death to complex arguments about words that are not true but have a hidden truth behind them. But it hangs on the idea that meaning is established in a completed communication, whereas, as already noted, God's words are true whether or not they are understood or comprehended by others. The meaning of words is determined by the speaker, not the hearer or the act of communicating with a hearer.

Somehow though Vanhoozer manages to separate hearers from interpreters, recognising that truth is not dependent upon what we make of the words: "Is the Bible's truth somehow dependent on the activity of interpreters? Hardly. The Bible teaches truth whether or not its students learn their lessons. ... God's words are wholly reliable: their human interpreters, not so much."[502] The implication is that

---

[500] Kevin J Vanhoozer in Merrick & Garrett (Eds) *Five Views on Biblical Inerrancy* (Counter Points: Bible & Theology/Zondervan) Kindle 2013, Kindle location 3701
[501] ibid
[502] Vanhoozer *Five Views* Kindle location 3821

the interpreter cannot discern meaning without being party to the original act of communication (speaker and hearer), which takes us to a concept of words that do not reliably convey meaning after they have been spoken and heard. The Bible is thus a reliable, inerrant record of God's word, but cannot be understood unless we can somehow discern, without reference to the meaning of the words recorded, how it was first understood (presupposing that it is different from what the words still say). To mix metaphors (which seems entirely appropriate in this context) Vanhoozer appears to want to have his quagmire of contextual interpretation and eat it too.

Consider the words I am presently writing. I am sufficiently a realist to know that it is possible no one will read this paragraph. Does it not have meaning then? Of course it does! Further, I am conscious that part of the function of this use of language, my writing this paragraph, is to help me clarify and record my understanding of language and its use in the Bible.[503] If no one else reads this, my using language here has still had a purpose, and what I have written is infused with fixed meaning. Should someone else read this at some time as indeed I intend and hope, is the meaning thereby changed; or even more stupid, is what I have written then given meaning for the first time? Or in a complete lack of sanity, does it only have meaning if it acts on someone or someone acts on it? What I have written may be misunderstood – something that happened regularly when Jesus spoke, and that through no fault of his use of language – but what he meant then and what I mean now is unchanged by our hearers' and readers' responses, even if they impute different meaning to it.

It is possible that confusion over the nature and function of language is also compounded by misunderstanding the way in which God speaks through prophesy. Vanhoozer claims that "Both the prophets and the apostles are divinely commissioned spokesmen charged with putting the word of God into words." [504] Not at all! They are not "spokesmen" given a concept around which to develop dialogue, but mouths (or scribes) to express the *words* (and not just the abstract "word") of God. Thus in Exodus 4 Moses is told that Aaron will be his "mouth" or "prophet": "You shall speak to him and put the words in his mouth ... he shall be your mouth/prophet." [505] This is exactly the process by which God has said he will put *his* words into *Moses'* mouth to speak to Aaron. From that point on Moses is said to speak to Pharaoh and the Israelites, who do indeed hear the exact words of Moses, but they hear them in Aaron's voice, with Aaron's accent and Aaron's cadence out of Aaron's mouth. Thus Jesus refers to the biblical text as words "that come from the mouth of God."[506]

Jeremiah's commissioning as a prophet[507] also clearly demonstrates that God's word is God's words. When Jeremiah objected that he was not suited to proclaiming

---

[503] It will not do to argue that in this case my language has acted on me, for in that case every use of language must act on the speaker, and Vanhoozer's demand that language act on someone becomes a nonsense.
[504] Vanhoozer *Five Views* Kindle location 3706
[505] Exodus 4:15,16
[506] Matthew 4:4, quoting Deuteronomy 8:3
[507] Jeremiah 1:4ff

God's word, God told him that he had set Jeremiah apart from before birth and known him from the womb in preparation for this task. Jeremiah had been prepared by God to be suited to the task. Further, God would be with him to ensure Jeremiah's prophesying went as God planned. Yet even more significantly, the message he was to pronounce was not only what God commanded him to say, but God "reached out his hand and touched my mouth and said to me, 'I have put my words in your mouth.' … Stand up and say to them whatever I command you."[508] God put God's words in Jeremiah's mouth. It was those words Jeremiah was commanded to proclaim.

So much for the spoken words of God; what of the written? God commanded Jeremiah, "Take a scroll and write on it all the words I have spoken to you."[509] When asked about the scroll, Baruch the scribe explains, "he dictated all these words to me, and I wrote them in ink on the scroll."[510] It was not just the message Jeremiah dictated to a scribe, it was the very words God had given him. When the wicked king Jehoiakim destroyed the scroll, God commanded Jeremiah, "Take another scroll and write on it all the words that were on the first scroll."[511] Jeremiah confirmed that the words on the second scroll were "all the words of the scroll that Jehoiakim king of Judah had burned in the fire."[512] Through the prophet he had created and prepared for the task, God spoke and wrote the words he wanted heard and read.

The prophets and apostles did not grope around to try to find in their idiom and in their literary forms an approximate reproduction of the words they were given by God; rather, God chose to speak through those speakers (those mouths) and those writers what he had to say with his chosen words in his chosen idiom utilising his chosen literary form – language in which God had no small mastery. What God said, was what the prophets said and the apostles wrote – and its meaning was expressed with God's exquisite mastery of language in a manner that was never, ever, dependent upon how it was received.

There is nothing in this to imply that God's words were given to the prophets and apostles in some mechanical way that bypassed their minds, gifts, character and literary styles: just the opposite. The God who was able speak in audible words understood by those listening,[513] and was able to give the apostles the instant ability to proclaim the gospel fluently in previously unknown languages on the day of Pentecost, is certainly able to cause his words to be proclaimed by people he has equipped for the event, people in whom he has nurtured the language, character and culture he has chosen to use. So the writer to the Hebrews alludes to the many ways God spoke through the prophets,[514] and Luke is able to describe how he set out to write an orderly account apparently based on careful research.[515] By such means God gave them the very words he was speaking, and in their mouths and writings those words were given exactly as received.

---

[508] Jeremiah 1:9 & 17
[509] Jeremiah 36:2
[510] Jeremiah 36:18
[511] Jeremiah 36:28
[512] Jeremiah 36:32
[513] Not Least in Luke 3:22 & 9:35
[514] Hebrews 1:1
[515] Luke 1:3

Collins' discussion does not at first deny that a text can have an objective claim to truth irrespective of a reader's response. But as we have seen, from that point, without showing any necessary connection, he next lists ways in which the truth claims can be verified by the reader, implying that without such verification, the text must not be treated as true. He makes the historical accuracy of anything but the "core" of biblical narrative subject to verification by the reader. This hybrid of communication theory, including a partial constructivism among others, is then assumed as a valid basis for sifting truth from fiction in the biblical text.[516] In effect he has set up a false dichotomy between truth claims and truth value, in that the Bible, in making truth claims that have eternal truth value irrespective of their reception, posits one further alternative to the two Collins lists: there are truth claims; there are truth values; and there is truth. In the Bible, the truth claimed *is* the truth value: what it says is true, is true. From his false dichotomy Collins asserts his three ways of verifying truth claims, and proceeds to apply them as a necessary consequence to the biblical text – again without demonstrating that the methods of verification or their application to the Bible are valid.

Words Without Messages, Messages Without Words

Where does all this lead? If, as Collins does, one claims that biblical authors can write a world picture that is not true to their worldview, the whole concept of truth is being reframed. Collins replaces reading for understanding of the truth in a statement taken to be true with a search for the "truth claims" or meaning in a text that may not in itself be a true statement after all.

Collins does not altogether abandon a conventional approach to Bible reading. He insists for example that Genesis is historical narrative,[517] understood by its writer and original readers as historical narrative, and to be read by us as historical narrative. Yet even this is ultimately diluted, asserting that the historical narrative is the Bible's content inviting "us to recognize the historical impulse."[518]

As "history" becomes "historical impulse," and infallible truth becomes "truth claims" more than a little biblical authority is being cast aside. It is hardly surprising then that the very next sentence warns, "We must be cautious about too high a level of literalism ... since it seems to follow some of the conventions of the literature of which it is a part."[519] This is so loaded! It is literal, but not too literal. It follows some conventions but not all – who knows which? Whatever conventions are followed, it appears they are the ones that belong to pagan literature, not the Bible.

How does Collins apply all this to Genesis 1? He discards almost all detail as conformity to the ways in which narrative was told in the ANE, but asserts that the "truth content" of the "broad strokes" of "inescapable metaphysical claims"[520] can

---

[516] He claims to have demonstrated the variegated fiction/non-fiction nature of biblical historical narrative in earlier discussion which, as discussed earlier, is itself unconvincing and replete with logical and exegetical fallacies.

[517] Collins *Genesis 1-4* Kindle location 2799 ff

[518] Collins *Genesis 1-4* Kindle location 2808

[519] Collins *Genesis 1-4* Kindle location 2808

[520] Collins *Genesis 1-4* Kindle location 2826

be found in stories that are not true. On what basis can these various theories he draws on be used to discern which things the Bible says are *not true in what is said but true in a message that does not match the words*, and which others are *inescapably true in what is said and true in a message that does match the words*? On the basis of personal judgement.[521] As one reads, one must decide if the data can be accepted at face value, or if some external criterion, specialist knowledge or literary mystery should be applied. The text presents as if the author intends historical truth. It reads as if it is historical truth. There is no pattern or structure that aligns it with other passages of Genesis or the corpus of biblical literature in a way that indicates it should be taken as anything but historical truth. All that is left is personal judgement (or submission to the personal judgement of an elite inducted into the mysteries of exegesis) as to what external data should be considered definitive.

All this seems incredibly arbitrary. It is. Collins takes much of the rest of Genesis at a much more literal level, although he never seems entirely comfortable with its complete historical accuracy. He recognises that, "the Biblical material speaks largely in terms of historical matters and of a worldview, and asserts they are true."[522] Yet in the next sentence he talks about the possibility of drawing "out just what assumptions underlie a good-faith act of communication" in the text that claims to be true history. He identifies what for him distinguishes one non-literal passage from another more literal one are various criteria that have no absolute certainty. He can point, for example, to a possible framework in the way the days of Genesis 1 are arranged. At best this is debatable.[523] But regardless of its validity, reading Genesis 1 within this framework is not required by a plain reading of the text: it must be conjured up by imposing the truth-concepts of pagan cultures and the literary devices by which they expressed such equivocation.

What happens if this approach is applied to a completely different passage, say one generally taken by evangelicals at face value such as Mark 9:7: "Then a cloud appeared and covered them, and a voice came from the cloud: 'This is my Son, whom I love. Listen to him!'"? The text purports to be a direct quotation from God, but is it influenced by Mark? Or perhaps Mark employs a literary device of the time: the use of "quotation" from deity to give a dramatic but not literal rendition of the truth content he is recording?[524] Is the cloud literal? After all, it so obviously and intentionally replicates God's presence on the mountain in Exodus that anyone discipled in discerning biblical imagery can see the symbolism and dismiss any literality. With the story of what really happened pictured in the language and imagery of ancient literature for dramatic impact, the intended readers should understand the convention the writer likely adopted and look beyond the story for the truth content. This pericope might well belong to the genre of "visionary literature" (by implication not true) since in Matthew, Jesus tells the disciples not

---

[521] Collins *Genesis 1-4* "In my judgement" Kindle location 487, 497; "I developed" Kindle location 2826

[522] Collins *Types of language* p11

[523] See above for discussion of the framework hypothesis.

[524] Least anyone read this paragraph superficially and subsequently misquote me, I am not writing in my own voice here but using the literary device of giving expression to an erroneous exegetical system – something that will be made manifestly clear by the end of the paragraph – an understanding of my text that will not be dependent upon external data!

to report what they have "seen" – sometimes translated as a command not to tell the "vision".[525] The truth claims behind the text are inescapable: there is a clear assertion of the metaphysical here. But are the details to be taken literally? Did God really say...? Someone asked that question once before.

Sadly, this is not hyperbole. There are plenty of examples of such readings of the Transfiguration, and every one of these non-literal readings of Luke 9 is consistent with any hermeneutic that supports a non-literal reading of Genesis 1. Once it is decided that one biblical passage presented as historical narrative, understood by its writer and original readers as historical narrative, and intended to be read as historical narrative, must be filtered through any additional criterion (in this case an extrinsic and subjective test of historical impulse and truth value behind the text), consistency demands that every similar passage is filtered in the same way.

If Genesis 1 is to be read as non-literal according to the criteria Collins advocates, every other biblical passage presenting as historical narrative must be subject to the same doubt, the same mining for hidden meaning, the same subjection to the magisterium of post-evangelical OT scholars. If God's Word is to have any reliability at all, there must be some more objective basis to determine which texts are historical; something more objective than gut-feelings, godless literature, or academic conclave vaguely hinting at which historical texts *seem* historical and which *seem* not.

In passages he considers historically true in the Bible, Collins is encouragingly clear and helpful in explaining and applying those portions. What makes it so is not conformity to tradition or culture (ancient or modern); it is not the application of literary or communication theories; nor is it the idolatry of orthodoxy or preference (mine or anyone's). What makes such commentary clear and stimulating is a simple treatment of the text as we have it, an exposition that anyone can check out and confirm against the text, the rest of Genesis, and the Bible as a whole. He accepts and movingly explains the plain meaning of Genesis and its implications when such a reading does not conflict with his scientistic world view.[526] As Vanhoozer rightly asserts, "It is the text, not some theory of truth, that ought to determine what kind of a claim is being made."[527]

Pastoral Care & Genesis

What response then can be made to Keller's call to offer pastoral help to those who struggle to reconcile their Bible with the cultural and scientific fashions of the day? The pastoral help of Genesis 1 is not only for those in the scientific community: it confronts and energises every aspect of life, every interaction with

---

[525] See the ESV

[526] While continuing to avoid attributing unstated motive, I note that one of Collins' greatest consistencies is that those passages that do not conflict with his scientism are mostly accepted at face value, and those that do conflict with his scientism are always subject to his "tests" which inevitably result in attributing a non-literality to the text. Whatever his intention, the result is a schizophrenic reading of the Bible: with one mind when science appears in conflict and another mind for all the rest.

[527] Vanhoozer *Lost in Interpretation* p99

the cosmos, every faithful engagement with culture, every inclination of the heart that loves God, and every act of those who serve God. Genesis 1, plainly read, equips God's people with a knowledge of their Creator who is unconstrained by and never conformed to culture or cosmos. It gives them confidence in a Bible that is the product of the word spoken miraculously by the same God whose words miraculously and supernaturally made out of nothing everything that is seen. Genesis 1 calls them to understand by faith "that the universe was formed at God's command, so that what is seen was not made out of what was visible."[528]

Genesis 1 is foundational for pastoral care, for it calls for faith in God not bound by cosmos or culture, who "calls into being things that were not."[529] It calls for trust in a Bible that is no ordinary literature locked in the conventions and culture of its day. It calls for submission to the word of God given in words delivered infallibly through otherwise fallible men prepared and controlled by the Spirit of God, delivered truly by the Spirit of God in a world lost then as now in lies and myths, and recorded in agelessly comprehensible clarity by the Spirit of God.

Genesis 1 reveals God the miracle worker, able to make things happen that would not and could not happen naturally. Genesis 1 makes known God who is able – who alone is able – to make the universe in a six-day event out of nothing by his word alone; the true and living God who with greater-than-cosmic-power can part oceans, incarnate his Son, raise the dead, save the lost, roll up the universe, and make a new heavens and a new earth. Genesis 1 introduces a Bible that God has spoken through men and language he has created and used to make himself and his word plainly known to all people in all time in all places irrespective of their human, linguistic, conceptual and cultural limitations. Genesis 1 proclaims a true understanding of the cosmos and life within it that radically differentiates God's revealed perspective from the arrogant philosophies, fallible observations and rebellious mythmaking of the godless. Genesis 1 is a profoundly wonderful foundation for confidence in the Bible that can be read without mystic induction into the foolish wisdom of the wise.[530] Genesis 1 is the charter for trust in God who is greater than what he has created, faith in a risen Saviour who is fulfilling his promise to do more for us than the creation ever can, confidence to think differently without shame, and the boldness to live differently without fear.

Genesis 1 is the foundation for a faith that does "not rest on human wisdom, but on God's power."[531]

---

[528] Hebrews 11:3
[529] Romans 4:17
[530] 1 Corinthians 1:17 – 2:16
[531] 1 Corinthians 2:5

The Misted World of Genesis One

Part 2:
A CLEAR MESSAGE
The Wonderful Message of Genesis 1 as God's Word

"In the beginning was the Word, and the Word was with God, and the Word was God. He was with God in the beginning. Through him all things were made; without him nothing was made that has been made. In him was life, and that life was the light of all mankind. The light shines in the darkness, and the darkness has not overcome it."

~ John 1:1-5

8. Genesis Regained

The Message: Reading Genesis 1 in the light of Genesis

"In the beginning, God created the heavens and the earth."

~ Genesis 1:1

God has chosen to start his self-revelation in the Scriptures with this simple, magnificent sentence: "In the beginning, God created the heavens and the earth." It is the foundation for the Bible, the interpretive framework for history and the theme song of heaven itself.[532] The profound depth and glorious scope of its meaning is exposed and explained in the biblical text that follows it, but even here the fundamentals are plain: God existed before and independently of the creation; God made everything that is not himself; there was a beginning, and that was the point at which God made everything. See it, hear it, sense it, learn about it: God made it. As there is a beginning, there is a progression (not a cycle). There was a beginning, there is a progression, there will be an end. Always, even from its first sentence, the Bible holds out an eschatological hope in which this marred, deformed and deforming creation is being moved to an end when it will be replaced with perfection, a perfection in which the Creator's glory will be transparent and we can have a place.

[532] Revelation 4:11

Genesis 1:1 – Summary or First Step?

The first verse of the Bible is without question a summary statement, a motto by which every generation can anchor its faith and philosophy, comprehend its place in history and its purpose in providence, motivate its life and worship, and frame its hope. Yet it is also the first verse of the book of Genesis: it has a particular role in the unfolding story of creation. For all the clarity it has as a statement on its own, the first verse of Genesis also poses a question: how does this verse relate to the rest of chapter 1?

There are two obvious possibilities.[533] The first is that verse 1 is a summary statement, a kind of "chapter heading," for the account that follows, and nothing more. The second is that while it does function as a summary statement, verse 1 describes an event – the creating of the heavens and the earth – which is followed by the events described in the rest of the creation account.[534] While there are variations on these two,[535] they are really the only two basic ways to read verse 1.

Genesis 1:1 – Summary?

Verse 1 can quite legitimately be used as a summary of God's creative work. Statements to that effect are found throughout the Bible. But is its function in this chapter only that of a heading? Read as such, verse 1 announces that God is the creator, and the following verses explain how he created. This understanding fits well with most English translations, and fits the sort of literary structure with which readers over the centuries are familiar.

With verse 1 taken as a heading, the creation account begins with verse 2 in which we find an "earth" that is "formless"[536] – that is, without shape; "void" – that is, without content; and "dark" – that is, without even light. In other words, God

---

[533] Over the centuries there have been numerous novel interpretations which I will not canvass here. Collins *Genesis 1-4* discusses a number of them. He has a helpful, detailed discussion (Kindle location 560 ff) of the relationship of verse 1 to the remainder of the creation account based on "discourse-grammar", the implications of which are not entirely dependent upon "discourse grammar", whatever the particular strengths and weaknesses of that approach might be.

[534] Attempts to resolve this choice can be – and in my view often are – unduly influenced by considerations of possible implications. The second view could allow for a vast period of time between verse 1 and the first day. (Sailhamer, for example, [J Sailhamer *Genesis Unbound* Dawson Media, Colorado Springs, 2011] argues that as "beginning" *can* mean "millions, or even billions, of years ... [although leaving] the duration an open question" it therefore *does* mean a vast period of time [Kindle location 258]. The only logic here is Sailhamer's forcing the text to agree with his presupposition of a long period of time in verse 1.) Convictions as to the period of time involved can unduly influence interpretation on this point, but they need not: reading verse 1 as a first-event does not necessitate a long period of time before the other events of chapter 1. Similarly, so much attention can be given to the structure and grammar of verse 1 that the light shed on it by other passages of scripture comes to be ignored.

[535] Most notably the "gap theory" in which it is envisioned that after the creation in verse 1 Satan came and messed it all up (hence the "chaos"), and verse 3 announces a recreation in preparation for man's habitation. Sufficient here to note that the gap theory does not adequately relate to the literary structure of Genesis 1, it is constrained to a particular, inconsistent theological construct, it has only very tenuous links to a couple of other Bible passages, and it does not fit the text of Genesis 1.

[536] This is the rendering of the King James/Authorised version.

begins creation with nothing. The creative work of God that unfolds in the following verses is in that context.

This approach however, runs into a number of problems. Firstly, description of darkness as being on the "face" or "surface" of the "deep" seems to imply there is something there that has a surface and a depth. Secondly, there does appear to be something there called "waters" and those waters seem to have real substance in the verses that follow. While one might read "waters" as some sort of poetic metaphor for "nothing" in verse 2, the waters are separated (verse 6) and dry land divides them (verse 9) whereupon the waters are called "seas" with no indication that they have just been created (verse 10): all of which implies the "waters" of verse 2 are actual created waters, and not a metaphor for nothing. Thirdly, the translation of the Hebrew *tohu wabohu* (rendered *formless and empty* in the NIV) has, as I will explain shortly, more to do with a description of what exists rather than what does not exist.

Fourthly, the structure of the Hebrew text raises questions about such a reading. There is considerable debate as to the implications of the grammar of this verse. These cannot be conclusive on their own, but Collins' analysis of the Hebrew grammar,[537] for example, gives a very strong argument for verse 1 being an event rather than a summary.[538] Yet in exploring the intricacies of Hebrew grammar it is possible to miss simplicity through immersion in complexity: John Sailhamer simply observes, "the conjunction at the beginning of 1:2 shows that 1:2-2:3 is coordinated with 1:1 rather than appositional," so that verse 1 "should be taken as an independent statement rather than a summary of the rest of chapter 1."[539]

Perhaps most significant however is the fifth difficulty: the text naturally reads as if verse 1 identifies an event, the outcome of which is described in verse 2; verse 3 identifies the next event, the outcome of which is then described, ... and so on. The simple story-line is always the best unless there is good reason to look for a more complex one.

These are all strong indicators that verse 2 describes what is there as a result of what happened in verse 1, rather than describing nothing.

---

[537] Collins *Genesis 1-4* Kindle location 560 ff

[538] Robert Reymond (*A New Systematic Theology of the Christian Faith*, Thomas Nelson, Nashville, 1998, pp389ff) has a discussion of the grammar along the same lines as Collins. Both agree that the traditional rendering of verse 1 should be "In the beginning God created ..." rather than "In the beginning God began to create ..." or similar, which is preferred by many modern scholars, particularly those rejecting creation *ex nihilo* and/or a factual/historical reading of Genesis 1. For both Reymond and Collins the primary significance of analysis of the Hebrew is that Genesis 1:1 is seen to assert God's creation of everything *ex nihilo* – "out of nothing." Reymond however, sees verse 1 as a summary statement which is explained from verse 2, while Collins argues that verse 1 records the act of creation of a universe which is made "good" for man's habitation from verse 2. For reasons explained in the next section ("Genesis 1:1 – First Step?") I find the latter position much more tenable. Whichever interpretation is accepted, however, two things stand out from their discussion of the text: verse 1 records the creation of the universe out of nothing, and the traditional rendering of verse 1 is accurate.

[539] John H Sailhamer *The Pentateuch as Narrative: a biblical-theological commentary* Zondervan Grand Rapids, 1992, p82 foot

Genesis 1:1 – First Step?

Without diminishing in any way the use of verse 1 as a summary statement of what God did (for his entire creative work can be summed up in this: he did create the heavens and the earth!), reading verse 1 as describing what God did first in the work of creation just makes sense. In the beginning, God made two things: the heavens and the earth (and the earth he made was formless etc).[540] Next God made the light. And so on. This is not only a perfectly natural way to read the text, it makes sense of verse 2.

What does it mean to be "formless and void"? Two Hebrew words are used: *tohu* and *bohu*, linked in Hebrew as *tohu wabohu*. Despite the confidence with which *bohu* is translated (after all, the translators have to put *some* word in the space!), nobody can be certain as to the exact meaning of *bohu*. It occurs three times in the Bible,[541] always in the *tohu wabohu* link, and never in any other known literature. The second and third occurrences clearly refer back to Genesis 1. In none of those three places is it defined. But the way it is linked to *tohu*, and the obvious rhythm and rhyme of *tohu wabohu*, serve unmistakably to reinforce the "tohu-ness" of *tohu* – whatever that might be. Whether it has a similar or nuanced meaning to *tohu*, or whether it is simply a nonce[542] word used to reinforce *tohu*, we cannot be certain. But its impact is clear enough in Hebrew and in translation the concept of *tohu* should be reinforced either by meaning, rhyme or both.[543]

Tohu is less challenging. Despite the confusion introduced by Walton,[544] it is used consistently to picture a wasteland or unproductive condition. Isaiah 45:18 is particularly helpful, referring to the creation of the earth in Genesis 1 with the

---

[540] Some see "Heavens and earth" as a description of everything rather than two things. eg Justin Taylor, in *Biblical Reasons to Doubt the Creation Days were 24-hour Periods* says, "I think Genesis 1:1 is describing the actual act of God creating "heaven and earth" (a merism for the universe, indicating totality …)" In that the heavens and the earth do comprehend everything created (cf Colossians 1:16), everything is included. However, as the following verses clearly treat both the earth and the heavens as objects created in verse 1, it will not do to consign verse 1 to a merism. Taylor himself makes this point: "In Genesis 1:1, God creates the 'heavens and the earth.' (In Joel 3:15-16 we see that "heavens" encompasses the sun, the moon, and the stars.)" In fact, Joel 3:15, 16 does nothing to locate the sun, moon and star in the heavens. It is mistaken exegesis to rely on the association of things in these verses to locate them in the same physical space; if that methodology is applied, it would be more consistent to locate the sun, moon and stars in the Valley of Decision or in Zion than in heaven! In any case, after the creation week of course the sun, moon and stars are located in the heavens: that proves nothing about day 1. For Taylor, categorising Genesis 1:1 as a merism (a classification he never justifies textually, relying on his speculative "I think") justifies separating verse 1 as a "background statement" isolated from the narrative in verse 2 and following. I will examine the chronological relationship of verses 1 and 2 shortly, by arguing that whether taken as a "background statement" or "antecedent event", there is no textual reason to suppose the events of verse 1 are separated from the events of verse 2 – and every reason for taking them to be intimately linked within the passing of the first day. Taylor's *Biblical Reasons to Doubt the Creation Days were 24-hour Periods* is here:
[http://www.thegospelcoalition.org/blogs/justintaylor/2015/01/28/biblical-reasons-to-doubt-the-creation-days-were-24-hour-periods]

[541] Genesis 1:2; Isaiah 34:11; Jeremiah 4:23

[542] "The second word of the pair looks like a nonce term coined to rhyme with the first and to reinforce it." Alter, *The Five Books of Moses* p17

[543] Alter opts for "welter and waste" which has the desired rhythm and its assonance comes close to rhyme, but not much more clarity of meaning! Alter, *The Five Books* p17

[544] See above

declaration, "He did not create it to be empty (*tohu*), but formed it to be inhabited." The earth created in Genesis 1:1 is created to be populated by plants and animals, and inhabited by humankind, but it is not yet ready for that: it is unproductive. It is dark, it is deep and it is wet. It is not difficult to see that more of God's creative work is needed before terrestrial plants and animals, along with mankind, can find a dry, light and productive place to inhabit. But for all that, it is not a chaos, a place out of control. This dark, damp, deserted place is not "bad," but it is not yet ready for its intended occupants and cannot therefore yet fulfil its ultimate purpose of revealing the full glory of God. God has made it and now his Spirit hovers over it as a protective bird watches over her chicks.[545] The earth is under God's care and control and is about to be shaped by his majestic creativity.

With verse 1 declaring that God made the universe out of nothing, verse 2 narrows the focus of Genesis 1 onto making the earth a "good" place for the gloriously variegated company of living things with which God intends to populate it. "The first verse of Genesis briefly records the creation of the universe in its essential form, and the second verse singles out a part of this universe, viz., the earth, and describes its condition in some detail."[546] But is verse one part of day one or some event prior to the first day?[547] By asserting that in "six days the LORD made the heavens and the earth, the sea, and all that is in them", Exodus 20:11 unequivocally includes Genesis 1:1 ("God created the heavens and the earth") in the six days of creation. "The beginning of the first day is not indicated, although, from Exodus 20:11, we may warrantably assume that it began at the absolute beginning, Genesis 1:1."[548] Verse one is part of day one.

---

[545] Deuteronomy 32:11 uses the same Hebrew word *rachaph* to describe "an eagle that ... hovers over its young." Some translate *rachaph* as "brooding" but Leupold comments on this with clarity: "The verb *rachaph* from which the piel participle is used, *mera (ch) chépheth*, signifies a vibrant moving, a protective hovering. No single instance of the Biblical usage of the verb would suggest 'brooding,' a meaning which was foisted upon the word in an attempt to make it bear resemblance to various old myths that speak of the hatching out of the world egg—a meaning specially defended by Gunkel, the strong advocate of mythical interpretation. Deut. 32:11 surely will not allow for the idea of 'brooding.' An eagle may brood over eggs but not over 'her young.' The fact that the Syriac root does happen to mean 'brood' cannot overthrow the Biblical usage, which takes strong precedence over mere similarity of root in kindred languages."
(Leupold *Exposition of Genesis* www.ccel.org/ccel/leupold/genesis.iii.html 1:48)
U Cassuto (I Abraham trans) *Genesis: Part 1 From Adam to Noah* Magnes Press, Jerusalem, 1944 had made the same points, with the lovely addition of "But the expression used in the Bible is *over the face of the waters,* and the waters of the deep are not an egg or anything resembling one." p25 (italics are his)
[546] Collins *Genesis 1-4* Kindle location 613 quoting Heidel, *Babylonian Genesis*, 1942 (see the 2nd edition), University of Chicago Press, Chicago, 1951, p93
https://oi.uchicago.edu/sites/oi.uchicago.edu/files/uploads/shared/docs/misc_genesis.pdf)
[547] Collins, like Taylor, proposes (or assumes) a significant chronological gap between verse 1 and 2, (Collins *Genesis 1-4*, Kindle location 579ff) but that is neither a necessary nor natural reading of the passage, and appears to be influenced by a scientism demanding a long period of time prior to the activities of verses 2 – 5
[548] Young *Studies in Genesis 1* p104

Genesis 1:1 – In "the Beginning"

The construction of the verse best sees the verse 1 creation of the heavens and the earth as an event, not a summary statement. That construction also indicates an event that precedes the story that is about to unfold. It is an "antecedent event,"[549] recording something that happened before the events that follow. Collins and others take this to imply that the verse 1 creation of the heavens and the earth happened at some point prior to the first day. What begins for Collins as an "antecedent event" becomes in his discussion a "background event,"[550] and finally an "action prior to the beginning of the first day"[551] without any textual evidence. The effect of this is to allow for an indeterminate period between verses 1 and 2. Inevitably for many adopting this scheme, that period is a long one in which various evolutionary things could have happened. There are three problems with this. Firstly, the way in which Genesis itself "bookends" the narrative[552] includes verse 1 in day 1; secondly, the inference that a chronological gap necessarily exists between the antecedent event and the narrative it introduces has no foundation, and is contrary to other instances where this construction is used;[553] and thirdly, it creates a point of reference for "beginning" that does violence to the passage.

It is obvious that the Genesis 1 account of the creation week does not end at the end of chapter 1. Some commentators end it at Genesis 2:1, and others at Genesis 2:4. Whichever verse is taken, it forms an inclusio or "bookend" with Genesis 1:1, indicating the beginning and end of the episode. Either way, that makes Genesis 1:1 part of the creation week.

Allowing for the sake of discussion that Genesis 1:1, the creation of the heavens and the earth, *is* an "antecedent event" upon which the subsequent narrative unfolds, there is nothing in either the text of Genesis 1 or the other uses of this construction that requires any chronological gap between the antecedent event and the subsequent events. Remarkably, two of the three other examples of this construction Collins points to[554] specifically recount the antecedent event happening on *the same day* as the narrated events that follow. In other words, when this construction is used in reference to a day (as it is in Genesis 1), it is not unusual for the antecedent event to have taken place on the same day in which the subsequent events took place. So Genesis 1:1 is part of the first day.

The construction is found in Leviticus 9:1 when "on the eighth day" Aaron and Moses instruct the elders in the sacrifice God requires for a sin offering. They then make the sacrifice. There is nothing to indicate a gap at all in these events, and everything to indicate that the "antecedent event" of giving instructions on the eighth day sees the making of that sacrifice immediately afterwards on that same day. Similarly, in Numbers 10:11, the "antecedent event" of God lifting the cloud from above the tabernacle is located in a very specific day (the 12th day of the 2nd

---

[549] Collins *Genesis* location 572ff
[550] Collins *Genesis* location 615
[551] ibid
[552] "Bookend" is used here for an *inclusio*: a literary device that frames a passage intended by the author to be considered as a unity by placing similar content, structure or wording at the beginning and end of the passage.
[553] See below
[554] Genesis 14:1,2; Leviticus 9:1; Numbers 10:11 (see Collins *Genesis 1-4* Kindle location 3728)

month of the 2nd year). The text makes clear that the event that follows this antecedent event is that Israel, that very day, set out on a three-day journey from Sinai to the mountain of the Lord.

Even if the text did not reveal this, it is ludicrous to imagine that after God lifted the cloud from above the tabernacle and instructed Israel to move, they hung around without moving for days (let alone the thousands of years an evolutionary model would require). The cloud went, God spoke, Israel moved: the events were immediately contiguous and occurred on that specific day. Far from the two events being chronologically distanced from each other, they are immediately sequential, occurring in intimate relationship on the same day. These examples underscore the plain meaning of Genesis 1: God created the heavens and the earth and with immediacy proceeded to bring light to that earth on the first day. That is consistent with the way the text of Genesis 1 is presented, and it is consistent with the particular grammatical construction used.

But since "the beginning" is used without telling us *which* beginning, could it not refer to some event – called "the beginning" – before (or long before) day 1? "The term 'beginning' in biblical Hebrew marks a starting point of a specific duration, ... In opening the account of Creation with the phrase 'in the beginning' the author has marked Creation as the starting point of a period of time."[555] Here is "the beginning of the history that follows."[556] The "beginning" of verse 1 is the beginning of the creation account that is unfolded in the rest of the chapter.

Does God create "from nothing" or is there something in the beginning from which he creates? The grammatical construction of Genesis 1:1 affirms "unequivocally the truth laid down elsewhere (eg Hebrews 11:3) that until God spoke, nothing existed."[557] This is *creation ex nihilo.*

So the first day of creation begins with God making the universe. Except, he doesn't call it "the universe," but "the heavens and the earth." Why? We regard the whole creation as a universe integrated and united in some way. Not so the ancient Hebrews. For the writer and his readers, there could be no universe, for only God has complete unity:

> The concept of the unity of the world was unknown among the Israelites till a late period ... the ancient Hebrew conceived God alone as a unity; what we designate the 'universe' they regarded as two separate entities: *the heavens are the Lord's but the earth he has given to the sons of men. (Psalm 115:16)*[558]

So the first day of creation begins with God making the *heavens and the earth* out of nothing, then creating light. Over five more days God will refine the earth part of that creation – moving and transforming water and land, and creating lights

---

[555] J Sailhamer "Genesis" in F E Gaebelein (Ed) *The Expositor's Bible Commentary Volume 2*, Zondervan, Grand Rapids, 1990, p20 In a footnote Sailhamer comments that as "beginning" does not have an article in the Hebrew, it can be argued – as many do – that rather than being an absolute "in the beginning" it should be read as a construct, "in beginning to create," leaving open the possibility that the Creator began with something rather than nothing. He goes on to point out however that there are numerous examples of "beginning" being used as an absolute without the article, citing Isaiah 46:10 as a critical example.

[556] F Delitzsch *A Commentary on Genesis* Translated S Taylor, T T Clarke, Edinburgh, 1888 p76

[557] D Kidner, "Genesis: and Introduction and Commentary" in Wiseman (Ed) *Tyndale Old Testament Commentaries Volume 1* IVP, Nottingham, 1967, p48

[558] Cassuto *Genesis* p20

and life – until it is perfectly suited to his plans. At the beginning the Cosmic Sculptor has formed his base material, an earth layered in darkness and deep, and now he watches over it, pondering, then taking, the next step with deliberation. He creates light.

Light

The first day's creativity is not complete with only darkness, deep and desolation: God created light on that first day too. He had wrapped the earth he created in darkness.[559] We frequently think of darkness as the absence of light, but before he created there was nothing, not even darkness. He created the darkness,[560] then he created light. "As a result of God's speaking, the light sprang into existence. This light is not an emanation from God, nor is it an attribute of God, but is the result of God's creative Word."[561] When he brought it into being, light existed as an entity in creation, with no other source than God's creative word, no continuing existence other than God's providence, and no continuity with God who shares nothing of his existence with the creation he made and sustains.

Even before he separated the light from the darkness, God called this light "good." Clearly, everything God does and makes is good in the sense that it conforms to his goodness, a goodness that cannot do what is not good. So in declaring the light "good" God was saying more than that it conformed to his good will and his good character as a morally good Creator. The context makes it clear: before he created light the earth was *tohu,* a desolate place not yet fully suited for the purpose for which it was made. But the light he created is *not-tohu*. That is, the light *is* suited for the purpose God was creating the earth. Creating light is the first step in making a *tohu* earth into a *not-tohu* earth – a good place for life to be lived by the plants, animals and man he will soon create. Creating light is the first step in transforming desolation to delight.

There is, however, more to the "goodness" of light, and of the goodness of the rest of creation as it unfolds, than making the earth a place where life can be lived. There is a very real sense in which each day's good creation fits the earth for life, and in particular for man, so that it can be said that what is good "is *beneficial* for man."[562] Yet if that is all that our concept of "good" in Genesis 1 encompasses, it falls far, far short of God's intent. If we read the Genesis narrative as a story about man, we might well see every pronouncement of good in that same context. But in doing that we fail miserably to lift our eyes to the true glory of creation. The heavens do not declare the glory of man, nor does the earth show man's handiwork. "The heavens declare the glory of God."[563] That becomes abundantly clear when in the Genesis description of climax of creation – the seventh day – there is no mention

---

[559] Job 38:9
[560] Isaiah 45:7
[561] Young *Studies in Genesis 1* p87
[562] Sailhamer *Genesis* p26 (his italics)
[563] Psalm 19:1

of man. Creation reaches is climactic very-goodness when it satisfies God's purpose to find satisfaction in a creation that glorifies him.

So light is good, not just because it will make the earth a good place for life, but because it answers to God's command with precision, with power and with glory. Whatever is good, is good because it fits God's purpose, it fits God's majesty, and it fits God's nature: it is befitting of God. It is good because it glorifies God, and because it pleases him: "This means that God made material reality (including visible light) and was pleased with it."[564] Certainly, what is God-centred good may also be good for man, and never more so than in Jesus who, radiating God's glory, made purification for our sins.[565] But goodness finds its clearest definition in God himself.[566]

> "Good" in Scripture is not an abstract quality, nor is it a secular ideal; "good" means first and foremost what God is ... It is not that the biblical writers assess God in terms of a prior concept of goodness, rather than contemplating the supreme glory of God's perfections, they apply to Him the ordinary word for acknowledging worth. By so doing, however, they give the word a new depth of meaning. They define good in terms of God; not *vice versa*.[567]

Paradoxically, darkness continues to have its place in a "good" earth. The darkness is not evil, for God even makes "darkness his covering, his canopy around him."[568] Darkness, like light, is created by God and given its place in the daily cycle of activity and rest. God separates the light from the darkness, putting both in their place in his creation. But in calling the light "good" he stresses that it is the light, not the darkness, that fits the earth for habitation and displays his glory. While darkness will have its place, it is light, not darkness, that makes this a good place for living. Light does not just make things visible, it makes life itself possible.

This goodness of light, this characteristic of light that makes the earth liveable, is a key to the wealth of imagery subsequently built around light. Much of that imagery hangs on light making things visible and knowable, and darkness hiding knowledge. The imagery of darkness associated with judgement as well as ignorance is extended to darkness becoming an image of a place where evil is hidden: "Everyone who does evil hates the light, and will not come into the light for fear that their deeds will be exposed."[569] But if all we see in this imagery is a contrast between knowing and not knowing, we miss its primary reference.

Who can miss the glory of the image of Jesus as breaking into the world like the light shining into the darkness that is powerless to overwhelm the light, [570] in just the same way as physical light burst upon a dark creation in Genesis 1? But that glorious image comes in the context of this: "In him was life, and that life was the light of all mankind."[571] The "Light" of John 1 does more than give knowledge: he gives life itself. Jesus makes this link between light and life when he said, "I am the

---

[564] Douglas Kelly *Creation and Change* Mentor (Christian Focus), Fearn (Scotland), 2015 (1997) p77
[565] Hebrews 1:3
[566] Mark 10:18
[567] J I Packer "Good" in *The New Bible Dictionary* IVP, London, 1962, p481f [italics his]
[568] 2 Samuel 22:12, Psalm 18:11
[569] John 3:20
[570] John 1:5
[571] John 1:4

light of the world. Whoever follows me will never walk in darkness, but will have the light of life."[572] This is not just light that shows the way to live, it is light that gives life. Thus when John announces his verdict, "Light has come into the world, but people loved darkness instead of light because their deeds were evil," it is not just good they reject and evil they love, but it is life itself they reject and death they love. Those who love to live in metaphorical darkness love to live as the dead, whereas those who love to live in the light of Christ love to live as the living. How thankful we should be that God sent Jesus like the rising sun "from heaven, to shine on those living in darkness and in the shadow of death."[573]

... and Darkness

Just as light has a number of metaphorical meanings, so darkness is used in different metaphors. When God is said to be covered in a canopy of darkness, we "see" that we *cannot* see him. He is unsearchable, unapproachable and unknowable – unless he makes himself known. Darkness here implies nothing evil. Rather it exalts the holiness of God. God is unsearchable, and he reinforces that by "covering" himself in unsearchableness. The metaphor draws on the physical darkness at Mount Sinai by which God kept his people separated from his presence.[574] But when John declares, "God is light; in him there is no darkness at all,"[575] the metaphor is different, and obviously so.

The physical darkness of Genesis 1:2 that renders the newly created earth as not yet good for life to be lived in is replicated in the physical darkness of judgement of Egypt in Exodus 10, in the physical darkness saving Israel from the Egyptians in Exodus 14, and in the physical darkness shielding God's holiness in Exodus 20. In the same way, the physical light of Genesis 1:3 that makes the earth good for humankind and the other living creatures to live in is replicated daily in covenant faithfulness[576] with the physical dawning of each day, until reality and metaphor become one in the new creation.

Four important points can be drawn from this:

1. Darkness and light are created entities, neither God nor eminences of God. Even when the visible glory associated with God's presence breaks into creation as light,[577] there is no suggestion that such light is ontologically divine even though that physical light is plainly distinguished from the ordinary light of creation.[578]

---

[572] John 8:12
[573] Luke 1:78,79
[574] Exodus 20; Deuteronomy 5
[575] 1 John 1:5
[576] Genesis 8:22
[577] Exodus 34:29ff & Matthew 17:2
[578] God's glory is associated just as dramatically in darkness, as in the impenetrable dark cloud of God's glory that filled Solomon's temple (1 Kings 8:10-12). In Ezekiel 10:4 this cloud of darkness is described as the "radiance of God's glory," a radiance to be fully seen in Christ (Hebrews 1:3) – a wonderful topic to explore another time!

2. Darkness and light are created as separate entities, not as a single continuum measured by some degree of evident or absent murk. God separates the light from the darkness, and while we might see a dusky overlap as light invades or gives place to darkness, they never share created existence.[579]
3. Darkness and light as metaphors are never considered by the Bible as a continuum: they are always absolute, diametrically distinguishable opposite attributes. There is no dark side to light, nor a light side to darkness: "God is light; in him there is no darkness at all. If we claim to have fellowship with him and yet walk in darkness, we lie."[580]
4. The overwhelming metaphorical use of darkness in the Bible as an image of ignorance,[581] evil[582] and judgement,[583] and its corollary, the overwhelming metaphorical use of light in the Bible as an image of knowledge,[584] righteousness[585] and blessing[586] both depend on the nature and function of physical light and darkness created in Genesis 1:2 & 3, and sustained by God throughout the history of this creation.

God Speaks

God spoke to make light. God spoke and there was light. God spoke and his command was fulfilled: there was light, not merely the beginnings of light or a process that would eventuate in light. God spoke, making his desire known, making his design clear, and by his speaking making it happen when he spoke. By immediately confirming that what was commanded was accomplished, the text shows "the precision and celerity with which the injunction was carried out: as He commanded, and as soon as He commanded."[587]

God could have created without speaking, but not only did he make his purpose known by speaking, he brought it into instant effect by speaking. This is no incidental detail of the creation, but an attribute of God the Scriptures mark as precious: "By the word of the LORD the heavens were made … For he spoke, and it came to be; he commanded, and it stood firm."[588]

There are at least five wonderful implications of God bringing creation into existence by speaking:

---

[579] "The creation of light ... was no annihilation of darkness, no transformation of the dark material of the world into pure light, but a separation of the light from the primary matter, a separation which established and determined that interchange of light and darkness, which produces the distinction between day and night." Keil & Delitzsch *Biblical Commentary on the Old Testament: Volume 1 The Pentateuch* T & T Clark, Edinburgh, 1822, p50. For those with a bent to chemistry, light and dark may mix at dawn or dusk but are never compounded.
[580] 1 John 1:5 & 6
[581] Psalm 82:5
[582] Ephesians 5:11
[583] 2 Peter 2:17
[584] John 11:9,10
[585] John 3:19-21
[586] John 9:5, 12:46 etc
[587] Cassuto, *Genesis* p26
[588] Psalm 33: 6 & 9

1. It is of the essence of God's being that he speaks to make himself and his purposes known, and to bring those purposes into effect. Even when (as in day one) there was nothing and no-one but God himself to hear, he speaks. The creation reveals God's glory,[589] God's power, and God's nature;[590] but it is in his speaking that he is most clearly revealed, it is through his speaking that his attributes are most clearly understood, and it is in hearing his voice that faith comes[591] and is energised in obedience. So it is that Jesus, being the most perfect revelation of God[592] is called the Word.[593] "In the past God spoke to our ancestors through the prophets at many times and in various ways, but in these last days he has spoken to us by his Son ... the radiance of God's glory and the exact representation of his being."[594]
2. By speaking creation into existence with words that express choice ("let us ...") God revealed he was not being forced to create. In saying "let us" God revealed that creation was what he wanted, not a consequence of something already there, or something compelled by God's nature. "'Let us make' is more than merely a poetic flourish in Genesis 1. It grounds the creation of all things in the will and purpose of God."[595] The Bible starts with this dramatic demonstration of God as completely free agent, which has significance too for another determined purpose of God: Jesus, the Word of God, came into this world, was handed over to wicked men to die, and was raised to life and victory "by God's deliberate plan and foreknowledge,"[596] planned and foreknown "before the foundation of the world."[597] God the Creator chose to show his glory through creating and chose to show his infinite love through the sacrifice of his Son. God's creation sets the context for the ultimate demonstration of his glory: a glory revealed in a freely made creation, a freely chosen incarnation, and a freely given saving love.
3. God's speaking is not merely the revelation of God or his will, it is the power by which he works. When God speaks, what he speaks happens. It is not merely that things obey God's word (which they do), but that things themselves come into existence by his speaking. So it is that "the word of God is alive and active."[598] When God makes his will known by word, creation is created[599] by that word.[600] By identifying Jesus as the "Word of God" through whom all things were made,[601] God is identifying him as the clearest revelation of himself, and as powerfully able to do all he has

---

[589] Psalm 19
[590] Romans 1:20
[591] Romans 10:17
[592] John 14:9
[593] John 1:1,14
[594] Hebrews 1:1-3
[595] Thompson *A Clear and Present Word* pp57f
[596] Acts 2:23
[597] Ephesians 1:4,11
[598] Hebrews 4:12
[599] Revelation 4:11
[600] Psalm 148:5
[601] John 1:3

promised and come into creation to do: as God's word accomplishes what God intends, so Jesus the Word accomplishes all that God intends.

4. There is knowledge that passes our understanding, which we cannot verbalise.[602] Yet even its existence is confirmed, not by shared mood or atmospheric empathy, but by verbal description. The key to knowing God better, to growing a personal relationship with God, to breaking into the realm of what presently surpasses understanding, is increasing our understanding of verbalised truth.[603] As Jesus is "the truth," without whom "no one comes to the Father,"[604] it is essential to know Jesus to know truth truly. Such knowledge, arising from the work of the Spirit nurturing within us a loving, growing relationship with Jesus, is the work of the Spirit of truth who teaches us and brings to mind God's words.[605] It is by language that we come to know Jesus, albeit it is also by the inward working of the Spirit of Truth, and by grace, and by faith, that we accept and trust in not only what God has said, but in Jesus himself. Knowing truth is of the essence of knowing Jesus the Truth through the work of the Spirit of Truth.
5. The first use of language in the created universe is in creating the universe. Language has its origins in God, not in his creation, much less in the needs of people. God speaking also indicates the nature of language: language has meaning formulated by the speaker. All sorts of language theories deny this, arguing in various ways that words only have meaning when heard. But when God first spoke, nothing "heard" and nothing "responded" so that the universe came into being. What God said was what God meant and what God did. Here is the foundation of all language: the speaker and writer imbues what is spoken and written with meaning irrespective of how well the hearer or reader comprehends that meaning. The best language use will always be that which most clearly makes the speaker's meaning understood as comprehensively as nothing comprehended God's spoken word at creation, and the best language use will always involve discerning just as comprehensively what is meant without imbuing it with novel meaning.

God Names

In naming the light and darkness "day" and "night" God did more than give them a label by which we can classify these two bits of creation. Naming is an exercise of superior authority, "the prerogative of a superior."[606] When God gave man dominion over the animals, one of man's first acts was to name the animals. So in naming light and darkness "day" and "night" God declared that he is not only their Creator: he is their sovereign. Day and night are not self-governing natural phenomena, but servants of the Creator. Verse 5 is no mere incidental detail, for

---

[602] Philippians 4:7
[603] 1 John 5:20; Colossians 1:9, 2:2
[604] John 14:6
[605] John 14:17,26
[606] J A Motyer "Name" in Douglas *et al* (Eds.) *The New Bible Dictionary* IVP, London, 1962 p862

there are no incidental details in this precisely crafted chapter. Verse 5 is a statement of cosmic proportions: God rules the cosmos, even governing day and night.

Yet day and night already had names: "light" and "darkness." So in giving them the names "day" and "night," something more was being done. The Bible has a "dynamic view of names and naming which runs throughout Scripture and which differs so dramatically from our static view of a name as a differentiating label."[607] In the Bible a name is often given to declare character or define function. That is the case here: in calling light and darkness "day" and "night" God not only declared his sovereignty over them, he declared that he is their creator and superior *and* that he was giving them function as his servants. Light and darkness are now corralled to function as day and night, never ceasing "as long as the earth endures,"[608] making the earth a good habitation in which man can live.

Days are not therefore "made" by the sun: the sun is created three days later to mark out the days as they already existed. Light "here precedes the sun, so in the final vision it outlasts it (Revelation 22:5)."[609] That we now see the sun marking out the days, and that we do not know how God marked out the days before he created the sun, is a springboard for a great deal of unnecessary angst and confusion. Unable or unwilling to accept that God could differentiate day and night without the sun, all sorts of novel ways of finding the sun in day 1 are employed.[610] Yet each one of those innovations not only fails to see God as not bound by the phenomena he creates, each also undermines the most basic message of this passage, that God is Creator and not like the idols. As Calvin points out, God "is not ignorant of [the] law of nature, which he has since ordained: but in order that we might learn to refer all things to him, he did not then make use of the sun and moon."[611] Here is "a polemic against idolatry"[612] in which the sun, unlike the Egyptian Ra, is merely a thing in the cosmos with no divinity or powers of its own, made in God's own time, run by God's own will, for God's own purpose. God made days happen.

---

[607] J A Motyer, "Name" in D. R. W. Wood, *et al* (Eds.), *New Bible Dictionary* (3rd ed.) IVP, Leicester, 1996, p800

[608] Genesis 8:22

[609] Kidner *Genesis* p51 [Referencing Barth *Church Dogmatics iii 1* T & T Clarke, 1958, p167.]

[610] Sailhamer, for example, argues that since the heavens were made in verse 1, the sun was there already for verse 3, since the phrase, according to him, "heavens and earth" invariably includes the sun and stars. [John H Sailhamer "Genesis" in *The Expositor's Bible Commentary* pp33f] This hardly does justice to the darkness of verse 2, let alone the fact that if the "earth" bit of "the heavens and the earth" is not yet complete and "good," there is no reason to expect – and every reason not to expect – that the heavens, being the other bit of "the heavens and the earth", were any different and needed no further work to become "good". Just as the earth is not yet suited to serving mankind and the other things living on the earth, so the sky is not yet suited to serving the living on the earth: the sky needs the sun, moon and stars before it can fulfil its function of being "good" for life. Even if one buys into Sailhamer's odd and inconsistent contention that "earth" after verse 1 refers to the land of Israel and not the whole earth, the same problems remain.

[611] John Calvin (tansl John King) *Commentary on Genesis* Banner of Truth Trust, London, 1965 (1554) p82

[612] Sailhamer *The Pentateuch* p83

One Day

So we have evening and morning, the first day. Well ... no, not quite! Yes, that was the first day, but that is not what the text says. Despite the way most translations render the last part of verse 5, the Hebrew says, "And there was evening, and there was morning, one day." Although the rest of the days are described by ordinal numbers ("second," "third," "fourth" ...) this first day is described with a cardinal ("one").

One of the basic tools for reading the Old Testament is recognising that a difference in a pattern signals something of significance. Not only does "one" not fit the pattern of the rest of chapter 1, but it uses a highly unusual Hebrew idiom, drawing attention to something special here. "The text is very carefully crafted so that an alert reader cannot read it as 'the first day.' Instead ... it must be read as 'one day,' thereby defining a day."[613]

God's intention when he created and separated day and night was not that they be static entities between which people could move, but a cycle within which people lived. So on the first day he begins the cycle with which we are now so familiar, causing day to pass to night and back to day again. "Thus the great cycle of time was put in place by the Creator."[614] That could have been reported as, "there was day, and there was night, one day" but that would have completely failed to describe the movement from one to the other. So the writer highlights the *transition* from day to night ("there was evening"), and from night to day ("there was morning"), as a way of describing the passing of a complete day, one day, the first day. "Having an evening and a morning amounts to having one full day."[615]

In this way, at the very beginning of the six-day narrative, God makes clear what he means by the word "day": a period of time in which day transitions through evening to night, and back again through morning to day. Here is a clear, straightforward identification of the period intended by the word "day": what we refer to as a 24-hour day.[616] Given that at the time Genesis was written the Egyptians were among those using precisely this terminology (what they called the two "twilight hours" of "evening" and "morning") to describe a day, what may seem to us to be an unusual way of describing a day, would have been perfectly understood by the original readers.

It is possible that the distinctive order – evening then morning – may be drawing attention to the celebration of God's goodness inherent in the creation days. Cassuto points out that in describing the ordinary passage of time, the Bible usually locates the beginning of a day at sunrise, but that festivals are described as beginning with the evening of the day before the anniversary.[617] Thus while the expression in

---

[613] Andrew Steinmann " אחד as an Ordinal Number and the Meaning of Genesis 1:5" in the *Journal of the Evangelical Theological Society 45/4* Louisville, December 2002 p583

[614] Walton *The Lost World* Kindle location 517

[615] ibid

[616] "In the absence of any Biblical evidence to the contrary, and the presence of frequent references to the narrative as historical narrative, the obvious way to read the text of Genesis 1 is the *obvious* way. It is impossible for God to use a misleading form of description. If Genesis 1 was not meant to be taken as a literal account, why was it written that way?" Noel Weeks *The Sufficiency of Scripture* p115 (italics his)

[617] Cassuto *Genesis* pp28ff

Genesis 1 clearly marks the passage of one day, it does so in a way that conventionally points to God-centred festivals. The days of creation are not merely days marking a passage of time, but days identified as festive celebrations of the glory of God. Truly they were "good."

It is worth noting that the description of this first day (and of each of the subsequent days) as having evening and morning renders rather odd the concept of those days being thousands or millions of years long to allow for some evolutionary process to take place. "Evening" and "morning" are so specifically used repeatedly they must have some impact on interpretation. If they have any relationship to the passing of time,[618] each of the so-called metaphorical days of an evolutionary construction would have to consist of tens of thousands of years of daylight, followed by tens of thousands of years of darkness. It seems difficult to fit any model of biological evolution to such a physical context.

Of course, if "day" is taken to be a metaphor for aeons of time, so "evening" and "morning" could also be metaphors. They could be metaphors for ... what? There is nothing they could symbolise that retains any meaningful relationship to the idea of "evening" and the idea of "morning." In any case, "evening" and "morning" are either points of time or transitions in a day (whether actual or metaphorical). Either way they mark a boundary between night and day, so whatever "morning" and "evening" symbolise as metaphors (if indeed they are metaphors), they mark out a period of daylight and a separate period of darkness that must each consist of aeons of time if "day" is a metaphor for aeons of time.

"Evening and morning" is used here to define a normal 24-hour day.[619] Not without reason R L Dabney comments:

> The sacred writer seems to shut us up to a literal interpretation, by describing the day as composed of its natural parts, "morning and evening." ... [Those reading "day" as a metaphor] cannot construe the expression ["evening and morning"] at all. The plain reader has no trouble with it. When we have had one evening and one morning, we know we have had just one civic day.[620]

---

[618] cf Collins *Genesis 1-4* Kindle location 877

[619] John Collins disputes this, claiming "The order of the items mentioned is crucial: it is evening *followed* by morning. This means that any effort to find this as defining the days runs counter to the author's own presentation. Evening and morning bracket the night." [Collins *Genesis 1-4* Kindle location 877] Collins justifies this by referring to the workday of Psalm 104:23 and the worker's rest in the night. This fails in three critical ways: 1. In Psalm 104 the expression "evening and morning" is not used. Psalm 104 uses a common idiom in which the morning and the evening are connected with a preposition (in this case "until') that indicates an action taking place in daylight hours. The other way in which morning and evening are commonly linked is in prescribing an action at each of those two points of the day (eg in making a sacrifice such as in Leviticus 6:20). Neither of these uses parallels Genesis 1. 2. If the order (viz evening then morning) is significant, then Collins would be admitting a different order (viz morning followed by evening) would not limit the description to half the 24-hour day: yet grammatically and linguistically the two ways of ordering those words are identical – in other words the order is irrelevant. In fact, as day 1 started in darkness, describing the passage of the day as evening followed by morning is not in the least extraordinary: that is what happened. 3. But the most compelling point is that the expression "there was evening, and there was morning" is immediately followed by a definition of what has just passed … "one day." What does "there was evening, and there was morning" refer to? According to the text, it refers to the passage of a day, one day. Least there be any confusion, that defining statement is repeated for each of the six days.

[620] R L Dabney *Lectures in Systematic Theology* Baker, Grand Rapids, 1985 (1878) p255

The *New American Standard Bible* (NASB) is among a few English Bibles that translate "one day" as "one day." The Septuagint does that also. Why then is "one day" so consistently translated "first day"? It will not do to blame evolutionary or process scientism, for English translations rendered it "first day" long before such models could have been an influence.[621] It is likely that where the significance of a jarring break with the pattern is not recognised, especially as the pattern is initiated with the "break" in the pattern as is the case here, translators would be likely to smooth the text to the beautiful consistency of "first day," "second day," and so on.

True, throughout the Old Testament cardinals are used as ordinals on numerous occasions. However, there is *never* an example that parallels Genesis 1:5. Andrew Steinmann's exhaustive study concludes, "אחד [one] may be used in place of the ordinal ראשון [first] when enumerating time periods, but only in two special idioms. One of these designates the day of a month, the other the year of a reign of a king."[622] While it is true then that cardinal numbers are *sometimes* used for ordinals, Genesis 1:5 does not conform to any of those instances. So unusual is the construction of Genesis 1:5, that if the writer meant "first" it would be the only place in the Old Testament where the word usually meaning "one" in a sentence structured this way had the intention of meaning "first."

There is therefore no textual reason for rendering "one" as "first", and very strong textual and contextual reasons for rendering it as it is written. God wants readers to be clear that what he called days in Genesis 1 is the same as what we call days today. "The use of אחד in Gen 1:5 and the following unique uses of the ordinal numbers on the other days demonstrates that the text itself indicates that these are regular solar days."[623]

Robert Reymond makes two pertinent comments. Firstly, "The recurring phrase, 'and the evening and the morning' ... occur together outside of Genesis in 37 verses (e.g., Exod. 18:13; 27:21). In each instance these words are employed to describe an ordinary day."[624] Secondly, "In the hundreds of other cases in the Old Testament where ... yom stands in conjunction with an ordinal number ... e.g., Exodus 12:15; 24:16; Leviticus 12:3, it never means anything other than a normal, literal day."[625] It is the clear intention of Genesis 1 that the days it describes be seen as ordinary, 24 hour days.

---

[621] Although the dominance of process scientism, informed by the fact (about to be discussed) that in the Bible cardinals are sometimes used as ordinals, may well have influenced the retention of a traditional rendering in many modern translations.

[622] Steinmann " אחד as an Ordinal Number" p580. It can also be used as an ordinal in listing a small number of things, but always with the definite article. There is no article in Genesis 1:5 and Genesis 1 is not in the format of a list of things to which that usage fits.

[623] Steinmann p584 (He is careful to distinguish a proper rendering of the text from the issue of accepting or rejecting the text by adding in a footnote, "Whether or not one believes in the veracity of the Genesis account of creation in six solar days is another matter altogether.")

[624] Reymond, *A New Systematic Theology*, p393

[625] ibid

Then Came the "Firmament"

On the second day God created a "firmament." Translators struggle with the Hebrew רקיע *raqia*, traditionally translated "firmament." "Expanse" is a good alternative that is now widely used, although "heavens" has been used, and "canopy," "vault" and "dome" are becoming popular. Despite all that, understanding what is referred to is really quite straight forward, for verse 8 tell us it is the sky. So on day two God made what he went on to name (and what we call) "sky."[626]

It is not difficult to see why translating *raqia* is problematic: few modern readers will have any real comprehension of "firmament," which was never the best translation anyway. It finds its way into English Bibles as a transliteration of the Latin Vulgate *firmamentum*. The Vulgate was attempting to reproduce the sense of the 3rd Century BC Septuagint's *stereoma* which does express a concept of something solid. However, the Septuagint's Greek appears to be less than accurate here, as there is nothing in the Hebrew to imply a solid *raqia*.

Nor is there anything in the word *raqia* or its usage to justify either "vault" or "dome." Earlier[627] I discussed the misguided attempts of some scholars to impose on the Hebrews a concept of the sky being a solid dome or vault. This mythology appears to influence some modern translations, such as the 2011 NIV (but not the original NIV which used "expanse"). Apart from Genesis 1, *raqia* is used in only four other Old Testament places. Three are in the Psalms[628] and in Daniel[629] where on each occasion the NIV translates it "heavens." The fourth is in Ezekiel[630] where the context fits the idea of a "vault": a sparkling and awesome "something like a vault" covers the arched wings of the four living creatures, and above this "something" sits a throne. The use of raqia in Ezekiel clearly implies a similarity with the "sparkling and awesome" sky in Genesis, but it is a limited similarity as, unlike the sky which extends limitlessly (so far as our observations go), Ezekiel's vault has a throne resting on top of it just above the heads of the creatures (which are below the obviously thin vault). Rendering *raqia* "vault" in Genesis 1 is therefore neither consistent with the context in Genesis, nor with the other instances of *raqia*.

Most agree that *raqia* has within its range of meaning a reference to something stretched or spread out.[631] This fits well with Psalm 104:2; Isaiah 40:22, 45:12, 51:13; and Jeremiah 10:12 in which the Lord is said to have stretched out the heavens like a tent. Once *raqia* is named "sky," every other use of *raqia* in Genesis associates it with "sky," rendering it "the *raqia* of the sky." Into this sky God placed

---

[626] Sometimes translated "heavens" as in sky/outer-space, rather than "heaven" as in God's dwelling place.

[627] pp68ff

[628] Psalm 19:1; 150:1

[629] Daniel 12:3

[630] Ezekiel 1:22-26 (four times) and 10:1 (once) all describing the same scene

[631] Its probable derivation is *raqa* which means beaten, stretched or spread out (such as in forming a metal plate or bowl, or spreading or stretching a cloth). Many attempting to force connotations of solidity see in the possible origins of *raqia* reference to the sky being beaten-out, made malleable, and stretched into position (whereupon it resumes a solid nature).

the sun, moon and stars. They move through the sky which rather hints at a less-than-solid *raqia*. Any remaining suggestion of solidness disappears in verse 20 when the birds are set flying in the "vault of the sky."[632] "Expanse" or "vast space" fits perfectly as does the associated idea of that expanse being stretched out as a covering over the earth. On day two, God stretched out and spread over the earth a vast expanse he called "sky."

Rick Lanser's description may be a little imaginative, but it does justice to the glorious event of the second day: "The Lord places His hands upon the ball of water, draws them apart, the *raqia* stretches out in all directions—and outer space is created, with light years passing in a moment of time."[633] On day one God created the heavens (as well as the earth), and now on day two he fills (or partly fills?) the heavens with the sky and outer-space, spreading it from the earth's surface upward and outward so that it separates the waters covering the earth from the waters beyond.

By identifying it as this stretched-out-expanse before naming it sky, God is drawing attention both to its attributes and to his ongoing work of naming. The sky – the earth's covering and the deep expanse of space – is spectacularly stretched out by God's hands, ready to be populated by the birds, ready to be made resplendent by sun and moon, and ready to be gloriously sprinkled with galaxies of stars. For the moment it stands empty apart from one watery globe, yet it will, for the rest of creation's existence, declare the glory of the Creator.[634] And by naming it, God affirms his complete dominion over it. It is his, and it will answer to him.

Where Are the Waters?

With the sky God separated the waters: beneath it the earth is covered in water, and above it the water...? Where is the water above the sky? That depends on what we are looking for and how we look. If we bring preconceptions to the text, we may only see what we are looking for ... or more likely not see what we are looking for and not see anything we are not looking for either! If we assume that the water above should look like the water below (that is, there should be a large ocean of water in the sky) we probably won't find it, and as likely as not nor will we find what God did put there. Or if, influenced by the mythology that falsely claims Moses thought the heavens were a solid dome, we look for a layer of water held up by that dome, we probably won't find that either. If, driven by a desire to find concordance between Genesis 1 and evolutionary theory or contemporary

---

[632] This is not infrequently accommodated by re-translating it so that the birds "fly *across* the vault of the sky." This necessarily implies a new, previously unidentified layer between the earth and the *raqia*. Up till this point almost every commentator takes the space above the earth's waters to be the *raqia*, and the sudden "creation" of this implied new layer is never discussed. The context however plainly implies that the birds fly *in* the raqia, rather than *across* it.

[633] Rick Lanser *Genesis 1 and the Raqia*
http://www.biblearchaeology.org/post/2009/08/05/genesis-1-and-the-raqia.aspx#Article

[634] Psalm 19:1

astronomy, we might find something related to water now in space[635] but as likely as not it won't fit the whole six-day narrative of Genesis.[636]

If though we just read the text as God has given it to us, there is remarkably little difficulty. The text says God used the sky to separate waters on earth from waters in the sky. What he doesn't say is that the waters in the sky have the same oceanic form as the waters on the earth, or that the waters in the sky are at the outer limits of the sky. All that he has said is that he put water up there as well as down here, and that he put an expansive separation between them. In common with all people down through the ages, on most days we can look up and see great bunches of water in the sky separated from us on the earth by a vast expanse. These may or may not be identical to what God created on day two,[637] but they indicate that placing vast quantities of water above the earth, separated by an expansive sky, is not at all improbable.

Bunches of water? Can water be held high in the sky without tanks or domed-vaults? Can it be "bunched" without containers? Indeed! That is precisely what clouds are: bunches of tiny water droplets and ice-particles (along with dust and various other stuff). It has always been obvious that rain comes from clouds, but just how it gets there and stays there without something solid holding it up has not always been so clear. Yet Job could see what so many have been blind to: "He wraps up the waters in his clouds, yet the clouds do not burst under their weight."[638] Once it became possible to fly into the clouds and to physically examine them, it has become accepted that the clouds contain millions of tonnes of water. There is indeed water above, separated from the earth beneath by a vast expanse of sky.

Of course the "sky" goes beyond where the clouds are found, beyond the atmosphere into the depths of space;[639] but that does not negate the fact that there is a vast expanse of sky between the clouds and the earth.[640] Whether the waters above in day two looked like clouds do today we have no way of knowing, but in preparing the earth as a "good" place for mankind and the other living things, putting water up there was part of that preparation. That water would, among other things, influence the atmosphere, impact on the earth's temperature, and moderate

---

[635] For example, "The 'waters above' ... represent all the bodies, large and small, that lay beyond Neptune in our solar system, including all the cometary material, mostly made of water ice. ... The 'waters above' are in a halo around the solar system, locked up in the form of frozen ices, dirty comets and other large chunks of frozen material." John Hartnett "The 'Waters Above'" in *Journal of Creation* Volume 20, Issue 1, March 2006, Creation Ministries International, Australia

[636] With constructs such as Hartnett's (above) space is filled on day two with stuff Genesis says is made on day four.

[637] Various speculators propose a permanent layer of water-vapour or mist with no apparent or visible clouds until after the Genesis 7 flood; eg Henry Morris & John Whitcomb *The Genesis Flood* Evangelical Press, London, 1969 (1961) pp240ff; and many others

[638] Job 26:8

[639] "The word רקיע (*rakia,*) comprehends not only the whole region of the air, but whatever is open above us ... the arrangement, as well as of the heavens as of the lower atmosphere, is called, רקיע (*rakia,*) without discrimination between them, but sometimes the word signifies both together, sometimes one part only." Calvin *Genesis* p79

[640] Leupold reasonably suggests that before the separation of the waters "the earth waters on the surface of the earth and the cloud waters as we now know them were contiguous without an intervening clear air space. It was a situation like a dense fog upon the surface of the waters." (Leupold *Exposition of Genesis* 1.60)

the levels of solar radiation reaching earth; and, of course, it would be caused to water the ground as rain. All of this helped make the earth a good place for life.

The significance of God providing for rain in creation should not be overlooked simply because that is what we expect from clouds. God describes the reservoir of water in the sky as "the storehouse of his bounty"[641] from which he will send the blessing of rain on favoured Israel, and on everyone: "Ask the LORD for rain in the springtime; it is the LORD who sends the thunderstorms. He gives showers of rain to all people, and plants of the field to everyone."[642] Rain is a symbol of God's good gifts of righteousness and salvation: "You heavens above, rain down my righteousness; let the clouds shower it down. Let the earth open wide, let salvation spring up, let righteousness flourish with it; I, the LORD, have created it."[643] Storing vast quantities of water above the earth on day two of creation, separated from it by the sky, is not only good because it is orderly and displays God's creative glory: it is good because it will be a means by which God blesses man on the earth he is preparing for him. In that it reveals even more of the glory of God.

A Separated Earth

What is also clear is that God makes a very definite distinction between the earth and everything else in the universe. Despite physical similarities between the earth and other heavenly bodies that were (and no doubt still are) waiting to be discovered, God separates the earth from everything else. The earth is not part of a pantheon of the universe. It is not one with the imagined being and forces of the planets and stars. It is separated from them. It has its own existence, a prior existence, an existence independent of the other created spheres. In the entire universe, the earth is special. It came first. It is set apart as the place where people will live, and where God will dwell with those people. With the creation of the sky the universe consists of two essential, separated parts: the earth, and everything else. The sky might be about to become spectacularly glorious, but the earth is where mankind and God will meet and be in fellowship.

The sky, when filled with stars, will declare the glory of God ... to whom? To people on earth. The sun and moon, when placed in the sky, will mark out the times and seasons ... for whom? For people on earth. Whatever other functions the universe might have in God's economy, the only ones revealed to us by God are those related to our life and worship on the earth. The heavens are not powers that control people or places in which to find God. The planets are not gods who influence events, or the locus of divine revelation. They are God's statements of his power and glory, statements enfolding the earth and its people with the unmistakable message of "God's invisible qualities—his eternal power and divine nature."[644] What becomes clear as the Genesis account of creation unfolds is that God's focus is on revealing the creation of the earth as a place in which people are to live in worshipful service of their Creator. God has something greater than the star-spangled universe for his people.

---

[641] Deuteronomy 28:12
[642] Zechariah 10:1
[643] Isaiah 45:8
[644] Romans 1:20

Down to Earth

With day three God continues to narrow the focus of his account of creation from the universe to the earth, and from the earth to the land. There is the temptation to begin to feel at home in the account of day three's making of the land. With our knowledge of the earth we can imagine water being gathered together in one place, exposing the land in others. But there is nothing natural here, nothing intended to seem ordinarily geological. We might assume that from day one the earth existed as a water-covered ball of rock, dirt, magma and so on that is exposed when the water is moved aside. There is nothing to indicate that in Genesis 1 – it may be so, but what God has said is that the earth was a water-covered deep, that the waters were moved, and that land "appeared" at the word of God. Whether the land appeared by creation or eruption at this point, the text focuses on the creative power of God with the simplest of mechanics: God speaks, it happens.

The enormity of this event is staggering. Not only does the land-mass appear, it does so instantaneously. Verse 9 not only allows no place for a gradual process over aeons of time, it allows no place for process over the third day: God speaks and "it was so." God parts the waters with a word, creates the land (positioning it in the spaces till then occupied with water) with another word, checks both out and names them, then moves on in the rest of day three to create vegetation to cover the land. It is difficult to conform this event to the time that would have been needed to naturally dry freshly exposed submarine land or to cool volcanic eruptions. "This ninth verse surely teaches that what we call geologic formations took place in titanic and gigantic measure at a vastly accelerated pace in a truly miraculous creative work as astounding as the rest."[645] From both looking at the text and considering the physical event itself, it would seem that the "appearance" of the land has more to do with an instantaneous creative action than to an instantaneous volcanic or seismic one!

> The magnitude of the work to be accomplished baffles the imagination and yet, in the simple words, "and it was so," the accomplishment is recorded. Nothing is said about the means or the method of accomplishment that we may concentrate in wonder and adoration upon him who alone can perform such a marvel.[646]

Remarkably, despite all the nonsense circulated about Genesis not being "scientific," these verses have an exquisite fit with science. Science seeks to observe the phenomena of the created universe; to classify, order and find relationships among those observations; if possible, to account for it all; and to bring some comprehension and meaning to existence. God starts at the other end. He reveals to us his purpose, he tells us how it was accomplished, he describes the relationships between it all, he classifies and names it, then he puts it all before us to be observed. Science postulates, God reveals. What God reveals is the true account. What science postulates may be true, but science can only explore consistently and validly when it acknowledges that the act of observing is only

---

[645] Leupold *Exposition of Genesis* 1.64. He also pertinently comments that there is no need to assume that evidence of the rapidity with which these formations were formed need be recorded in the formations themselves.

[646] E J Young *Genesis One* p91

possible when empowered by God; and observations are only true when conforming to what is truly there as God has made and sustains it all. In other words, the best science starts with revelation from God, knowing that every phenomenon and every observation must fit that frame of reference before it is fitted to any other.[647] Right here in Genesis 1 God gives us the precise, accurate and scientifically consistent key for the work of science.

God is very specific about the order here: having created the land and set the boundaries of the seas[648] he pauses his creative work, he names the land then the seas, then reflects on what he has done. Equally specifically, he declares that what he has created is good. God declares by this that the earth is becoming fit for the purpose for which he has created it, and part of that fitness is located in dry land now separated from the seas.

The earth is still the only place in the universe, the only sphere in space. Systematically covered in a cycle of light and darkness, its surface now a patchwork of water and land, it hangs beneath a void of nothing, a vast empty sky of deep space.[649] There is light but there is no sun, there is no moon, there are no stars. The earth is the first place made, the only place existing. There is no room here for the galaxies to have given birth to the earth, or for pre-existing planets to be the determiners of the earth's destiny. There is no accommodation possible in this account for a "big-bang" filling the universe with emergent energy, coalescing galactic bodies and an eventual earth – whether by accident or design. In two and a half days, from nothing, by his words, God has created a universe, and created in it a single place of earth and water. It is a good place – he says so. It is good for people he has planned to put there. It is a good display of his glory. It is good, but it is not yet good enough. Before he creates mankind and installs them in his creation, before creation is fully fitted to reveal the Creator's glory, God wants the earth to have life and greater order. That will be next.

---

[647]From time to time notable scientists who do not believe the Bible recognise a consistency between Genesis and science that they express in quite surprising ways. Among favourites are these few sentences from astrophysicist Robert Jastrow (NASA Medal for Exceptional Scientific Achievement, Arthur S. Fleming Award for Outstanding Service in the U.S. Government, Columbia University Medal of Excellence, Columbia Graduate Facilities Award to Distinguished Alumni) "Now we see how the astronomical evidence supports the biblical view of the origin of the world. The details differ, but the essential elements in the astronomical and biblical accounts of Genesis are the same: the chain of events leading to man commenced suddenly and sharply at a definite moment in time, in a flash of light and energy. … For the scientist who has lived by his faith in the power of reason, the story ends like a bad dream. He has scaled the mountain of ignorance; he is about to conquer the highest peak; as he pulls himself over the final rock, he is greeted by a band of theologians who have been sitting there for centuries." Robert Jastrow, *God and the Astronomers*, W.W. Norton, New York, 1978, p14 & p116

[648] Proverbs 8:29

[649] Albeit with the "waters above" within the earth's atmosphere.

9. Genesis Life

The Lonely Planet Awakes: Reading Genesis 1 in the light of what God calls "Good"

"But ask the animals, and they will teach you, or the birds in the sky, and they will tell you; or speak to the earth, and it will teach you, or let the fish in the sea inform you. Which of all these does not know that the hand of the LORD has done this. In his hand is the life of every creature and the breath of all mankind."

~ Job 12:7-10

God speaks again.

Plants arrive.

But this time, what God creates does not come out of nothing; it comes out of the earth. The ESV's "Let the earth sprout vegetation ... the earth brought forth" beautifully captures the sense of this. God speaks, and "Sprout!" the earth fills with vegetation. The dry, dull earth becomes a verdant spectacle: valleys, hills and plains in variegated texture, form and colour – each plant from shoot to succulent maturity at God's word, each according to its kind, and each niche growing what fits. Again God evaluates it all and again declares it good: one more good step towards a good place for mankind to live in good fellowship with God in a good creation that reveals his glory.

What are we to make of the change in creative method? In day four God will revert to creating out of nothing. But here he reveals very specifically that he causes the plants to be created "out of the earth." A change in the pattern of a text is a sure signal of something significant. What is being signalled here?

What is *not* being signalled is that plants spontaneously or naturally arose from the earth. Three things make that clear:

1. God pauses in the middle of his day-three creativity. Having made the dry land, there is a break in the narrative while God considers the goodness of the dry land separated from the waters. He also engages in naming: something that till now has coincided with the end of a day. This naming closes off an episode: the plants are not coming on their own. The plants are not coming till something else happens.
2. It is not till God speaks again that the plants sprout up. Plants come, not because the earth produces them but because God does. John Calvin pulls these two thoughts together with clarity:

> For though it [the earth] was already destined to bring forth fruit, yet till new virtue proceeded from the mouth of God, it must remain dry and empty. For neither was it naturally fit to produce anything, nor had it a germinating principle from any other source, till the mouth of the Lord was opened.[650]

3. When in day six God creates animals, they too come from the earth. There is no idea evident that the earth somehow has inherent capacity to produce fully formed animals in all their variety. It is consistent with this to also see no inherent capacity in the earth to produce plants.

That last point helps, for just as the creation of plants out of the earth is a break in the pattern of creation out of nothing, the creation of animals out of the earth repeats that break. In other words, the creation of something out of the earth is a new pattern rather than an isolated event. Putting the whole picture together helps identify the message: the earth sprouts with life that lives in the earth, the waters swarm with life that lives in the water, the air is filled with life that lives in the air, and the earth produces animals that live on the earth. The living things God made belong to the earth God made.

That too will be true of mankind: man will be made from the earth. The earth will be the place where he lives. The other living things – the plants and animals – have been created earth-bound to make the earth a good place for earth-bound mankind. Even as the ruler over all those other living things, mankind still is earth-bound. Neither mankind nor anything else living is divinity in any form. Neither mankind nor anything else living has its origin or its ontology in the galaxies, or the planets, or the forces of the universe. God is creating an environment for life which, far from being derived from the universe, is served by the universe.

Which Plants? What Kinds?

The specific repeated reference to seed-bearing plants and fruit trees causes some to wonder if all plants were created on day three, or only seed-bearing and

[650] Calvin *Genesis* p82

fruiting plants were created on day three.[651] "Let the land produce vegetation ..." seems sufficiently comprehensive: all plants are created. Any doubt about that is dispelled by verse 29 and 30 which finishes up with "green plants" not just seeding or fruiting plants. The Hebrew can be read as if "seed-bearing plants and fruit-trees" defines the particular vegetation referred to. However, even Sailhamer who insists verses 11 and 12 are not comprehensive, also insists that verses 29 and 30 are comprehensive of all plants.[652] So if technically verses 11 and 12 do not list every type of plant, this is a synecdoche in which some listed plants stand for all. Either way, if it is living and rooted in the ground, it was created on day three.

Of greater significance however is the reference here and in subsequent verses to "kind." Repetition of "kind" draws attention to its significance. Reference to "kind" is not an incidental detail but a feature of the creation of everything living: each is conformed to and will reproduce according to the pattern or kind in which it is first created.

Confusion arises when some attempt to identify "kind" as "species" or something similar. This doesn't work with any degree of satisfaction, and for good reason: importing a man-made concept (in this case, "species") into the biblical text almost inevitably produces confusion. But the text is actually very clear: every living thing God created on day three looked like the sort of living thing it was. Fruit trees had a similarity, and they all produced fruit, which in turn produced trees similar to the trees the fruit came from. Seed bearing plants had a similarity, and they all produced seeds, which in turn produced plants similar to the plants the seed came from. The implications are just as clear. Firstly, nothing created on day three morphed into something else found in day three (or later). Secondly, they would continue to be the sorts they were created as – they would reproduce a likeness not a difference.

The concept of "kind" is going to be developed over the next three creation-days. There is a danger that while we engage in a fruitless quest to determine the scientific definition of "kind" we miss what God is saying about what he created.

---

[651] eg "This suggests that the description of the land sprouting plants on the third day had only man's nourishment in view." (J H Sailhamer in "Genesis" p33.) And in *Genesis Unbound* [Kindle location 310] he argues, "At the conclusion of the chapter, other plants are mentioned that also are for the nourishment of human beings, as well as food for the animals (Genesis 1:30). Yet the creation of those plants is not mentioned anywhere in the first chapter; clearly they are not created on the third day. Only 'fruit trees' were created at that time. The account thus assumes that such plants already were present in God's world. This means that all these things were created as part of the 'heavens and the earth' in Genesis 1:1." Sailhamer's logic here escapes me. The text mentions vegetation, seed bearing plants and fruit trees which according to Sailhamer is to be read as "only fruit trees." The end of the chapter mentions other plants. According to Sailhamer those could not have been created on day three because only fruit trees are mentioned on day three. Therefore, according to Sailhamer those other plants must have been made in Genesis 1:1 where they are not mentioned either. The transparent lack of logic seems driven by Sailhamer's presupposition that Genesis 1:1 records the creation of the universe – probably over billions of years – while the rest of Genesis 1 records a literal week in which the land of Israel (his interpretation of reference to "the earth" in day 3) was functionally prepared for mankind. Sailhamer concedes that at the beginning of the Genesis week the earth is covered with water ... one wonders how the animals and plants got on under water for all that time before popping up to be ready for man on days three and six. The greatest consistency here is that credibility is strained to the extreme on all fronts: exegesis, logic and biology!

[652] ibid

When he created plants, he created them to be the sorts of plants they were created as. Evolution is not the first myth to postulate things changing into other things. What God is unequivocally saying here is that the plants he created did not come from other kinds of things and would not change into other kinds of things. Whatever kind each plant was, is what it will be; and what its seeds or fruit produced will be like the parent plant. "The repetition [of 'after its kind'], along with the clear allocation of separate creative events to different days, is meant to teach us something. The obvious thing ... is that living things were created to reproduce within prescribed limits. Thus the theory of evolution is excluded."[653]

God will say the same about the birds and the fish created at the same time on day five: not only are the birds created in "their kinds," and the fish created in "their kinds" but it is abundantly clear that birds and fish are different. God says he made fish that are fish and are going to be fish; he says he made birds that are birds and are going to be birds. The animals created on day six are all created in their kinds: whatever "kinds" means, it means that one kind of animal does not change into another kind of animal. As we will see, this concept of "kind" becomes of greatest significance in the creation of man.

Yet again God declares it all good. It brings glory to God now, with the promise of more to come! The first three days of creation have narrowed the locus of mankind's dwelling place from a dark universe to light; from there to the earth, then to land, and now to a green and lush living environment. There are three more days to go till creation is finished.

The Lonely Planet Waits

The blue-green earth hangs alone in the vast universe. This is the dawning of day four. Once totally immersed in water, earth is now a patchwork of aquas and emeralds bathed in a daily cycle of light and darkness. Above it, beyond the water gathered above the earth, stretches a sky of complete emptiness. That sky will soon contain the myriads of stars, galaxies, nebulae and mixes of energy and particles we call "the universe." But though he has already spread the sky out as a vast space above the earth, no place other than the earth has yet been created, no other cosmic body has yet been inserted by God into this space. Empty space and the lonely planet await God's will.

Again God speaks. "Let there be lights in the expanse of the sky," says God. And it was so. With those few words on day four God populated the universe.

To do this, God again uses an expression that indicates creation out of nothing. In day three he said, "let the earth produce plants," but here he does not say, "let the sky produce lights." God does not use something already existing "in" the empty universe to make the sun, moon and stars. By his simple command they exist. God speaks and space is colonised. But the contrast with his creation of plant-life has greater significance than that: plants were made from the earth because they belong to the earth. The sun, moon and stars were not made of the heavens, for they do not

---

[653] Weeks *The Sufficiency of Scripture* p104

belong to the heavens: they too are servants of man on earth; they too are "good" because they make the earth a good place for mankind, and that brings glory to God.

The text draws special attention to this. Nothing else so far created has had function declared at its creation. God's day four "let there be" statement goes way beyond the previous "let there be" statements." On this day he says "Let there be lights in the expanse of the sky *to separate ... to serve as signs ... to give light ... to govern*." Lest the point be missed, there is immediate repetition. As with previous creative acts, the creation of the sun, moon and stars is summed up with "And it was so." But immediately after that the text records that God made these heavenly bodies for earthly purpose, repeating that they were created to govern, to give light, and to separate. They are put in the sky for what they will do on earth. Yes, they will declare the glory of God,[654] but that glory is best seen, not in their sparkling spectacle, but in their earth-ward purpose and in their submissive service. They show the glory of God supremely because they show God's glorious, spectacular, powerful provision for life on earth.

Rulers of Day and Night

The heavenly bodies are given four specific, interrelated, earth-bound functions. Firstly, they are to mark out the separation between light and darkness. God has already separated the light from the darkness on day one. Separated light and darkness have already washed over the earth in three cycles of day and night. So how can the sun and moon do what is already done? "To separate one thing from another means to mark the distinction between two things *already in existence*."[655] We don't know how God marked out the separation between day and night before day four, but we certainly do know how he has done it ever since. The rising of the sun unmistakably declares a new day separated from the darkness. God has given us a definitive way for knowing the separation he created on day one. That is why God saw their creation as "good": fitted to God's ultimate purpose of exalting his name and glory through creating a good home for mankind.

Secondly, the heavenly bodies "serve as signs to mark sacred times, and days and years." Note that since they "serve" they are *servants*. The heavenly bodies are not creators of times and seasons. The times and seasons – secular and sacred alike – do not have their origins in the spinning of the heavenly spheres. The earth does not follow their dictates, and mankind is not expected to bow to these servants. They are markers, mere signs to help us know when seasons are changing, when days God (not the universe) has set aside for rest, thanksgiving, sacrifice, worship or work have dawned. They are our helpers. That is why God saw their creation as "good": fitted to God's ultimate purpose of exalting his name and glory through creating a good home for mankind.

Thirdly, the sun, moon and stars are created to give light on earth. Note again the earth-centeredness of this function. These celestial bodies are not created to give light to the universe, but to give light to the earth. This is reinforced by God's

---

[654] Psalm 19:1

[655] Cassuto *Genesis* p43 (italics his)

declaration that he has apportioned "the sun, the moon and the stars – all the heavenly array" to "all the nations under heaven."[656] But light was already shining on the earth daily. "Day four, we may assert with all confidence, presupposes the existence of the light which was created in day one."[657] Why create the heavenly array to do what was already being done? Light exists from day one, but by creating the sun as the vector by which light is given to the earth, God is making clear that light for living is a gift of specific focus: there is light, and there is light given to the earth.

These heavenly bodies are God's servants in the heavens called to praise him by giving light to his servants on earth.[658] Light for living comes to earth by things God has created: that should point us in thankfulness and praise to the Creator on a daily basis. How ironic that instead people so quickly worship the created things – created themselves to praise God – instead of the Creator. Job aptly expresses how the glorious light-providers (ie not light-givers!) can entice us to kiss the creation rather than the Creator.[659] These celestial things of glory are but creatures given to serve us, not deities for us to serve. Thus, without bringing light itself to an end, God can bring judgement on the earth, when "The stars of heaven and their constellations will not show their light. The rising sun will be darkened and the moon will not give its light. I will punish the world for its evil, the wicked for their sins."[660]

Fourthly, they govern. How so? Not absolutely as law-givers, for God alone is supreme Sovereign and law-giver. Rather, theirs is the government of administration. Theirs is just the same sort of government as the government to be given to mankind. People will be given rule over the earth and living creatures – not as determiners of the boundaries of creation or the functions of creatures, but as administrators of the limits and laws God has given. Not only do the celestial bodies mark out the days and seasons so that people can know what they are and respond faithfully, but the heavenly array will force people to comply. Despite the signs, we might want a season to continue or a dawn to wait: but God's governors will sort us.

Also the Stars

Vast and spectacular though this universe is, the stars are a mere "also made"! Creation of the stars comes in the text almost as if an afterthought. Here is how it reads: "He made the sun and the moon ... he gave the sun and moon specific functions ... and it was so ... and the sun and moon governed day and night ... and he also made the stars." There can be no doubt that the vast array of the universe is a staggering display of the power, glory and majesty of God. The heavens *do* declare the glory of God, and the expanse *does* show his handiwork.[661] Yet with the account of the cosmic creation dropped into the text like this, God is declaring the

---

[656] Deuteronomy 4:19
[657] Young *Genesis* p97
[658] Psalm 148:3-6
[659] Job 31:25-28. cf Romans 1:25
[660] Isaiah 13:10,11
[661] Psalm 19:1 (again!)

sun and the moon – the prime focus of verses 14-19 – to be of far greater significance. As he calls them into existence, he gives the sun and moon functions: he gives them a range of duties that will serve mankind. *That* is why the sun and moon are given pride of place against the spectacular backdrop of the glorious cosmos.

Not that this should be a cause for missing the significance of a back-drop filled with stars. The number of stars and the enormity of the space they fill is truly staggering.[662] Yet this is not a random scattering of star dust, as it were, but a deliberate placement of each star, known to God by its unique name, in its unique place in space: "He determines the number of the stars and calls them each by name. Great is our Lord and mighty in power; his understanding has no limit."[663] That vast array is created with precision and determination.

The question can arise that if some of the stars we see are thousands of light years away, how can we see them if creation is much younger than that? This is only an issue if one ignores the creative power of God who put space and the stars there in the first place, and ignores the fact that he was not then – nor is he now – bound by the laws of the creation he created. God who placed a star, for example, ten thousand light years away, and wanted people on earth to see it, was as capable of filling the universe with a matrix of light imaging that star and all the other stars, as he was of making light in the first place and later adding stars to the space he had prepared.

It only takes a moment too to realise that not only could God fill the universe with a matrix of radiating light, that when any light reaches the limits of creation it will stop – or at least stop moving in that direction. For the universe to exist within created boundaries, its "laws" have limits. Time, space, matter and energy are all created things within a limited creation. They do not exist beyond the creation. At the edge of creation, does energy cease, transform, bounce back in a new direction? For that matter, why should creation have an edge? We can only think in terms of the physics we observe, but we are observing something that in its creation, in its continuing, and in its determined end, is not conformed to the normality we observe from within it, or the "laws" embedded and maintained by God in creation's limited normality. What if our conventions of "shape" are just inadequate for describing this cosmos? The incredible vastness of the cosmos should be sufficient cause for hesitating to impose on it the engineering concepts we understand and use in our tiny little corner of creation. And all that is just the setting, the backdrop for God's communion with man on earth. With such a backdrop, how glorious is God's principal work on earth!

How empty was space before it was filled with the stars? The picture that comes from all this is that when in verse 1 God created the heavens and the earth, the heavens were a vast, defined space containing only the earth. There are lots of reasons proposed as to why this space was occupied with something, but none arise

---

[662] The numbers of stars and the distances involved are beyond counting: anything other than estimates based on limited observations and framed within tentative theories of astrophysics is impossible. But there is no biblical reason for rejecting the possibility of the number of stars being in or beyond the region of 1×10^{24} or more, and the distances across the universe exceeding tens of thousands of light years (figures of these magnitudes are commonly given in contemporary astronomy).

[663] Psalm 147:4,5

from the text. We can make the mistake of thinking empty space is not a creation: but before God spoke there was only God, not even space. When God spoke, empty space was created, ready to be filled and given purpose on day four.

Geocentric? Oh Yes! – But.

Doesn't all this present a picture of a universe with the earth at its centre? Yet we know that the earth is a tiny planet in a small solar system tucked away in a corner of a vast galaxy. And we know that not only is our galaxy but one of millions, we are nowhere near the centre of the universe. Actually, we don't *know* that, because we don't know everything there is to know about the universe, but on the data we do have it is reasonable to see our little world as not a terribly significant spot in the universe. How does that fit with the Genesis 1 picture of a universe created to serve the earth? Perfectly! Physically, the universe may well be as it appears: not in the least geocentric. But functionally, that is exactly how God has put it all together: the earth is at the centre of the work of the universe in the service of God.

Consider the destiny of this universe: the "present heavens and earth are reserved for fire ... The heavens will disappear with a roar."[664] By the same word of God that made them they will be destroyed. Because Adam by his sin, and all the descendants of Adam by our sin, have dragged the whole creation into the "bondage of decay,"[665] the universe will end.[666] It is under the sentence of destruction, not because it failed, but because those it was created to serve – people – have failed. Were the universe not geocentric, the failure of people on a little planet in the corner of space would have no significance at all. But because a day of judgement and destruction is coming to the ungodly, so a day of judgement and destruction is coming to the entire universe. When the universe can no longer serve man, the universe will be terminated, and replaced: "See, I will create new heavens and a new earth."[667]

Genesis 1 not only describes the creation of the universe, but it also reveals why that universe was created. God made a place for people to live, and he made a surrounding universe that would serve him by making that people's place a perfect place in which people would live and worship. In that sense God reveals a totally geocentric universe. But that is only part of the story, for in reality it is a Creator-centric universe, serving man *in the service of the Creator*. That, in its turn, makes it a Christo-centric universe:

> The Son is the image of the invisible God, the firstborn over all creation. For in him all things were created: things in heaven and on earth, visible and invisible, whether thrones or powers or rulers or authorities; all things have been created through him

---

[664] 2 Peter 3:7-11

[665] Romans 8:21

[666] Some question the totality of the destruction indicated by "burned up" or "destroyed," preferring "laid bare" or similar indicating a radical cleansing and purifying that nonetheless does not see the earth totally destroyed. The issue does not need to be resolved here to understand the impact of man's sin on the universe, indicative of the geocentric nature of the creation.

[667] Isaiah 65:17

and for him. He is before all things, and in him all things hold together. And he is the head of the body, the church; he is the beginning and the firstborn from among the dead, so that in everything he might have the supremacy.[668]

Teeming Life

Day five, and the earth teems with animate life.[669] This is no gradual oozing of one or two prototypical animals from primeval mud. Unlike the coming creation of one man and one woman as first parents of all people, the seas suddenly teem with every kind of fish and the air is filled with every kind of bird. On day four the seas and air are empty; on day five they are vibrant with life.

There is a subtle but significant change in wording in the account of day five. Two different Hebrew words are used in this chapter to describe the creative work of God. In v1, v21 and v27 *bara* "created" is used; elsewhere *asah* "made" is used. Although these two words are sometimes used independently, and (unlike *asah*) *bara* always has God as its subject, some of God's creative acts are described using both words[670] which would indicate that a difference in meaning is not intended.[671] Whether *bara* or *asah* is used, the Bible is declaring that God made these things by his word. So when, as in verse 21 *bara* is again used, the text is indicating something of significance that does not relate to its meaning "made" or "created." *Bara* is used in verse 1 of the creation of the universe, in verse 21 of the creation of living things, and in verse 27 of the creation of man. "Each new step in the account is marked by the use of *bara*: the universe (v1), the living creatures (v2), and man (v26). The orderliness of the account is evident."[672] In other words, God is making definitive distinctions between the universe, living things, and man.

Life is a critical element of God's creation, for "he alone is the living God who has life in himself, as opposed to idols that have no life. He alone is the uncreated Life who speaks life into existence."[673] To reveal the glory of the God who lives,

---

[668] Colossians 1:15-18

[669] Modern biological science classifies plants as "living things" but the Bible distinguishes animals and man as living things having the breath of life as opposed to plants which do not have the breath of life.

[670] As discussed p50 above *asah* (made) and *bara* (created) are both applied to the creation of the sun, moon and stars (Genesis 1:16 made & Psalm 148:5 created); man (Genesis 5:1, 6:6-7, 9:6; & Genesis 1:27); the heavens and the earth (Genesis 2:4 and Genesis 1:1); and all (Genesis 1:31 and Genesis 2:3).

[671] Justin Taylor is among those who claim a different meaning is intended. "It helps to remember that in Hebrew there are distinct words for create and make. ... if the sun, moon, stars, and lights were created in Genesis 1:1, then they were made or appointed for a particular function in Genesis 1:13, 14, 16—namely, to mark the set time for worship on man's calendar." [*Biblical reasons to Doubt*] His logic fails along with his exegesis. Apart from the presupposition that the sun moon and stars were made on day 1 (see above), he takes the fact that they were appointed to function in a particular way to mean that they were not made at that point (even though "made" is used) as if the appointment to a particular function cannot coincide with being made. As discussed above regarding Walton's similar differentiation, nothing in the text demands a reading that would make God a rather odd creator: making things that have no purpose or function but hang around purposelessly for aeons of time (since according to Taylor the days are not really days at all but aeons of time) until God steps back into the cosmos and gives them something to do.

[672] Sailhamer *Genesis* p35

[673] D H Johnson "Life" in Alexander et al (Ed) *The New Dictionary of Biblical Theology* IVP Leicester/Downers Grove, 2000 p641

creation is filled with living things. For creation to be "good" by the standards of God who is life it must be a theatre for life displaying the glory of God who lives, and now on day five the Creator brings his good stage to life.

Although *in* the universe, living things are not *of* the universe; and although living, man is *not* the same as the living creatures. This has significance for exposing all forms of pantheism. It has significance for the traditional false religions along with their cloned New Age manifestations that find some form of continuity between the universe, living things, and man. It has significance also for the scientific pantheism that imbues the universe with forces and chance through which material evolves into living things, and living things evolve into people. Particularly significant is the distinction between people and animals: despite biological and behavioural similarities, God made man "in his own image," [674] not only in distinction from the animals, but given rule over them.

Life in living things is described using the Hebrew נפש *nephesh*. Unlike plants, "living things" move.[675] Living creatures "breathe and are animated and have power of their own volition to go from place to place."[676] This *nephesh* "life" is frequently associated with breath[677] and symbolised by blood.[678] *Nephesh* "life" is found in both animals and mankind.[679] Because *nephesh* has sometimes been translated "soul" in Genesis 2:7 (as in "man became a living soul"), there can be confusion here. Genesis 2:7 is better translated "man became a living being."[680] As we will see shortly, that does not mean the life in mankind is the same as life in animals. In fact, there are clear distinctions made here between animals and man, but the point of this text is to attribute to God the life found in living things. While animals and man both have the breath of life given them from God, it is only into man that God breathes that breath "into his nostrils"[681] – face to face as it were, in "a sign of great intimacy."[682] Yet animals and man alike live because God gives them breath.[683]

Genesis also makes a distinction between sea-creatures, air-creatures, and land-creatures. There is no basis here for a scientific classification based on biblical-biology, and it is futile to attempt that. But the classification God does make directly relates to the unfolding themes of Genesis 1. Every living thing is after its kind, in its place, serving him. God said, "Let the water teem ..." and the water teemed with every sort of living thing that moves in water ... "after their kind." The water "swarmed forth of each kind."[684] God uses the same form of expression as he used in day three ("Let the land produce ...") to the same end: what he creates in the water lives in the water. What God creates to fly through the air flies through the

---

674 Genesis 1:27
675 Genesis 1:20-25
676 Leupold *Exposition of Genesis* 1.81
677 Genesis 6:17
678 Genesis 9:4,5
679 Johnson "Life" p641
680 So in Genesis 9:4,5 God demands an accounting of everyone for the blood of animals and man, albeit there is a difference: animals can be killed and eaten so long as the blood is drained from the flesh. The letting of a man's blood is not permitted.
681 Genesis 2:7
682 Johnson "Life" p641
683 Numbers 27:16; Job 33:4; Isaiah 42:5
684 Alter's translation

air. Every one of those living things is after its own kind, neither product nor propagator of a different kind. In one day a multitude of unchanging diversity populates sea and sky. And again, God looked at what he had made and "saw that it was good." The creatures he had made fitted his purpose to glorify him both in their creation and in creating a place in which people could live well. But there is also something different here.

On day five there is a new pattern introduced into the text. Having seen that the created fish and birds were "good," God blessed them. When God blesses he bestows good.[685] God's blessing is thus more than a wish that all might go well (as we might bless our friends with a hope of well-being but with no hope of being able to ensure that), but an affirmation that the good promised will be good received. Throughout both the Old and New Testaments God's blessing includes a sense of being secured in a good relationship with God,[686] and it is frequently fulfilled with the birth of offspring and the giving of life.[687] Accordingly here we find the blessing is directly linked to the command to be fruitful, to increase and to fill the earth. When God blesses the fish and birds, he not only commands them to reproduce and fill the earth, he affirms that they will do this, and that he will give life as they do; and that in reproducing and filling the earth they will fulfil their relationship with him as his good servants. "This blessing of God ... is not a mere wish or a wishing-well on the part of the Almighty. It is a creative word of power which makes possible the things that it commands, and continues to this day. The Creator is glorified by the multitudes of beings which His creative word makes."[688]

Animal Life

On day six God created more living things: all the animals. They too come forth from the earth as belonging to the earth. Indeed, the expression commonly translated "wild animals" is literally "beasts of the earth."[689] But though they come from the earth,[690] and belong to the earth, they are not made by the earth: they are made by God as he speaks: "Let the land produce …" In the words of Genesis 2:19, God "formed" them "out of the ground." It was an instantaneous creation: God spoke, "And it was so." It was a comprehensive creation: there are the wild animals, there are the domestic animals, and there are all the other animals that move on the earth. It was a stable creation: having said that at the voice of God the land produced animals "after their kinds … each according to their kinds," (v24) verse 25 underscores that the animals are established in their kinds by specifying that each of the kinds *was* according to their kind. As Calvin comments, "this distribution carried with it something stable."[691] The text presents the creation of *all* the animals,

---

[685] W W Wessel "Blessing" in Douglas et al (Ed) *The New Bible Dictionary* IVP, London, 1962 p160

[686] M J Evans "Blessing/Curse" in Alexander *The New Dictionary of Biblical Theology* IVP Leicester/Downers Grove, 2000 pp397ff

[687] See Sailhamer on vv20-23

[688] Leupold *Exposition of Genesis* 1.82

[689] Alter *The Five Books* p18

[690] Genesis 2:19

[691] Calvin *Genesis* p91

stable in their kinds, in an it-was-so *instant* at the *voice of God* in the first part of the sixth day.

It seems something is missing in the text at this point. We read that when God created the fish he commanded them to fill the seas, and he blessed them. We read that when God created the birds he commanded them to fill the sky, and he blessed them. But when we read about God creating the animals, there is no command to fill the earth, no blessing. Some pass over this by noting that clearly God intended the animals to reproduce: "What Moses before expressed on a similar occasion is here also to be understood, although he does not repeat it word for word."[692] In fact, he doesn't repeat it with different words either! That God intended the animals to reproduce can hardly be doubted, but the significance of there being no reference to this in the text cannot be so easily side-stepped. One of the things agreed by almost all commentators – perhaps the only thing agreed by almost all commentators – is that this chapter has been most carefully crafted. There are no accidents of omission or commission in Genesis 1. The lack of instruction to reproduce, to fill the earth, to be blessed when a pattern of stating those things has been established, must be deliberate and must point to something significant.

The lack of blessing for the animals is simple enough: God's blessing of the fish and birds was his affirmation that he would enable them to fulfil his command to reproduce and fill their habitats. With no explicit command for the animals to reproduce and fill their habitat, there is no explicit blessing pronounced. So the issue becomes, "Why is there no command for the animals to reproduce and fill the earth?"

Was the land not to be "filled" in the way the seas and sky were filled? Oh yes! "God blessed them and said to them, 'Be fruitful and increase in number; fill the earth …'"[693] This, of course, was God's declaration and blessing for Adam and Eve, *not* for the animals. Once again, the way in which God has given us Genesis 1 highlights the centrality of man in God's creation and in God's purpose. When God commanded the fish to "fill" the waters, he set them free to possess their habitat, to go where they would, to do in it what they could. They would be subjected to man's dominion, but even so the seas were theirs. When God commanded the birds to "fill" the skies, he set them free to possess their habitat, to go where they would, to do in it what they could. They too would be subject to man's dominion, but even so the skies are theirs. But the earth is human kind's habitat, created for people to populate and possess. The animals were created guests in the habitat mankind was to fill.

The animals, made from the earth belong to the earth on which they live, but over which they should never have dominance. Think of the seas, and one thinks of the fish that God commissioned to fill them. Think of the sky and one thinks of the birds God commissioned to fill it. Think of the land and one thinks of the people God commissioned to fill it. While we inevitably associate certain lands with particular animals, the primary focus for the earth is people.

That is not to say that the animals exist only for man. Some will come to serve man quite directly: supplying labour, providing food, and even being food. Yet only

[692] Calvin *Genesis* p90f

[693] Genesis 1:28

a tiny portion of the vast variegated menagerie of God's creation will serve man in such a way. So much diversity, so much vibrancy, so much differentiation – yet all with commonality that makes them "animals" means there is more to animals than what they do for man. The same can be said about the birds, the fish, and the plants. Living things make the world a "good" place in which man lives in God's service; but more than that, living things join in creation's song, declaring the glory of God.[694]

God makes plain from the very beginning that the similarities in biology, the "closeness" of mankind and animals, is not one that can fill the void of Adam's incompleteness. God brings the animals to Adam so that he and we can see there is no fitting helper or companion to be found in animals. Some might become pets; none can ever be wives. Regardless of similarities, animals are made in indissoluble distinction from man: despite commonality, there is no continuity either in origin or existence.

There was however at creation a harmony in living things – implied in Genesis 1 but reinforced in the promises of the New Creation. This is not just a harmony of existence, nor only a harmony in praise of God: it is a cosmic orchestration of what can be known about God. When later in Day 6 man is introduced into the concert hall of creation, he will not only know God from his relationship with his Creator, but the chorus of creation – especially of living things – will fill the earth in which man lives with the knowledge of God. So much of that was lost and marred in the fall, but not forever. When the victory of Christ over sin and its consequences is brought to its full realisation, there will be a return to Day 6 harmony, the knowledge of God revealed and declared in transparent perfection everywhere in everything:

> In that day I will make a covenant for them with the beasts of the field, the birds in the sky, and the creatures that move along the ground. Bow and sword and battle I will abolish from the land, so that all may lie down in safety. The wolf will live with the lamb, and the leopard will lie down with the goat, the calf and the lion and the yearling together; and a little child will lead them.... They will neither harm nor destroy on all my holy mountain, for the earth will be filled with the knowledge of the LORD, as the waters cover the sea.[695]

It is still day six. Everything God has created is good: it is ready to fulfil God's purpose. It is ready to praise its Maker. But something is missing: the universe is not finished. God will now add what he has been preparing for. Creation waits again.

---

694 Psalm 19 cf Job 38-41

695 Hosea 2:18 & Isaiah 11:7,9

10. Genesis Image

The Last Act of Creation: Reading Genesis 1 in the light of Man in God's Image

"Then God said, 'Let us make man in our image, after our likeness. And let them have dominion over the fish of the sea and over the birds of the heavens and over the livestock and over all the earth and over every creeping thing that creeps on the earth.'
So God created man in his own image, in the image of God he created him; male and female he created them."

~ Genesis 1:26,27[696]

It is the last act of creation, the penultimate event in the prologue of the Bible. It sets the scene for the story of the descendants of the first man Adam and the history of redemption through the Second Adam. With it the cosmos is complete: God stops creating. There will be one more climactic event after this in the creation week, but it will not involve creating.

Again God speaks: "Let us make man."[697] Without doubt the creation of people is so significant it deserves a chapter of its own. That is what God gave us in Genesis 2: a more detailed account of the creation of Adam and Eve that is the beginning of the story of humanity. Some mistakenly see Genesis 2 as giving a different account of creation from Genesis 1, as if Genesis 2 also somehow covers creation from

---

[696] ESV used here rather than the NIV for reasons made clear below.
[697] Genesis 1:26

nothing to completion. Refuting this, Young explains how Genesis 2 expands on the Genesis 1 account of man's creation, without conflicting in any way with Genesis 1. He draws attention to the significance of the expression, "These are the generations of the heavens and the earth,"[698] which in Hebrew, he explains, begins an account of what is begotten from what is named. For example, he notes that Genesis 11:27 uses the same expression, "These are the generations of Terah."[699] This "does not mean that we are now introduced to an account of Terah; rather, the account of Terah is completed. ... [The section] is concerned with an account of those begotten of Terah."[700] In the same way, Genesis 2:4 is not beginning a recapitulation of the Genesis 1 account of the creation of heaven and earth, but beginning "an account of those things which are begotten of heaven and earth. This is not to say that it is silent of the subject of the heaven and earth themselves, but it is not an account of their origin. It deals rather with what was begotten of them, namely, man."[701]

But before God takes up that more comprehensive account, he makes clear in chapter one how humanity's creation fits into the creation of the earth and everything else. The text signals that the creation of man, although a part of the creation week, is significantly different from everything that has gone before. There is a change in the way the events of creation are told. Everything so far has been created by the repeated impersonal decree: "Let there be ..." The account of the creation of man however is introduced by God reflecting with himself the desire to create man in God's own image: "Let us make man in our image, in our likeness, so that he may rule ..." The change in the repeated pattern is signal enough to the alert reader that this is different, but the personal nature of God's reflection, the explicitly personal nature of God's involvement in the proposed creative act, and the personal nature of making man in God's image signal this as a dramatically different act of creation.

The God who can say "Us"

Why does God use the plural "us"?

"Hear, O Israel: The LORD our God, the LORD is one." These definitive words begin the great *Shema*,[702] the daily Jewish prayer drawn from Deuteronomy 6:4. It affirms that God alone is God and that he is one. How God could therefore use the plural pronouns "us" and "our" of himself has sometimes puzzled readers.[703]

The plural pronoun is no accident: it is used three times in this verse alone, with God's name also in the plural form. But along with that, "said" is singular. God

[698] The ESV uses "generations" where the NIV obscures this with "account."
[699] The ESV again, although this time the NIV conveys a similar sense: "This is the account of Terah's family line."
[700] Young *Genesis One* p60
[701] Young *Genesis One* pp59f
[702] Sh'ma Yisrael; Hebrew: שְׁמַע יִשְׂרָאֵל
[703] A plural noun (or pronoun) associated with a singular verb is a Hebrew idiom likely indicating that the object represented by the plural noun is in fact singular – context determines the number, while the plurality of the noun is indicative of some other particular feature of the object named apart from number.

speaks in the singular, as one, with reference to himself in the plural, as if more than one. God who is one said "us," "our" and "our."[704] Further, it is God alone who creates: "the verbs make and create have only God as their subject throughout this account: no one joins him in the work."[705] There is consultation, but there is only one God; he is the only one there he can consult, and he alone is man's Creator.[706]

God uses plural pronouns in reference to himself in two other instances: Genesis 3:22 and 11:7. In both cases God is unmistakeably consulting with himself about what he will do with regard to man on earth. In Genesis 1 God consults with himself about the creation of man in his own image; in Genesis 3 God consults with himself about man distorting that image; and in Genesis 11 God consults with himself about an even greater distortion of that image. In each case the consultation is not in the form of deliberation in which possibilities are considered.[707] Rather, it is an expression of agreed determination to undertake a particular action. Further, each case relates to man's image bearing. Not only is the plural pronoun no accident, it is pointing very deliberately to unusual, personal action by God with regard to the creation or judgement of man as his image bearer. By way of plural pronouns in Genesis 1 God gives clear expression to a determination he shares with himself to make man in his own image.

At the very least the writer is stressing that God took his own counsel. Cannot the God who makes things by speaking clarify his intent – for himself and for us – by speaking, addressing himself in that plurality? "Yes," he says to himself, "what we have pondered, let us do." So great is the step he is to take, such significance given by God himself to the creation of man, he makes known to readers that he does it with reflection and deliberation. People are neither an accident nor an inevitable outcome of naturalistic forces, much less a whim God somehow found himself caught up in. Creation of people is a choice of God who planned for people in his image, prepared a universe for people in his image, then considered what he was about to do and consciously committed to creating them in his image.

Yet such reflection and deliberation could have been conveyed in the singular: "Let *me* make man in *my* image, after *my* likeness." So God intends to convey something more in using plural pronouns.

But discussion of the plurality should not distract us from something far more fundamental. The pronouns by which God alludes to himself are *personal* pronouns. This is the first time God addresses himself, and he does so in explicitly personal language. Each of his creative commands to this point has been impersonal: "Let there be ..." or "Let something produce ..." But now God says, "Let us make ..." This is the action of God who is personal. And what does he make? He makes man – a person – "in our image." The use of personal pronouns highlights the act of a personal God creating persons; people who have personhood like God.

---

[704] Let *us* make man in *our* image, after *our* likeness (Genesis 1:26)

[705] Collins *Genesis 1-4* Kindle location 686

[706] cf Collins *Genesis 1-4* Kindle location 678

[707] Where God appears to deliberate between alternatives, the singular pronoun is used; eg in Genesis 18:17 (cf Sailhamer *Genesis* p38)

Image and Likeness

God describes man at his creation as being "in our image, in our likeness."[708] Does God refer to something different in likeness compared to image, or is likeness and image the same? Various traditions distinguish between the two. Some have held the "image" describes man's essence which cannot be lost, while "likeness" is the part of man that can be lost. Others have seen a distinction between the physical and ethical parts of man. The Roman Catholic position, built on the teaching of Irenaeus, is that "image" references man's free will and reason while "likeness" references God's gift of spiritual communion with himself. Yet for all the theological variegation such differentiation might provide for, the terms are used so interchangeably "that it is impossible to avoid the conclusion that the two Hebrew terms are not referring to two different entities. In short, use reveals the words are used interchangeably,"[709] and when used together, are used this way for emphasis.

In Genesis 1:26 "image" and "likeness" are used together. In the next verse, "image" is used twice with no use of "likeness" even though it clearly references the fulfilment of God's intent to create man in the "image" and "likeness" of the previous verse. The "image" of verse 27 covers both "image" and "likeness" in verse 26. In Genesis 5:1 "likeness" is used in apparent reference to the whole man created earlier in God's "image" and "likeness." This is reinforced in verse 3 where "image" is appended as a qualifier for "likeness." They appear to refer to the same thing. Of equal significance, while in Genesis 9:6 fallen man is described as in God's "image," here in chapter 5 fallen man is described as in God's "likeness" a "likeness" passed on to his son. Man is created in God's "likeness" and in God's "image"; and fallen man is in both the "likeness" and "image" – for they are the same thing.

Plurality of God in Man?

Having announced his determination to make man in his own image (v26) the next verse records that creation taking place, and immediately confirms that man is created in God's image. It also declares that man is created male and female, and that both male and female image God. At this point it is very easy to read more in the text than the text says, and extrapolate the idea that being male and female somehow images God. As Scripture unfolds, it does indeed become evident that the relationship between male and female is sometimes linked to imaging God, but that is not the issue addressed in these verses. The focus of Genesis 1 is not the relationship of male and female, but their creation: God creates man; God creates man in his image; God creates man male and female; God creates man, male and female, each in his image.

Nevertheless, it is common to find in this text reference to male and female as indicating a plurality in the creation of man that reflects a plurality in God. Along

---

[708] Genesis 1:26

[709] Charles Lee Feinberg "The Image of God" in *Bibliotheca Sacra 129* Dallas Theological Seminary, July 1972, p237

with many others Sailhamer asserts that the text points to relationship between the man and the woman, which in turn images a relationship within the Trinity:

> The one God (wayyōʾmer ʾelōhîm, "And God said") created man through an expression of his plurality (naʿaśeh ʾāḏām beṣalmēnû, "Let us make man in our image"). Following this clue the divine plurality expressed in v26 is seen as an anticipation of the human plurality of the man and woman, thus casting the human relationship between man and woman in the role of reflecting God's own personal relationship with himself.[710]

"Relationship" is one of those words loaded with pleasant connotations and obfuscating imprecision. Its sematic range is broad: "the way in which two or more people, groups, countries, etc., talk to, behave toward, and deal with each other; a romantic or sexual friendship between two people; the way in which two or more people or things are connected."[711] Contemporary Christian usage additionally imbues the term with warm fuzzies and a never spelt-out sense of spirituality. Exactly what is meant is seldom clear. Sailhamer can hardly be faulted for attributing "relationship" to the first man and woman – they are "linked" by virtue of being created, they are in or about to enter a sexual union which one hopes knew something of friendship and romance in their 900 years together; and their behaviour towards one another could have been catalogued as "relationship." But which part of this reflects God's personal relationship – and what is God's "relationship"?

There is nothing in the text that overtly points to relationship beyond the fact that both are created and both are God's image bearers:

> It is quite a leap… to claim that this *defines* the image, and a much greater leap to find in this a paradigm of all relationships. It is much simpler to see that mankind consists of both males and females , both of which are in the image of God and both of which are necessary to carry out the commission 'to be fruitful and multiply.[712]

In fact, as I will show shortly, the emphasis is on likeness rather than any difference that could become a fulcrum for relationship, whatever is meant by the term. However, the *following* chapter in Genesis quite specifically addresses relationship between Adam and Eve united in "one-flesh-ness," in unity of likeness, life, commitment, service and purpose; in sexual union; and in a specific social dynamic. Genesis chapter 2 does this in a way that is entirely consistent with the text of chapter 1. Exposition of chapter 2 will legitimately and necessarily describe the relationship between the man and the woman. That is entirely consistent with chapter 1, yet its being consistent does not mean it is implied or is a truth hidden in the text of chapter 1.[713] Relationship is not even hinted at here (ie contra Sailhamer, there is in reality no "clue" to relationship). Progressing directly to discussion of relationship on the missing "clue" supposed to be expressed in chapter 1 can leave the significance of verses 26 and 27 of chapter 1 undervalued.

---

[710] Sailhamer *Genesis* (who references Barth). p. 38.

[711] *Merriam-Webster Dictionary* http://www.merriam-webster.com/dictionary/relationship 2016

[712] Collins *Genesis 1-4* Kindle location 762 (italics his)

[713] See discussion of *sensus plenior* below p225

Male and Female

What do verses 26 and 27 say about male and female? A key theme running through this chapter is that of likeness in the living. The plants are created with a likeness to their kind: plants are like plants. The animals are created with a likeness to their kind: animals are like animals. Man is created with a likeness to … God! And least there be any mistake, the text stresses that both of our first parents were like God. The decedents of the first couple will indeed be like them; but in saying that, Genesis 1 is making it clear that the likeness of people to their parents is this: they are like God.

In the creation of man something not evident in the creation of other living things happens. As with other creatures having "the breath of life" in them, Adam and Eve will reproduce after their kind: their children will be "like" *them* and not like some other living creature. But man was not created after his own kind, in the likeness of other men; God created him in the likeness of God. There are not multiple "kinds" of man, although, of course, each man has a likeness to his forebears, such that all are men. But the essence of that likeness of men to men is that every man is in the likeness of God. The "likeness" associated thus far with "kinds" is – unlike the plants, fish, birds and animals – a likeness to God. The pattern of "likeness" in created living things brings into focus the distinguishing likeness of man: a likeness to God.

It is this concept of likeness that drives Adam to declare of Eve when he first sees her, "Bone of my bones, and flesh of my flesh."[714] He has searched in vain for an animal with enough likeness to himself to find in it a "good helper" to fulfil God's mandate to rule the living things of the earth. But there was none like enough. In fact, the text goes further: it was not just that Adam couldn't find a suitable helper, none could be found for him. In other words, God demonstrated that as *he* searched through his creation he could not bring to Adam what he needed. But on seeing Eve, Adam sees one taken from his own flesh and bone with flesh and bone like his, a person like him, an image bearer of God like him. The ESV captures Adam's delight in finally finding a companion, after the unfulfilling search among the animals, with its translation of Genesis 2:23, "This is *at last* bone of my bones …" (my italics).

Only then, but truly then, was Adam to be found with a good helper. Only then, but truly then, was man ready to fulfil his commission. Only then, but truly then, God could say of what he had created on the sixth day, "It was very good."[715] It was not good merely because man had what he needed to fulfil his commission: it was good because creation was complete, ready to fulfil its commission, ready and able to display the glory of God in the fullness God had purposed.

Yet in the definitive likeness there is also definitive difference. Yes, male and female are both in the image of God. Just as emphatically, the woman is in the image of the man. And just as emphatically again, the man and the woman are different. "She shall be called woman,"[716] being taken out of man so as to be the same flesh and bones, but different so as to be known from the outset as "woman"

---

[714] Genesis 2:23
[715] Genesis 1:31
[716] Genesis 2:23

in contrast to "man." Gender difference is not rooted in biology or cultural practice or upbringing or personal preference: it is a matter of distinct creation by God. Male mankind and female mankind are both like and different in the created order, and they are no more interchangeable than are worms or whales with people. "God depicts the existence of a man and a woman as essential to his creational plan. The two are neither identical nor interchangeable."[717] Regardless of what people think and do with the fact that they are created in God's image, that is what God has made them. Regardless of what people think and do with the fact that they are created male or female, that is what God has made them.

Being male and female is not incidental to God's creation. In contemplating the creation of man, God said, "Let us make man in our image, in our likeness, so that they may rule."[718] As soon as they are created, God repeats this goal as a commission: "Rule over every living creature."[719] Being male and female is not incidental, but it is man and woman together who are made rulers of creation. Yet this is only part of the commission: "Be fruitful and increase in number; fill the earth and subdue it. Rule over …" Ruling over the living on the earth is simply not possible for man limited to space and time (even though he is in the image of an omnipresent God) without reproduction, migration and colonisation. So this rule for which man was created is dependent upon man and woman being like God, man and woman being united in one life and mission, and man and woman being sufficiently different in their likeness to reproduce in their likeness. God's image can rule only as he populates the earth, meaning that being distinctly male and female while being distinctly like each other is foundational. That will be examined more closely in the next chapter.

What Did They Know?

What it means to be in God's image will be explored shortly, but for now this question remains: "If the relationship between man and woman is not the point of this passage, what can still be said about the use of plural pronouns in reference to God?" God with God consults with God. So Sailhamer states that the use of plural divine pronouns reflects "God's own personal relationship with himself."[720] Even Bruce Waltke, who interprets the Genesis account in an evolutionary framework, concedes as a possible reading of the text what he ultimately rejects:

> The traditional Christian interpretation, that it represents a plurality within deity, has some textual support and satisfies Christian theology of the Trinity (John 1:3; Eph. 3:9; Col. 1:16; Heb. 1:2). That God is a plurality is supported by the mention of the Spirit of God in 1:2 and the fact that the image itself is a plurality. This

---

717 Kevin DeYoung *What Does the Bible Say About Transgenderism?* September 2016 *https://blogs.thegospelcoalition.org/kevindeyoung/2016/09/08/what-does-the-bible-say-about-transgenderism/*

718 Genesis 1:26

719 Genesis 1:28

720 Sailhamer *Genesis* p38 (who references Barth). As noted already, he argues that this is not only consistent with v26 itself, but with context provided by the following verse in which man is created in plurality, in the image of God who is a plurality. However, the fact that God consults with God revealing plurality in God stands on its own and is not dependent upon any idea of plurality in man.

interpretation would explain the shifts in the text between the singular and the plural.[721]

What is important to note here is that, taken at face value in the context of Genesis 1, some form of consultation within the Godhead is the most natural way to read this text. In Genesis 1, apart from what he creates, there is only God, so that in verse 26 there is only God who could be consulted by God.

Did the writer and first readers of Genesis have such an understanding of divine plurality? A wide variety of scholars say, "No." Given that it is only as Scripture unfolds that God reveals himself as a Trinity, and given that written formulation of the doctrine first appears no earlier than the 2nd Century AD,[722] it is argued that no concept of divine plurality could have existed when Genesis was written.

But to argue that since there is no evidence they understood the doctrine of the Trinity as we do, they could have had no doctrine of God encompassing a plurality, is simply not logical. Worse, it is also arrogant. It is not logical to claim that since they didn't know what we know they knew nothing; and it also presents an arrogant view of our own knowledge, given that though we have a doctrine of the Trinity, it is hardly one fully comprehended by the mind of modern believers! Objectors say we cannot bring a doctrine of plurality to the text. Equally we must argue that we cannot bring an *exclusion* of a doctrine of plurality to the text. There is no basis for bringing to the reading of Genesis 1 a presupposition that a divine plurality *could not* have been within the original writer's and readers' understanding.

The most basic assumption of contemporary approaches to Genesis (and all biblical text for that matter) is that we must read the text on its own terms.[723] We must aim to read the text without imposing on it concepts not evident in the text or in its earlier context (a context that does not exist for Genesis 1). So what happens when Genesis 1 is read as it is presented? We have a text in which God appears to speak as one God to himself in plurality. Both the original author and the original readers can reasonably be expected to be conscious of this, not only because it is clearly there, but also because it has such obvious significance for understanding who God is.

This should not surprise us. Given that

1. the *original* author of Genesis is God himself who, being at the time Genesis was written the self-conscious triune God, is hardly likely to be unaware of his own Trinitarian Being; and that
2. although God's inspiration of the writing of his word involves his using men whose minds are engaged in expressing with understanding what they wrote, he nevertheless not infrequently caused his writers to record things they did not *fully* understand;[724]

---

[721] Bruce Waltke *Genesis, A Commentary*, Zondervan, Grand Rapids, 2001, p64

[722] This is when most Christian doctrines first appear in written form apart from the Bible, so no special significance need be attached to the doctrine of the Trinity being formulated then apart from the fact that it was by then seen as part of the expression of orthodox Christianity.

[723] That does not deny the importance of reading the Old Testament in the light of the New (cf an historical/redemptive approach); but it does assert any analogical, typological or other New Testament framework for understanding the Old must approach the Old on its own terms to make any consistent sense of its New Testament meaning or application.

[724] 1 Peter 1:10-12

it is entirely consistent with his Being and his self-revelation that he speaks to himself as he is, and records that speaking faithfully in Scripture.

One of two arguments leads to the rejection of the plain biblical text. While virtually everyone claims to approach the text on its own terms, once they get there objectors reject the plain meaning either because it does not fit their presupposition that Moses and his contemporaries could not have had a concept of divine plurality, or that the text is not after all plain. Appeal is then made to extra-textual sources, or to cultural/linguistic contexts supposed to prevail at the time Genesis was written. I consider these in more detail below, but sufficient to note here, that taking the text on its own terms means that God must be seen to be addressing himself in plurality.

Whom did the Lord Consult?

The idea that God took counsel from someone other than himself is untenable in the light of Isaiah 40:13,14 which explicitly reinforces the plain teaching of the entire Old Testament that God is all wise, all knowing and in need of no-one's counsel. That he took the advice of angels, as favoured by many Jewish scholars, introduces angels as a presupposition into a text in which they have neither an explicit nor implicit place. "No others can be included here, such as angels, for none has been even intimated thus far in the narrative."[725]

In a similar vein some modern scholars contend that "God meets with a group of spirit beings to decide what happens on earth."[726] The concept rests on eccentric interpretations of a handful of texts, interpretations that tend to ignore the literary form of those texts and override both immediate and wider contexts. But whatever one makes of such claims with regard to the rest of Scripture, to apply such a concept to Genesis 1 requires the reading-back into this passage of ideas that are neither expressed in it nor consistent with it.

When God makes man in "our image" it is in God's image alone, not in the image of God and consulting angels or spirits. So even if God had consulted angels or spirits, the "us" that makes man in his own image refers to God alone. Not surprisingly, nowhere does the Bible hint at our being in the image of angels, or of other spirit beings. If there was any interaction between God and angels or spirit beings regarding the creation of man, Genesis 1 does not record it.

God could be using some form of regal "us" or a "Royal We," by which some intensification of an attribute takes place, or some special dignity is indicated. Some

---

[725] Feinberg "The Image of God" p238

[726] Michael S Heiser *Super Natural* Lexham Press, Bellingham, 2015 Kindle location 74. Heiser appeals to a number of passages, one of the clearest of which (he claims) is Psalm 82:1 in the Good News Version. [Kindle location 143] Here, as typically in much of his exegesis in this book, his presupposition of a "Divine Council," and God's "task force of divine beings [which he calls 'Gods'] that carry out his decisions" overrules the obvious context. The "gods" of verse 1 know nothing, understand nothing, and walk about in darkness according to verse 5. I am sceptical therefore that they have much to offer God! Does God take counsel from the "gods"? Well, according to God, "I look but there is no one—no one among the gods to give counsel, no one to give answer when I ask them. See, they are all false! Their deeds amount to nothing; their images are but wind and confusion." [Isaiah 41:28,29] Heiser demonstrates that the images are not alone in their confusion. In any case, Jesus identifies these "gods" as not gods but those "to whom the word of God came" (John 10:35).

distinguish between a) a *Plural of Excellence* (a literary device of intensification) where a plural is attached to a singular, and b) a *Plural of Majesty* (in which the speaker uses a plural to imply he and God speak as one). Not all make the distinction, but it is not uncommon for a claim to be made that the plural pronouns in Genesis 1 carry something of the idea of dignity and/or intensification.

Kidner expresses this well: "It is rather the plural of fullness, which is found in the regular word for God (*'ĕlōhîm*) used with a singular verb; and this fullness, glimpsed in the Old Testament, was to be unfolded as triunity, in the further 'we' and 'our' of John 14:23 (with 14:17)."[727] There can be no question that the verses concerned intensify the text: as readers, we become acutely aware that God in all his majesty is about to undertake something momentous. But what is really meant by a "fullness" revealed by God who is not thought of as plural speaking as if he is plural? In any case, Genesis 1 does not match any of the instances in which a "plural of fullness" might be found. There are several examples in the Old Testament where singular and plural are mixed in a way that may intensify the allusion,[728] but none of these is similar to the use of plural pronouns in Genesis 1.[729] It is only a presupposition that God is not revealed in plurality in the Old Testament that forces interpreters to look for alternative readings of Old Testament references to God in plurality. But if, as seems apparent, God reveals himself in plurality in the very first book of the Bible, why should it be so difficult to see references to plurality in the rest of the Old Testament as being a continuing, progressive revelation by God of his plurality?[730]

Nor are there any examples in the Old Testament of Israel's kings (or of pagan kings for that matter) using a plural pronoun to declare "We say …" in reference to themselves in partnership with God. The very idea is intrinsically repulsive to Old Testament reverence for God. Some make allusion to such practices in ANE cultures, but even if there was some basis for attributing such pagan literary idioms to biblical authors (which there is not!), no examples can be found in those cultures until around the 4th Century BC.[731] It seems clear then that God could *not* be using some form of regal "us" or a "Royal We" in Genesis 1.

---

727 D Kidner "Vol. 1: Genesis: An Introduction and Commentary." *Tyndale Old Testament Commentaries*, Nottingham, England: Inter-Varsity Press 1956 p56

728 This is contended among commentators.

729 In the examples of intensification, there is said to be a mismatch of number between noun and adjective; in Genesis 1 there is no adjective attached to the pronoun.

730 There can be little hermeneutical basis for reading back into Genesis 1 later idiomatic readings (real or imagined) that depend upon a presupposition that Genesis 1 cannot be read at face value. If Genesis 1 makes such an idiomatic reading *necessary*, then the later readings can throw light on Genesis 1. But in the argument as presented, we have an essentially circular argument that goes like this: Later uses of divine plural pronouns cannot be references to divine plurality because the Hebrews had no concept of that despite what they wrote; therefore, Genesis 1 cannot be a reference to divine plurality despite what is written; therefore, later references to divine plurality must have an idiomatic meaning; which means Genesis 1 has an idiomatic meaning. But once the possibility is accepted that what was written gave plain expression to what was intended, not only do the difficulties fall away across the entire Old Testament, but there is – as one might expect – a wonderful consistency apparent to God's self-revelation.

731 Thus to claim the author of Genesis was adopting a pagan idiom, one has to argue that he adopted an idiom for which there is no evidence that it existed.

Glimpsing the Trinity

Christian interpreters have frequently found a reference to the Trinity in these plural pronouns. Are they right? God the Trinity consulting with himself (ie Father with Son and with Spirit) is undoubtedly consistent with the use of plural pronouns. The opening lines of John's Gospel, "In the beginning was the Word, and the Word was with God, and the Word was God. He was with God in the beginning,"[732] fit perfectly, especially as they go on to confirm the Word's participation in creation.

As the Bible unfolds there is a great deal made plain that was obscured to the original writers. The writers were not fully aware of all that is meant in what they wrote, "but God, who inspired them, was explicitly aware, and when this meaning becomes explicit in the New Testament, the 'blurred vision' becomes clear and it is truly something that is organically 'unfolded' from the Old Testament author's original meaning."[733] At times those writers even knew there was something hidden from them that would be revealed to later generations: "It was revealed to them that they were not serving themselves but you, when they spoke of the things that have now been told you."[734] So here, at the very beginning of the Bible, we can see that the doctrine of the Trinity fits consistently with the text. Here is a glimpse of what will later become much clearer.

Although the writer and original readers would have been conscious of plurality, reference to the Trinity (as Father, Son and Spirit) would almost certainly not have been apparent. But the fuller sense of what has been written can now be seen in the text without in any way changing the text or its original meaning. This is what is known as a "*sensus plenior* ('fuller sense') ... [that] occurs when a later passage amplifies an earlier one in a way consistent with the intent of the earlier one."[735] We find this in the Messianic Psalms and in the "Suffering Servant" passages in Isaiah, where, in the light of the New Testament, Christ is unmistakably to be seen in a way that was obscured to the original writer and readers. Here in Genesis 1 is a text that in the same way, in the light of the New Testament, shows the Trinity at work in harmony; yet on its own it leaves such rich meaning partially hidden. "This is not the same as claiming that the author or a pious Israelite reader must have been able to see it, only that the narration allows it."[736]

The Spirit of God

The significance of Genesis 1:2 should not be overlooked: "… and the Spirit of God was hovering." From the very opening of the creation account there is an inescapable complexity in the way in which God works and is revealed. The plural pronouns of verse 26 have a context in which complexity is no surprise. For some, the "Spirit of God" is no more than "a term for God's outgoing energy, creative and

---

[732] John 1:1,2
[733] Beale & Gladd Hidden but Not Revealed p364
[734] 1 Peter 1:10-12
[735] Collins *Genesis 1-4* Kindle location 696
[736] ibid

sustaining."[737] But this hardly does justice to the personal nature of the Spirit's engagement in the creation; and it is difficult to comprehend the writer describing such a "force," hovering over the earth as a mother bird.[738] The Genesis "Spirit of God" not only hovers protectively and nurturingly, but strives with men,[739] and evidences the presence of God.[740] The same difficulties arise for those who, conscious of the fact that the Hebrew allows for "Spirit" or "wind," want to translate it as "a mighty wind hovering over the earth." In fact, "wind" fits neither the context nor the Hebrew.[741] Further difficulties in such a translation arise: "Dan. 7:2, which glances at this passage, shows that a writer who meant to convey such a meaning could do so without requiring his readers to divine it from the familiar expression for the Spirit of God, construed in an unfamiliar way."[742] In contrast, for many from the foundation of the Christian church, the Genesis "Spirit of God" is so obviously the New Testament's "Holy Spirit" that it is assumed without discussion.[743] Using the same expression, "Spirit of God," Job attributes his creation to this Spirit of God, and his life to the breath of God.[744]

God speaks in plurality because he is in plurality: One God – Father, Son and Holy Spirit.

Adam, an adam, mankind, or people?

Who does God create? Translations vary, as do the implications. Does God create a man called "Adam," an anonymous "adam" (man), mankind, or people? The Hebrew word אדם "adam" is used in all these ways in the Old Testament, so each time it is used, questions arise as to how best to translate it:

1. Is it naming a man called "Adam"?
2. Is it alluding to a man (not called "Adam")?
3. Is it a generic reference to people? And if so,
4. Should it be translated with a neuter "people" or "human-kind," or with gender overtones as "man" or "mankind"?

In 1 Corinthians 15:45, Paul makes an unmistakable reference to Genesis 2:7 with the words "the first man Adam became a living being." It is clear therefore that the first *adam* is properly called "Adam". He does not have to be known as "a man" or "the man" as some are wont to render the text. It is critical to God's salvation of mankind that there is a single individual who is the first parent of all people. So God made, not just "a man," but Adam, the first man. From him he made

---

737 Kidner, *Genesis* p49
738 ibid
739 Genesis 6:3
740 Genesis 41:38
741 Cassuto *Genesis* p24 presents a cogent argument to this effect.
742 Kidner, *Genesis* p49 (footnote)
743 eg Reymond, *Systematic Theology*, p392
744 Job 33:4

Eve, the first woman; and from them came all people. Whenever that first man is referred to, he is properly called "Adam."[745]

It is not just Adam however, who is called "adam" (man). It is the name God applies to all humanity. Contemplating the creation of man, God says "let us make *man* ... let *them* have dominion ..."[746] so it is apparent that for God the term "man" includes all humanity. The same concept is apparent in verse 27: "So he created man ... male and female ..." What is implicit here could be seen to be made explicit in Genesis 5: "When God created man, he made him in the likeness of God. He created them male and female and blessed them. And when they were created, he called them 'man'."[747]

However, translation of *adam* at the end of Genesis 5:2 is not so straight forward. It ranges in Bible versions from "Adam"[748] through man,[749] mankind[750] and humankind,[751] to human/humans.[752] While "Adam" as a proper noun identifying the first man is clearly a biblical usage, "Adam" rather than "man" is not suited to every instance of אדם "adam." On the other hand, it is difficult to find in this text, or in any other in which *adam* is used, any justification for completely neutering *adam*. Translations in which this is done appear to be driven by the gender-philosophy and cultural context of the translators rather than by the text or original context. The NIV 2011 attempts to preserve the masculine of the original *adam* while indicating a more generic reference than is self-evident in "man": "When God created mankind, he made them in the likeness of God. He created them male and female and blessed them. And he named them "Mankind" when they were created." With the NIV 2011's appropriate commitment to rendering neuter references to people with a neuter translation,[753] it is clear that by their retaining a masculine translation of *adam* here, those translators recognise that the text is inescapably masculine. "Mankind" resonates with the emphasis throughout the creation account of "after its kind." "Man" resonates, especially in Jewish tradition, with man being made from the earth *adama*. From the text therefore it can be

---

745 There is nothing in the text of verse 27, or in the verses around it, that would indicate "Adam" is to be preferred to "mankind" in that verse; and the rest of verse 27, with its identifying "adam" as being male and female, would indicate a generic reference to mankind is appropriate.

746 Genesis 1:26

747 Genesis 5:1,2 (NIV 1984. cf the ESV. The NIV 2011 appears to attempt to soften "Man" with "Mankind," but without really obscuring the obvious gender specificity.)

748 KJV, ASV

749 ESV, NASB

750 NIV 2011

751 NET, Alter

752 ISV, NLT

753 "The original NIV (1978) was published in a time when 'a man' would naturally be understood, in many contexts, to be referring to a person, whether male or female. But most English speakers today tend to hear a distinctly male connotation in this word. In recognition of this change in English, this edition of the NIV, along with almost all other recent English translations, substitutes other expressions when the original text intends to refer generically to men and women equally. Thus, for instance, the NIV (1984) rendering of 1Co 8:3, 'But the man who loves God is known by God' becomes in this edition 'But whoever loves God is known by God.' On the other hand, 'man' and 'mankind,' as ways of denoting the human race, are still widely used. This edition of the NIV therefore continues to use these words, along with other expressions, in this way." [*Preface* to the NIV 2011]

confidently asserted that either "man" or "mankind" is appropriate: which is the best translation will be determined by wider contextual issues.

God named humanity, men and women, "Man/Mankind."

It would be a mistake to see this naming of humanity by God "man" or "mankind" as an insignificant incidental incursion into the text. It is not incidental: in such a carefully crafted text it could not be more obviously intentional. Nor is it insignificant: God declares his intention to make man, makes a man, then makes a woman from that man. There is clearly something about the first man Adam that has significance: Adam (not Adam *and* Eve) is the prototype for mankind. And just as clearly there is something about humanity that makes calling us "Man" of significance.

Further, God has chosen to reveal himself in masculine terminology. Clearly that has nothing to do with sex or sexuality, for God is not sexual nor does he engage in sexual activity.[754] Yet to use masculine terminology when neuter is available either constitutes a sustained deception on the part of God (which is unthinkable!) or is representative of God's nature in some way: "In his personhood, God is clearly 'masculine' ... In himself, God is beyond the limitations of human gender or sexuality, but that does not mean that his masculinity is purely conventional."[755] Bruce Ware notes that God not only refers to himself in male terms, but specifically identifies Father and Son in gender-specific terms.[756] As Ware goes on to assert, by deliberately choosing this language, God has chosen to deliberately indicate something of significance. In a detailed response to common assertions that in a number of places the Old Testament uses feminine language to describe God, David Clines concludes, "There is not a single instance of female language about the deity in the Hebrew Bible, that is, of language suggesting that the deity is viewed as female."[757] God reveals himself in the Old Testament in exclusively male terminology.

God is God: he alone knows himself, he alone decides how he reveals himself, and he alone chooses how he is to be addressed. It is not for us to neuter him or feminise him. There "is one God, the Father, from whom all things came and through whom we live."[758] But God's self-revelation is not something to apologise for! Every aspect of his self-revelation draws our attention to a thing of wonder, to a cause for adoration, to a reason for delight, and to a call to faith. That God the Creator and Lord of all space, people and time should bind himself to us as our Father[759] is staggeringly remarkable: "Praise be to the God and Father of our Lord Jesus Christ, the Father of compassion and the God of all comfort."[760] "Sing to God,

---

[754] That is one of the distinctives of the God of the Bible compared with the pagan gods surrounding Israel at the time Genesis was written, and in multitudes of cultures since.

[755] Gerald L Bray "God" in Alexander *The New Dictionary of Biblical Theology* IVP, Leicester/Downers Grove, 2000, pp514f

[756] Bruce Ware The Man Christ Jesus: Theological Reflections on the Humanity of Christ Crossway, Wheaton, 2013, Kindle location 1489

[757] David J.A. Clines *Alleged Female Language about the Deity in the Hebrew Bible* the Society of Biblical Literature, Seoul, 2016

[758] 1 Corinthians 8:6; cf Ephesians 4:6

[759] Isaiah 63:16; 64:8

[760] 2 Corinthians 1:3

sing in praise of his name, extol him who rides on the clouds; rejoice before him — his name is the LORD. A father to the fatherless, a defender of widows, is God in his holy dwelling."[761]

It is as the Trinitarian nature of God is unfolded that the significance of God referring to himself in male terms become clearest: "God wishes by this language to indicate something of the authority and submission that exists within the relationships of the members of the immanent Trinity."[762] It is as Son to the Father that Jesus makes the Father known because it is as a Son that "All things have been committed to me by my Father. No one knows the Son except the Father, and no one knows the Father except the Son and those to whom the Son chooses to reveal him."[763] This is a relationship of Father to Son love: "The Father loves the Son and has placed everything in his hands."[764] It is a relationship of Son to Father dependence: "I tell you, the Son can do nothing by himself; he can do only what he sees his Father doing, because whatever the Father does the Son also does."[765] It is a relationship in which the Son offers reverential submission and obedience.[766] The biblical concept of sonship – for all its variegation and complexity – means at the very least that the Son is from the Father, and thinks and acts like him and for him.[767]

It is hardly surprising therefore that in turn God represents gender in the mankind he has made in his image. I will look more closely at the significance of created gender shortly, but for now it is important to briefly consider three things:

1. God is very explicit in using a gender specific term for humanity: therefore, to use "man" or "mankind" in generic reference to people has a proper and necessary place in our language and theology. Whatever that place is, and whatever significance it has, to always resile from referring to people as "man" or "mankind" can be less than biblical.
2. The generic "man" transcends sexuality. It does not minimise sexuality or sexual distinctives. There is never any attempt to reduce those distinctives. Yet Genesis 1:27 and Genesis 5:2 stress that both men and women are in the image of God. From the very beginning, mankind is constituted of men and women who are different and who have different roles. But they are given a generic name by God that has masculine reference. They are all in the image of God; they are "man."
3. While "man" is the appropriate translation of a generic "adam", in the context of God creating man living beings "after their kind" it would seem "mankind" could be a perfectly appropriate translation of a generic "adam." That would seem particularly appropriate in any text where it might not otherwise be clear "man" is intended to be generic.

---

761 Psalm 68:4,5

762 Ware *The Man Christ Jesus* Kindle location 1470

763 Matthew 11:27; cf Luke 10:22

764 John 3:35; John 5:20

765 John 5:19

766 Hebrews 5:7,8

767 cf D A Carson *Jesus the Son of God* Crossway. Wheaton, 2012

In His Own Image

To be in God's image is to be imbued with enormous personal dignity:

> What is mankind that you are mindful of them,
> human beings that you care for them?
> You have made them a little lower than the angels
> and crowned them with glory and honour.[768]

Man is made lower (just a "little" lower!) than the angels, but unlike them, man is crowned "with glory and honour." In Psalm 8 David considers the heavens, the moon and the stars – put in place by the finger of God – and asks, "What is man" compared to that? His answer is that God has made man glorious; that God has given man a glory that surpasses that of the sparkling expanse of the universe in its entirety. Every person – from the unborn to those constrained in awful disability – has a glory (and thereby a dignity) above and beyond any other created thing. Man is honoured with imaging God in a way that the rest of creation – the impersonal creation and angels – could not and cannot do.

Creation announces the glory of God;[769] man images that glory. Through creation we know that God is glorious. Through man we know the nature of that glory, and never more so than in the perfect man, Jesus, whose glory is the fullness of "grace and truth."[770] "God did not make Adam and Eve to resemble rocks, trees, or animals. Nothing so common was in his design for us. Instead, God carefully shaped the first man and woman so that they were in *his* likeness. He determined to make us creatures of incomparable dignity."[771]

It is not that man is in himself so glorious that he can stand in the universe and declare, as Renaissance man claimed, "I am," proclaiming that "Man by himself will tear himself out of nature and free himself from it."[772] That has been the arrogant, pathetically silly claim of man in the face of creation and eternity from Adam to today! Equally pathetic is the attribution of dignity to man who "originally bearing the image of an orangutan and chimpanzee … gradually pulled himself up from a state of raw brutishness to that of a noble humanity"[773] in some evolutionary process. According to such concepts "the essence of man is situated not in what he was or is but in which he, in an endless process of development and by his own exertions, may become."[774] Both concepts leave man completely bereft of anything but a fluid and pliable dignity founded on the shifting sands of ethics unanchored in transcendence. Such a liquid dignity can at one moment condemn such things as abortion, euthanasia and genocide, and at another moment acclaim them with no sense of the utter futility of finding anything of more than momentary value in people or what they do. Man is then but what he has made himself or what he is becoming. In such a framework what man makes of himself and what he becomes – regardless of the cost to himself or to others – is by definition the sum and

---

[768] Psalm 8:4,5
[769] Psalm 19:1
[770] John 1:14
[771] Richard L Pratt *Designed for Dignity* P & R, Phillipsburg, 1993, p9 (his italics)
[772] Francis A Schaeffer *How Should We Then Live* Crossway, Wheaton, 2005 (1976) p71
[773] Herman Bavinck (J Bolt ed) *In the Beginning: Foundations of Creation Theology* Translated by John Vriend, Baker, Grand Rapids, 1999, p165
[774] ibid

substance of what passes for the time being as human dignity. Such transient dignity lacks any real dignity at all.

For the Genesis man however, true and lasting dignity and glory resides not in himself or his deeds, and much less in his potential; Genesis man's lasting dignity and glory reside in his being the image of his Creator. In a world besotted with the search for self-image – an image not only "self" in terms of perception by self, but as actually or virtually created by self – the Genesis revelation posits man's dignity in God: it is "other-made" not self-made, "other-centred" not self-centred. For this reason, the search for personhood needs to be the search to realize our "God-image" not our "self-image."

It is this "God-made-ness" which makes each person's dignity non-negotiable: because they are man they have a dignity that is not dependent upon class or achievement, gender or self-image, youth or maturity, heritage or hope. Personal dignity is given by God in creating each individual in God's image. This was as radical in Moses' day as it is in ours:

> In those ancient times, only kings could rightly claim to be images of divinity. Commoners and peasants had no such value; they had no importance. It was their destiny to suffer and die for the gratification of kings. These beliefs were behind Israel's terrible suffering in Egypt. What gave Pharaoh the right to subject the Israelites to cruel slavery? How could the Egyptians justify their attempt to destroy the Jews? The answer was very simple for ancient Egyptians. The lowly Israelite shepherds should not have expected honourable treatment. They had no dignity; they did not deserve any respect. Only Pharaoh represented divine authority on earth.
>
> Moses' words in Genesis directly opposed these lies. He boldly claimed that *all* people were royal images of God. Every descendant of Adam and Eve possessed the same honoured status. God bestowed great value and dignity not on a few, but on all of the human race.[775]

It is that, too, which should restrain any pride in our self-image, any arrogant satisfaction in what we are, or any claim to be more than God-made images for God-made purposes. "We are both magnificent and dust. Like God, and yet also one of his creatures."[776] Adam and Eve "were finite, physical representations of their Creator. As astounding as this description may be, we must not miss how it discloses our humility. We are images of God, but that's all we are – images."[777] As Calvin comments, "that those should glory in their excellence who not only dwell in tabernacles of clay, but are themselves in part dust and ashes," should curb pride.[778] "You return to the ground, since from it you were taken; from dust you are and to dust you will return."[779]

The fact that man's creation is in God's image is made abundantly clear in Genesis 1; what is not so clear is all that it means to be in God's image. Dabney states the obvious: "The general idea here is obviously, that there is a resemblance

---

[775] Pratt, *Designed for Dignity* p9 (his italics)
[776] Claire Smith *God's Good Design* Matthias Media, Kingsford, 2012 p163
[777] Pratt, *Designed for Dignity* p4
[778] Calvin *Institutes* Book 1 Chapter 15, 1, p160
[779] Genesis 3:19

of man to God,"[780] and goes on to point out that man's resemblance to God is not to be found in man being of the same essence as God (whose essence is incommunicable) or of the same bodily shape as God (for God has no body or shape).[781] Lutheran Nathan Jastram also goes to the obvious plain meaning: "The simplest and most comprehensive definition of the image of God is that it means 'to be like God.'"[782] While conceding that a narrow association of the image of God in reference to righteousness is traditional, he goes on to point out that righteousness "does not exhaust the many ways in which people can be like God."

Luther himself proposes caution, noting that "when we speak about that image, we are speaking about something unknown. Not only have we had no experience of it, but we continually experience the opposite; and so we hear nothing except bare words." [783] Until we are fully reformed into the image of God in Christ, he writes, "we cannot have an adequate knowledge of what that image of God was which was lost through sin in Paradise."[784] He sees the image of God in Adam as comprehending all that Adam was, all the graces gifted to Adam, and all that Adam did. Nevertheless, he is willing, as we should be, to look more closely at what it is to be in the image of God, albeit we will not see with the clarity in which Adam began.

Image Lost or Image Perverted?

But is the image of God still to be found in fallen, unregenerate, rebellious man? Some answer, "No!" For example, Dabney asserts, "This image has been lost, in the fall, and regained, in redemption."[785] His argument, along with others who hold his position, is that the unregenerate have nothing of the image of God in them, but do retain the potential for the image to be remade in them. None of this can be plainly read in Scripture; it is a concept arrived at through a series of conditional inferences, starting with Scripture but dependent upon reason with only tenuous reference back to Scripture. It is a methodology that superficially appears consistent but raises more questions than it answers.

A more modern writer, Angus Stewart, presents a detailed exposition of this position asserting that the image a man bears at any point must either be the image of God (*imago dei*) or the image of Satan (*imago diaboli*). "Both believing and unbelieving men are necessarily image-bearers but they differ regarding the one whose image they bear. For one it is God; for the other it is Satan."[786] Perhaps the

---

[780] R L Dabney *Lectures in Systematic Theology* Baker, Grand Rapids, 1972 (1927) p293.
[781] Similarly, "It is clear enough that the likeness does not remove the difference between man and God, and that the insistence on this likeness at the same time witnesses to the uniqueness of man in comparison with other creatures." Berkouwer *Man: The Image of God* p70
[782] Nathan Jastram "Man as Male and Female: Created in the Image of God" in *Concordia Theological Journal Volume 6:1* Concordia, Fort Wayne, 2004 p7
[783] Martin Luther (J Pelikan ed) *Luther's Works: Volume 1 "Lectures on Genesis 1-5"* Concordia, Saint Louis, 1958, p63
[784] Ibid p65
[785] Dabney *Lectures* p293 [Dabney *does* put commas in strange places!]
[786] Angus Stewart "The Image of God in Man: A Reformed Reassessment"
http://www.cprf.co.uk/articles/imageofgod.htm#.Voh0kvl96Uk

most basic error here is missing the point of Genesis: God did not make man an image bearer with capacity to image whatever man took up as a mirror might image whatever faced it, but specifically as God's image, imaging God no matter what faced him. Man is not created "necessarily an image-bearer" of something, but necessarily an image-bearer of God.

For Stewart and those who share his understanding the image of God cannot remain in fallen man, albeit in a corrupted form, for that would mean "if unregenerate man is the image of God (in some sense) then there must be some good in him. ... The image of God cannot be bad, nor can it be merely neutral. God is good and, therefore, the image of God is good."[787] In a footnote he goes further, asserting, "It is hard to deny that if unbelieving men are in the image of God they must also be 'partakers of the divine nature' (II Peter 1:4) to which belongs 'all things that pertain unto life and godliness' (v. 3)." Actually, it is not hard to deny that at all! One simply has to control one's reasoning by Scripture instead of imposing reason on Scripture. By demanding any image be a complete and perfect representation, Stewart (and others with him) not only distort the biblical concept of image, but make nonsense of any ordinary concept of imaging that does not involve comprehensive identity. Just as Jesus truly came in the likeness of sinful flesh[788] yet without man's sin,[789] so man can have the likeness of God without God's good. But to Stewart an image must take on the absolute good or absolute bad of what is imaged. The necessary implication of this must be that regenerate man, partaking of the divine nature (2 Peter 1:4) must be an absolutely good image of God. I for one am reasonably confident that though regenerated by the grace of God in Christ I have not yet attained such a state of perfection. An image can be corrupted yet clearly image what is referenced.[790]

Some years ago a provincial newspaper published a satirical cartoon of a man I know well who was thrust into prominence through a national morals campaign. He was instantly recognisable as referenced in the cartoon, yet the context of the image and the activity portrayed so distorted the message of the campaign and so perverted the character of the man imaged, that it could only be described as a corrupted image. Who and what was imaged was obvious; that it referenced that particular man and the morals campaign he championed was indisputable; but that it was a corrupted image devoid of truth in its imaging was also plain.[791] Images can still be recognisable images even when totally corrupted. So it is with fallen man imaging God, yet doing so with an image wholly perverted.

---

[787] ibid

[788] Romans 8:3

[789] Hebrews 4:15

[790] It is possible to read texts that are commonly read as confirming the continuing imaging of God in fallen man in ways that mean the image is completely absent in fallen man. Genesis 9 can be read as referring only to those men who are in God's image rather than to all men as being in God's image; 1 Corinthians 11:7 can be read as addressed to believers (ie those who are renewed in the image of Christ); and while James 3:9 naturally reads as a generic reference to all men, it can be read as referring to the particular men who are made in God's image. Such readings however appear to arise from a presupposition of a totally lost image, rather than from any necessity in a plain reading of the texts.

[791] The cartoon was not making overt claims about a hidden meaning in the campaign's message or imputing some moral imperfection to the man, but in satirising them both attempted to use ridicule to marginalise their impact.

The Second Adam

In such a condition, man is truly lost: without God, under God's judgement, without hope. But there is hope! In Christ, what has been lost is recovered, and more. The renewal of God's image in man through Christ prompts Paul to call Jesus "the last Adam" and "the second Adam":

> So it is written: 'The first man Adam became a living being'; the last Adam, a life-giving spirit. The spiritual did not come first, but the natural, and after that the spiritual. The first man was of the dust of the earth; the second man is of heaven. As was the earthly man, so are those who are of the earth; and as is the heavenly man, so also are those who are of heaven. And just as we have borne the image of the earthly man, so shall we bear the image of the heavenly man.[792]

The first adam, Adam, gave Adam-likeness to Adam-kind; the second adam, Christ, gives Christ-likeness to Christ's-kind. Man is created with a body. Christ took a body; he became flesh.[793] He was "made in human likeness,"[794] "in the likeness of sinful flesh,"[795] "born of a woman."[796] Christ took our "body-likeness" to redeem us, so that we could be given incorruptible "God-likeness," a God-likeness that was and is perfect in Christ and will be perfected in those who are Christ's.

Not that man becomes divine. Never! Though "man is the son, the likeness, or offspring of God,"[797] man is and remains eternally creature. Through Christ we are gifted a share in his glory,[798] in his inheritance,[799] in his holiness,[800] in the covenant blessings,[801] in uninhibited life itself.[802] We are brought into unblemished fellowship with God himself as his sons and daughters.[803] But we will remain man: perfected man perfectly imaging God.

Perfect likeness of God is found in Jesus, "who is the image of God."[804] That image comes with such perfection in Jesus that the writer to the Hebrews sees in Jesus greater clarity of the revelation of God than all the inspired words of the prophets:

> In the past God spoke to our ancestors through the prophets at many times and in various ways, but in these last days he has spoken to us by his Son, whom he appointed heir of all things, and through whom also he made the universe. The Son is the radiance of God's glory and the exact representation of his being, sustaining

---

792 1 Corinthians 15:45-49
793 John 1:14
794 Philippians 2:7
795 Romans 8:3
796 Galatians 4:4
797 Bavinck *In the Beginning* p186 (citing Genesis 1:26; 9:6; Luke 3:38; Acts 17:28; 1 Corinthians 11:7; and James 3:9)
798 Romans 8:17; 2 Thessalonians 2:14; 1 Peter 5:1
799 Colossians 1:12
800 Hebrews 12:10
801 Romans 11:17
802 Revelation 22
803 2 Corinthians 6:18; Hebrews 2:10; 12:8
804 2 Corinthians 4:4; also Colossians 1:15-20

all things by his powerful word. After he had provided purification for sins, he sat down at the right hand of the Majesty in heaven.[805]

It is not just that Jesus shows what God is like. In his being Jesus is the "exact representation" of the being of God. It is not just that Jesus radiates the glory of God. Jesus "is the radiance of God's glory." It is not just that Jesus does things that image what God does. Jesus does the work of God: what Jesus does is God doing.

In 2 Corinthians 4 Paul describes this likeness, not in terms of physical similarity or behavioural imitation, but in displaying "the knowledge of God's glory." Of course, Jesus does do the works of his Father, but according to Jesus, this indicates not merely image-identity, but divine-identity: "I do the works of my Father … that you may know and understand that the Father is in me, and I in the Father."[806] Jesus does not just bear God's image: he is God.

God's glory is seen in Christ because he has full, personal knowledge of that glory: it is his! Paul takes us right back to the creation: "God, who said, 'Let light shine out of darkness,' made his light shine in our hearts to give us the light of the knowledge of God's glory displayed in the face of Christ."[807] There can be no mistaking Paul's intention that Christ's image-bearing be understood in the context of creation and God's making of man in his own image. It is not just that God's glory is reflected in the face of Christ, but that it is seen in Christ as something belonging to him, something he *knows* in his being, giving us "the light of the knowledge of God's glory." An image in a mirror is but a reflection that does not belong to the mirror; but the image of God in Christ belongs to Christ: "The Son is the image of the invisible God … For God was pleased to have all his fullness dwell in him."[808] The image of God in Christ is seen because God is so intimately known[809] by Jesus as to make God's nature inevitably evident wherever Jesus' nature is evident.

That glorious imaging of God in Christ has always been his. God's image has always belonged to the Son and been evident in him. When Jesus took flesh, the glory seen in him[810] is the glory that always was his. In referring to the image of God in Jesus, Paul's "phraseology is dealing with Christ not so much as the incarnate Saviour as the eternal Son."[811]

Just as the image of God belonging to Jesus is seen in Jesus, the image of God in man belongs to man and is seen in him despite the distortions and corruptions of the fall. Something of the nature of God is still visible in man because that likeness is embedded in man's being. Fallen man's knowing is light-years short of the intimate knowledge the Son had and has of the Father. Yet there *is* a knowledge of God given to each person so that each is "without excuse" for the image-defacing wickedness that suppresses such truth as they know.[812] Even in such a state, "They

---

[805] Hebrews 1:1-3
[806] John 10:37
[807] 2 Corinthians 4:6
[808] Colossians 1:15 &19
[809] The concept of "knowledge" here is not merely knowledge about, but intimate existential knowledge.
[810] John 1:14
[811] Feinberg "The Image of God" p244
[812] Romans 1:18-32

show that the requirements of the law are written on their hearts, their consciences also bearing witness."[813] The knowledge of God and his law is indelibly intrinsic to man as created. An apple rotten to the core may not be desirable, but it still exhibits something of the nature of apples. Man, rotten to the core, and even given over by God to self-selected depravity, is still man; and to be man *is* to image God in some measure. "Even fallen man is man and is not shorn of his humanity."[814]

> This living creature, then, and not some distillation from him, is an expression or transcription of the eternal, incorporeal creator in terms of temporal, bodily, creaturely existence—as one might attempt a transcription of, say, an epic into a sculpture, or a symphony into a sonnet. Likeness in this sense survived the fall, since it is structural. As long as we are human we are, by definition, in the image of God.[815]

Man as created imaged God. Man as fallen, despite the fall, images God. But in what way does man image God, and what is this man, this human, this living creature?

---

[813] Romans 2:15
[814] Feinberg "The Image of God" p245
[815] Kidner *Genesis* p55

11. Genesis Man

The Man of Creation and New Creation: Reading Genesis 1 in the light of Christ

"So it is written: 'The first man Adam became a living being'; the last Adam, a life-giving spirit. The spiritual did not come first, but the natural, and after that the spiritual. The first man was of the dust of the earth; the second man is of heaven. As was the earthly man, so are those who are of the earth; and as is the heavenly man, so also are those who are of heaven. And just as we have borne the image of the earthly man, so shall we bear the image of the heavenly man."

~ 1 Corinthians 15:45-49

So much has been written over the centuries on how man is in God's image that it can come as a surprise to find that the Bible has very little to say about it. A handful of Old Testament verses highlight the fact of man being in God's image; none directly explain what that means. None. Several identify outcomes of that image-bearing, most imply various attributes or behaviours are associated with image-bearing, but none define it. Genesis 1:26,27 is undoubtedly the key passage, but it does no more than unmistakably declare man is – men and women are – in God's image, and that as image-bearer man is given dominion over creation. Genesis 2 makes no mention of man's image-bearing. Misleading reference to it plays a significant role in Genesis 3[816]... but there is nothing in Genesis 4. The opening three verses of Genesis 5 recapitulate Genesis 1:26,27 and add that Adam's son Seth was in Adam's likeness and image. There is silence on the subject in Genesis 6, 7 and 8; then in Genesis 9 the killing of a man is declared a capital crime because man is in God's image. After that ... silence. There is no direct mention of man in God's image for the rest of the Old Testament.[817]

It would be a mistake to think that the absence of explicit definition of what it is to be in God's image means nothing can be learnt about it from these passages. The opposite is true. The obvious inference from repeated reference to man being in God's image is that man is in God's image! That is, man as man (and since the woman is also identified as being in God's image, woman as woman) is in God's image. It is not about particular aspects, certain attributes or selected behaviours: to be human is to be God's image. The absence of any more specific definition simply reinforces that.

In the New Testament a little more light is shed on the concept. It reveals Christ as the true image of God,[818] reinforces that all men are in God's image,[819] and shows how believers are being recreated in God's image with attributes of that image-bearing.[820] Yet even these references do not give a detailed or comprehensive account of what it is to be God's image; except that in taking all these passages together it becomes apparent that for God man images God in man's total being. Man *is* – men and women *are* – in God's image. The image of God is not linked to an assortment of attributes that image God. Nor is man to be seen as having "bits" that image God and "bits" that don't.

Learning About God from the Image of God

Is God like us or are we like him? To say we are in God's image is to say we are like him; but as the Bible is read, this concept can effectively be turned on its head. Much of the language of the Bible is "anthropomorphic." Many

---

[816] Satan's distortion "then you will be like God, knowing good and evil" (v5) sets a context for God's judgement "man has now become like one of us, knowing good and evil" (v22). Satan's distortion ignores the message of chapter 1 that man was already in God's likeness, which implies that knowing good and evil is *not* like God. What is meant by "a knowledge of good and evil" is a question for another time. Depending on that, God's statement, that they are *now* like God, implying they were not like God till that point, could best be considered (a) ironic (eg Calvin) for they are now demonstrably less like God; (b) factual, recognising they have an existential awareness of good and evil that is not good for them (eg Cassuto); or (c) mocking, exposing their false claim to be either independent discerners of good and evil (eg Sailhamer) or independent determiners of good and evil.

[817] "Relevant passages on man as the image of God are Genesis 1:26-27 (the creation account); 5:1, 3 (the transmission of the image from Adam to his posterity); 9:6 (the doctrine of the image relative to homicide); 1 Corinthians 11:7 (discussion of headship in the family); Colossians 3:10 (exhortations to the believer to put on the new man); and James 3:9 (treatment of the proper use of the tongue). Psalm 8 does not contain the words "image of God," but the passage deals in poetic form with the creation of man and the area of his dominion. Cf. also Heb. 2:6-8." [Feinberg "The Image of God" p236] To that list I would add John 1:1-14, 2 Corinthians 4:4, Colossians 1:15-17 and Hebrews 1: 1-4 in that Jesus is the perfect man who perfectly images God.

[818] Hebrews 1:3; 2 Corinthians 4:4; Colossians 1:15

[819] 1 Corinthians 11:7

[820] 2 Corinthians 3:18; Colossians 3:10 See below p267

commentators take that to imply God is accommodating himself to the language and likeness of men. When the text uses the language of human emotions, actions and being to portray God, is not God reduced to being like us? Jewish scholar Yochanan Muffs presents the problem in this way:

> There is a root tension in the nature of YHWH, the God if Israel. On the one hand, He is utterly other than the stuff of the world or its laws. He is the principle of absolute nondependence. Neither magic nor fate controls Him. Destiny is not prior to Him. He is not born, and He does not die. And yet, at the same time, this being of total nondependence is portrayed in the Bible as having qualities that can only be described as human.[821]

The tension Muffs sees arises from reading all biblical text in which God and man have shared qualities as anthropomorphic. Muffs goes so far as to speak of the "humanness of God" asserting that "this anthropomorphic deity is, on the whole, a paragon of human virtue."[822] This inverts the created order, making God the image of man rather than seeing man as the image of God. The qualities Muffs says "can only be described as human" can really only be described as divine. When seen in man those qualities are not so much human, but rather imperfect images of the perfect qualities of God.

When God is said to love, to be angry, to listen, and suchlike he is not adopting human qualities to show what he is like. Rather, they are the true qualities of God seen imperfectly and incompletely in man, his image. So, for example, God and man both love. Both love in expression of their nature: one loves in unchanging, eternal nature, and the other in created, imaging nature. One loves in perfection and completeness, the other imperfectly and incompletely. One *is* love,[823] so love is a natural expression of his being: he loves like God loves for he is God. The other loves because he is the image of the One who loves: he loves like God loves for he is God's image (albeit as the image is less than the imaged, man's love is less than God's).

True, the Bible is full of anthropomorphic language, such as: "Give ear, Lord, and hear; open your eyes, Lord, and see."[824] As God does not have a body like us, reference to ears and eyes is clearly anthropomorphic. It is anthropomorphic in that God does not use an ear to turn the sound-waves generated in spoken prayer into electrical impulse for mental processing – but he does listen. He does comprehend our prayer and respond … without ears! Anyone who has raised children knows the difference between hearing and listening: how often I have said to my children when they were young, "I know you can hear me, so listen!" In this sense listening means comprehending and responding to what has been said. If God does not listen, then prayer is pointless. So likening God to man as if God has ears is anthropomorphism, but it is no anthropomorphism to speak of God listening. Rather, when men truly listen they imitate or image God who listens.

An approach to the Bible that sees all qualities shared by God and man as anthropomorphic shapes a concept of God as man-like. In contrast, the Bible sees qualities shared by God and man as God revealing man as (in some senses) God-

---

[821] Yochanan Muffs *The Personhood of God* Jewish Lights Publishing, Woodstock, 2005 p47

[822] Muffs *Personhood of God* p21

[823] 1 John 4:8,16

[824] 2 Kings 16:19

like. God is revealing himself as he is through the God-like qualities which he has imprinted on man in his image. Man has such qualities not because he is man (as if God is like man) but as God's image (in that man is like God). Rather than lowering God to human level, the imaging of God in man raises humanity to heights of dignity in which he is found "just a little lower than the angels."[825]

So to truly grasp what it is to be in God's image, we must look at God rather than man. If man's imaging of God was primarily about revealing who God is, then we would look at man to know God. But man's imaging of God is primarily about representing God and ruling for God. By this we are pointed by man to God from whom we learn about God. And as we know God better, we know better how to be faithful in our imaging, filling the earth and ruling it as his representatives. The best way then to learn what the image of God is in man is not to look at man, much less "to contrast man with animals, as has often been done, and then to find the divine image to consist in those qualities, abilities, and gifts that man has in distinction from the animals."[826] To learn what it is to image God, we must look at God.

Turning to the Word of God, the Bible, by which God reveals himself to man, gives a much clearer view of God than turning to man! Of course, there is another aspect of God's revelation of himself – creation (or "natural revelation"), but that fails. It does not fail in lack of clarity for "For since the creation of the world God's invisible qualities—his eternal power and divine nature—have been clearly seen, being understood from what has been made, so that people are without excuse."[827] It fails because fallen man suppresses that truth by outright wickedness.[828]

Yet God makes himself known with even greater clarity than by his spoken and written word, and he does so in a perfect image of himself: "he has spoken to us by his Son, whom he appointed heir of all things, and through whom also he made the universe. The Son is the radiance of God's glory and the exact representation of his being, sustaining all things by his powerful word."[829]

> We must learn to know what the image of God is by looking at Jesus Christ. What must therefore be at the centre of the image of God is not characteristics like the ability to reason or the ability to make decisions (important as such abilities may be for the proper functioning of the image of God), but rather that which is central in the life of Christ.[830]

The First Adam vandalised the image of God vested in him and populated the earth with mutant gargoyles who at the same time resemble and distort the glory of God in which they were shaped. The Second Adam exactly imaged God in whom he has his being, with a glorious radiance enabling mortals to "see his glory, the glory of the one and only Son, who came from the Father, full of grace and truth."[831]

---

[825] Psalm 8:5
[826] Anthony A. Hoekema *Created in God's Image* Eerdmans, Grand Rapids, 1986, p22
[827] Romans 1:20
[828] Romans 1:19
[829] Hebrews 1:1-3
[830] Hoekema p22
[831] John 1:14

Being Man

That Son, the Lord Jesus, did not merely cloth himself in a body to become man. He, who was and is pure Spirit *became* flesh.[832] "Being in very nature God … [was] made in human likeness … in appearance as a man." Flesh and spirit united makes him man.

There are things about being human that can be identified. Without those attributes, we would not be human. Yet those attributes – even if we could compile a comprehensive list – do not exhaust what it is to be human. What we are, in the totality of our being, is human. In the same way, what we are, in the totality of our being, is God's images. "*Everything we are* is like God. We *are* the image of God. … Human nature itself is the image of God. … The image of God embraces everything that is human."[833]

What is it that is the image of God? What is man? Man is, most fundamentally, man. We instinctively recognise man as distinct, although that distinction is confused when biology aligns man too closely to animals, when new-age and old-age pantheism conspire to make man one with everything, and when myths ancient and modern attribute some form of divinity to man. But the Bible is clear: man is not an animal, a plant, a bird, a fish, an earth, moon, sun or star. Man is not God. Nor is man of the substance of angels.[834] By reporting the specific, distinctive, particular creation of man by God, the Bible makes it clear that man is in a category of existence that uniquely belongs to being man. Man is man.

Creature

Man is a creature. To be sure, he is a creature who, unlike other creatures, is in the image of God. But nonetheless it is as a created being he is his Creator's image. The text that reveals God's declaration, "Let us make man …" also reveals to man that God makes man's relationship as creature to God the Creator of more importance than any consideration of the makeup of man. "The Scriptures are not primarily interested in the constituent 'parts' of man or in his psychological structure, but in the relationship in which he stands."[835] Whatever constitutes man, he is there at the will of and for the glory of his Creator.

> Your true identity is who God says you are. You will never discover who you are by looking inside yourself or listening to what others say. The Lord gets the first word because he made you. He gets the daily word because you live before his face. He gets the last word because he will administer your final "comprehensive life review."[836]

We are who and what God has made us to be. We can never know who we are or be at peace with what we are until we accept we are made. Contemporary man

---

[832] John 1:1,14

[833] John Frame "Men and Women in the Image of God" in Piper & Grudem *Recovering Biblical Manhood and Womanhood* Crossway Illinois, 1991 pp225, 231 [His italics]

[834] Psalm 8:5

[835] Hoekema *Created in God's Image* p204

[836] David Powlison *Brother, Where is Your Identity?* http://www.thegospelcoalition.org/article/brother-where-is-your-identity November 2015

is besotted with a search for identity; yet searching for our identity is searching for the wrong thing in the wrong place. We cannot know who we are until we know God. In the ultimate act of rebellion, the modern search for identify has become the creation of identity. The fashionable trend to define gender according to personal choice is not only a denial of creation reality, it is a denial of the Creator. If you are what you want to be, you are your own maker and there is no God.

But we *are* created, and there is a Creator. To know who we are we need to go to our Creator. God has made us what he wants us to be, and along with all the individuality and difference, one core attribute is shared by us all: we are in God's image. He defines us, and he defines us in reference to himself as Creator, Lord, Life-giver and Judge. More than that, in Christ he *redefines* us so that we are rescued from being creatures at enmity with our Creator to being creatures in harmony with our Creator: those who are in Christ "are God's handiwork, created in Christ Jesus to do good works, which God prepared in advance for us to do."[837] "True humanity is found not by trying to mold myself into who I perceive myself to be; rather, true humanity is found as I daily die to my own way of being and conform myself, in the Spirit's power, to the image of Christ who shows me what true humanity really is."[838]

Person

We almost instinctively recognise people as people, persons who have personhood. Cultural, religious and faddish ambiguities that surround the concept of personhood are multiple: the personhood of some in various cultures (such as those practising slavery or genocide) may be diminished or even extinguished, but only so as to enhance the personhood of those who dominate; sentimental animism attributes personhood to pets because we interpret their behaviour as loving, but they are rarely accorded equal dignity with ourselves or our children (and when they are, such recognition is seen by most as grounds for mockery if not assessed as almost indecent eccentricity); and personal dignity is faddishly attributed to whales because they share human traits,[839] but recognition of those common traits is inevitably given by elevating whales to a personal status rather than identifying people as animals.

The example of whales is particularly telling, for the definitions of personhood that embrace whales are creation-bound and must therefore fail. Such definitions fail at the rational level for all such definitions hang on traits to be found in some measure in non-persons. William Lane Craig identifies three broad categories by which personhood is defined: "consciousness, intentionality, or capacity for inter-

---

[837] Ephesians 2:10

[838] Wesley Hill *A New Way of Being Human* https://spiritualfriendship.org/2016/09/21/a-new-way-of-being-human/#more-6946 September 2016

[839] cf http://uk.whales.org/ June 2016 "Whales and dolphins share traits once believed to be unique to humans: self-awareness, abstract thought, the ability to solve problems by planning ahead, understanding such linguistically sophisticated concepts as syntax, and the formation of cultural communities (Herman, 1984; Norris et al., 1991; Reiss & Marino, 2001)." Thomas I. White, PhD *Whales, Dolphins and Ethics: A Primer*

personal relations,"[840] each of which can be attributed to whales and many other animals. Such definitions also fail at the biblical level, for they frame the issue of personhood without reference to God. The Creator has revealed himself as having personhood. By virtue of his revealing himself to man, it is "established that God is a person, a conscious and free-purposing being, not shut in by the narrow confines of this universe but highly exalted above nature."[841]

The classical Trinitarian formula sums this up: "God is three Persons in one." Here is the key to what it is to be a person: "The Christian understanding of personhood flows from the Christian doctrine of the Three Persons who are God."[842] Man is person because God is Person, and for all the personal traits that might be evidenced in some degree in animals, man alone – and not animals – is made in the image of this Personal God.

In grasping what it is to be a person, the danger is of trying to do so with reference to man alone. We then grapple with the concept of personhood in God by imposing man-referenced criteria on God. It is an error to try to

> grasp how God can be *three* persons, based on what we know of human personhood. … The danger is of importing modern concepts of personhood into our thinking on the Trinity. … We need to approach the matter from the other end. Personhood is to be understood (insofar as we can ever understand it) in terms of the way God is three. He is an eternal communion of three *hypostases* in undivided union. He creates human persons.[843]

When we turn to Genesis 1, one trait of personhood stands out through constant repetition: God is good. God chooses good, does good, bestows good, and commands good. Everything God determines to do in Genesis 1 is good; everything he does in Genesis 1 is declared to be good; in creating man male and female he bestows good on the man he has made because it was "not good that he should be alone;" and he commands man to rule and populate the earth in the image of God's goodness.

As Adam's personhood is tested through the unfolding events of Genesis 3, interpersonal relations are indeed at play, but he is not ultimately judged for failure there; intentionality also plays a part, but he is not judged for his intentions but for his disobedient action; and there can be no doubt that intense self-consciousness is evident, but that does not become an issue of judgement either. As God confronts the newly sinful Adam, he does not ask, "How has your relationship with Eve changed?" Nor does he ask, "What did you intend?" Adam's awareness of his nakedness is not condemned by God, but is a cause for probing deeper: "Who told you?" immediately becomes, "Have you done what I told you not to do?"[844] Adam is judged because he has done wrong.

---

[840] William Lane Craig *Divine Timelessness and Personhood* http://www.lewissociety.org/divine.php June 2016

[841] Herman Bavinck *The Doctrine of God* The Banner of Truth Trust, Edinburgh, 1977 (1951) p15

[842] Peter Toon *Our Triune God: A Biblical Portrayal of the Trinity* Bridge-Point, Wheaton, 1996 p 241 cited by Robert Letham *The Holy Trinity* P&R Phillipsburg, 2004, p474

[843] Letham *The Holy Trinity* pp461f (citing Thomas F Torrance *The Christian Doctrine of God: One Being, Three Persons* T&T Clark, Edinburgh, 1996, pp159f) [italics and parentheses are his].

[844] cf Genesis 3:11

While it is true that "Man's whole personality was to be a manifestation and revelation on a finite scale of the personality of God,"[845] I would suggest that it is God's moral perfection that is the personal trait that comes to the fore in Genesis 1, and it is the calling to image God's goodness and the accountability that goes with that calling that marks man out as person. To be a person is to be morally directed and morally accountable; and the reference point for both is the unchanging moral perfection of God.

Living

Man is living. He is a *living* person. He is the image of the *living God.* Unlike the pagan idols that are lifeless,[846] God lives and his image lives. In vain men call to the idols of wood to come to life and to the idols of stone to wake up: they do not live, there is no breath in them.[847] In contrast to this God reveals himself throughout the Old and New Testaments as the living God: "The Lord is the true God; he is the living God, the eternal king."[848] "We are the temple of the living God. As God has said: 'I will live with them and walk among them, and I will be their God, and they will be my people.'"[849] "We have put our hope in the living God."[850] "He is the living God and he endures forever; his kingdom will not be destroyed, his dominion will never end."[851] As such he speaks,[852] rescues his people,[853] and is the desired comforter and companion of those who live.[854] The living God sees and hears those who mock him[855] and those who call on him in faith, coming to *live* in the midst of believers and giving them the name, "Children of the living God."[856] So man is created *living*, imaging and relating to the living God as only living people could.

Man lives because God "breathed into his nostrils the breath of life."[857] This unexpected imagery draws attention to simple but basic facts about man in God's image, and also becomes the excuse for a plethora of imaginative interpretations. It is not that God inserts a soul into man up his nostrils! Such a concept could be reinforced by a misreading of older translations that render the end of Genesis 2:7,

---

845 Cornelius Van Til *In Defense of the Faith Volume 3: Christian Theistic Ethics* P & R Phillipsburg, (undated) p41
846 Psalm 135:15-18
847 Habakkuk 2:18-19
848 Jeremiah 10:10
849 2 Corinthians 6:16
850 1 Timothy 4:10
851 Daniel 6:26
852 Deuteronomy 5:26
853 Joshua 3:10; Daniel 6:20
854 Psalm 84:2
855 Galatians 6:7
856 Hosea 1:10
857 Genesis 2:7

"and man became a living soul."[858] But "soul" here is not a reference to the inner being of man but to his whole being.[859]

Nowhere in the Genesis account is man pictured as anything but a unity. Body and soul are not spoken of as parts that make up the whole: in fact, neither body nor soul get specific reference. It is man in unity who is made, man in unity who lives, man in unity who communes with God, man in unity who is called to image God and man in unity who is given dominion. Only with the judgemental introduction of death are body and soul considered as separate or separable entities.

The emphasis of the text is that man became *living* as opposed to the non-living nature of the dust from which he was formed. With the breath of life man became a *living* being. The "breath of life" is the same breath of life – the same expression denoting the same thing – by which God had earlier identified the birds and land animals as living.[860] The breath of life is not here the characteristic of man that distinguishes him from animals: it is something he shares with animals. By stressing, as the text does, that this breath of life entered man "through his nostrils" the writer could not make it more clear that it is physical breath and physical life that is being spoken of, not some metaphor for a spiritual infusion or a spiritual livingness.

The corollary to this is that when man dies at the fall, he dies physically. Physical death is not immediately realised albeit it is immediately assured. In light of the unrealised physical death, many attempt to limit the immediate consequence of the fall to "spiritual death." Both occur. Nor should "spiritual death" be defined as "separation from God" as is common, for while the relationship with God changes, God remains – he is present, he communes with Adam, he effects his judgement personally, he protects and guides man, he sustains him, and he covenants with him. For the spiritually alive, God is close companion; for the spiritually dead, God is imminent judge.

When Paul speaks of the lost being dead in their transgressions and sins, he identifies what that spiritual death involves. It is not separation from God but following "the ways of this world and of the ruler of the kingdom of the air … gratifying the cravings of our flesh and following its desires and thoughts."[861] Collins is helpful in describing spiritual death as "estrangement from a life-giving relationship with God," by which he alludes to a covenantal life-giving relationship rather than one in which God provides physical life.[862] Estrangement from a life-giving relationship with God is replaced by a death-giving relationship with God. When Adam fell he died physically – disease, decay, and the unrealised certainty of death made him a "dead man walking" knowing he would die;[863] he also died

[858] KJV; similarly the Geneva Bible and numerous translations since.

[859] "As נפש חיה,ψυχὴ ζῶσα , does not refer to the soul merely, but to the whole man as an animated being, so נשׁמה does not denote the spirit of man as distinguished from body and soul." Keil and Delitzsch *OT Commentary* http://www.studylight.org/commentaries/kdo/view.cgi?bk=0&ch=2 1866 (Edinburgh, T & T Clark 1885)

[860] Genesis 1:30; see also Genesis 6:17; 7:15; 7:22

[861] Ephesians 2:1-3

[862] Collins *Genesis 1-4* Kindle location 1312 (contrasting it with Proverbs 12:28)

[863] Ecclesiastes 9:5 with 3:18,19 & 12:13,14

spiritually – he could no longer desire or do good. He was estranged from God and under his judgement even as he remained dependent upon him.

Reading the text in this way is not to deny that man has a soul that distinguishes him from animals. It is rather to see that the text is making a very big issue of man being living. Why?

Genesis is a text that can undoubtedly stand on its own – but it is also a text written to a people consciously and dramatically separated from surrounding pagan cultures from which they have just been "exited." Genesis is, to a significant degree, a polemic against the dead pagan gods of those cultures, and a call to Israel to follow the only true, living God. So when God creates man in his image, he creates a *living* image instead of a *dead* idol.

This is beautifully reinforced in Genesis 3:20: "Adam named his wife Eve, because she would become the mother of all the living." Clearly Eve is not the mother of the animals who also have the breath of life in them. To be living in the sense of Genesis 3:20 is to be living as Adam was made a living being; it is to be a son or daughter of Eve. The "livingness" of people is different from the "livingness" of animals. The unique "livingness" of people is theirs because they, coming from the uniquely living Eve, are living images of the living God. But the text goes beyond the mechanics of passing on life. "*Eve* sounds like the Hebrew for *life-giver* and resembles the word for *living*."[864] Eve is, as are women after her, dignified with a unique role in imaging God. She is the giver of life. As God gives life, Eve in God's image gives life.

Typically, pagan idols were said to be functional when they became infused with or indwelt by the god or some eminence of the god. In some cultures specific rituals would transform the idol into the god – or at least into a vivified conduit to the god.[865] Yet despite the rituals, as already noted, the idols do not live. They are dead.[866]

---

[864] ESV footnote to Genesis 3:20

[865] cf Joshua Matson "Idol Remains: Remnants of the Opening of the Mouth Ritual in the Hebrew Bible" in *Studia Antiqua: A Student Journal for the Study of the Ancient World* 12:1 (2013), 33-50

[866] Our commitment to the idea of rational man can obscure the reality of beliefs that hold rationally inconsistent ideas to be simultaneously true. Pagan pantheism (eg my own Māori heritage) can hold both that the image is in reality the god (or in the case of Māori belief, more likely the deified ancestor) while at the same time holding true the scientific view that the image is merely wood or stone worked by craftsmen. If this is missed it becomes necessary to affirm that pagans are not stupid: eg "It seems so stupid to carve an idol from wood or stone or make one from clay and then worship it. But ancient people did not believe their gods were actually images of stone or wood." (Michael Heiser *The Unseen Realm* Lexham Press, Bellingham, 2015, Kindle location 594). Perhaps … or perhaps not! Those ancient people, like many today, held a world-view not bound by Heiser's rationality: it is a world-view that allows for a man-made object and a god to share identity. They would find Heiser's inability to think in such terms as just as stupid as Heiser's implication of stupidity to thinking that does not fit his rationality. But the biblical writers did indeed regard the idols as the "gods": in 1 Samuel 5 when Dagon falls it is not described as the image of Dagon falling, but Dagon himself. This is entirely consistent with the biblical view of such idols: not only are they dead, but they are also not indwelt by gods or infused with god-stuff because there are no gods! The image of Dagon does not represent Dagon, for there is no Dagon apart from the idol to be represented. The image *is* Dagon, a lifeless fall-on-your-face lump of carved stone.

Genesis presents a bold contrast to this. It is neither the indwelling of God nor the infusion of some divine part or product – much less the insertion of a soul up man's nostrils – that causes man to live: it is air up man's nostrils. True, there is spiritual life too in man. But the pagan idols were said to have spirituality in some form or other. Genesis declares that the living images of the living God live; not so the dead images of the dead[867] gods.

To be sure, it is God who breathes the breath of life into the man's nostrils. Life is given by God, and given in a particularly personal way. There is nothing mechanical or inevitable about this: God takes the man he has made, and with face-to-face intimacy the living God gives life to the man who now becomes the living image of the living God. But it is nonetheless air that he breathes that identifies the first man as living.

Man/mankind becomes a living being by this one-off act at man's creation. By this act man is declared to be living. There is nothing here to suggest that each person becomes living when at birth they begin to breathe. Rather, the new-born breathe because they live. In those tragedies when a new-born does not take a breath despite heart, muscles, reactions and brain functioning, they are rightly deemed to have died after birth. Man is from the creation of Adam a living being. Babies in the womb are certainly living, and are not considered dead because they do not breathe. But more importantly, they are living because they are man/mankind: they are not man because they breathe but they breathe at birth because they are man.[868]

Body and Soul

This is not to imply that God does not also make man a spiritual living being. Man became a living being in two senses: by giving man breath, he became a physically living body rather than dead one; by (congruently) giving man a soul, he became a spiritually living person. He would not be man without a body, and he would not be man without a soul.[869] In Genesis 2, Adam's declaration of Eve as "bone of my bones and flesh of my flesh"[870] unmistakably affirms both have a body, though as we saw above their shared identity embraces more than having bodies. The very fact that at creation the creation of man is complete makes certain that anything subsequently revealed about who man is as man, is applicable from the moment of his creation. It is worth repeating that the emphasis of Genesis 1 is on man comprehensively – and not in various parts or attributes – as the image of God. That there is no mention in Genesis 1 of God giving man a soul simply means there is no redundancy: to say he made man is to say he made man, body and soul.

It is to the immaterial soul or spirit that the Bible attributes the affections, will and spiritual communion.[871] It is also the seat of sin, in stark contrast to the Greeks

---

[867] ie non-existent gods.

[868] There are some who, in the contemporary madness that sees thousands of unborn children poisoned, crushed, torn limb from limb, or chemically burnt to death *in utero* justify their wickedness by appealing to a concept of living that depends on breathing. Thus they argue that until a child breathes on its own it is not living, missing (or avoiding) a most basic aspect of personhood: people breathe because they are people; they are not people because they breathe. cf the next section below.

[869] Ecclesiastes 12:7; Matthew 10:28

[870] Genesis 2:23

[871] eg Psalm 42:1,2

and the ascetics who attribute sin to the body, or moderns who blame nurture and/or the environment. Both Old and New Testaments attribute such an inner being to man. Various words are used for this soulishness, mostly translated *soul* or *spirit* or *heart*. Sometimes, too, any of those words can stand for the whole man, which is hardly surprising given that it is as God breathed into man that he became a living image of his Creator. Man may have an animal-like body, but when soul is united with body, you have not an animal, but man; not something that merely points in glory to God, but God's image; not something merely material but spiritual.

Man, body *and* soul (rather than body *with* soul) became God's living image bearer. That is to say, man does not consist of a body that houses the real spiritual person as the Greeks argued, with their equally erroneous antithesis between body and soul. They wrongly viewed man as parts in tension: the visible, material, evil, body in conflict with the invisible, spiritual, good soul or spirit. God's picture is radically different: the material world is not evil, but a creation God describes as "very good."[872] That "very good" creation expressly includes man, body and soul.

Some see the nature of man as body and soul in some way imaging the Trinity. While having bi-partite man said to represent tri-partite God is, at the very least, conceptually awkward, there is no way in which either spirit or body is wholly man as each of the Trinity is wholly God.[873] It is better to see man as like God in his being spirit; unlike God in being body; but imaging God in the person who is body and spirit.

The unity of man as body and soul explains why the resurrection is an essential part of the redemption by which Christ will bring the promised perfection to believers. The souls in heaven await the redemption of their bodies, which brings to completion the promised adoption to sonship.[874] Why not just give those souls new bodies? Why must they await the resurrection of their decayed dust? Because men are not souls who can cast off one body and slip into another. The conceived and birthed body and soul is the person, and though death separates body and soul, restoration comes only with the reuniting of *that* body and *that* soul. Even Christ was raised with the body with which he was conceived, born and died.[875]

---

[872] Genesis 1:31

[873] Genesis 1 & 2 offer a view of man as bodily and soulish: that is, bipartite. Any concept of tripartite man must be found elsewhere. Whether or not that concept can be found in other biblical texts (something I remain unconvinced of – see Matthew 10:28 for example), it does not appear to bear greatly on understanding the imaging of God in man in Genesis 1. If for example it is argued that man as body, soul and spirit represented God as Father Son and Spirit, one is still left with the fact that the complete unity of the Godhead contrasts with the incomplete unity of fallen man (in which some absence or disfigurement of spirit is proposed), and in the incomplete unity of man and woman. The text does not link the existence of body and soul (or body, soul and spirit) to man's being in God's image. Apart from the fact that man is created "living" in reflection of God who is life, there appears nothing in the text to consider the constituent parts of man (if man can be spoken of as having constituent parts) as relating to being in God's image. Here man is body and soul, and if he is to be regarded as body, soul and spirit, that is a discussion for another time, another place, and other texts.

[874] Romans 8:23

[875] John 20:17, 20, 27 To be raised bodily, Christ became bodily. He did more than clothe himself in flesh: he became flesh (John 1:14).

To be sure, the risen body is transformed in some way. Christ in his risen body appeared in a room of locked doors, [876] and "flesh and blood cannot inherit the kingdom of God."[877] So "the dead will be raised imperishable, and we will be changed. For the perishable must clothe itself with the imperishable, and the mortal with immortality."[878] Yet it is the dead bodies that are raised and transformed, not some substitute or replacement. Immortality replaced mortality in the body of the risen Saviour, but the nail marks and spear slash were still visible in the raised but not-yet glorified body. The perishable will clothe itself with the imperishable: the body that could die, the body that bore the stamp of Adam, will be raised the body that cannot die, the body that bears the stamp of Christ.

> Man must be understood as a unitary being. He has a physical side and a mental or spiritual side, but we must not separate the two. The human person must be understood as an embodied soul or a "besouled" body.[879] He or she must be seen in his or her totality, not as a composite of different "parts." This is the clear teaching of both Old and New Testaments.[880]

> The Bible makes man a unity: acting, thinking and feeling with his whole being. This living creature, then, and not some distillation from him, is an expression or transcription of the eternal, incorporeal creator in terms of temporal, bodily, creaturely existence.[881]

That unity extends to every act of man as well as to his being: "Every act of man is seen as an act of the whole man. It is not the soul but man that sins; it is not the body but man that dies; it is not merely the soul, but man, body and soul, that is redeemed in Christ."[882]

Male and Female in Imaging God

"Male and female he created them."[883] As noted earlier, being male and female is not incidental to God's creation.[884] Genesis lays stress on the fact that each images God, yet each is distinct. The gifting of the woman to the man as his good helper, the commission to reproduce and fill the earth, and Adam's moving identification of himself with Eve inescapably images the union of the Trinity. Some go so far as to assert that this union, this relationship, is the essence of man's imaging God.

But what is the nature of the "relationship" that is said to be found here? It can hardly be that man reflects the Trinitarian formula of "One in Three and Three in One," for although man is two, the two are not truly one in the way God is one. In marriage husband and wife remain substantially different even though they become one flesh – which is about as close as the image can come to what is imaged.

---

[876] John 20:19
[877] 1 Corinthians 15:50
[878] 1 Corinthians 15:52,53
[879] Here Hoekema references Barth, *Church Dogmatics*, III/2, p 350
[880] Hoekema *Cràted n God's Image* p216
[881] Kidner *Genesis* p55
[882] Louis Berkhof *Systematic Theology* Banner of Truth, London, 1958 (1941) p192
[883] Genesis 1:27
[884] See p220.

Sailhamer, following Barth, argues "the image and likeness of the being created by God signifies existence in confrontation."

It is doubtful Barth intended anything as aggressive as "confrontation" generally implies in present usage, but rather he was speaking of the Trinitarian face-to-faceness that is so dramatically portrayed in John 1:

> In the beginning was the Word, and the Word was with God, and the Word was God. He was with God in the beginning. Through him all things were made; without him nothing was made that has been made. In him was life, and that life was the light of all mankind. The light shines in the darkness, and the darkness has not overcome it.[885]

Mere confrontation does not do sufficient justice to the concept of God "with" God. Created man does not exist merely as male and female in confrontation (however benign), but as man "with" woman as husband and wife: "That is why a man leaves his mother and father and is united to his wife." I will discuss the place of singleness shortly, but for now the unmistakable prototype for man is marriage. The primary characteristic of the marriage relationship is not order, morality, or function, but loving unity, something that images the primary relationship of God with himself.

Among all the attributes of God, there is one his use of plural pronouns in Genesis 1 points to above all others, just as man in unblemished created plurality images that same attribute: love. Just as in the Trinity God loves and is loved, so man is to love and be loved, and God is to be loved by man he loves. And to make all this possible, that eternal love within the Trinity was turned toward us: "God so loved the world, that he gave his one and only Son,"[886] the Son of his love. Who cannot therefore echo John's outburst of praise, "See what great love the Father has lavished on us!"?[887]

Use of plural divine pronouns reveals plurality in the Godhead. As Scripture unfolds, we see that God's own personal relationship with himself within the Trinity is, above all, one of love, for "God is love." Man is created as man and woman to image in their own relationship of love the God who is love. That loving relationship between man and woman, imaging Trinitarian love and unity, is not primarily sexual. Although sexual union between husband and wife expresses and nurtures intimacy and unity, godly love is a necessary condition for godly sex, not its outcome. In fact, the relationship between husband and wife is more than a loving relationship. It is a "oneness" that Genesis declares to be such as to make of the two "one flesh".[888] It is not just in ontological commonality and difference that man images God: the becoming one flesh involves a created communion of complementarity that images the communion and complementarity of the Trinity. Collins, in reference to 1 Corinthians 6:16,17, points out that being joined in one flesh also involves holding fast to one another in loyalty and faithfulness.[889] That too images the loyalty and faithfulness of the Trinity.

---

[885] John 1:1-5
[886] John 3:16
[887] 1 John 3:1
[888] Genesis 2:42
[889] Collins *Genesis 1-4* Kindle location 1633

Male and Female in Union

As already noted, to be one flesh involves a communion of common interests and pursuits. That is what it means to be "united." Yet there is more than this in being "one flesh." By reference to the oneness of the "flesh," the text emphasises that there is a bodily aspect of the marriage companionship. If the reality of living, labouring and loving in intimate physical closeness was not a necessary element of marriage, it would have been sufficient for God to have declared simply that they become united as one. But the text stresses that they become united as one flesh.

While being "one flesh" means more than sexual union, it can never mean less. A man and a woman in marriage have more in common than their interests, pursuits and covenant commitment: they have a oneness in body. Of course that includes sex, and the very nature of sex is that it joins two bodies in one. That is one reason sex outside of marriage is so evil: sexual union with a prostitute, declares Paul, is making of two one body. But it also includes the intimacy of companionship expressed in confronting (in the sense of replicating the face-to-face confrontation of the Father and Son), sharing, caring, touching, being together, and in doing things together. A couple's sexual union may not – should not – be observed, but their physical unity as much as their unity of interests and pursuits ought to be observable. A couple's most intimate unity ought to be hidden, but their oneness of flesh should be patently obvious. It is a real, physical unity that no man should separate.

Gender in a Fallen Image

The relationship between men and women that God unfolds from Genesis 2 onwards could be taken, wrongly, to assume that women are not image bearers of God as men are. Before any discussion of the relationship between men and women takes place therefore, God makes this clear: both men and women are equally and truly in God's image, and the relationship of men and women to God and to each other has its foundation in this.

Such a reading is underscored by the way that, at this point in the narrative, "male and female" is specified. Animate life in its various kinds is clearly given male and female form and sexual reproductive function by God. It cannot be without significance that while the creation of all animate life involves the creation of male and female in each kind, it is only in the creation of man that we are give specific reference to gender. Gender is noted both in the intention to create and in the creation that occurs. In this way attention is being drawn to something apart from either male and female form or sexual reproductive function. The most distinctive aspect of the creation of mankind is his image-bearing: so as God declares man will be made and has been made in his image, he is saying that both men and women will be and are his image-bearers.

> To define humanity as bisexual is to make each partner the complement of the other, and to anticipate the New Testament doctrine of the sexes' spiritual equality ('all one', Gal. 3:28; 'heirs together', 1 Pet. 3:7b; see also Mark 12:25). This is

reaffirmed in Genesis 2:18–25, together with their temporal inequality (cf. 1 Pet. 3:5–7a; 1 Cor. 11:7–12; 1 Tim. 2:12, 13), and again in 5:1, 2.[890]

By nature, man is in the image of God; hence mankind is in the image of God. By nature, man and woman were created in the image of God; hence men and women are in the image of God. By nature, man and woman were different; hence by nature men and women are different. Men and women both image God, yet "Male and female have unique, non-interchangeable glories."[891]

This may explain the intensity of the contemporary gender revolution: if meaningful gender distinctives can be obliterated, a primary imaging of God is obliterated, and man is one step closer to obliterating the consciousness of God in a vain attempt to obliterate God himself. Denying created gender, mutilating bodies to express that denial in self-delusion, the likes of cross-dressing, and interchanging sexual roles are just more hiding from reality behind fig leaves!

Sexual Distinction without Sex

The Bible entertains not even a hint of sexual differentiation within the Godhead, much less any form of sexual activity as is portrayed of the gods in pagan myths. So while differentiation is of the essence of the Godhead (the Father, the Son and the Spirit are differentiated even as they are one God), and therefore differentiation between men and women is consistent with our bearing God's image, sexual function – albeit the significant created thing that it is – is not of the essence of man or of imaging God. Men and women image God, are different, and can love, without sex. They are sexually differentiated in being and function that can be evidenced and expressed without sex.

Yet the anatomical differences and complementarity of men and women are not without significance. Within marriage the differentiation of being and function between men and women also finds expression in God-given and God-honouring sexual union. The unmarried have distinct sexual being and function that does not entail sexual union, but for the married, sexual union is a part of the creation God declared "good."[892] It is so good that at creation, the man and the woman were unashamed in their nakedness – that is, the exposure of their sexual organs and

---

[890] Kidner *Genesis* p56

[891] Keller *The Bible and Same Sex Relationships: A Review Article* Redeemer Presbyterian Church, June 2015
http://www.redeemer.com/redeemer-report/article/the_bible_and_same_sex_relationships_a_review_article Matthew Vines makes a fundamental error in claiming that, "It is not enough to say that 'male and female have unique, non-interchangeable glories.' In order to make a persuasive argument from Scripture, Keller—and anyone else taking this approach—must define specifically what those 'unique, non-interchangeable glories' are." [http://www.matthewvines.com/a-response-to-tim-kellers-review/ June 2015]. No. It is enough to demonstrate that the Bible confirms such a unique non-interchangeable glory. God makes woman as a suitable complement to man, and thereby specifically rejects man as suitable for man, with specific reference to a "goodness" or "suitableness" for fulfilling God's mandate for man (see below). That establishes Keller's point. We might like to explain those unique glories – we may even be able to – but the fact of the uniqueness is made known by God and is therefore indisputable whether or not we can describe it or quantify it.

[892] Genesis 1:23

sexual activity did not shame them – not because they were insensitive to their shame but because there was nothing to be ashamed of.[893] They were created to

> consummate and deepen their unity and companionship in their sexual relation – after all, the most obvious way in which a woman and man correspond to one another is in their complementary sexual anatomy. The biblical picture endorses sexual enjoyment within the marriage commitment as a good part of a good creation.[894]

A Good Helper

Even so, God declared that it was "not good for man to be alone."[895] As we have seen, to be "good" in the context of creation is to be suited to God's purpose, fitted to glorify God. For man to be suited to his created calling, he needed another. Adam's situation was not one that could merely be made better by woman: he needed her, and without her he was not yet "good." That does not mean he was morally less than good, but that without woman he was not as fitted for God's purposes as God planned.

This is not Adam doing "ok but would be more comfortable if he had a companion." Nor is this "it's ok for man to be alone but *better* he has a companion." Rather, it is "man *cannot* fulfil his calling without a companion any more than the earth could fulfil its calling without light. .... Hence the companion is called a 'helper'".

The creation of woman for man is presented as filling of man's need for a helper suited to his calling.[896] Despite the goodness and necessity of sex (for the mandate to fill the world cannot be fulfilled without sex) sex is not the reason for the creation of woman. For the creation of man to be completely good, God saw that man needed a companion helper united with him as one. Clearly this is not a surprise observation by God: it was always his intention and considering the mandate to fill the world could not have been otherwise. But by saying "God saw" the writer is affirming that just as God considered and affirmed what he had created fulfilled his good purposes when he "saw" everything as good, so he affirms that having made man, his work of creating is not yet done.

A companion is needed, but companionship is not the issue; having help to fulfil God's calling is. Every step of creation so far has been judged "good" by God, but created man on his own is not good! The goodness of each progression in creation has been good in that it is preparing a place for man; but having man in a good creation alone will not fulfil his calling to be and to serve to the glory of God. Two things are need in the companion he is to be united to:

1. The companion Adam needs must be a "helper"
2. The helper needs to be "suitable"

---

[893] Genesis 2:25
[894] Collins *Genesis 1- 4* Kindle location 1620
[895] Genesis 2:18
[896] Genesis 2:20

Adam needs someone[897] who can help him fulfil his calling to image God in creation. She will join him and be with him to help him to do what he is called to do. In the context of contemporary social values, there is sometimes comfort found in fudging the distinction between helper and helped. For example, it is not unusual to hear Ephesians 5:21-24 expounded as calling for "mutual submission." On that basis, Christ would have to be submitting to the church (mutually of course!). It won't do. When God explains that "man did not come from woman, but woman from man; neither was man created for woman, but woman for man,"[898] he is not denying the fact that women bear God's image just as do men. In fact he reinforces man's dependence on woman: "man is born of woman."[899] But he is also reinforcing the enduring relationship of helper and helped he created in the beginning. There is a God-ordained order in marriage, established in Genesis and confirmed in the New Testament. It is an order that does more than give help to the man: it an order in union that images the union between Christ and his church in which he is the head and the church is the body in submission. That, in its turn, images the Trinitarian union in which the Son is in submission to the Father, albeit they are united.

It might be a little too simplistic to assert that "A 'help(er)' is one who takes a subordinate role."[900] Helping necessarily involves practical commitment to the goals and needs of the one helped. That may mean subordination, but not necessarily so. A teacher, for example, may help a student while retaining a superior role. The goals and needs of helper and helped can be congruent, or can require of one or the other significant submission. Nevertheless, when God announces his intention to bring a helper to the man, there is an order evident: the woman will help the man fulfil the task God has given him. Although it will become clear that the man has duties of love and care for the woman, the helping the woman is created to provide is unidirectional: she is to help him.

But there is great dignity attached to that helping, a dignity that directly images God: "It is so startling to read of God being the 'help' of his faithful ones, as in Deut. 33:7 and Ps 33:20"[901] Over and over again God himself steps into the life of his people as their helper. Clearly there is no loss of God's dignity when he helps Israel; rather his unfailing love and his saving strength magnify his dignity. Nor is there any subservience in God's helping! A helping role is not inconsistent with employment of greater authority or power, or even of leadership and rule. Helping has to do with advancing the goals and good of the helped, not with relative status or submission, albeit submission might also be required – and in the case of marriage, is required.[902]

The greatest of divine humility in helping man is seen in Christ, "Who, being in very nature God … made himself nothing by taking the very nature of a servant."[903] Yet he is at the same time, even in his humble humanity, God the Son, gloriously

---

[897] Presupposing "someone" rather than "something": see the next section.
[898] 1 Corinthians 11:8,9
[899] 1 Corinthians 11:12
[900] Collins *Genesis 1-4* Kindle location 3900 (footnote)
[901] ibid
[902] eg Ephesians 5:22
[903] Philippians 2:6,7

revealing God the Trinity.[904] There was no suitable helper to be found in creation to rescue man from sin and hell: so Christ humbled himself "by becoming obedient to death – even death on a cross!"[905] There is no greater dignity or love[906] to be found than in this humble serving of those who deserve nothing of the sort.

> Therefore God exalted him to the highest place and gave him the name that is above every name, that at the name of Jesus every knee should bow, in heaven and on earth and under the earth, and every tongue acknowledge that Jesus Christ is Lord, to the glory of God the Father.[907]

It is in such a context that God calls for submission "to one another out of reverence for Christ."[908] Submission to one another is not some bizarre leaderless mush of indifference and indecision. The context makes it abundantly clear that just as Christ is the head of the body, there is submission and leadership in the church and in the family. In one way or another we are all placed in roles of submission, albeit we may also have roles of leadership. So the passage goes on to give practical examples. Children are to be in submission to both parents (although the image really is of parents in a unity rather than as distinct individuals). Husbands are to be in submission to Christ, but they are to lead in the marriage in which wives are to be in submission to husbands (which is part of the submission of both to Christ). The created order of marriage is to be upheld in an injunction anchored in Genesis 2:24: "Wives, submit yourselves to your own husbands as you do to the Lord."[909] At the same time, husbands are to image Christ by serving their helpers in love: "Husbands, love your wives, just as Christ loved the Church and gave himself up for her."[910] This does not overthrow the created order; it enhances it with dignity that images the glory of Christ.

A Suitable Helper

The "suitedness" of that helper is also emphasised. There were numerous animals that on their own or in concert with others could have helped man with many of the tasks for which God created him. Indeed, to this day many animals fulfil that role. But a helper "suited" to him is more than a fellow labourer or technical specialist. She is, above all else, an image-bearer who is suited to help man fulfil his calling in a way that man could not achieve without her (or she without him). She will advance his mission with skill, wisdom, work and biology. She is a companion with whom a lasting relationship of love and intimacy can be established, experienced and expressed. Yet it goes further than loving intimacy: "'Becoming one flesh' involves the complete identification of one personality with the other in a community of interests and pursuits, a union consummated in intercourse."[911] Together they progress the cause that could not be completed by

---

[904] John 1:1-14; Hebrews 1:1-3
[905] Philippians 2:8
[906] John 15:13
[907] Philippians 2:9-11
[908] Ephesians 5:21
[909] Ephesians 5:22
[910] Ephesians 5:25
[911] Leupold *Genesis* p74

man alone. This too images God whose Trinitarian fellowship is with a complete harmony of interests and pursuits.

The suitedness of woman for man is founded in our being human: we share a human nature that distinguishes us both from God and all other created beings. That shared nature means we can help and be helped in a communion of likeness that Adam discovered the animals could never offer. Ontologically we are human. But the suitedness of woman to be man's helper is also founded in difference: she brings to the communion of likeness what man lacks. She brings help where by nature man needs help, and by nature she is created with the differences that equip her to bring that help.[912] Her nature, her being, somehow fits with man in a way that enables them to become one flesh, a harmony of identity, interests and pursuits. There is then an ontological distinction between men and women – a sub-set if you like of the ontological commonality. We are firstly human, but within that we are either male or female.

Woman is woman and not man, not only because she is biologically or functionally differentiated, but because she is ontologically differentiated. Man is man and not woman, not only because he is biologically or functionally differentiated, but because he is ontologically differentiated. Whatever biological and functional differences there are between men and women, they exist because there is first and foremost a created distinction – and union – between them.

Yet the creation of Adam as man and Eve as woman reinforces the fact that each was given a body to match their gender and the role that aligns with that gender. Gender and biology are expressly linked. "The Bible believes in the organic unity of biological sex and gender identity. … [it assumes] equivalence between the biology of sexual difference and the corresponding identities of male and female."[913]

While the fall perverts the inclinations of the heart in all sorts of ways (including inclinations expressing or experiencing gender), created gender and created body align. While the fall corrupts the flesh in all sorts of ways (including biological function), created gender and created body align. Adam and Eve were not invited by God to decide on their gender, then to adapt bodily function to their choice. "We do not have an inalienable right to do whatever we want with our physical selves. We belong to God and should glorify him with our bodies (1 Cor. 6:19-20)."[914] He made Adam man and Eve woman and they confirmed that by looking at their bodies.[915] Biology does not determine gender, but it is aligned to it.

Among other things, that excludes the possibility that inclinations to deny gender alignment or identity with biological sex, no matter wherever, however or from whatever those inclinations may arise, are wrong. It is hardly surprising that with man's fall into sin, it is the most fundamental aspects of our creation in God's

---

[912] It is worth reiterating the point made earlier that irrespective of our ability to describe or quantify woman's uniqueness, the fact that such uniqueness is made known by God makes her uniqueness indisputable.
[913] DeYoung *op cit*
[914] ibid
[915] Genesis 2:23 makes it clear that Adam identified the distinction; Genesis 2:24 makes it clear that such a distinction applies to all their descendants.

image that are most forcefully and commonly assailed. And it need not be merely an inclination: a genuinely held perception of who we are is – if in conflict with God's revelation – as distorted as every other sinful construct. We cannot see ourselves truly without submitting to Scripture because we are so out of touch with reality that God declares us dead in sin[916] and incapable of pleasing God.[917] It follows that when inclination or perception conflicts with revelation, we need Christ to liberate inclination and perception:

> If Christ, the firstborn from the dead, is the prototype of the new humanity—if he is the first fruits of the resurrection, if he is the one who shows us what we too will one day become—then our daily task is one of saying "no" to everything in us, no matter how deeply inborn or hardwired it may seem or feel, that does not conform to what we know of Christ as he we learn of him through the teaching of the apostles and prophets.[918]

Further, all Adam's descendants – including those who will never marry and so will never engage in legitimate sexual activity – are also "in God's image."[919] That is a fairly convincing indicator that it is not sexuality or sexual activity that is the primary reference for being in God's image, man or woman.

This is why the unmarried can and do image God. While God created the love to be found in and expressed in marriage as a dramatic imaging of his Trinitarian love, each person is born into the world as unmarried image bearer. The unmarried can surely love God and love their neighbour, even as the Perfect Man, our unmarried Saviour, perfectly and completely loved God the Father and his neighbours. While God created marriage to image the intimate, redeeming and enduring love of Christ for the church,[920] the unmarried can surely image God's love by committing to personal, sacrificial and enduring love for others. The unmarried are not called to give or receive the intense intimacy of sexual union, but every other aspect of man in God's image is theirs by nature, by calling and by opportunity. And they are called to a unique devotion to Christ unavailable to the married,[921] albeit the married have their own special expression of devotion to Christ in marriage.

Weaker Vessels?

Is distinction in roles based on gender a put-down of women? Peter for example calls wives "weaker vessels."[922] But Peter is identifying a characteristic of wives that is, according to the text, worthy of honour. In any biblical context, honour is accorded that which is honourable. It is not made worthy of honour by being honoured, but is honoured because it is worthy of honour. Nor is this some sort of gratuitous compensation for actually being less worthy. It is giving honour because honour is due. Wives are to be regarded as weaker vessels, and on that basis they

[916] Ephesians 1:1-3
[917] Romans 8:5-8
[918] Hill op cit
[919] Genesis 9:6; 1 Corinthians 11:7; James 3:9
[920] Ephesians 5:22-32
[921] 1 Corinthians 7:32-35
[922] 1 Peter 3:7

are to be honoured. Their "weakness," whatever that is, is an honourable thing, on account of which wives are to be actively accorded honour by their own husbands.

The likely reaction to this in contemporary culture is hesitation, cringe, or outright rejection as if in identifying wives as "weaker vessels" they are demeaned in some way. Yet that can hardly be the case, for it is because they are "weaker vessels" that they are worthy of honour. Whatever it is then that makes wives "weaker vessels," it is something of value, something good, something to be treasured and nurtured, something worthy of respect and honour.

The NIV uses "respect" for "honour." It would appear that "respect" is included in the concept but that on its own is too reserved for the context here, in which "honouring" is surely more than an attitude, and even more than respectful conduct, but an active attributing to the wife of honour. For a comparison, consider the difference between respecting God (in which cognisance is taken of who he is and how we conduct ourselves in his presence) and honouring God (in which our actions and words are directed to God in a manner that brings him praise and worship). So husbands are to actively give honour to their wives because of their "weakness."

As always, the context is important. Here Peter is addressing the issue of the relationship of men and women in their marriages. It may be that there are general applications in this verse for understanding distinctives in gender and relationships. But the starting point is the relationship of a husband to his wife in marriage. Peter's injunction is not a generalised one for all men to treat all women in a particular way, albeit there may be some such extrapolation available to the text. Peter addresses each husband with regard to his own wife. His concern is that each husband should actively accord his own wife honour, because she is the "weaker" of the two "vessels." In what way?

Some see the weakness in terms of vulnerability to abuse, in that the submission enjoined in the previous verses could, if misapplied, leave the wife open to such abuse. While that is a valid concern, it does not appear to be what Peter is addressing here. It is difficult to see why a man would praise his wife because she is potentially vulnerable to his abuse. Others align this weakness to a claim, based on a gross misapplication of 1 Timothy 2:14, that women are more prone to sin than men. That fits neither 1 Timothy nor 1 Peter, for 1 Timothy is discussing the exercise of teaching authority in the church, and as already noted, 1 Peter is not discussing any impropriety but the very opposite: the need to give honour because honour is due.

The word translated "weakness" here is used with a range of meanings in the New Testament, always with some comparative sense of lack of strength. It can refer to inability to combat more powerful spiritual forces[923] but more commonly to an immaturity in faith[924] or spiritual effectiveness (actual[925] or apparent[926]). It is also used for disease,[927] sickness[928] or basic physical weakness.[929] And there are

---

[923] Matthew 26:41
[924] 1 Corinthians 8 & 9
[925] Galatians 4:9; Hebrews 7:18
[926] 1 Corinthians 1:27
[927] Acts 28:39
[928] Numerous instances including Matthew 25:36; Philippians 2:26,27
[929] Hebrews 11:30

those passages where it could be either or both physical and spiritual, such as in Pauls' reference to a "thorn in the flesh. "[930] That "thorn" which reinforces to him his "weakness" is likely some physical impediment that is having a spiritual impact.

That the "weakness" characteristic of wives is a thing of honour however, suggests that those uses indicating some form of spiritual deficiency, physical disability, or less than desirable maturity, just don't fit. None are praiseworthy, albeit the manner in which such things are borne may well be. The only thing that might fit from this list is physical weakness, which in and of itself casts no aspersions on anyone other than those wanting to be recognised for outstanding bodily strength. Even so, why would physical weakness be a thing of praise?

Is Peter really asserting that to be an honoured wife a woman must necessarily be physically weaker than her husband? It is true that in general men are physically stronger than women, so it can be expected and observed that most husbands are physical stronger than their wives. Could it be that Peter is teaching that God has gifted husbands with a strength that fits them for their purpose of "husbanding"; wives have been fitted with something other than strength that fits them for "wifing," making that worthy of praise? Husbands often have physical strength wives characteristically do not have, but in its place wives can be deemed to have an honourable weakness that is fitting for their calling. Generally, husbands are masculine, wives are not – not merely in lacking physical strength, but in possessing "the imperishable beauty of a gentle and quiet spirit, which in God's sight is very precious."[931] Wives' lack of masculinity *and* their contrasting attribute of femininity is a gifting of value that their husbands should treasure and honour. But that interpretation of Peter's identifying wives as weaker vessels only works for a marriage in which the wife is actually physically weaker than the husband. It would make invalid any marriage in which the wife was physically stronger than the husband. Worse, it just doesn't fit the context Peter is addressing in his letter.

Vessels of Purpose

Word studies like this do little on their own to define the sense intended in a particular passage. Context, vocabulary, and concepts of the whole passage most likely indicate which of a range of semantic meanings is intended. Because of our cultural setting we are inclined to focus on the "weakness" but Peter links it to "vessel." Therein lies more than a clue.

We tend to think of a vessel as a container, but New Testament usage predominantly has in mind not merely containing, but function, utility and purpose. In other words, when Peter refers to husbands and wives as "vessels" it is unlikely he views them as containers of – or receptacles for – something of value. Rather, he views them as possessing qualities of value that have honourable *purpose*.

By referring to husbands and wives as "vessels" there is both a sense of purpose in their being, and a sense of their having been created with that purpose. Both are called and equipped by God to serve God: they are both vessels through which God

---

[930] 2 Corinthians 12:1-10

[931] 1 Peter 3:4

is working out his purposes. One is a vessel of headship and the other a vessel of submission.

Peter has just addressed the issue of slaves, who are instructed to submit to their masters, good and bad alike.[932] The slaves are in a weaker position in the relationship than their masters, not because of abuse (albeit some slaves are, Peter acknowledges, subject to abusive masters) but simply because a place of submission is one where preference and assertion give place to submission and service. He then points to Christ who submitted himself to abuse for our sakes without retaliating or threatening, entrusting "himself to him who judges justly."[933] Again, it is a relationship in which the one who is in submissive service exhibits a weakness in authority and power, sacrificing self for the good of those served, while trusting God to resolve any injustice involved. Then as Peter turns to wives, it is firstly to wives who are in submission to unbelieving husbands: theirs is to be a gentle submissive service of a quiet spirit. In comparison to their husbands, such wives are on the weaker side of a relationship that requires headship by one and submission by another. So they are to put their trust in God and adorn themselves with gracious and winsome helping.

It is in this context that Peter instructs husbands to honour their wives as the weaker vessels. In the relationship in which they offer submission, wives are dependent on the decisions and leadership of their husbands in all their strengths and weaknesses. The leadership a husband gives, the decisions he makes, and the way he does those things impact on his wife through her willing submission. So each husband is to *honour* his wife: he is to lead her with the deliberate intent of doing good to her and for her. He is to honour her with an awareness of his wife's dependence upon his words, actions and attitudes. She is worthy of honour because in herself and in her submission is treasure beyond measure. Such honouring, I would suggest, will not only seek to do and say what benefits his wife, and will not only make known to her and to others how greatly he esteems her, but will mine his wife's wisdom and grace for help that he might otherwise fail to accept from a vessel who exhibits service and submission in place of assertion and control.

Wives' weakness is not a flaw. Nor is it an absolute, but a comparative weakness in the relationship of husband and wife. Wives are not to be pitied or abused as if they have an undignified weakness, but honoured because they give place to their husbands. This is indeed a weakness that is dignified by femininity: but it is the femininity of a helper of Christ-modelling service and submission that is not necessarily linked to the superficial behaviours any particular culture might expect women to exhibit. So the outstanding wife of Proverbs 31 is unmistakably a woman, is unmistakably her husband's helper, is unmistakably industrious and multi-skilled, is unmistakeably involved in the management of business and staff, is unmistakeably a decision-maker and trader, and is unmistakably honoured by a husband who trusts her.

How is a husband's honour to be given? In the same way we honour God. How do we honour God? By faithful service, by clarity of testimony to others, and in giving him praise for his attributes and his works. In like manner, Peter's direction

---

[932] 1 Peter 2:18

[933] 1 Peter 2:23

for husbands to honour their wives is fulfilled when each husband, as the head of his wife, leads her faithfully; it is fulfilled when his response to her submission is care, protection, and attentiveness to her help in its various forms; it is fulfilled when he tells others how he is helped by her God-given gifts, so that together they are what he could never be on his own; and it is fulfilled as he makes known to her how he values – no, treasures – her faith, work, insights, wisdom, grace, personal attributes, and perhaps above all, her personhood.

Gender in Protest

The core issue for protests against God's creation order for relationships between men and women over the last two centuries – and indeed, the core issue for all social convulsions – is denial, choice and control.[934] It is really just one issue. Denial, choice and control are facets of the same flawed diamond: man in his own image. Clearly the Bible legitimises choice and control within particular boundaries.[935] But it is the existence of those boundaries against which men and women have rebelled since Genesis 3. To be human is to be a creature subject to the Creator. "You, LORD, are our Father. We are the clay, you are the potter; we are all the work of your hand."[936] The Creator establishes individual being, gives laws, assigns roles, and prescribes boundaries for those he has created.

Not only does fallen man seek to obliterate created gender distinction at the ontological and biological levels, but he seeks to do the same at the relational level. Each person of the Trinity is fully and equally divine, and equally and fully worthy of our worship. Yet there is an ordered relationship within the Trinity in which the Son is in submission to the Father ("I have come from heaven not to do my will but to do the will of him who sent me."[937]), and the Spirit is in submission to the Father and the Son ("… who I will send you from the Father – the Spirit of truth who goes out from the Father."[938]). That order, that rule and submission, in no way diminishes the dignity or divinity of the Son or the Spirit.[939] In the same way, the church's

---

[934] That is not to say that everything about the reform of women's roles and rights is wrong. For example, it is to be applauded that there is a dignity and integrity accorded women today that shamefully has not always been evident in western society. That such dignity and integrity were always available through submission to Scripture rather than the convulsions of protest and social revolution does not diminish the value of those things that now prevail that are truly good. At the same time, there are also things that now prevail that are not good.

[935] eg "You are free to eat from any tree in the garden; but you must not eat from the tree of the knowledge of good and evil." Genesis 2:16,17

[936] Isaiah 64:8

[937] John 6:38

[938] John 15:26

[939] It is not necessary here to take up, let alone resolve, the debate as to whether or not the Son is in eternal submission to the Father. In his incarnation, at least, there is a submission of the Son to the Father through which the Son learnt obedience [Hebrews 5:8] without in any degree diminishing his divinity, dignity or glory; in fact, the glory of God is most perfectly seen in this submissive Son [Hebrews 1:3]. Whether or not John Owen's statement is comprehensive of the Son's submission, it makes a sufficient case for recognising that submission does not necessarily diminish ontological equality: "This indispensably introduceth an inequality and subordination in the covenanters [ie the Father and the Son] as to the common ends of the covenant, however on other accounts they may be equal." [John Owen (Goold Ed) *The Works of John Owen DD* Johnstone & Hunter, London 1854, Vol

submission to its Head, Jesus,[940] in no way diminishes the dignity or being of the church or its members. And in just the same way, the submission of a wife to her husband in no way diminishes the dignity or divine image-bearing of the wife, but rather displays it.

It follows that every attempt to obliterate gender distinctives is a defiance of God's created order. Every concept of gender being fluid or a matter of personal choice is a rejection of God's created order. Every inclination to misuse gender is dishonouring of God's created order. Every abuse of gender in marriage is an abuse of God's created order. That does not mean that in our fallenness we, and those around us, will not experience all sorts of struggles in conforming to our created gender in a faithful and God-honouring way. We will. They will. But it does mean that such struggles have a context of right and wrong that needs the enlightening, cleansing, redeeming, empowering and guiding work of Christ.

Rosaria Butterfield's writing on this subject is particularly pertinent and helpful. Her convictions and way of life were radically transformed on being brought to faith in Christ by Christ while immersed in life-long lesbian culture: "I was not converted out of homosexuality. I was converted out of unbelief. I didn't swap out a lifestyle. I died to a life I loved."[941] In seeking to understand her identity she came to realise that her feelings and desires did not define her but distorted who she truly was:

> I learned through conversion that when something feels right and good and real and necessary—but stands against God's Word—this reveals the particular way Adam's sin marks my life. Our sin natures deceive us. Sin's deception isn't just "out there"; it's also deep in the caverns of our hearts.
>
> How I feel does not tell me who I am. Only God can tell me who I am, because he made me and takes care of me. He tells me that we are all born as male and female image bearers with souls that will last forever and gendered bodies that will either suffer eternally in hell or be glorified in the New Jerusalem. Genesis 1:27 tells me that there are ethical consequences and boundaries to being born male and female.[942]

Having Dominion Like God

What else is involved in man being in God's image? Theories abound! They generally fall into one of three categories: man is in some way like God in his relationship to God and others, man is in some way like God by nature, or man in some way functions like God.

The latter concept of functioning like God might appear to fit the text of Genesis 1:26: immediately after declaring his intention to make God in his own image, God

---

19 p83]. On the eternal submission of the Son see Bruce Ware "Eternal in Essence, Distinct in Roles *Journal for Biblical Manhood and Womanhood* Louisville, Fall 2008, Volume 13 #2 p43ff http://cbmw.org/uncategorized/equal-in-essence-distinct-in-roles/

940 Ephesians 4:15

941 Rosaria Butterfield, *Love Your Neighbour Enough to Speak the Truth* The Gospel Coalition, October, 2016 https://www.thegospelcoalition.org/article/love-your-neighbor-enough-to-speak-truth

942 ibid

goes on to say he will give man dominion. Does having dominion then define what it is to be in God's image? Collins suggests it doesn't:

> To appeal to the sentence in Genesis 1:26, "and let them have dominion" as defining the image is to mistake the grammatical function of that sentence; as Delitzsch put it, "the dominium terrae ... is not ... its content but its consequence." ... the syntax is waw followed by a volitional form, which commonly indicates a purpose or result clause.[943]

If exercising dominion is a consequence of being in God's image, clearly something more than having dominion is involved in image-bearing. However, the fact that "having dominion" is grammatically dependent on being "made in God's image" does not exclude the exercise of dominion from being a *part* of what being in God's image means. The 2011 NIV tends to reinforce the idea that having dominion is a consequence of being God's image that is not of its essence, translating the more traditional "and let him have dominion" as "so that they may rule." In such a translation, rule is a possibility arising from created ability or potential, but not a necessary function arising from being. Yet even in that translation, it is inescapable that the two – image bearing and having dominion – are inextricably linked. Alter's translation "to hold sway"[944] seems to capture the sense of consequence Collins and Delitzsch highlight, while retaining the intense congruity of the two that God's declaration makes evident.

Images were and remain common objects in pagan cultures. The Bible forbids the crafting of images. God cannot be pictured or represented in anything man-made. Yet God uses the concept of "image" to identify what distinguishes man from all other created being. Although images of deities and kings in ancient cultures often (though no always) took a form intended to portray a visual representation of the deity or king, they also inevitably expressed the rule and virtual presence of the deity or king in a place where he was not physically present.[945] Making man God's image on the earth would be commonly understood to mean man is God's representative and so is created to rule and subdue in God's name. By specifically expressing this, the writer of Genesis confirms that the common understanding of the place and function of an image is applicable here.

> The image does not primarily mean similarity, but representation of the one who is imaged in a place where he is not. ... The function of the image is as representative of one who is really or spiritually present, though physically absent. ... The primary function of an image is to express, not to depict.[946]

A king's image in a city was intended to show something of what the king looked like, but more importantly, to express the fact that though not visible, his rule was as real in the city as if he were physically there. Thus in linking man as God's image to man's dominion, that dominion is properly seen as a function intrinsic to his image-bearing even though not definitive of it.

However, everything about man in this chapter and in the unfolding biblical account that follows indicates that being in God's image is not something that can

---

[943] Collins *Genesis 1-4* Kindle locations 3765-3766 citing Jouon, *Grammar of Biblical Hebrew*, §116a

[944] Alter *Five Books* p18

[945] D J A Clines "The Image of God in Man: Tyndale Old Testament Lecture 1967" in *Tyndale Bulletin 19* Tyndale House, Cambridge, 1968 pp 87-90

[946] ibid

be flattened as if it consists of only one or two aspects of man's being and calling. Rather, the meaning of what it is to be in God's image is comprehensive and complex, holding a number of aspects in coordinated unity that together provide a rounded definition of what it is to be in that image. "The image of God extends to everything in which the nature of man surpasses that [of the animals]. [It] constitutes the entire excellence of human nature, as it shone in Adam before his fall."[947] Being in God's image "must be seen as having both a structural and a functional aspect – as describing both what we are and what we do."[948]

Having dominion does not define what it is to be in God's image, any more than being male and female defines it. But it is an essential part of that definition. As David addresses God in Psalm 8, the crowning of man with glory and honour is directly linked to the fact that "You made them rulers over the works of your hands; you put everything under their feet."[949]

Put simply, man could not exercise dominion if he is not by nature in God's image; but that which by nature images God will by nature exercise dominion. It is not as if God made man like an animal, then added God-like appendages, "bits" of God or God-likeness. Man as man is in his totality in the image of God, and without that image he is not man. God made man in his image, and explicitly declares that as image-bearer he will have dominion. Man is made like that to be like that to do what belongs to being like that: that is his image-bearing.

Genesis, and a wealth of other Scripture, points to the nature of man being what is indelibly imprinted with the image of God. It is, if you like, the "human-ness" of man in which the image of God is to be found.

Invasion or Home-Coming?

In this discussion of man's having dominion however, something of significance has been overlooked. Exercising dominion is the *fourth* instruction given to man. Not that God calls them "instructions." He calls them "blessings": "God blessed them and said to them, 'Be fruitful and increase in number; fill the earth and subdue it. Rule over the fish in the sea and the birds in the sky and over every living creature that moves on the ground.'"[950] Here then are four *blessings*: God blesses man with the call to do what he has been created for: to reproduce, occupy, subdue, govern.

At first glance this looks very much like an invasion: "Expand, take the land, take the occupants, take the resources." Nothing could be further from the truth! "Emigrate, occupy, subdue, and govern" are blessings because God in his good grace has made creation for this and has made man to do this, and to be in this relationship. Man has been created to reproduce as a good thing for himself and for the creation he is to occupy. The land has been created to be occupied by man who has been made for living in the good place God has made for him. The earth has

---

[947] Calvin *Institutes* pp164f

[948] Hoekema, *Create in God's Image* dust-jacket blurb.

[949] Psalm 8:6

[950] Genesis 1:28

been created to be subdued by man who has been made to subdue it as a good way to live in the environment God has made him for.[951] Creation has been made to be governed by man who has been made to live as God's co-regents in the good service that God has made him for. Man is blessed – as creation is blessed – when man takes up the roles for which he was created in the creation prepared for man in this role.

So for man to fill the earth no invasion is proposed, but a home-coming. The earth would welcome man as each new generation migrated further across its face, taking residence and responsibility for previously unfilled territory prepared as their home. The creatures of each territory would welcome man's subduing them as at last receiving the long anticipated home-coming of their governors. And the earth would be filled with the knowledge of God as man in God's image exercised dominion for God in every place called "home" on mountain, plane and valley; and in every ocean; and even in the sky above. God made an earth that needed man to take up his prepared home in it, and God made man to image him by living at home in the place prepared for him.

The force of God's injunction to multiply and fill the earth is at the heart of the audacious rebellion at Babel. Fulfilling God's command, Adam's descendants multiplied and migrated – until they came to Shinar, "and settled there."[952] They decided to stop spreading out, and instead to build up, to "build ourselves a city, with a tower that reaches to the heavens."[953] Instead of possessing the earth they arrogantly set out to possess heaven!

Contrary to what the English romanticists would have us believe, there is nothing intrinsically evil in cities or intrinsically innocent in rural settlement. In fact, the ultimate dwelling place for man is pictured as the perfect city, the city of God, the New Jerusalem from heaven.[954] No, the rebellion here is not about city v country, but about *them*, putting themselves in the middle of the story. "They said, 'Come, let us build ourselves a city ... so that we may make a name for ourselves;

---

[951] Note that this is diametrically opposed to those "green" movements that would make man subject to the rule of the earth.
[952] Genesis 11:2
[953] Genesis 11:4 [The introduction to this rebellion is with emphasis on their choice to make bricks instead of using stone (v3). The suggestion that they had to do this because of a lack of stone on the plain misses the point. Swedenborg's argument (http://www.biblemeanings.info/Words/Artifact/Brick.htm) that bricks are intrinsically evil cannot be sustained on any sensibly construed biblical evidence. Nor can later references to the use of bricks in Egypt (Jeremiah 43:9), in Israel's captivity (Exodus 1:14), in false worship (Isaiah 65:3), or in unfaithful cities (Isaiah 9:10) be read back into Genesis 11, albeit that when Genesis was written, writer and readers would already have been more than familiar with the connotations of bricks in Egypt. Rather, the use of bricks here in the context of rebellion provides a reference point for the later biblical references to bricks used in rebellious contexts. What makes the bricks of Genesis 11 so wrong then? The context is clear: they made bricks because this was to be *their* creation, *their* city. Stone would have inevitably symbolised the creation and Creator they wished to dissociate from. That paradigm carries through from Genesis 11 to God's insistence on the use of stones for his altars – uncut stones at that (eg Exodus 20:25) – and for his temple; while the use of bricks thereafter in places of worship is associated with false worship (eg Isaiah 65:3).]
[954] Revelation 3:12 [The imagery is complex: what begins in Revelation as a city ultimately becomes the bride of Christ; ie the church. The point of the present discussion is not what physical form our ultimate dwelling will be, but that the image of a city is used to represent God-created perfection and harmony.]

otherwise we will be scattered over the face of the whole earth.'"[955] Their two-fold evil objective was, "stay here and make a name for ourselves in our place." They were meant to keep going from there and to make a name for God in God's place.

Subduing a Passive Earth

We instinctively assume that subduing a fallen world inevitably involves conflict and domination. But the blessing of subduing the earth was given to man with regard to a pre-fall earth that was not resistant, and in which conflict, oppression and domination – normally of the essence of "subduing" – were utterly alien concepts. What is meant by "subdue" when all sense of coercion, tyranny and unwelcome bondage are necessarily absent?

Had the injunction to subdue the earth been given after the fall, we would all immediately identify with the labour, the difficulty and the conflict involved.[956] But that is not the context of God's blessing man with the tasks of subduing the earth, and when we take the wrong concept into our daily tasks we further pervert both the earth and our service in it.

It is not that our concept of "subdue"[957] is misplaced with regard to normal usage throughout the rest of the Old Testament. Enemies are subdued by being vanquished;[958] the strong are subdued by being tied down with restraints of rope and hair;[959] nations are "put under-foot."[960] Even when used in a benevolent context as in Micah 7:19, "he will tread our sins underfoot,"[961] it clearly has the sense of forcefully overthrowing. But in every case, something other than force is also implied: in every case order and governance is established, and, especially in the case of our sins, *good* order and governance is established. Take conflict and force out of "subdue" and one is left with the establishment of management. The context determines whether that management is good or bad.

Subduing creation before the fall – *and after it* – involves the establishment of good management. The earth awaited what it had been created to have: good management by man created to be its manager. The earth is not a self-sustaining and self-managing entity: "nature" does not know best. It was created with the intent that man would subdue it (ie bring good management to it) and exercise dominion over it (ie maintain that good management).

The idea of "subduing" creation also reflects the fact that creation is not an idol to be kept at a reverential distance; nor is it an untouchable, unusable treasure to be preserved unchanged, much less a deity to be appeased or submitted to. God gave it to man for his use. Man was to subdue it, exercise dominion over it, and use it. Initially man was given the seed-bearing plants for food,[962] but that was extended

---

955 Genesis 11:4

956 Genesis 3:17-19

957 Hebrew *kabash*

958 Numbers 24:24; Deuteronomy 9:3; Isaiah 45:1

959 Judges 16:5,19

960 Psalm 47:3

961 ie "subdue": the same Hebrew word *kabash* is used

962 Genesis 1:29

to animal life for food[963] and clothing.[964] Stone, minerals, timber, water: all were to be legitimate resources for man's harvesting and use. Man and creation are blessed when man exercises a dominion over creation that manages it well and uses it well.

What is involved in "good" management and use? As discussed above, when God declared his creation to be "good" he declared it beautifully fitted for the purpose he had in mind. So it follows that for man's *management* of creation to be "good" it must be management that is fitting to God's purposes. For man's *use* of creation to be "good" it must be use that is fitting to God's purposes. And God's purposes are that God should be glorified. So while indeed God's purpose is that man should benefit from creation, his purpose is that man should benefit from creation in a way, and exclusively in a way, that glorifies God. While this validates man's governance and use of creation – in fact, it commends it – it also excludes two extremes: the extreme of idolising "nature" to the extent that it cannot be used or consumed for the good of man, and the extreme of plundering creation beyond what it can bear. The former rejects God's gift by refusing to use it; the latter abuses God's gift by destroying it.

To be sure, following the fall, management of creation involves toil, sweat, pain, opposition, tiredness and the testing of perseverance. But despite that, God's intent is that our management of his creation is benevolent and harmonious, not conflict and exploitation. A creation that would have welcomed man's subduing and dominion – man's bringing joyfully anticipated order and continued mutually beneficial management and use – is now under the curse, frustrated from achieving what would have been revealed through faithful dominion:[965] a dynamic display of the glory of God. And in our fallen-ness we tend to abuse what has been entrusted to us in what was meant for the blessing of both man and creation. Not till the old has been replaced with the new creation will that struggle end with concord and unblemished good. Nevertheless, the task for us today remains what it has always been: the establishing and maintaining of control and dominion that is good for creation, good for man, and good for the glory of God.

Having Attributes Like God

When James speaks of man being "made in God's likeness"[966] it appears he is alluding to man as created being rather than what man does. The likeness is to be found in man's nature. That does not exclude it also being found in man's works; it is just that James finds man being by nature in the image of God is a basis for man's dignity. James says that we should not curse man because he is God's image (with no reference to what men have done that might provoke cursing). What is striking here is that James does not describe man as merely having God's image or showing God's image but being made in God's image. Man as man images God. "The whole being … and not *something in man* but *man himself*, is the image of God. … a

---

[963] Genesis 9:1-3
[964] Genesis 3:21
[965] Romans 8:20,21
[966] James 3:9

human being does not *bear* or *have* the image of God but he or she *is* the image of God."[967]

Similarly Paul, in describing the recreation or renewal of the redeemed "into the new man" links image-bearing to true knowledge,[968] and to "righteousness and true holiness."[969] In other words, there are attributes of God's nature in man that characterise man as God's image bearer, and those attributes are not merely outward dressing but essential to the nature of the image- bearer. Yet those attributes are just that: attributes – albeit necessary attributes – of the "new man" who in his entirety is the image of God.

The fall has horribly corrupted man's God-likeness so that the image we are is distorted and perverted – yet it in some degree remains. It is fallen man that James says is made in God's image. "After the fall, man is still said to be in God's image (Gen. 9:6) and likeness (Jas 3:9); nonetheless he needs to be 'renewed … after the image of him that created him' (Col. 3:10; cf. Eph. 4:24)."[970]

The promise that the redeemed will be restored to "true knowledge" reminds us that fallen man knows, but oh! So imperfectly! There comes a day when we will be "restored" to the image bearing of man at creation, knowing truly (but not exhaustively) as God knows. A residual consciousness of right and wrong and the need for justice hangs around fallen man, but oh! How distorted and malleable and fickle it is! But the redeemed have been given a righteousness in Christ that has destroyed all that separates us from fellowship with God, and are being sanctified by Christ into the image of perfect righteousness. Fallen man, having rejected God as the centre of life, service, and being, gropes for something in which some sort of transcendence can be located. And what a miserable confused, self-centred mess he makes of that vain search! But the work of Christ and the gift of the Spirit that has transformed the hearts and inclinations of God's people to God-centeredness is transforming us to that place where at last we will be holy: unimpeded in "Godwardness." "Now we are children of God, and what we will be has not yet been made known. But we know that when Christ appears, we shall be like him, for we shall see him as he is."[971]

C H Spurgeon's declaration, "A man, a real man, who died on a [cross], has risen from the dead, and we are one with that glorious man, who was also God, and because he lives, we shall live also!"[972] is matched by Joseph Hart's hymn:

> A Man there is, a real Man,
> With wounds still gaping wide,
> From which rich streams of blood once ran,
> In hands, and feet, and side.
> 'Tis no wild fancy of our brains,
> No metaphor we speak;
> The same dear Man in heaven now reigns,

---

[967] Bavinck *In the Beginning* p186 (italics his)
[968] Colossians 3:10
[969] Ephesians 4:24
[970] Kidner *Genesis*, p55
[971] 1 John 3:2
[972] C H Spurgeon, "A Sermon and a Reminiscence" *Sword and Trowel*, March 1873, http://www.spurgeon.org/s_and_t/srmn1873.php

That suffered for our sake.
This wondrous Man of whom we tell,
Is true Almighty God;
He bought our souls from death and hell;
The price, His own heart's blood.
His blood can cleanse the blackest soul,
And wash our guilt away;
He will present us sound and whole
In that tremendous day.[973]

Glory

The entire creation displays the glory of God, but mankind, and only mankind in all of creation, is "crowned with glory and honour."[974] So it was that the Son of God, on becoming man, radiated the glory of God.[975] He, as perfect man, displayed God's glory with perfection; yet even fallen man cannot hide the indelible brand embedded in his being: "Made by God." Our fallenness, despite its putrid permeation of our whole being, cannot obscure the remarkable thing that man is by God's creation. Man is hallmarked by his Creator with the Creator's gift: a crown of glory and honour, that sets him apart in creation to be in God's image endowed with a glory that reveals God's glory.

There is a surpassing glory that belongs to the "Creator made a creature; that he that was clothed with glory should be wrapped with rags of flesh."[976] There is the surpassing glory that is his because he humbled himself in obedience to the Father to redeem us.[977] And there is the surpassing glory that is his because creation is his. He made it. He sustains it. He is served by it. It exists for him.

Beyond that, there is a glory belonging to Christ because he is God the Son. This was the glory John testifies to: "The Word became flesh and made his dwelling among us. We have seen his glory, the glory of the one and only Son, who came from the Father, full of grace and truth."[978] Of all the attributes of God to be seen in Christ, those two are at the very heart of John's testimony to the radiance of God's glory seen in Jesus.[979] Exodus 33 and 34 tell how God's glory had been shown to Moses in God's goodness, mercy, compassion, grace, slowness to anger, forgiveness, love and faithfulness. Carson shows that the last two, love and faithfulness – recurring repeatedly through the Old Testament – are what John appears to be alluding to: "The divine goodness characterised by ineffable grace

---

[973] Joseph Hart 1822 (verses 1, 2, 3 & 6)
[974] Psalm 8:5
[975] Hebrews 1:3
[976] Thomas Brookes *Precious Remedies Against Satan's Devices* Banner of Truth, London, 1968, (1652) p36
[977] Philippians 2:9
[978] John 1:14
[979] Hebrews 1:3

and truth, was the very same glory John and his friends saw in the Word-made-flesh."[980]

As man was created in God's image, man was created imaging God's glory in grace and truth. To be God's image is then, perhaps above all else, to image grace and truth. It is the restoration of this glory that is a particular focus of the restoration of man in Jesus Christ. It is this glory of grace and truth in imaging God the Son as he images God the Father to which all who are Christ's are being transformed "with ever-increasing glory."[981] It is not that we are so transformed at regeneration, nor is it something that awaits the new creation (although not till then is it perfected for only when we see him face to face will we be perfectly like him[982]). It is that which Christ is now doing in every disciple in restoring the true image of God.

How is Christ making this transformation? Not by what we do, but by the only way fitting for grace: by grace through the work of the Spirit of God as we behold Christ.[983] As Calvin puts it, in the Gospel God shows his unveiled face that "we should be transformed in God's image … (as) by continual progress we increase both in the knowledge of God and in conformity to His image."[984] To truly image God is to live in face-to-face communion and conformity with God seen in Christ, made possible by Christ, effected by Christ, and promised with ultimate perfection through Christ.

All is Christ's

With the making of man God finished creating a creation that by his unimpeachable evaluation was very good. That glorious creation was set in place to be man's place, and man on his creation as man and woman was set in it as the spectacular image of the invisible God in his place. That image was to fill God's earth, to subdue it, and to govern it – all for the glory of the Son of God to whom every motion of the stars, every movement of the atoms, every breath of life by its very being renders worship.[985] To that Son every man renders worship: whether in faith and submission or in sinful rebellion that nevertheless is overwhelmed by God for his glory.[986] And to that Son every knee will one day consciously bow.[987]

> The Son is the image of the invisible God, the firstborn over all creation. For in him all things were created: things in heaven and on earth, visible and invisible, whether thrones or powers or rulers or authorities; all things have been created through him and for him. He is before all things, and in him all things hold together. And he is the head of the body, the church; he is the beginning and the firstborn from among the dead, so that in everything he might have the supremacy. For God was pleased to have all his fullness dwell in him, and through him to reconcile to himself all

---

[980] D A Carson *The Gospel According to John* Apollos (IVP), Leicester, 1991, p129
[981] 2 Corinthians 3:18
[982] 1 John 3:2
[983] 2 Corinthians 3:18
[984] John Calvin, *The Second Epistle of Paul the Apostle to the Corinthians*, Eerdmans, Grand Rapids, 1964 (1547), p50
[985] Psalm 47; Psalm 98
[986] cf Exodus 50:20; Acts 2:23; Romans 8:28; etc
[987] Isaiah 45:23 & Philippians 2:10

> things, whether things on earth or things in heaven, by making peace through his blood, shed on the cross.[988]

Truly, "You are worthy, our Lord and God, to receive glory and honour and power, for you created all things, and by your will they were created and have their being."[989]

---

[988] Colossians 1:15-20

[989] Revelation 4:11

12. Genesis Finished

Creation's Climax: Reading Genesis 1 in the light of the Seventh Day

"Thus the heavens and the earth were completed in all their vast array. By the seventh day God had finished the work he had been doing; so on the seventh day he rested from all his work.
Then God blessed the seventh day and made it holy, because on it he rested from all the work of creating that he had done."

~ Genesis 2:1-3

The seventh day dawned on a gloriously complete and perfect universe. God stopped, creating finished, creation completed. From the nuclear radiance of the furthest star to the beat of Adam's heart and Eve's rhythmic breathing, everything was as God had created it. Everything moved to God's plan, animated by God's power. Nothing more would be created because there was nothing lacking: everything in its place, everything after its kind. The climax of creation is God at rest from creating; God beholding, sustaining, governing and finding satisfaction in a finished and perfected creation.

> Genesis 1 is monumental in character, and exhibits a stately cadence of grandeur as it reveals the sovereign Creator uttering His will, and that will coming to immediate

fulfilment. So the narrative proceeds until it reaches its mighty climax. The Lord beholds the finished world and pronounces it very good.[990]

"God saw all that he had made, and it was very good."[991] Each day has concluded with God's declaration that he judged his work to be "good"; but on the last day of creating, God declares his work to be "very good." It is now complete. The change in wording is as indicative of the fulfilment of growing goodness as is the use of the superlative: it was *very* good. The previous days were "good" because they were fitted to God's purposes, but with each day there was more to come. Not now. God's purpose has been achieved, and the creation fitted for man's occupation and Godward-worship is now finished: it is as good as good can be. In its completeness it renders glory to God as God had planned: that is truly good.

So with the heavens and the earth completed in all their vast array, God rested from all his work.[992]

God Rests

How could God rest? Very easily – he stopped doing what he had been doing. That is stressed by the text: "he rested from all the work of creating that he had done."[993] This was not total cessation of all activity, but the end of the work of creating. "By resting, God declared that his work as Creator was completed, as we observe in Genesis 2:1, where God pronounces that he has completed his work as Creator."[994] He continued to sustain and rule his creation: "God's rest, however, was not a cessation from all work, for he continues to work in providence, governing the processes of life and all aspects of his created order."[995]

Nor was it a rest for recovery from tiredness or the rejuvenation of expended energy. "Do you not know? Have you not heard? The LORD is the everlasting God, the Creator of the ends of the earth. He will not grow tired or weary."[996] We tend to think of rest in terms of recovery and rejuvenation because, unlike God, we do tire and we do drain our reservoirs of energy. But even in reference to men, the Old Testament consistently uses *rest* to mean *stopping* rather than rejuvenating.

With men, stopping may lead to rest and refreshing, but biblical reference to rest is always about stopping, and any congruent refreshing is a consequence of rest not of its essence. In contrast, we use the word quite differently: we stop to rest. In such a rest, refreshing self and ministering to self is often of the essence, although it is just as likely to be a rest of indolence and mere self-indulgence. This is not biblical rest.

---

[990] E J Young *An Introduction to the Old Testament* (revised) Tyndale Press, London 1960 (1949) p51
[991] Genesis 1:31
[992] cf Genesis 2:1-3
[993] Genesis 2:3
[994] Joseph Pipa "The Sabbath as a Creation Ordinance" *New Horizons*, Orthodox Presbyterian Church, April 2009, http://www.opc.org/nh.html?article_id=600
[995] ibid
[996] Isaiah 40:28

With the institution of the Mosaic Sabbath-rest as a covenant sign,[997] and with every subsequent reference to it, the point is always that Israel is to stop working in obedience to God, with no allusion at all to any sense of Sabbath observance as such reviving them physically, mentally or even spiritually. In fact, Sabbath observance becomes a symbol of denying self[998] rather than reviving self. The Sabbath is a day when man is to rest from (stop) doing what he wants – "not going your own way and not doing as you please"[999] – so as to do (work diligently at) what God wants.

Although the Mosaic seventh-day rest was named "the Sabbath Day," there were in fact a number of sabbaths unrelated to the seventh day, all of which required stopping and none of which had as their purpose the refreshing of man, albeit when properly observed they resulted in joy and refreshment. There was a sabbath on the first day of the seventh month on which a food offering was to be made to the Lord,[1000] and on the Day of Atonement, the tenth day of the seventh month whether or not it was the seventh day of the week. Anyone failing on that day to "deny yourselves and present a food offering to the Lord" meant they "must be cut off from their people."[1001] While atonement certainly brought benefits to the people ("it is the Day of Atonement, when atonement is made for you"), the whole day's focus was on satisfying God's requirements, not theirs: three times they are warned to deny themselves, and four times they are told to stop work. Then on the 15th day and the 23rd day there are also sabbaths. These too were workless, Godward days, devoted to serving God in God's way, completely devoid of any sense of personal preference or gain:

> These are the LORD's appointed festivals, which you are to proclaim as sacred assemblies for bringing food offerings to the LORD … in addition to those for the LORD's Sabbaths and in addition to your gifts and whatever you have vowed and all the freewill offerings you give to the LORD.[1002]

So as well as the regular seventh day sabbaths in the seventh month, there were four other days that were "sabbaths." Although the calculations for the Sabbath Year and the Year of Jubilee revolved around sevens, they were still there as times when work ceased.[1003] They were still times when personal preference and benefit were set aside in obeying God in observance of a "sabbath to the Lord."[1004]

In Nehemiah's judgement of Judah for breaking the Sabbath, there is not a single mention of how the people miss out on some benefit: it is God who "misses out" the obedience and worship that he has commanded.[1005] Interestingly, the ox and the slave are given rest (that is, they are given a stop-work time or "sabbath") through their master's Sabbath observance.[1006] But while the slave and the ox benefit from

---

997 Exodus 20:10; 31:14-16; 35:2,3; Leviticus 23:3 etc
998 Leviticus 16:31
999 Isaiah 58:13
1000 Leviticus 23:24
1001 Leviticus 23:26-32
1002 Leviticus 23:37,38
1003 Leviticus 25:4-11
1004 Leviticus 25:2
1005 Nehemiah 13:15-22
1006 Exodus 23:12

the Sabbath in that they get a stop-work time away from serving their masters, Israel itself is never induced to keep the Sabbath for personal benefit. They never rest from serving their Master, only from serving themselves. Rather than for refreshing themselves, their inducement to sabbath keeping is "keep it for God, or die."

True, Isaiah does identify benefit from Sabbath keeping. But it is not that in keeping the Sabbath Israel or outcast is benefitted, but in the blessing God brings to the obedient.[1007] To keep the Sabbath, *ordinary* or *regular*[1008] work must stop, but in its place they are to choose the *extraordinary* activity that puts the worship of God God's way ahead of personal preference or benefit. This was the case from the outset. Obediently keeping the Sabbath was no reward in itself. Keeping the Sabbath would have been personally unrewarding had not God added to that his reward for obedience. The rewards for Sabbath keeping, along with keeping the other provisions of the Mosaic Covenant, were exclusively rewards given by God rather than anything intrinsic to observance of the Sabbath or law-keeping. The rewards were God-given peace in the land, God-given prosperity, and the presence of God in fellowship.[1009] Correspondingly, the judgement promised for failure to keep the Sabbath and the other provisions of the covenant was God-given famine, God-given defeat at the hands of their enemies, and the presence of God in judgement,[1010] none of which could ever be construed as "natural" outcomes of a failure to keep the Sabbath.

Not that the Sabbath was meant to be a burden: for those who would keep the Sabbath as God's day, delighting in doing what God wanted instead of what they wanted, it would be a day of finding "your joy in the Lord."[1011] There would be joy in Sabbath keeping: it would be a joy arising from doing what God wanted, not what man wanted. A God-centred Sabbath day would be a day of God-centred joy in God-centred activity.

God Rests *and* is Refreshed?

Yet later we are told God not only rested on the seventh day of creation, but that he was refreshed then too.[1012] How can God "who does not grow tired or weary" be refreshed? The temptation is to impute to this "refreshing" some concept of "refreshing" we use, and try to make sense of reading that meaning back into Exodus. But the Hebrew word used here (*nāpas* or *naphash*) is unusual. It is only found in two other places,[1013] while a variety of other words are also sometimes translated as "refreshing." *Nāpas* is generally recognised as related to breathing, with Alter translating it, "catch their breath" in reference to servants in Exodus

---

[1007] Isaiah 56:1-8
[1008] Leviticus 23:25
[1009] Leviticus 26:1ff
[1010] Leviticus 26:14ff
[1011] Isaiah 58:13,14
[1012] Exodus 31:17
[1013] Exodus 23:12 & 2 Samuel 16:14

23:12 and as "caught his breath" in reference to God in Exodus 31:17.[1014] His reasoning is that

> It is cognate with *nefesh* most probably in the sense of "breath," and is related to the verb *nashaf*, "to breath hard or pant." The idea of catching one's breath is consonant with the representation in Job and elsewhere in the Bible of the labourer panting from his work and longing to draw a long breath of relief after labour.[1015]

This "refreshing" then has the sense of stopping hard work, of relief from the intensity of labour, rather than on receiving something that rejuvenates a tired soul or restores sapped energy. That makes the meaning of Exodus 31:17 much clearer, such that God not only stopped what he had been doing (ie "rested") but gave up the intensity with which he had been working. Thus it reads as a *parallelism of intensity*:[1016] "on the seventh day God stopped the work of creating, he completely stopped the intense work of creating."

At the same time, God's being refreshed "seems to point to a refreshment of delight in work fully accomplished." [1017] When God stopped the work of creation, he had completed a creation in which he rightly could – and did – delight. "The divine recognition that the work of each day had been well done reached its climax in a sabbath of cessation and delight. The sabbath is not a sabbath of endless inactivity. It is rather a climax of satisfaction in work fully accomplished."[1018]

It is possible for a labourer to stop work, while, as a result of having been fully involved in that work, retaining a sense of still being burdened by it. One can stop the actual labour but still be mentally and emotionally engaged in it. God has something else in mind for his Sabbaths. Tied, as *nāpas* is, to the command in Exodus 31:17 for Israel to make every seventh day a Sabbath (ie a rest, a stop-work), the implication is that on every seventh day Israel is to stop all work *and* put an end to the intensity of their work, just as God did on the seventh day of history. Not only that, they are to delight in God's work as God delighted in his work. They are to so stop that mind and body are wholly engaged in other: the worship of God.

With Stopping He Stopped

The degree of repetition makes inescapable that at the end of the sixth day creating stopped and that creation had been brought to a finished completion. Genesis 2:2 declares the work finished. God stopped. Creating is now in the past. This was nothing short of the absolute end of creating, with a creation "complete in its vast array." God "had finished." It was work "he had been doing" with no continuing tense in the language or opportunity in the context. So he "rested from

---

[1014] He calls the latter a "flagrant anthropomorphism [which] would not have been a problem for the ancient audience." [Alter *Five books of Moses* p492] Translated as "caught his breath," it can hardly be less than an anthropomorphism. It would appear that an anthropomorphic translation is not necessary (eg "took a pause"), albeit that the image of God catching his breath dramatically conveys the sense of God completely resting.

[1015] Alter *Five books of Moses* p450

[1016] The pun is accidental

[1017] Weeks *Sufficiency of Scripture* p114

[1018] ibid

all his work." Least we miss the point, verse 3 repeats and explains: "He rested from all the work of creating he had done."

"In six days the LORD made the heavens and the earth, the sea, and all that is in them, but he rested on the seventh day."[1019] In six days from nothing to everything. In six days from nothing to everything in perfection. In six days from nothing to everything in perfection completed. There is simply no room here for a mere "intelligent designer" who with bumbling ineptitude makes things that are not "good" then takes aeons of time to tinker with them until they come out "good," but with potential to further evolve into something even more "good." He spoke and what he spoke became. No mistakes. No twisting of days into years or years into epochs so that the imperfect could be perfected. Creation was complete and perfect. Creating was ended. After just six days God stopped what he had started on the first day.

There no room here either for any evolutionary process. Evolution, by its very definition, has no terminus: it cannot be said to have ended, to have reached a stage whereby God could call it "very good." There can be no "finished" or completed universe in an evolutionary construct, for embedded in the very nature of an evolutionary universe is constant change and transformation so that there will always be a "next," and what is next has never been before. But creation in day six was completed in all its array.

That is not to say the created universe of Day 6 was fixed and unchanging. Creation is dynamic: life gives birth to life; matter and energy are transformed; atomic particles are rearranged; and mutations bring to dominance various attributes embedded or made available at creation. Yet, as we have seen, there are boundaries fixed by God. Time is anchored to days and seasons, and the earth will not revert to a formless deep.[1020] Living things are conformed to their "kind," and mankind in particular is not on a journey to a new and higher evolution. There will be many a "next" in history, there will be many a "next" in geological and astronomical events, there will be many a next in the reproduction of living organisms after their kind, and there will be many a "next" in changes in genetic codes, in rearranging atomic structure, and in transformation of existing energy. But there will never be a "next" of God creating in this finished universe. True, there is a "new heavens and earth" to come;[1021] but it is a creation that will replace what God made in those first six days. The creation we now live in is the creation God finished on day six.

The Day the Creator Rested

It was the seventh day of creation in which God rested. He stopped creating this creation because it was then all that he wanted it to be. Each of the first six days had been carefully numbered: one day, the second day, the third day … then, the seventh day. It was that particular day God rested, and it was that particular day

---

[1019] Exodus 20:11

[1020] Genesis 8:22

[1021] 2 Peter 3:10-13 see Chapter 13 below p291

God blessed and made holy.[1022] It was a day in the same way as the previous six days were "days." It differed from the previous six days because of what God did in it, not in its nature as a day. "The seventh day referred to here is unquestionably the seventh day in sequence with the six days of creative activity, the seventh day in the sphere of God's action, not the seventh day in *our* weekly cycle."[1023]

It was that day God blessed: that seventh day of creation, that seventh day of history. One day. His rest continued and continues, but not the day. And because God continues to rest without again taking up the finished work of creating, no new day of God's ceasing from his work occurs.

The text says God blessed that day, but an overwhelming tradition reads it to say God blessed tens of thousands of days. It has become traditional to read "the seventh day" as "the seventh days" as if God blessed every seventh day in every week that follows. But this distorts the text. Not only is the text specific ("on it [the seventh day] God rested") in identifying a single day, the idea that this text calls for rest – ceasing from work – every seventh day shifts the reference from God to man. Without question, one of the sabbaths (ie rest-days) God instituted in the Mosaic covenant involves God's people resting from their work every seventh day. Without question, that seventh-day anniversary is imbued by God with symbolism that is intended to cause every seventh-day-rest observer to remember that God created the cosmos in six inaugural days of history which he marked as work finished by blessing the seventh day of history. As Jesus said, the seventh-day Sabbath rest-day "was made for man,"[1024] and it was made for man to (among other things) remember what God did on day seven in history. The Sabbath day of the law was for man, a day in which man rested, a day repeated every week, and a day in which man, remembering God's rest in the seventh day of history, was to rejoice in God his creator with worship and self-denial. In contrast, the seventh day of history was for God, a day in which God rested, a day that is never repeated, and a day in which God rejoiced in his creation.

Day seven of history, the day God blessed, was for God, not man:

> An essential statement is made by these verses, namely, that Genesis 1:1-2:4 does *not* speak primarily about man or recognize the climax of creation in the creation of man ... This can only indicate that the goal of creation is not mankind, that the crown of creation is not man, but that all creative activities of God flow into a universal rest period.[1025]

The concept of an eternal rest will be considered shortly, but at this point it is important to note that day seven is about God, not man. In this text, "the divine rest is not ... made normative for the rhythm of human life ... nothing is said here of the Sabbath law."[1026] The focus of the day – as the focus of the text and the focus of all creation – is on the glory of God. On this day we read nothing of man, of the spinning of the galaxies, or of geological formations. It is God's day.

[1022] Genesis 2:3
[1023] John Murray, *Principles of Conduct* Tyndale Press, London, 1957, p30 [His italics.]
[1024] Mark 2:27
[1025] Harold Dressler "The Sabbath in the Old Testament" in D A Carson (Ed) *From Sabbath to Lord's Day* Wipf and Stock, Eugene, 1999 (Zondervan 1982) p29
[1026] Gerhard von Rad *The Problem of the Hexateuch and other Essays* quoted by Dressler "The Sabbath in the Old Testament" p28

A Creation Ordinance?

But is not the Sabbath a "creation ordinance"? The term "creation ordinance" is widely used to speak of institutions ordained for all mankind at creation. Each is regarded as normative – that is, applying to all men in all ages – and all are undoubtedly blessings for our good. Among those are the institutions of marriage[1027] and the dignified calling to work.[1028] Despite the fact that there is no direct reference to a Sabbath in Genesis, and no instruction to man to take part in God's rest on day seven, a creation ordinance of Sabbath-keeping is found by many in Genesis 2:2,3. Joseph Pipa puts it as clearly as any: "God instituted the Sabbath, along with work and marriage, to govern the lives of all mankind. Just as the ordinances of work and marriage are permanent, so is the ordinance of the Sabbath."[1029]

There are two very significant implications. Firstly, if the Sabbath is a creation ordinance, it does not matter how the Decalogue (containing, as it does, the fourth commandment requiring Israel to keep the Sabbath Day holy) is related to Christian living, for in the creation ordinance there remains the necessity of Sabbath-keeping for Christians. Secondly, if the Sabbath is a creation ordinance, a duty of Sabbath-keeping extends to all men in all ages and in all places. Further, a creation ordinance Sabbath is not just an issue of duty, but of blessing for a well-ordered society in the same way marriage and work are blessings.

The concept of the Sabbath as a creation ordinance is so entrenched in the theology of the seventh day that it can be a surprise to those familiar with the discussion to learn that both the term and the concept of "creation ordinance" are relatively new. John Murray coined the term in developing his approach to Christian ethics in the 1950s.[1030] For Murray, a creation ordinance was an "ordinance which had been revealed to man at the beginning. ... standards and criteria of holy living which had been established by God at the beginning."[1031] That is, a creation ordinance was a specifically revealed command of God to man at creation about how man was to conduct himself.

Before Murray there were a number of fluidly overlapping ideas about laws embedded in nature, about God's providential governance of nature, and about expressly enunciated commands of God given at creation. Abraham Kuyper, for example, saw both laws in nature ("Everything that has been created was, in its creation, furnished by God with an unchangeable law of its existence ... God has

---

[1027] Genesis 2:18-25
[1028] Genesis 1:28; 2:15
[1029] Pipa The Sabbath as a Creation Ordinance
[1030] The earliest use of the term I can find in any place by any writer is in Murray's *Principles of Conduct*. After a couple of passing uses of the term "creation ordinances" he begins Chapter 2 (which is headed "Creation Ordinances"), "We have had occasion already to refer to the commandments or mandates given to man in the state of integrity. These creation ordinances, as we may call them ..." [p27] This was published in 1957, but is an expansion of talks delivered in 1955 in response to an invitation in 1953 [see the Preface to *Principles*]. Westminster Theological Seminary identifies Murray's Creation Ordinance ethics as one of a number of "new concepts of theology and ministry," of which they boast. [http://www.wts.edu/about/history/theologicalpursuit.html]
[1031] Murray *Principles* p16

fully ordained such laws and ordinances for all life."[1032]) and specific commands given at creation ("the order of creation: 'Replenish the earth, subdue it and have dominion over everything that lives upon it.'"[1033]). While for Kuyper the "order of creation" was limited to those three things, the ordinances in creation covered everything from "the blood that courses through our arteries and veins" to "the orbit of the mightiest star."[1034]

So far as the seventh day and any concept of a Christian Sabbath is concerned, rather than finding a creation command or ordinance in Genesis 2:2-3, the idea of a Sabbath was said to be embedded in nature. The *Westminster Confession of Faith*, for example, makes no appeal to anything at all like a creation ordinance, but appeals instead to nature and to the fourth commandment:

> It is the law of nature, that, in general, a due proportion of time be set apart for the worship of God; so, in his Word, by a positive, moral, and perpetual commandment binding all men in all ages, he hath particularly appointed one day in seven, for a Sabbath, to be kept holy unto him (Exodus 20:8ff).[1035]

How the Sabbath as such or even a "due portion of time ... for worship" (in distinction from natural evidence for the benefit or even necessity of some "due portion of time" for rest) is made evident in nature is often assumed but never discussed. It is difficult to see how looking at nature – however faithfully that was done – would discover a law requiring a weekly Sabbath. But that aside, while the *Confession* makes no reference to Genesis 2 as to the institution of the Sabbath, it does cite Genesis 2 in support of its subsequent statement that the Sabbath has been observed as the last day of the week "from the beginning." The *1689 Baptist Confession of Faith* mimics the Westminster in its Scripture proofs *except* that it excludes the Genesis 2 reference. The reluctance of these Confessions to anchor institution of the Sabbath in God's day of rest on the seventh day of history can hardly be accidental. In contrast, assured that the Decalogue is applicable to all men in all ages, both Confessions expressly validate Sabbath observance on the basis of the fourth commandment. Exegesis of the text and context leads to an explicit assertion that the seventh day of history was God's day, but can give no credence beyond assumption or implication that the institution of a Sabbath for man can be found in Genesis 2.

After Murray coined the term, "creation ordinance" is widely used, but the concept to which it refers differs significantly among users. It is used with such flexibility that one needs to check what is meant each time it is used. It can include, for example, "the cultural mandate given at creation ... to build the city"[1036] for "City building is an ordinance of God just like work and marriage."[1037] But the

---

[1032] Abraham Kuyper *Lectures on Calvinism* p53 This is reinforced on page 70: "all created life necessarily bears in itself a law for its existence, instituted by God Himself. There is no life outside us in Nature, without such divine ordinances, – ordinances which are called the laws of Nature."

[1033] Kuyper *Lectures* p130 What is also striking here is that while Kuyper comes close to Murray's "creation ordinances," he makes no attempt to include the Sabbath in such ordinances.

[1034] Kuyper *Lectures* p70

[1035] *Westminster Confession of Faith* Chapter 21, paragraph 7. The *1689 Baptist Confession of Faith* has almost identical wording (chapter 22, paragraph 7).

[1036] Meredith G. Kline, *Kingdom Prologue* (no details supplied) quoted by Tim Keller *A Theology of Cities* https://www.cru.org/content/dam/cru/legacy/2012/02/A_Theology_of_Cities.pdf

[1037] Tim Keller *A Theology of Cities* CRU, (undated), https://www.cru.org/content/dam/cru/legacy/2012/02/A_Theology_of_Cities.pdf

primary association of the term "creation ordinance" is with marriage, work, an ordered society, and the Sabbath. It is the concept of a Sabbath established for man at creation that has particular relevance in considering the seventh day of history. Exactly how the Sabbath is said to be established for man at creation varies significantly across users of the term, though claiming that the Sabbath is a "creation ordinance" is usually assumed to settle the issue, even if what is meant by "creation ordinance" is equivocal.

Confirming the Sabbath as a creation ordinance can be critical to the place of the Sabbath in the Christian life. It can be argued – and often is – that the institution of the Mosaic Sabbath in Exodus 20 is mandated only for Israel under the Old Covenant, and is not therefore mandated for contemporary believers.[1038] If the Sabbath is a creation ordinance however, there is still a Sabbath to keep regardless of the outcome of the debate about how applicable the Mosaic Sabbath is to contemporary believers; but if there is no creation ordinanced Sabbath, it leaves open, so far as Genesis is concerned, the question as to whether or not there is a contemporary Sabbath that must be kept, either by Christians in particular, or mankind in general.[1039]

Murray listed seven creation ordinances: "the procreation of offspring, the replenishing of the earth, subduing the same, dominion over the creatures, labour, the weekly Sabbath, and marriage."[1040] For six of these he references specific commands in Genesis 1; but for the Sabbath there is no such command. Through a series of conditional suppositions that form a possible foundation for further supposition, Murray reaches the point where "in Genesis 2:3 there is at least an allusion to the blessing of the seventh day in man's week."[1041] He also finds in Genesis 2 a model for man in a divine cycle of work and rest – overlooking the fact that no such cycle exists, for God worked, then rested from his work … and never cycled back to working.[1042] As Murray himself points out, God continued to rest. Rather than a cycle, there is a progression: God worked, then rested unendingly. This, as will be seen below, is indeed the prototype for man: man is to work, then enter an unending rest.[1043] Murray does in fact describe things in this way too, finding in God's eternal rest an eschatological promise for man; but nevertheless

---

1038 eg "This commandment [Exodus 20:8ff] is not a mandate for Sabbath observance by all humanity, for the lesson of creation is applied narrowly to the Israelite Sabbath." [A G Shead "Sabbath" in Alexander *The New Dictionary of Biblical Theology* p746]

1039 It needs to be stressed that the absence of a Sabbath institution for man in Genesis 2 does not resolve the debate about the institution or not of a Sabbath for all men or more specifically for Christians in the fourth commandment. My aim here is to give expression to a faithful exposition of the text and teaching of Genesis 2. Discussion of a universal and/or Christian Sabbath is for another time and place.

1040 Murray *Principles* p27

1041 Murray *Principles* p32. Murray asserts "there can be little doubt" as to this; I would suggest however that there is nothing in Murray's argument that does anything but induce very great doubt about such an allusion!

1042 True, as Jesus said, God continues to "work" but the work he continues is the work he continued on day seven. The work he stopped on day seven – the work of creation – he has not cycled back to for he is finished with it. The work he continued in on day seven he continues in now, and there having been no stopping it, it cannot be argued he has cycled back to it even once, let alone in a repeated cycle that would form a model for man's week.

1043 See below p289

he also sees a cyclical paradigm for man in the absence of a cycle of work and rest in God's seventh-day rest.

On this basis Murray makes what he calls "the most reasonable supposition" that Adam received the same revelation as us (viz Genesis 2:2,3) which Murray now imbues with a creation-ordinance Sabbath, albeit he has previously affirmed that the text is about God and does not refer to man's weekly cycle.[1044] The conclusion is inescapable that, despite Murray's semantic gymnastics, the point he starts at – that Genesis 2:2,3 is about God and not about man – is the point at which the text must rest.

Joseph Pipa takes the less complex approach typical of those who see in the sanctifying of the seventh day the institution of a seven-day cycle of work and rest for man.[1045] Pipa begins by affirming that on the seventh day of creation God stopped his creative work. He then discusses the meaning of "rest" and "refresh," morphing rest from "stopping" to "being refreshed." At the same time he begins calling the seventh day of creation "the Sabbath," even though it is never called that in the text; and goes on to assert that God "rested on the Sabbath." Further, in discussing God's sanctifying the seventh day, there is a subtle shift in defining sanctifying: this morphs from setting aside for God's "special use and service" to become setting aside for God's "worship and service." The former allows for a day God sanctified for his use – which the seventh day of history undoubtedly was; the latter can only be setting the day aside for man's use in worship – which (as discussed below) the seventh day of history could not have been. For these shifts there is no textual justification at all. All this forms the context for an unspoken and unexplained transition from the seventh day being the seventh day of history to it being a generic seventh day of every week. To begin with, the "seventh day" is the single day that ends the creation week. At some point, with no explanation, the "seventh day" becomes tens of thousands of weekly seventh days. In short, the assumption is made but never acknowledge or explained, that when God blessed and sanctified the seventh day of history he simultaneously blessed and sanctified every seventh day in every week for the rest of time.

The wording of Exodus 20:11 "binds the two days together, but we should beware of the simple equation of the Seventh Day with the first Sabbath day."[1046] The seventh day of history, and the seventh-day-rests of Exodus 20, share the idea of work stopped and God's blessing and sanctifying, but they are not identical. The seventh day of history is the unrepeated and unrepeatable day God *chose* to stop his own work *of creation*; the seventh day of Exodus 20 is the day repeated each week on which God *commanded* Israel to stop their work *in creation*.

Conjuring Up a Creation Sabbath

Three propositions are generally used to validate morphing the seventh day of history into the Sabbath: Firstly, day seven of creation is deemed to have no ending; Secondly, the sanctifying of day seven of creation is said to be for man's use; and

---

[1044] See above p280

[1045] Pipa The Sabbath as a Creation Ordinance

[1046] Shead "Sabbath" in Alexander *The New Dictionary of Biblical Theology* p746

Thirdly, the Sabbath of Exodus 20:8-11 is read back into Genesis 2, so that the seventh day of history is called "The Sabbath" and becomes indistinguishable from the Mosaic Sabbath.

It is practically and exegetically awkward to assert that the seventh day of creation has no end. Even for those who count all the days of Genesis 1 as metaphorical, the metaphor has no meaning if the days have no closure. But if days one to six are, as I have argued above, literal 24 hour days, then day seven, being part of the same sequence and being identified by the same term "day," must have closure.

The argument advanced for a never ending seventh day is twofold: firstly, the rest never ends so it is argued the day cannot end; secondly, the fact that there is no statement ending day seven (as there are statements ending each of the previous six days) is said to indicate that day seven does not end. It only requires a very little reflection to see that arguing that the day on which an event begins cannot end if the event does not end is transparently illogical as well as being semantically inconsistent. I took up marriage on a particular day that has long ago ended, but by the grace of God my marriage continues with great blessing. I ceased from my work as a school teacher on the day of my retirement, a day that has also long passed – but I continue in that rest. So God stopped his creative work on a particular day, but the fact that his rest continues has nothing at all to say about the day he did that being unending.

The change in language is most certainly significant. Each of the previous six days ends with a formulaic statement, "There was evening, and there was morning, the nth day." No such refrain appears at the end of day seven. For some, this becomes the springboard into fanciful speculation: "This day lacks the refrain because it has no end – it is not an ordinary day by any stretch of the imagination."[1047] There is ambiguity here that obfuscates: truly, it is no "ordinary day," but has there been an ordinary day in creation's six-day history yet? Does the extraordinary nature of what happens on that day necessarily change the length of that day? Because God's rest does not end does the day not end?

If it is "no ordinary day" because it is the day God stopped creating, because it is the day God set aside for his rest, it is indeed "no ordinary day." With that point of reference, it stands out as extraordinary even in the context of the previous extraordinary six days. But Collins shifts that extraordinariness to make it no ordinary day in length – no ordinary 24 hour day. Declaring it to be a day of extraordinary event (an obvious extrapolation), he morphs it into a day of extraordinary length (an irrational extrapolation, but an inevitable one in view of his presupposition that this day in particular and all the days of this week are of extraordinary length). In his typically circular argument, he goes on to assert, "This makes us question whether the other days are supposed to be ordinary in their length."[1048] Collins wants us to see the seventh day as extraordinarily different from the other six days, and therefore not of ordinary length; while at the same time taking the seventh day as typical of the previous six days, wanting us to see all

---

[1047] Collins *Genesis 1-4* Kindle location 1396

[1048] ibid

seven days as being not of ordinary length and therefore not different but the same. This may or may not stretch the imagination, but it certainly does stretch credibility.

Yet the lack of refrain has both obvious and clear significance. The first part of the refrain "there was evening, and there was morning" has been used to indicate transition from one day of creation to the next. That is, it has not been primarily used to identify the completeness of each day[1049] – *that* has been signalled by numbering each day, just as this seventh day is numbered ("on the seventh day, God …"). So when at the end of the seventh day there is no transition to the next day of creation, guess what? There is no further day of creation to transition to. Seven days of extraordinary creation and rest are clearly numbered as seven days of ordinary length. The week of creation has been contained, in a literary sense, by an introduction, by six bridging/transitional refrains, and by a clearly marked change in language to bring it to an end. Rather than indicating day seven is not of ordinary length, the lack of refrain signals that the first week in history of seven days of ordinary length has been completed.

The Day the Creator Blessed

What is meant by God's "blessing" the seventh day? The term has already been used with both animals and man in affirming God's purpose in and promise of their fruitfulness. As Genesis unfolds, men are blessed as they enjoy good from God and the promise of its expansion. So when God blesses day seven he affirms it is very good, and that its goodness is a foretaste of what he will continue. Day seven is not just a marker in history making known that the Creator created and finished his work. It is a marker in history that the Creator created a *good* creation, and that his good would continue to be gifted to creation. It would continue to be gifted to man in the place created for him. But above all, it would continue to serve and exalt God as Creator: it glorified God. That first day after he stopped creating, creation glorified God by what it was, and because it was sustained by God's power and answered to God's sovereignty. By "blessing" that day, God declared creation fulfilled its purpose in glorifying him, and that it would be fruitful in continuing to do so.

What is meant by making day seven holy? Things are made holy (sanctified[1050]) when set aside exclusively for the worship of God. A bowl, for example, when made holy for temple service was exclusively for temple service and not available for other uses. There is a very real sense in which everything is for God's glory, and never more so than days one to six. Yet those days were also for man: God makes a place for man (that does indeed glorify God) and places man in it (also glorifying God) to serve God (that is, to glorify God). But this day, creation's seventh day, is God's alone. He continues to sustain creation, and man lives as God's servant: but the entire focus of day seven is God's and God's alone.

It is worth considering a little more closely what God's purpose was in creating. That purpose includes the creation of a place for man, a place where man could

---

[1049] It does of course confirm the completeness of the day indicated by numbering, but its *primary* use, dependent upon the concept of completeness, is to indicate transition.

[1050] KJV

fellowship with and serve God, and so join with creation in in displaying God's glory and rendering praise to him. That is true, so far as it goes. Creation is for man, albeit not man independent, but man as God's image bearer. But that is only part of the picture, for man is part of creation too. While man is served by the rest of creation, and is given dominion over it as God's agent on earth, man is also part of the creation that declares God's glory. God's objective of establishing a creation in which he could fellowship with man in grace and love is a staggering on-going demonstration of God's glory. But even that is a subset of his purpose. It is a glorious objective in itself, and at the same time contributes to the greater glory seen in God's ultimate purpose.

The ultimate purpose of God's creating is to satisfy God: "For from him and through him and for him are all things. To him be the glory forever! Amen."[1051] God created a universe for himself, and in resting (stopping) from creating on the seventh day, he declared it perfectly ready for its purpose. He stopped making his universe and began sustaining and governing it for his pleasure, unfolding his plans for history and eternity, nurturing and saving his people while holding cosmos and time in his hands for his glory:

> Come, let us sing for joy to the LORD;
> let us shout aloud to the Rock of our salvation.
> Let us come before him with thanksgiving
> and extol him with music and song.
> For the LORD is the great God,
> the great King above all gods.
> In his hand are the depths of the earth,
> and the mountain peaks belong to him.
> The sea is his, for he made it,
> and his hands formed the dry land.
> Come, let us bow down in worship,
> let us kneel before the LORD our Maker;
> for he is our God
> and we are the people of his pasture,
> the flock under his care.[1052]

A great painting can display the artist's glory, but the universe is no static work of art in a star-spangled setting: it is a dynamic and vibrant creation pulsating with energy, movement, life, and enormity; momentarily and constantly sustained and governed by God for himself. The glory of creation is to be found in more than its first six days, for in six days he made it all, and for ever since he has held it all. Nor is the universe some gigantic super-computer running automatically to divine algorithms installed at creation. Every moment, every movement, every stillness, every existence, every outcome is consciously and deliberately sustained and ruled by God for God.

[1051] Romans 11:36
[1052] Psalm 95:1-7

It is this "work" that Jesus alluded to when he affirmed, "My Father is always at work to this very day."[1053] So the seventh day of history is a marker not only for the completion of creation, but for the initiation of God's sustaining and governing that creation for his glory. In other words, God's "rest" is not only the stopping of his creating activity: God's rest is his unending, unfaltering sustaining and ruling of the cosmos.

This picture would be incomplete without also recognising two things:

1. The Trinitarian nature of this "rest." It is the Holy Spirit, present at creation[1054] and giving life to man,[1055] who is sent by the Father to bring living things to life on the earth, and who renews the earth on which they live.[1056] It is by the Son "through whom also he made the universe" that he sustains "all things by his powerful word."[1057]
2. The significance of his doing this by "word." The mechanism by which the Father sustains all things through the Son and the Spirit is by word. As he created by speaking, he sustains by speaking and rules by speaking.

God's rest day was a day God set aside for himself, and marked it down in time as the end of creating, and the beginning of his sustaining and ruling his creation, the beginning of history. The finishing post of history, though announced, is hidden from us, but the starting post is revealed. It is the seventh day of creation and it has God's names: "Creator, Sustainer, Ruler."[1058]

Who Rested?

God rested. Man? No, not man. Firstly, there is no mention of man resting on the seventh day of history. In fact, there is no mention of man at all on the seventh day of history. Why would there be? Man had not been creating, and that day's rest was a rest from creating: it says so very explicitly. The text is very clear: this was God's day of rest/stopping creation; it was God's day of enjoying the declaration of his glory by a perfect creation.

But for argument's sake, say that on that day man did rest from the work he had been doing … but he hadn't been doing six day's work to rest from. God has just told him – the day before – to fill the earth, subdue it, and govern it. I suppose it is possible he had started to fill the earth: but if Eve was pregnant by the end of Day 6, it wasn't something that could be stopped by a sabbath rest. True, naming the

---

[1053] John 5:17 Jesus by-passes the issue of the legitimacy or otherwise of man working on the Sabbath by claiming he is one with the Father who has never stopped working. When he says, "My Father is always at his work to this very day, and I too am working," Jesus is making three very important points. The first, which the Pharisees completely understand and as a result set out to kill him, is that he is equal with God: the work he does is the Father's. The second is that there has never been a sabbath (ie rest) for God from that work he refers to when he says "My Father is always working." Whatever rest God had on the seventh day of history did not involve stopping the work that he has done every day since. The third point is that the Sabbath does not apply to God.

[1054] Genesis 1:2

[1055] Job 33:4 cf Genesis 2:7

[1056] Psalm 104:30

[1057] Hebrews 1:2,3

[1058] Revelation 4:11

animals in a search for a helper on Day 6 was part of the mandate to subdue and govern, but that was work that was finished on Day 6, so there was nothing in that activity to stop for a day before taking it up again. In any case, one does wonder how "stopping" after half a day's work fits with the idea of working six days then taking a seventh day rest. While that really misses the point, Collins does get the point, and explains it with clarity. He asks

> What does God rest from? It must be from his work of furnishing the earth to be a place for mankind to live, love, and worship: he 'enjoys' the product of that workweek, which is finished. In other words, this Sabbath [Collins capitalisation] rest continues into the present, a notion that underlies John 5:17 and Hebrews 4:3-11.[1059]

It is worth repeating that God's seventh-day-sabbath (ie God's seventh-day-rest, or God's seventh-day-stopping-work) is not the Sabbath of Exodus 20. The latter is identified as the Sabbath Day (the Rest Day, or the Stop-Working Day) Israel is to keep every seventh day, and as such it is given the proper noun, "The Sabbath Day." God calls *this* sabbath "his holy day"[1060] in a similar way to which the seventh day of history was his holy day, for every Sabbath reminds Israel of God's sabbath. God's seventh day sabbath or rest, in reference to which the word "sabbath" is never used as a proper noun, is a rest from work which he never takes up again. It is a rest that God enjoys by sanctifying that seventh day of history without ever calling it "the Sabbath."

But Collins – as with many others – does not hesitate to go where God never went: "The Father is 'working' on his Sabbath, which only makes sense if we suppose that his creation Sabbath [ie day] continues."[1061] No! It confuses what Jesus is saying. It only makes sense if God's sabbath and Israel's Sabbath are different. Jesus is not saying that God kept working on his seventh-day-in-history-rest (albeit that is true), but that God also keeps working on Israel's Sabbaths. The moment the seventh day of history is given the proper noun "Sabbath" and made identical with the Sabbath of the Mosaic Covenant, the real nature of God's rest from creating, the real nature of God's continuing gracious work on every Sabbath Day (and every other day!), the real nature of Israel's Sabbaths, and the real nature of the rest we are moving towards when our work ends, are all obscured.

God's Rest, Our Promise

The significance of God's setting aside the seventh day of history as a sanctified/holy day lies firstly in this: God has done it! That should be more than enough to cause us to worship; him with awe. We rightly see the six days of creation as awesome, yet with shameful diffidence we so often somehow pass off the seventh day with a sort of, "And God rested. Ho hum." Yet for all the awesomeness of the first six days, God makes the seventh, and only the seventh, his set-aside holy day. God's greatest glory as Creator is not in the making of the cosmos, but in the

---

[1059] Collins *Genesis 1-4* Kindle location 1396
[1060] Isaiah 58:13
[1061] Collins *Genesis 1-4* Kindle location 1049

complete package: God creating the cosmos, *and* God taking up his created cosmos to sustain and govern it. That is what God is saying by making the seventh day holy.

The seventh day also has significance in what God memorialises and foreshadows by it. The fact that God created the world in six days, and stopped on and sanctified the seventh, is foundational for identifying who God is according to his own self-revelation,[1062] and to everything that follows. It is the foundation upon which God unfolds the outworking of his history and his sovereignty over man in every age and nation. It is the basis for Israel's worship.[1063] It is the starting point for John[1064] and for Paul[1065] as they announce the Gospel for Jew and Gentile alike. And, as I alluded to at the beginning of the second section of this book, it is the theme song of heaven.[1066] Deny, dilute or distort the biblical doctrine of the seventh day of history and you congruently deny, dilute or distort the Gospel.

But God's Rest *Is* For Us!

God's seventh day rest is also critical to the promise of eternal rest for God's people. "There remains, then, a Sabbath-rest for the people of God; for anyone who enters God's rest also rests from their works, just as God did from his."[1067] So "with regard to His work of creation, God's rest was final and grounded in the completion and perfection of that work; with regard to humanity, this rest pointed forward to a future state that it was to share."[1068] The rest that God began on the seventh day of history – his rest – is not one that on that day man took up. But when man has finished his work, he will then enter into that rest. There comes a day when God's people will, like God, stop work never to take it up again, for to enter God's rest is to rest the same way God rests. "Because there is no concept in Genesis 2:1-3 of a *cycle* of work punctuated by rest, its lesson is not that rest is good as a regular relief from work or as a means of making work more efficient, but that there is more to life than work; rest is the goal and fulfilment of work."[1069]

That rest will have fully come when this cosmos is replaced: "See, I will create a new heavens and a new earth."[1070] The old will go as the old came: "Long ago by God's word the heavens came into being and the earth was formed out of water and by water. ... By the same word the present heavens and earth are reserved for fire."[1071] Then

---

[1062] Deuteronomy 32:6; Psalm 106:1-9; Isaiah 45:12; Jeremiah 33:2; Amos 5:8; Jonah 1:9; Revelation 14:7

[1063] 2 Chronicles 2:12; Psalm 24:1-4; Psalm 100:3

[1064] John 1:1-5

[1065] Acts 14:15; Acts 17:24

[1066] Revelation 4:11

[1067] Hebrews 4:9,10

[1068] A T Lincoln "Sabbath, Rest and Eschatology in the New Testament" in Carson (Ed) *From Sabbath to Lord's Day* pp198f

[1069] Shead "Sabbath" in Alexander *The New Dictionary of Biblical Theology* p746 Here Shead also argues that inescapably, the Sabbath command of Exodus 20 "is not a mandate for Sabbath observance by all humanity, for the lesson of creation is applied narrowly to the Israelite Sabbath."

[1070] Isaiah 65:17

[1071] 2 Peter 3:5-7

we will all be changed— in a flash, in the twinkling of an eye, at the last trumpet. For the trumpet will sound, the dead will be raised imperishable, and we will be changed. For the perishable must clothe itself with the imperishable, and the mortal with immortality. When the perishable has been clothed with the imperishable, and the mortal with immortality, then the saying that is written will come true: "Death has been swallowed up in victory."

"Where, O death, is your victory? Where, O death, is your sting?"

The sting of death is sin, and the power of sin is the law. But thanks be to God! He gives us the victory through our Lord Jesus Christ.[1072]

[1072] 1 Corinthians 15:51-57

13. Genesis Replaced

The New Creation: Reading Genesis 1 in the light of promised perfection

"See, I will create new heavens and a new earth. The former things will not be remembered, nor will they come to mind. But be glad and rejoice forever in what I will create, for I will create Jerusalem to be a delight and its people a joy. I will rejoice over Jerusalem and take delight in my people; the sound of weeping and of crying will be heard in it no more."

~ Isaiah 65:17-19

The universe will end. This creation is not forever. "The present heavens and earth are reserved for fire, being kept for the day of judgment and destruction of the ungodly. … The heavens will disappear with a roar; the elements will be destroyed by fire, and the earth and everything done in it will be laid bare."[1073] The heavens and the earth created in six days will be destroyed by God and replaced by him with a new heavens and a new earth. There is judgement resting on this creation and there is a better creation to come. "In keeping with his promise we are looking forward to a new heaven and a new earth, where righteousness dwells."[1074] Unlike the creation in which sin now dwells, this will be a sinless creation in which righteousness dwells. The spectacular declaration of God's glory in the universe that he created and sustains – the Genesis 1 creation – is to be replaced by a new creation that is even more spectacular and even more revealing of God's glory.

[1073] 2 Peter 3:7 & 10

[1074] 2 Peter 3:13

In Christ we have a glorious hope, a hope that surpasses the glory of this present creation and our pilgrimage in it, a hope that is the fulfilment of the Sabbath rest, a hope in which we will stop work and take part in God's rest God's way. "See, I will create a new heavens and a new earth."[1075] The old will go as the old came: "Long ago by God's word the heavens came into being and the earth was formed out of water and by water. ... By the same word the present heavens and earth are reserved for fire."[1076] Even though we will stop work when we enter this new creation, it is not on account of our work that we get there! "Ultimately life comes as a gift through the Messiah, the possessor of the Spirit, the pioneer of life, who restores God's people to life. He holds the keys of death and Hades because he was dead but now lives. This restoration to life is salvation." [1077]

In a sense the new creation and the rest it brings "is a return to the Garden where life began."[1078] But the new creation surpasses the garden of Genesis 2 by far.[1079] It is a far, far better rest that we go to, than we have ever known.[1080] Even had the old creation not been marred by sin, even if it were not destroyed, its glory would fade out of sight in the face of the new creation. Glorious though it is, the old must go and give place to a far, far better place; a far, far better life; and a far, far better hope than man could hope to have without the new creation. It is a place prepared for God's people, the people of his love, where Jesus will be always present in the fullness of that love,[1081] leading us to springs of life.[1082] It will be a creation in which God will remove every tear and every cause for sorrow – even death itself.[1083]

The new creation is a place for the people of God. Although it is a rest to which all mankind is called, it is not a rest into which all mankind will enter. It brings to all who trust in Christ – and only to them – the full redemption he won at the cross. In Malachi's description of the day God ends this creation and creates the new,[1084] God makes clear that the sun of righteousness that brings healing to those who fear the Lord, is also the sun that burns like a furnace, setting every evil doer on fire like stubble. For God-fearer and God-hater alike, there is only righteousness from the sun of righteousness – the personification of Jesus coming as King of Kings, Saviour and Judge. The righteous release of God's people from the bondage of a fallen creation in which sin abounds, from the bondage of law that can never be fulfilled by us, from the bondage of guilt and accusation, is likened by Malachi to a calf – born and bred inside a barn – suddenly released into the open where it leaps for joy. All that Christ won at Calvary will be experienced in its fullness that day in which they are joined with a new creation in which righteousness rules. But for those who spurn God's grace and salvation, deny God's glory and authority,

---

[1075] Isaiah 65:17
[1076] 2 Peter 3:5-7
[1077] Johnson "Life" in New Dictionary of Theology p643
[1078] ibid
[1079] 1 Corinthians 2:9
[1080] Adapted from Dickens, *A Tale of Two Cities*
[1081] John 14:2,3
[1082] Revelation 7:17
[1083] Revelation 21:4,5
[1084] Malachi 4:1,2

worship the creation more than the creator, and idolise their pathetic self-images, there is nothing but righteous judgement from the sun of righteousness.

It can rightly be argued that "Creation's raison d'étre then is to serve the redemptive ends of God."[1085] But God's redemptive purpose in creation and new creation goes beyond individual redemption. God's redemption saves individuals on whom God has set his love, *and* unites them in a community of life and faith, the church of his love. Paul, speaking of God as the Creator of all things says, "His intent was that now, through the church, the manifold wisdom of God should be made known to the rulers and authorities in the heavenly realms."[1086] His picture of the church is that of the fulfilment of a unity pictured in marriage. For God, marriage is an image of Christ's love for and union with the church: "Christ loved the church and gave himself up for her to make her holy, cleansing her by the washing with water through the word, and to present her to himself as a radiant church, without stain or wrinkle or any other blemish, but holy and blameless."[1087] Redemption "is communal as well as individual."[1088] The new creation is a place for the people of God united as one, and as one united with Christ.

Rest in the New Creation

It is in that new creation that man in Christ will find rest from his work. When man's work is finished, he will stop by entering into God's rest, never again to take up the work he has finished. It will not be merely *like* God's rest: it will be participation in God's rest.[1089] Man will not find satisfaction in what he has done or in who he is or in independent sovereignty over creation. Instead, God's people will enter God's rest: that is, they will be brought into fellowship with him as he dwells with them,[1090] find satisfaction in what God has done and who God is,[1091] and with God, rule over God's new creation[1092] in which righteousness is completely pervasive. The goal of his work accomplished, the fulfilment of work will be taken up.

What work will man stop to enter this rest, "for anyone who enters God's rest also rests from their works?"[1093] What work will man keep doing, for in God's rest, God "is always at work to this very day?"[1094]

Hebrews 4 is the complex key for answers to those questions. It takes the concept of our promised rest back to Genesis 2 so that it clearly involves what the writer calls our entering into God's rest. He compares that with the promises of rest anticipated for Israel on entering the Promised Land, but points out that "If Joshua

---

1085 Reymond p398
1086 Ephesians 3:10
1087 Ephesians 5:25-27
1088 Johnson "Life" in New Dictionary of Theology p643
1089 Hebrews 4:9,10
1090 Revelation 21:3
1091 Revelation 7:9,10; 15:2-4
1092 Revelation 5:10
1093 Hebrews 4:10
1094 John 5:17

had given them rest, God would not have spoken about another day."[1095] He then calls on us – his readers – to persevere, working to find that rest in which we will no longer have to work. Although he later talks of our need to strive against sin,[1096] he never suggests anything but that our sin is forgiven through Christ, and not by our own efforts.[1097] This leaves us with this challenge: "You need to persevere so that when you have done the will of God, you will receive what he has promised."[1098] From this it appears that what we will rest from in God's rest is not labouring to subdue creation (which Genesis originally pointed to), and most certainly not labouring to cleanse ourselves from sin, for that is Christ's accomplished work; but our rest will be from the labour and fiery trial[1099] of persevering in faith and holiness in the life he has called us to in this world.

At creation God worked in creating his universe, then rested from that work so as to rule it. He set man to work to subdue that creation, and to rule it. As with God's creating, man's subduing sets the stage for ruling. As with God's creating, man's subduing is work from which he would rest upon its completion. Once that work had finished (had man not abandoned God's plan, plunging into sin with alacrity) man would have joined God in his rest of ruling the earth. That gives us more than a hint of what our rest in God's rest will be like. Our rest in God's rest will involve both not working to subdue all that is inimical to the new creation characterised by righteousness, for it will already be completely and harmoniously subject to God; and ruling with him over that new creation to ensure its good fulfilment of its created purpose. Why?

Firstly, it is *God's* rest Christ leads us towards. It is not just a rest for man from man's labours, but "entering into God's rest" which, as we have seen, is a rest from creating with an ongoing work of sustaining and ruling that creation. It is inconceivable then that when man enters into God's rest he becomes an indolent slug. Man's initial commission was to fill, subdue and rule: and if for God ruling is rest, then it would seem that for man ruling will be of the same sort – rest from the labours of subduing the earth, but enjoying the calling to rule that earth in the same harmony with which God rules the cosmos.

Secondly, as God models his redemption through Israel's separation to himself, he makes the "rest" of residing in the Promised Land a cessation of the struggle to subdue it and an enjoyment of God's presence in its daily life: "You will cross the Jordan and settle in the land the LORD your God is giving you as an inheritance, and he will give you rest from all your enemies around you so that you will live in safety … to the place the LORD your God will choose as a dwelling for his Name."[1100]

Thirdly, such a rest with on-going rule seems to be what Paul has in mind when he says "The Lord's people will judge the world."[1101] Further, sitting with Christ on

---

[1095] Hebrews 4:8
[1096] Hebrews 12:4
[1097] eg Hebrews 10:17 – but this is really what the whole book of Hebrews is about!
[1098] Hebrews 10:36
[1099] 1 Peter 4:12
[1100] Deuteronomy 12:10,11
[1101] 1 Corinthians 6:2

his throne as a "right"[1102] – an extraordinary right indeed! – implies some ruling role in fellowship with the King of Kings.

But whatever else God envisages in the rest he will bring us into, it involves settling his people in a new creation; it involves a union with Christ fulfilling what has been imaged in marriage;[1103] and it involves a fellowship with God dwelling, working, and ruling in our midst, compassionately making *everything* new:

> Then I saw "a new heaven and a new earth," for the first heaven and the first earth had passed away, and there was no longer any sea. I saw the Holy City, the new Jerusalem, coming down out of heaven from God, prepared as a bride beautifully dressed for her husband. And I heard a loud voice from the throne saying, "Look! God's dwelling place is now among the people, and he will dwell with them. They will be his people, and God himself will be with them and be their God. 'He will wipe every tear from their eyes. There will be no more death' or mourning or crying or pain, for the old order of things has passed away." He who was seated on the throne said, "I am making everything new!"[1104]

Why a New Creation?

"The great work whereby God designed to glorify himself ultimately in this world was that of the *new creation*, or of the recovery and restoration of all things by Jesus Christ."[1105] This statement form John Owen has huge significance. In recognising the bondage and corruption into which man's sin has dragged the creation, we can mistake God's revealed purposes, and mistakenly impugn the perfections of God. When we ask, "Why is a new creation needed?" it is common to respond that it is because of man's sin. That is true so far as it goes. But if that is all we say, it implies that God tried Plan A (creation) and when that did not work, was forced by man's rebellion to go to Plan B (new creation). Owen rightly affirms that God was neither surprised by a "failure" of Plan A, nor forced to adopt a Plan B. Rather, a new creation was needed because only "the recovery and restoration of all things by Jesus Christ" would glorify God in a way that could not otherwise happen. The creation is and always was terminal, albeit in God's sovereignty he brought it into judgement on account of man's sin. There was no "Plan A" and "Plan B," but one plan to create then to create anew. The new creation was always part of the only plan of God. "God's eternal plan never included the human race locked in the garden of Eden with the potential for self-destruction. Rather, it always included the work of Christ and his gospel, with a redeemed people in the new creation. This is the Sabbath rest for the people of God."[1106]

The Genesis creation was indeed very good. It perfectly fitted God's plan and purpose; but that plan and purpose went beyond what he accomplished in those first six days. God planned something even better:

1102 Revelation 3:21
1103 Ephesians 5:32
1104 Revelation 21:1-5
1105 Owen *Works* Volume 3 p157
1106 Graeme Goldsworthy *The Son of God and the New Creation* Crossway, Illinois, 2015, p117

> That which God ordereth and designeth as the principal means for the manifestation of his glory must contain the most perfect and absolute *revelation* and declaration of himself, his nature, his being, his existence, and excellencies; for from their discovery and manifestation, with the duties which as known they require from rational creatures, doth the glory of God arise, and no otherwise.[1107]

It is not in the creation of the new heavens and the new earth that this more glorious declaration of the glory of God will be displayed most clearly, for the new heavens and earth will come in a supporting role for the new creation. "The creation waits in eager expectation for the children of God to be revealed … in hope that the creation itself will be liberated from its bondage to decay and brought into the freedom and glory of the children of God."[1108] First comes the new creation of God's people, for "if anyone is in Christ, the new creation has come: The old has gone, the new is here!"[1109] Second comes the new heavens and the new earth that *enter into the freedom of God's people.*

Believers are "Created after the likeness of God in true righteousness and holiness"[1110] surpassing Adam in God-likeness. As Jesus is the "radiance of God's glory, the exact representation of his being,"[1111] so in Christ the redeemed will be "like him"[1112] revealing God's glory in God's image as only those imaged in true righteousness and holiness in Christ and created after the likeness of Christ can display. What the First Adam foreshadowed, the Second Adam accomplished, and fulfils in his people by making them his new creation. This "new creation," this people of God united with Christ, living in holiness and righteousness in God's rest, will be joined by the new heavens and the new earth. When the redeemed are free in new creation, so creation too can be freed into new creation. "The reversal of the curse that befell the whole creation will be achieved when we experience the final redemption of our bodies in the resurrection."[1113]

No wonder Paul tells the Romans to persevere in their sufferings in this present time, for those sufferings are "not worthy to be compared with the glory that shall be revealed in us."[1114] It is a glory revealed *in* us, not merely to us! It is not for its own display of God's glory that creation waits, "groaning as in the pains of childbirth,"[1115] but it "waits in eager expectation for the children of God to be revealed,"[1116] groaning with us as we wait eagerly for "the redemption of our bodies."[1117] What sort of new heavens and new earth could fit so glorious a revelation in God's people?

[1107] Owen *Works* Volume 3 p157 (his italics)
[1108] Romans 8:19-21
[1109] 2 Corinthians 5:17 Goldsworthy aptly comments that this "is often understood to be referring to the individual becoming a new creation rather than to an individual being swept up into the broader new creation Christ brings." [*The Son of God* footnote 1 p30]
[1110] Ephesians 4:24
[1111] Hebrews 1:2
[1112] 1 John 3:2
[1113] Goldsworthy *The Sons of God* p105
[1114] Romans 8:18
[1115] Romans 8:22
[1116] Romans 8:19
[1117] Romans 8:23

God can contrive matter so that there shall be other sort of proportions that may be quite of a different kind, and may raise another sort of pleasure in the sense, and in a manner now inconceivable, that shall be vastly more ravishing and exquisite. And in all probability the abode of the saints after the resurrection will be so contrived by God that there shall be external beauties and harmonies altogether of another kind from what we perceive here.[1118]

Creation Refreshed or Creation Replaced?

"The Bible begins in Genesis 1 and 2 with creation and ends in Revelation 21 and 22 with the new creation."[1119] But is it a completely new creation replacing a destroyed first creation or a renewal of the old creation in better form? Peter speaks of a heavens that pass away and an earth burnt up.[1120] This reads as a radical annihilation of the first creation, replaced by a new creation, a new heavens and earth.

There are however passages that appear to indicate the present creation will be reformed and renewed – albeit radically by a purging fire – rather than being destroyed and replaced. Calvin contends that the elements of the world "are to be consumed, only in order to receive a new quality while their substance remains the same."[1121] The result of such renovation is undoubtedly something so radically different that it can fittingly be described as a new creation, but is such a description a fitting exegesis of the Bible? As already noted, Peter's announcement of the final destruction of the present creation certainly reads as a complete annihilation: "The heavens will disappear with a roar; the elements will be destroyed by fire, and the earth and everything done in it will be laid bare … everything will be destroyed in this way ... That day will bring about the destruction of the heavens by fire, and the elements will melt in the heat."[1122]

This is in the context of scoffers who "deliberately forget that long ago by God's word the heavens came into being and the earth was formed out of water and by water." The implication is that as God spoke to create he will speak to destroy, and to make a new creation.

Psalm 102 appears equally definitive: "In the beginning you laid the foundations of the earth, and the heavens are the work of your hands. They will perish, but you remain; … they will be discarded."[1123] The writer to the Hebrews quotes this Psalm,[1124] and later expands on this with the promise of "the removing of what can

---

[1118] Jonathan Edwards *The Works of Jonathan Edwards*: Volume 2, The Banner of Truth Trust, Edinburgh, (1834) 1974 p618

[1119] Goldsworthy *The Son of God* p17

[1120] 2 Peter 3:10

[1121] J Calvin *Hebrews and I and II Peter* Calvin's New Testament Commentaries, Trans W B Johnston, Eerdmans, Grand Rapids, 1970 (1963) p365. Other translators [eg the 1885 Thrussington edition in the public domain] have "that they may be renovated, their substance remaining." However, Johnston's "new quality" is particularly helpful in informing the discussion below.

[1122] 2 Peter 3:10-13

[1123] Psalm 102:25,26

[1124] Hebrews 1:11

be shaken—that is, created things,"[1125] contrasting the removed creation with the kingdom of God that "cannot be shaken" or removed. Then in Revelation,[1126] John records his vision in which the "earth and the heavens fled from his presence, and there was no place for them," and "the first heaven and the first earth had passed away." These appear definitive of total destruction and replacement of the material creation.

Prophetic and eschatological writing is frequently imbued with metaphor and non-literal imagery, as these passages demonstrate with reference to God's hands, creation perishing and being discarded like worn-out clothing, and the earth and heavens fleeing. Yet even allowing for the imagery, those images all convey one basic idea: creation goes!

Creation Reconciled, Renewed and Restored?

In apparent contrast with these passages, there are texts that indicate a "renewing" or "restoring" of creation, implying a reformation of what is already there, a "material continuity between the present and the eschatological future."[1127] Do these descriptions of the destruction of the earth allow for something left (what Calvin calls the "substance" of creation) from which God will fashion the new creation? Significant among those texts is Paul's declaration that "God was pleased to have all his fullness dwell in him [Christ], and through him to reconcile to himself all things, whether things on earth or things in heaven, by making peace through his blood, shed on the cross."[1128] The concept of created things being reconciled to God through Christ does not seem to fit well with the idea of their total destruction, but rather that "the destiny of the natural world is not destruction but transformation."[1129] Similarly, Paul asserts that "the creation itself will be liberated from its bondage to decay and brought into the freedom and glory of the children

---

[1125] Hebrews 12:27

[1126] Revelation 20:11 & 21:1

[1127] Mark Stephens, *Annihilation or Renewal* Mohr Siebeck, Tubingen, 2011, p4. Stephens' extensive work is helpful in places, especially in surveying new creation language and concept in Revelation, but his presupposition of "creation" meaning "rearranging" or at best "effecting" [pp25ff etc] so colours his discussion as to make renewal the only possibility, leaving the impression at times that his exegesis is shaped by that presupposition. Add to that his commitment to eclectic use of a range of critical methods [pp12ff etc] that undermine confidence in God's plenary inspiration of the biblical text conveying transcendent meaning, and the book can be as unhelpful as it is helpful. Despite his very detailed discussion of texts, it is not always clear why he adopts one approach with one text and a contrary one with another; one reviewer, for example, comments "Stephens at numerous points chides those interpreters who dismiss the language of creational abundance in the OT prophets as being a merely metaphorical depiction of the divine removal of sin and dysfunction from the world. Yet at the same time, Stephens is content to argue that the apparent indications of creational destruction and judgment in the biblical writings should not be pressed in a hyper-literal fashion." [Ben Dunson "Annihilation or Renewal" (Book Review) *Themelios* Volume 37 # 2 July 2012 http://themelios.thegospelcoalition.org/issue/37-2] For another example, see Michael Williams *2 Peter 3 and the Destruction of the Earth* Third Millennium Ministries (undated) http://thirdmill.org/answers/answer.asp?file=44426

[1128] Colossians 1:19,20

[1129] Douglas Moo "Nature in the New Creation: New Testament Eschatology and the Environment" in *Journal of the Evangelical Theological Society* 49 (2006) p454

of God,"[1130] which, although part of a quite complex passage, seems strongly to suggest some form of continuity of old and new creation.

Various other passages incline one way or the other, although most have enough ambiguity to allow for either view.[1131] Two that are frequently referred to erroneously however are Jesus' allusion in Matthew to "the renewal of all things, when the Son of Man sits on his glorious throne,"[1132] and Peter's reference to the time coming "for God to restore everything."[1133] Matthew's "renewal" is a translation of *palingenesia*, a word used only twice in the New Testament. Here it possibly refers to 'the world that is to be',"[1134] or more precisely, "the consummation of the kingdom,"[1135] rather than the new creation. Its focus is the kingdom not the cosmos. It carries with it none of the connotations the English suggests of a remaking of the existing universe. That too applies to Peter's sermon, where the "restoration of everything" refers not to the material creation but to full recognition of and submission to the authority and majesty of the Messiah.

There can be confusion also with consideration of the "goodness" of creation. It is sometimes argued that as God declared creation "good" in Genesis 1, he would not destroy it: "It is difficult to think that God would entirely annihilate his original creation, thereby seeming to give the devil the last word and scrapping the creation that was originally good."[1136] There is no biblical basis for this: when God has finished with something why should he not finish with it? In this case, God's declaration that creation was good was not a description of its moral character but of its suitability for the use for which it was created.[1137] With the return of Christ and the introduction of the new creation, the old is most certainly finished with. In any case, Grudem bases his reasoning on 2 Peter 3:10 which is intimately linked with verse 6: "The world of that time was deluged and destroyed," so it seems entirely consistent with the revealed character, acts and purposes of God for God, having once destroyed a significant portion of his "good" creation, to finally and totally destroy the creation he has once declared good.

There is also the possibility that apocalyptic language would indicate dramatic but not literal fulfilment. It is commonly recognised that in Revelation John "frames his vision of cosmic eschatology"[1138] by drawing upon the imagery and language of Isaiah, Ezekiel and Daniel. On that basis one might legitimately expect a similar use of metaphor and hyperbole as in the prophets. There, for example, "the Lord is going to lay waste the earth and devastate it … the earth will be completely laid waste"[1139] still leaves the heavens and earth in place. Images of fire are used in those prophets for judgement that does not totally annihilate. On such evidence many assume hyperbole and metaphor of similar nature in Revelation. Caution would be

---

[1130] Romans 8:21
[1131] eg Isaiah 24:1-3; 65:17; Revelation 6:12-17; 20:11
[1132] Matthew 19:28
[1133] Acts 3:21
[1134] Leon Morris *The Gospel According to Matthew* (Pillar New Testament Commentary, Eerdmans Grand Rapids, 1992, p495 (foot)
[1135] D A Carson *Expositor's Bible Commentary* Volume 8, Zondervan, Grand Rapids, 1984, p425
[1136] Wayne Grudem (Jeff Purswell Ed) *Bible Doctrine* IVP, Leicester, 1999, p468
[1137] See p143 above
[1138] Stephens *Annihilation or Renewal* p20
[1139] Isaiah 24:1-3

prudent however, in that Revelation, as the final consummation of all that is foreshadowed, may well take to the full what is only partially effected at the time of the prophets. That John uses the same language as the OT Prophets does not mean he uses it in exactly the same way. He may by this means be drawing attention to the fulfilment of promises never fully realised in earlier events. While such considerations make renewal compatible with those texts, they do not compel such a reading.

The same caution is warranted in other passages where commentators invert the convention of reading the Old Testament in the light of the New by insisting that the way the language of total destruction was used in the Old Testament defines its use in the New. Philip Church notes that the quotation of Psalm 102 in Hebrews 1[1140] seems to "predict the dissolution of the cosmos,"[1141] but goes on to argue that as the Psalm predicted "not dissolution, but renewal after destruction resulting from exile," a restoration of the cosmos rather than its replacement is the expectation of Hebrews 1.[1142] Interpreting Hebrews in the immediate context of Psalm 102 may give eschatological renewal of the cosmos traction; but interpreting Hebrews (and with it, Psalm 102) in the context of Hebrews does not! For the writer of Hebrews, the heroes of the faith admitted "they were foreigners and strangers on earth … looking or a better country – a heavenly one."[1143] Contrasting their expectation with that of returning exiles, Hebrews records that had these heroes "been thinking of the country they had left, they would have had opportunity to return."[1144] By asserting they were "looking forward to the city with foundations, whose architect and builder is God,"[1145] the writer is not denying God is the creator of the present cosmos, but that the heavenly city is to be a better creation than what had been known because God will build it differently. Looking for a new earth, a new country and a new city really does look more like replacement than return, and read in that context Hebrews 1 takes the return from exile in Psalm 102 to its typological completion in the dissolution of this creation and the building of a new one.

Nevertheless, Romans 8 and Colossians 1 on their own do present compelling evidence for a renewal of some sort that fits well with those other texts.

[1140] Psalm 102:25-27 in Hebrews 1:10-12

[1141] Philip Church "Hebrews 1:10-12 and the Renewal of the Cosmos" *Tyndale Bulletin*, 67.2, Tyndale House, Cambridge, 2016, pp 269-286

[1142] He also proposes that the context of Hebrews 1, being the exaltation and of the unchanging Son (in contrast with a changing cosmos) who upholds the cosmos and the expectation "of the dominion of humanity over the world to come," indicates renewal. There is no logical necessity for that: the unchanging Son is exalted to at least the same standard in a replacement cosmos as in a renewed one, and humanity's rule over the world to come belongs to the world to come however it comes.

[1143] Hebrews 11:13 & 16

[1144] Hebrews 11:15

[1145] Hebrews 11:10

What Difference Does it Make?

Does it matter if the new heavens and the earth come with the destruction or the renewal of the old? To that question, many answer, "No,"[1146] and they have a point. If it is not clear *how* the old is to go and the new comes, the *fact* that the old will go and the new comes is what matters. "Many texts … do not seem to give a clear answer about continuity, although they do clearly emphasize that new creation means the eradication of sin and evil from God's creation as well as the perfect communion that will exist between God and his people in the new creation."[1147] That is surely Peter's point. He is not discussing the intricacies of the end of the old creation and the inauguration of the new. But because the fiery destruction of the old creation is certain, and the coming of "the new heavens and new earth where righteousness dwells"[1148] is certain, he calls on God's people to live holy lives. Knowing this about the future should change how we live now: "Since everything will be destroyed in this way, what kind of people ought you to be? You ought to live holy and godly lives as you look forward to the day of God … make every effort to be found spotless, blameless and at peace with him."[1149] John makes the same point: "And now, dear children, continue in him, so that when he appears we may be confident and unashamed before him at his coming."[1150] The outcome of either destruction or renewal is a new heavens and a new earth, and the knowledge of such an outcome is inducement to faithful and holy living and hope, irrespective of destruction or renewal.

The unremitting instruction of God's word to his people – in Old and New Testaments – is to live holy lives befitting God's holiness. Whether we turn to the Pentateuch ("be holy, because I am holy."[1151]) or the New Testament Epistles ("Be holy; without holiness no one will see the Lord."[1152]) God's call is for holiness. And in the face of the trial that is besetting his readers, Peter sees the coming destruction of the world and the coming of Christ and his kingdom as a critical encouragement to holiness:

> Therefore, with minds that are alert and fully sober, set your hope on the grace to be brought to you when Jesus Christ is revealed at his coming. As obedient children, do not conform to the evil desires you had when you lived in ignorance. But just as he who called you is holy, so be holy in all you do; for it is written: 'Be holy, because I am holy.'[1153]

[1146] eg D M Lloyd-Jones "I say it does not ultimately matter which of the two views we believe; but what does matter is that, as Peter puts it, 'we, according to his promise, look for new heavens and a new earth'." [*Expository Sermons on 2 Peter* Banner of Truth Trust, Edinburgh, 1983 (1948-50) p193]

[1147] Ben Dunson "Annihilation or Renewal"

[1148] 2 Peter 3:13

[1149] 2 Peter 3:11-14

[1150] 1 John 2:28

[1151] Leviticus 11:45

[1152] Hebrews 12:14

[1153] 1 Peter 1:13-16

Neither, Either or Both?

Yet the Bible is not as obscure regarding replacement or renewal as popular indecision suggests. If the Bible is sufficiently clear as to provide for a definitive view, faithful Bible reading demands we align our thinking with the text, whether or not we can see significance in the point God has chosen to make specific.

In focusing on the tension between renewal and replacement however, we may be asking the wrong question. Paul reminds the Corinthians that "'no eye has seen … no ear has heard, and … no human mind has conceived'— the things God has prepared for those who love him."[1154] If what God is going to do is inconceivable to man, it ought not to be surprising that we cannot conceive of it! The Bible

> must, in the nature of the case, seek to describe what is unique and quite beyond our experience – the transition from the temporal world to the eternal state – with language and analogies drawn from our own world. … There is continuity as well as discontinuity in the shift from the present heavens and earth to the new heaven and earth.[1155]

In other words, neither replacement nor renewal adequately describes what God is going to do; and to recognise that the Bible asserts both will happen is only an issue of conflict or tension within the frame of thinking confined – as we must be – to this terminal cosmos.

Consider that in 2 Corinthians believers are described, in their present state of new-birth and faith, as "new creations."[1156] There is a complex mix of imagery around Christians' present state, involving dying, being buried, being reborn, and being new – but without hesitation we must assert that we are the people we were before we came to faith and regeneration, albeit we are also new creations. There is a type of existence here that simply does not fit categories of existence as we know them within the created cosmos. Is it not possible that in the same way the new creation is of a sort that does not fit the existing creation? Is that not what every mention of the new creation points to?

In fact, Paul goes beyond saying believers are new creations: "if anyone is in Christ, the new creation has come: The old has gone, the new is here!"[1157] Believers constitute the new creation come. True, there is more to come. We have a hope of a new creation in which righteousness rules. What we have is the beginning but not the completion. But if the old has gone and the new has come, the new is radically different from the old. The terms renewal and replacement therefore both convey something of what God is doing and has promised, yet neither is sufficient to comprehend the continuity of the new with the old and the comprehensively new of the new.

The doctrine of the resurrection illustrates perfectly the discontinuity and continuity between the old and the new. The reality is that the bodies of most of the dead, having returned to dust, are by now even less than dust! Yet from these totally annihilated bodies, bodies that are but scattered molecules unidentifiable as belonging to anyone, God will raise the bodies of the dead – the actual bodies of

---

[1154] 1 Corinthians 2:9
[1155] Moo "Nature in the New Creation" p202
[1156] 2 Corinthians 5:17
[1157] 2 Corinthians 5:17

those people. We are not to be given replacement bodies, but our bodies in new form. It can be described as a different type of body, yet one that has continuity with the body that was totally destroyed. In writing to the Corinthians, Paul highlights the fact that this is a different type of body. He calls it a "spiritual body," not as if it is spirit without body but body of a sort fitted to the spiritual dimension:

> But someone will ask, "How are the dead raised? With what kind of body will they come?" How foolish! What you sow does not come to life unless it dies. When you sow, you do not plant the body that will be, but just a seed, perhaps of wheat or of something else. But God gives it a body as he has determined, and to each kind of seed he gives its own body. Not all flesh is the same: People have one kind of flesh, animals have another, birds another and fish another. There are also heavenly bodies and there are earthly bodies; but the splendour of the heavenly bodies is one kind, and the splendour of the earthly bodies is another. The sun has one kind of splendour, the moon another and the stars another; and star differs from star in splendour.
>
> So will it be with the resurrection of the dead. The body that is sown is perishable, it is raised imperishable; it is sown in dishonour, it is raised in glory; it is sown in weakness, it is raised in power; it is sown a natural body, it is raised a spiritual body. If there is a natural body, there is also a spiritual body.[1158]

Douglas Moo points to the resurrection body, especially the resurrection body of Jesus, as possibly "the best way to resolve the tension between destruction and transformation with respect to the universe."[1159] Just as in the resurrection, old-creation bodies have a new-creation form that exhibits both continuity associated with renewal and discontinuity associated with replacement, so the new creation may exhibit both renewal and replacement:

> Here also we find a puzzling combination of continuity and discontinuity. Jesus' resurrection body is able, apparently, to dematerialize and materialize again; it is not always recognizable; it is, as Paul puts in with respect to the resurrection body in general, a new kind of body, suited for existence in the spirit-dominated eternal kingdom (1 Cor 15:35-54). Yet there is continuity in the body: in some sense, the body that was in the grave is the same as the body that appears to the disciples after the resurrection.[1160] This 'transformation within continuity,' as Colin Gunton puts it, furnishes an apt parallel to the future of the cosmos.[1161]

Is there renewal or replacement of the old creation in the coming of the new creation? Both.

Waiting in a Terminal Creation

As already noted, the certainty and perfections of the new creation give impetuous to faithful living characterised by what we will be in the creation that will be. Perseverance, faithfulness, holiness, the suppression of evil desires and the cultivation of moral and spiritual purity are all addressed specifically by New

---

[1158] 1 Corinthians 15:35-44

[1159] Moo "Nature in the New Creation" p445

[1160] The body of Jesus the disciples saw was indeed "in some sense, the body that was in the grave." It carried the wounds of nail and spear [John 20:24-26].

[1161] Moo "Nature in the New Creation." p445 [His reference is to Colin E. Gunton, *Christ and Creation* Eerdmans, Grand Rapids, 1992 p31]

Testament writers as necessary response to believers' looking forward to the new heavens and the new earth. What is not so clear – because it is not directly addressed in the New Testament – is how believers should regard this present, terminal creation. It is not uncommon to find allusion to a contempt for (or at least an indifference to) the present creation among Christians who believe this creation is to be destroyed. On the other hand, commitment to the care of this creation among those who look for its reformation can assume concepts of transformation and improvement (a man-managed "redemption of the earth") that reduces all mention of cosmic judgement (and in many cases, personal judgement) to mere myth or metaphor. These extremes should not be allowed to obscure the plan of God that man maintains his first calling to subdue and rule this creation for the glory of God until God brings about the promised dramatic change in the locus of our service.

It is a false assumption that creation is disparaged by an expectation that it is to be replaced. In his discussion of Hebrews 1:10-12, Philip Church, for example, observes, "It does seem incongruous that a Psalm reflecting the traditions of the restoration of Zion … should then deconstruct it with the suggestion that the earth … will ultimately disappear."[1162] His discussion mistakenly ties God's declaration of creation as "good" to necessary renewal and links any idea of replacement with a disparaging of creation.[1163] There is no reason at all why God should not discard something he has made and called good when he has finished with it: in all his works of judgement, temporal and eternal, what he has created is no longer sustained as good. Further, the destruction of a cosmos once called good is not to be compared with the eternal wrath of God upon Adam's unbelieving descendants in hell, albeit Adam was part of the creation declared by God to be good.

Indifference towards the environment is frequently attributed to Christians committed to belief in the total destruction of the cosmos, even if they are not said to be disparaging it. In some senses this can be considered the environmental equivalent of the cultural pessimism of apocalyptic premillennialism.[1164] An expression that seems to have quite wide currency is this: "It's all going to burn, anyway." On that basis careless treatment of the world in which we live, and abuse of its resources, is said to be excused if not impelled. Yet strangely, the expression has currency almost exclusively among those committed to a belief in the transformation of the cosmos.[1165] While transformational writers frequently allude

---

[1162] Philip Church "Hebrews 1:10-12" p274 Church argues credibly that the thrust of the passage is not so much the endurance of the cosmos but how a deteriorating cosmos contrasts with the enduring reign of the Son, their Creator. But the future of the cosmos is still a critical issue in the passage.

[1163] Philip Church "Hebrews 1:10-12" p285

[1164] A close look at apocalyptic premillennialism is beyond the scope of this book. Sufficient to say that its popularity (if not dominance) in American evangelicalism through much of the 20th century led variously to forms of engagement with, or fear of, secular society that has some congruency with evangelical insecurity with more contemporary environmental issues.

[1165] Non-Christian environmentalists also use it to beat-up Christians, as also when used by liberals (defining themselves as Christian but rejecting traditional Evangelical doctrine) such as John Mabry in *Crisis & Communion* Apocryphile, Berkley, 2005 p131 in which he reduces the second coming and new creation to myth to be fulfilled in the liberation of all from fear, oppression and poverty in a benign earth. But the expression's currency (and the credibility of non-Christian critiques) is maintained by transformationalists' constant reference to it, not by any evidence of significant use among Christian writers, teachers or churches holding to such a view.

to it, and a few give anecdotal references to individuals who have used it, I can find no use of the expression in any replacement writing at all, let alone in any serious writing on 2 Peter or similar passages by replacement writers; nor can I find any credible citations to such use in the allusions made by transformationalists.[1166]

There are many examples, but two will do for this discussion: In her essay, "Isn't It All Going To Burn Anyway,"[1167] Nancey Sleeth reports having encountered the expression throughout the United States, leading people to ask, "If Revelation says it is all going to burn up in the end, why should Christians care?" and "Why care for the earth when God's just going to destroy it?" Matthew Tallman argues for something more than occasional use of the expression: "Has not an eschatological emphasis upon an imminent Parousia caused all Pentecostals to completely disregard any future hope for the rest of creation by suggesting that 'it's all going to burn anyway'?"[1168]

Two things can be said in response: 1. There is no biblical warrant to use the concept that God is going to destroy this cosmos to excuse abusing it or simply not caring for it; much less for disparaging it. In fact, there is clear biblical direction to do the opposite. 2. Disdain for the environment is neither a necessary nor sufficient consequence of taking 2 Peter (or any other passage) to announce the total destruction of the cosmos. On the contrary, the normal position of those who anticipate the total destruction of the heavens and the earth is arguably identical to that of transformationalists such as Sleeth: "Life on earth matters. What we do on earth matters. God created the earth and cares for it. God called it 'good' and gave us responsibility to care for it. When we care for the earth, we are participating in the work of God."[1169] That's because our duty of care for the earth is not based on the terminus of the cosmos, nor on its relative goodness, but on God's command at its origin, the command for man to subdue and rule over creation as God's agents.

None of the Bible's passages about the replacement or renewal of the cosmos have anything to do with our present care of it. As already noted, Peter uses his description of the end of the cosmos, not to validate or invalidate environmental care, but to urge God's people to "live godly and holy lives." True, caring for the environment can be extrapolated from the instruction to live godly and holy lives; not, though, as a consequence of the earth's destruction or renewal, but as a result of what God declares is holy: obedience to his commands.

Present popular rebuttal of the "It's all going to burn, anyway" error attacks a straw man.[1170] In rebutting the idea that replacement of the creation implies carelessness towards it, transformationalists go on to turn the argument on its head

---

[1166] That is not to say that such writing and references do not exist: I have searched quite assiduously but by no means exhaustively! But I am happy to assert that the overwhelming use of the term appears to be by transformationalists critiquing the complete destruction/replacement model.

[1167] Nancey Sleeth "Isn't It All Going to Burn Anyway?" in Trip York & Andy Alexis-Baker *A Faith Encompassing All Creation* Cascade, Eugene 2014 [the quotations that follow are from pp111f]

[1168] Matthew Tallman "Pentecostal Ecology" in Amos Yong (Ed) *The Spirit Renews the Face of the Earth* Wipf and Stock, Eugene 2009 [Here especially one can see the influence of apocalyptic premillennialism.]

[1169] Sleeth "It's All Going to Burn Anyway" p119

[1170] By referring to it as a "straw man" I do not intend to deny *some* give voice to this error; but they do not appear to constitute a body of serious or significant commentary.

and claim that the promised renewal of the creation implies we must care for it. The error of carelessness towards creation, espoused by a few, is elevated in significance so as to become a foil against which renewal theology is used to underpin an eco-evangelicalism. Evangelical concern for godly management of the environment can easily be justified – and should be – in terms of the creation command, but basing it on loose exegesis of Romans 8, Colossians 1, and 2 Peter 3 almost always involves minimising the fiery destruction of the cosmos that is promised along with its renewal.[1171] We ought to care for this creation, but not as if we thereby stave off the death of the planet.

This minimising or overlooking God's promised destruction of creation in renewal theology frequently synthesises renewal theology with populist hopes of ecological salvation. Sleeth, for example, seems to leave the way open for this by arguing that "Because God is making all things new, we get the honor of participating in this renewal process by protecting God's earth now."[1172] In other words, what we do now for creation in some way contributes to the new creation, and our ecological advances will carry through to the new creation. This denies both the promise of creation's destruction and of God's creating the new creation as *his* creation by *his* word.

Christians should undoubtedly be committed to minimising pollution, and nurturing creation even as we use it in sustainable ways. We should respect it as God's creation and strive to ensure it is kept well for future generations. But when caring for God's creation gives place to preserving creation we may not be far removed from "serving created things rather than the Creator."[1173] Good ecological management is a good to which every Christian should be committed in response to God's command to rule creation on his behalf, but it will not preserve creation beyond God's planned termination. Nor will pollution or unsustainable consumption destroy it, albeit they deface God's creation and render life for others a greater struggle than loving them would provide. In his time, and only in his time, God will destroy creation in judgement with a destruction that consumes even the "laws" of nature that environmental care utilises – and render utterly insignificant anything global warming or nuclear holocaust could achieve.

This Creation: Glory & Life Now!

Yet it is *this* creation that displays the glory of God and reveals his handiwork, even though it is passing. This creation will give place to a better one, but it is *this* creation that God declared to be good for man, and it is *this* creation he sustains through its seasons and days. This creation is a place of struggle, sweat and pain; yet it is in *this* creation we are called to mediate God's dominion and serve him with perseverance. This creation is a theatre of decay, devastation and death; yet it is in *this* creation we are given life in all its richness and called to live holy lives. This creation is host to a multitude whose whole being is at enmity with God; yet it is in *this* creation to these people we are called to bring care, compassion, love, and

---

[1171] For the most part fiery destruction doesn't even get a mention, but where it does, it is taken as hyperbole or metaphor.
[1172] Sleeth "It's All Going to Burn Anyway" p116
[1173] Romans 1:25

the good news of Jesus Christ. This creation is terminal, but it is for now our home away from home. It is marred, but it is for now our place of service and worship. And why not! It may be terminal, it may be marred, but overwhelmingly, it is glorious. Every day dawns in fulfilment of his faithfulness, passes with myriad spectacles great and small of his creative power, and ends with the certainty of the coming dawning of not just a new day, but a new creation. There is no moment in history nor place in the cosmos that does not shout God's glory and call for his praise:

> LORD my God, you are very great;
> you are clothed with splendour and majesty.
> The LORD wraps himself in light as with a garment; …
> He set the earth on its foundations;
> it can never be moved. …
> How many are your works, LORD!
> In wisdom you made them all;
> the earth is full of your creatures.
> There is the sea, vast and spacious,
> teeming with creatures beyond number—
> living things both large and small. …
> May the glory of the LORD endure forever;
> may the LORD rejoice in his works— …
> I will sing to the LORD all my life;
> I will sing praise to my God as long as I live.[1174]

Creation's Message

Creation declares the glory of God, and the seventh day of history, the day God stopped creating and made his own, anchors that display of that glory in a six-day burst of unparalleled, completed, creative power. Samuel Marsden's response to creation is one that every man, woman and child should give voice to:

> How great and marvellous are the works of God in creation. How wonderful and infinite in power must be he who spake and every creature was made from the largest to the most minute. How happy are those who are graciously protected by this almighty power! May I at all times put my trust in the Lord for with him is everlasting strength.[1175]

Creation sings in harmony with Genesis 1. In the beginning God made everything, and he did so as he now sustains it, and as he will end it, by his powerful word.[1176] It did not begin, it does not continue, and it will not end naturally, as if nature is self-generating and self-sustaining, for from beginning to end creation is

---

[1174] Selected verses from Psalm 104

[1175] Andrew Sharp *The World, the Flesh & the Devil* Auckland University Press, Auckland, 2016, p93 quoting Samuel Marsden's Journal Entry for 15 November 1793, in response to his first sighting of a whale while on his journey to New South Wales from where he would eventually launch the first Christian mission to New Zealand.

[1176] Hebrews 1:2,3

the work of his hands declaring his glory.[1177] From creation to new creation, everything that happens in the cosmos – whether in the ordinary events that follow the patterns by which he normally governs nature or in the extraordinary events that do not fit those patterns – God decrees and nature obeys.

Whether "heard" from the wordless voice of creation[1178] or the inspired words of Genesis 1, creation's message calls for faith in, submission to, and worship of the Creator from every created man, woman and child. Such a response will rejoice in the perspicuity of Genesis 1, and delight to trust it as the foundation for faithful and energetic engagement in man's gifted dominion of creation through the sciences, community and the arts and all that belongs to the glory of life in its fullness in Christ.[1179]

When the "Teacher" declares, "Remember your Creator,"[1180] he goes on to say, do it "in the days of your youth," before age dims the eyes, making the glory of creation increasingly incomprehensible. But it is not only age that opaques creation's display. For many, long before old age intervenes, it is simple unbelief[1181] that generates denial of the plain wording of God's revelation in Scripture and denial of those seven days of creation; and with that denial, denial of creation's Creator, denial of the Creator's judgement on sin, sinners and a sin-corrupted creation, and denial of the Creator's new creation:

> Who is this that obscures my plans
> with words without knowledge?
> Brace yourself like a man;
> I will question you,
> and you shall answer me.
> Where were you when I laid the earth's foundation?
> Tell me, if you understand.
> Who marked off its dimensions? Surely you know!
> Who stretched a measuring line across it?
> On what were its footings set,
> or who laid its cornerstone—
> while the morning stars sang together
> and all the angels shouted for joy?[1182]

To creation's message faith, submitting to God's self-revelation in the words of the Bible, explains seen reality, gives substance to imminent unseen reality,[1183] and responds, "Now my eyes have seen you."[1184]

[1177] Psalm 19:1
[1178] Psalm 19:3
[1179] John 10:10
[1180] Ecclesiastes 12:1
[1181] Unbelief need not be expressed in outright denial of the inspiration of Genesis 1. Whether confused by experts claiming that what Genesis 1 says is not what it means, or beguiled into accommodating Genesis 1 to the naturalism of this age, rejecting, doubting or distorting the plain meaning of Genesis 1 without warrant in the text of the Bible itself is unbelief. Neither the "wisdom" of academics, nor the motifs of pagan literature or their myths – much less our own good intentions – can justify a "faith" that fails to submit to the text God has spoken.
[1182] Job 38:2ff
[1183] Hebrews 11:1
[1184] Job 42:5

God
formed clay
Spirit
breathed life
Man

Man
glory surrendered
Born
cross-nailed
Dead

God and Man
risen
Life-gifting Saviour
eternally
Man and God

God for man
Redeemer
God with man
Rest
Redemption accomplished

New Creation

Bibliography

Alliance of Confessing Evangelicals *Statement on Biblical Inerrancy*

Laidlaw College, Understanding Genesis 1-3: Exploring Two Contrasting Evangelical Perspectives, 17 July 2013. See and

Merriam-Webster Dictionary 2016

New Zealand Council for Educational Research *Scientific Language*

Westminster Confession of Faith

Alter, Robert *The Five Books of Moses* Norton, New York, 2004

Banks, E J in James Orr (ed) International Standard Bible Encyclopedia 1951

Barrett Matthew (ed) *Reformation Theology: A Systematic Summary* Crossway, Wheaton, 2017

Bauckham, Richard *The Gospels as History*[no date given]

Bavinck, Herman *The Doctrine of God* The Banner of Truth Trust, Edinburgh, 1977 (1951)

——— (J Bolt ed) *In the Beginning: Foundations of Creation Theology* Translated by John Vriend, Baker, Grand Rapids, 1999

Beale, G K *Eden, the Temple, and the Church's Mission in the New Creation* in Journal of Evangelical. Theological. Society 48/1 (March 2005) pp5-31 http://jbburnett.com/resources/beale_eden-temple-mission.pdf

——— The Erosion of Inerrancy in Evangelicalism: Responding to New Challenges to Biblical Authority Good News Publishers/Crossway, Wheaton 2008

——— The Temple and the Church's Mission: A Biblical Theology of the Dwelling Place of God IVP Academic, Downers Grove, 2004

Berkhof, Louis *Systematic Theology* Banner of Truth, London, 1958 (1941)

Bratcher, Denis *Enuma Elish: "When on High ..."* Christian Resource Institute, 2013,

Bray, Gerald L "God" in Alexander *The New Dictionary of Biblical Theology* IVP, Leicester/Downers Grove, 2000

Brookes, Thomas *Precious Remedies Against Satan's Devices* Banner of Truth, London, 1968, (1652)

Buchan, John *The Thirty-Nine Steps* (London 1915) this edition Chatto & Windus, London 1985

Burridge, Richard *What Are the Gospels? A Comparison with Graeco-Roman Biography* (2nd Ed) Eerdmans, Grand Rapids 2004 (1992)

Butterfield, Rosaria *Love Your Neighbour Enough to Speak the Truth* The Gospel Coalition, October, 2016

Calvin, John (tansl John King) *Commentary on Genesis* Banner of Truth Trust, London, 1965 (1554)

——— *Hebrews and I and II Peter* Calvin's New Testament Commentaries, Trans W B Johnston, Eerdmans, Grand Rapids, 1970 (1963)

——— *Institutes of the Christian Religion* Henry Beveridge (Trans), James Clarke, London, (1536) 1962

——— The Second Epistle of Paul the Apostle to the Corinthians, Eerdmans, Grand Rapids, 1964 (1547)

Carson, D A *Exegetical Fallacies* Baker, Grand Rapids, 1984

——— *Expositor's Bible Commentary* Volume 8, Zondervan, Grand Rapids, 1984

——— *Jesus the Son of God* Crossway, Wheaton, 2012

——— *The God Who Is There* Baker, Grand rapids, 2010

——— *The Gospel According to John* Apollos /IVP, Leicester, 1991

Carson, D A & **Moo**, D *An Introduction to the New Testament* Apollos/IVP Leicester 2005

Cassuto, U (I Abraham trans) *Genesis: Part 1 From Adam to Noah* Magnes Press, Jerusalem, 1944

Church, Philip "Hebrews 1:10-12 and the Renewal of the Cosmos" *Tyndale Bulletin*, 67.2, Tyndale House, Cambridge, 2016, pp 269-286

Clines, D J A "Alleged Female Language about the Deity in the Hebrew Bible" the Society of Biblical Literature, Seoul, 2016

——— "The Image of God in Man: Tyndale Old Testament Lecture 1967" *Tyndale Bulletin 19* Tyndale House, Cambridge, 1968 pp 87-90

Collins, John *The Evolution of Adam* (book review)

——— Did Adam and Eve Really Exist? Who They Were and Why You Should Care Crossway, Wheaton, 2011

——— "A Historical Adam: Old-Earth Creation View" in Barret & Caneday (eds) *Four Views on the Historical Adam* Zondervan, Grand Rapids, 2013

——— in *Interpreting Adam: An Interview with Jack Collins, Part 1* Biologos, 2014

——— John Collins Replies to Richard Belcher, Jr 2014

——— *Types of Language and Biblical Interpretation*, [paper distributed by Collins at his Auckland lectures, July 2013] 2012

Craig, William Lane *Divine Timelessness and Personhood* C S Lewis Society of California, June 2016 from Craig, William Lane. "Divine Timelessness and Personhood." *International Journal for Philosophy of Religion* 43 (1998)

Currid, John *Against the Gods* Crossway, Wheaton, 2013

——— Ancient Egypt and the Old Testament Baker Books, Grand Rapids, 1997

——— "Exodus," in Miles V Van Pelt (Ed) A Biblical-Theological Introduction to the Old Testament: The Gospel Promised Crossway, Wheaton, 2016

Dabney, R L *Lectures in Systematic Theology* Baker, Grand Rapids, 1972 (1927)

——— *Lectures in Systematic Theology* Baker, Grand Rapids, 1985 (1878)

DeYoung, Kevin, Taking God At His Word: Why the Bible Is Knowable, Necessary, and Enough, and What That Means for You and Me Crossway, Wheaton, 2014

——— What Does the Bible Say About Transgenderism? The Gospel Coalition, 2016,

Delitzsch, F *A Commentary on Genesis* Translated S Taylor, T T Clarke, Edinburgh, 1888

Drake, Lyndon, "Abba isn't Daddy" Auckland Baptist Tabernacle, 2013

Dressler, Harold "The Sabbath in the Old Testament" in D A Carson (Ed) *From Sabbath to Lord's Day* Wipf and Stock, Eugene, 1999 (Zondervan 1982)

Dunson, Ben "Annihilation or Renewal" (Book Review) *Themelios* Volume 37 # 2 July 2012 http://themelios.thegospelcoalition.org/issue/37-2

Edwards, Jonathan *The Works of Jonathan Edwards*: *Volume 2*, The Banner of Truth Trust, Edinburgh, (1834) 1974

Enns, Peter The Evolution of Adam, What the Bible Does and Doesn't Say about Human Origins Baker Publishing Group, Grand Rapids, 2012

——— Inspiration and Incarnation: Evangelicals and the Problem of the Old Testament Baker Academic, Grand Rapids, 2005

——— The Firmament of Genesis 1 is Solid but That's Not the Point Biologos, 2010

——— Peter Enns on the Incarnational Model of Scripture Biologos, 2010,

——— Preliminary Observations on an Incarnational Model of Scripture: Its Viability and Usefulness Biologos, [no date given]

——— Still in the Weeds of Human Origins Book Review of C John Collins Did Adam and Eve Really Exist)

Evans, M J "Blessing/Curse" in Alexander *The New Dictionary of Biblical Theology* IVP, Leicester/Downers Grove, 2000

Faulkner, R O in William Simpson (ed) *The Literature of Ancient Egypt* New Haven, 1973

Feinberg, Charles Lee "The Image of God" in Bibliotheca Sacra 129, Dallas Theological Seminary, July 1972

Frame, John "Men and Women in the Image of God" in Piper & Grudem *Recovering Biblical Manhood and Womanhood* Crossway, Illinois, 1991

Gaffin, Richard *By Faith, Not by Sight* Paternoster, Waynesboro, 2006

Geisler, Norman, *Explaining Hermeneutics: A Commentary on the Chicago Statement on Biblical Hermeneutics* International Council on Biblical Inerrancy, Oakland, 1983 [on Article XXIV)

Godowa, Brian *Mesopotamian Cosmic Geography in the Bible* Biologos, (undated)

Goldsworthy, Graeme *The Son of God and the New Creation* Crossway, Illinois, 2015

Grudem, Wayne (Jeff Purswell Ed) *Bible Doctrine* IVP, Leicester, 1999

Hartnett, John "The 'Waters Above'" in *Journal of Creation* Volume 20, Issue 1, March 2006, Creation Ministries International, Australia

Hawking, Stephen *The Origin of the Universe* (Undated)

Heiser, Michael *I Dare You Not to Bore Me with the Bible,* Lexham Press, Bellingham, 2014

——— *Super Natural* Lexham Press, Bellingham, 2015

——— *The Unseen Realm* Lexham Press, Bellingham, 2015

Helopoulos, Jason,

Hill, Wesley *A New Way of Being Human* September 2016

Hodge, A A & **Warfield,** B B "Inspiration" in *The Presbyterian Review 6* (April 1881), pp. 225-60

Hoekema, Anthony A *Created in God's Image* Eerdmans, Grand Rapids, 1986

Holding JP & **Peters** Nick *Defining Inerrancy: Affirming a Defensible Faith for a New Generation* Tekton, (Kindle) 2014

Horton, Michael "What Are We Celebrating?" in Matthew Barrett (ed) *Reformation Theology: A Systematic Summary* Crossway, Wheaton, 2017

Jastram, Nathan "Man as Male and Female: Created in the Image of God" in *Concordia Theological Journal Volume 6:1* Concordia, Fort Wayne, 2004

Jastrow, Robert *God and the Astronomers*, W.W. Norton, New York, 1978

Johnson, D H "Life" in Alexander et al (Ed) *The New Dictionary of Biblical Theology* IVP Leicester/Downers Grove, 2000

Keil and **Delitzsch** *Commentary on the Old Testament* T & T Clark, Edinburgh, 1885 (1866)

Keller, Tim *The Bible and Same Sex Relationships: A Review Article* Redeemer Presbyterian Church, June 2015

——— *Creation, Evolution and Christian Laypeople* The Biologos Foundation, p2

——— *Counterfeit Gods* Hodder & Stoughton, London, 2009

——— A Theology of Cities CRU, (undated)

Kelly, Douglas *Creation and Change* Mentor (Christian Focus), Fearn (Scotland), 2015 (1997)

Kidner, D "Vol. 1: Genesis: An Introduction and Commentary." *Tyndale Old Testament Commentaries* IVP, Nottingham, 1956

——— "Genesis: and Introduction and Commentary" in Wiseman (Ed) *Tyndale Old Testament Commentaries Volume 1* IVP, Nottingham, 1967

Kline, Meredith G "Space and Time in the Genesis Cosmogony" in *Perspectives on Science and the Christian Faith* 48:1, March 1996, The American Scientific Affiliation, Ipswich

Kuyper, Abraham *Lectures on Calvinism* Cosimo Classics, New York, 2007 (1931)

Lloyd-Jones, D M *Expository Sermons on 2 Peter* Banner of Truth Trust, Edinburgh, 1983 (1948-50)

Lanser, Rick *Genesis 1 and the Raqia* Associates for Biblical Research, 2009

Leithart, Peter "Genesis 1 in Ancient Perspective?" in *First Things First* 20 June 2014

Lenzi, Alan "John Walton: Ancient Near Eastern Thought and the Old Testament" [Book Review] *RBL 10/2007* Society of Biblical Literature, 2007,

Letham, Robert *The Holy Trinity* P&R, Phillipsburg, 2004

Leupold, *Exposition of Genesis* Baker, Grand Rapids, 1950

Lewis, C S *Fern-seeds and Elephants* 1998 ["Modern Theology and Biblical Criticism," essay read at Westcott House, Cambridge, 11 May 1959 and published under that title in *Christian Reflections* 1981]

——— "The Language of Religion" in *Christian Reflections*, Eerdmans, 1964

Luther, Martin *Assertio omnium articulorum M. Lutheri per bullam Leonis X. novissimam damnatorum* (1520), WA 7:98.40–99.2. quoted by Mark Thompson "Sola Scriptura" in Matthew Barrett (ed) *Reformation Theology: A Systematic Summary* Crossway, Wheaton, 2017

——— *The Bondage of the Will* 1525, translated by Packer & Johnston, James Clarke, London, 1957

——— (J Pelikan ed) *Luther's Works: Volume 1 "Lectures on Genesis 1-5"* Concordia, Saint Louis, 1958

Mabry, John in *Crisis & Communion* Apocryphile, Berkley, 2005

Matson, Joshua "Idol Remains: Remnants of the Opening of the Mouth Ritual in the Hebrew Bible" in *Studia Antiqua: A Student Journal for the Study of the Ancient World* 12:1 (2013)

Melanchthon, Philipp *Epistolas ad Hessum, CR 1*:141; *Melanchthon: Selected Writings,* 51 quoted by Mark Thompson "Sola Scriptura" in Matthew Barrett (ed) *Reformation Theology: A Systematic Summary* Crossway, Wheaton, 2017

Moo, Douglas "Nature in the New Creation: New Testament Eschatology and the Environment" in *Journal of the Evangelical Theological Society* 49 (2006)

Morris, Henry & **Whitcomb,** John *The Genesis Flood* Evangelical Press, London, 1969 (1961)

Morris, Leon *The Gospel According to Matthew* (Pillar New Testament Commentary), Eerdmans, Grand Rapids, 1992

Motyer, J A "Name" in Douglas *et al* (Eds.) *The New Bible Dictionary* IVP, London, 1962

——— "Name" in D. R. W. Wood, *et al* (Eds.), *New Bible Dictionary* (3rd ed.) IVP, Leicester, 1996

Muffs, Yochanan *The Personhood of God* Jewish Lights Publishing, Woodstock, 2005

Murray, John *Principles of Conduct* Tyndale Press, London, 1957

Oswalt, John N The Bible Among the Myths: Unique Revelation or Just Ancient Literature? Zondervan, 2009

Owen, John (Goold Ed) *The Works of John Owen DD Vol 19* Johnstone & Hunter, London 1854

Packer, J I *Fundamentalism and the Word of God* IVF, London, 1963 (1958)

——— "Good" in *The New Bible Dictionary* IVP, London, 1962

——— *Statement on Biblical Hermeneutics* Alliance of Confessing Evangelicals

Pipa, Joseph "The Sabbath as a Creation Ordinance" *New Horizons* Orthodox Presbyterian Church, April 2009,

Powlison, David *Brother, Where is Your Identity?* The Gospel Coalition, 2015,

Pratt, Richard L *Designed for Dignity* P & R, Phillipsburg, 1993

Pyle Rod "Stephen Hawking: Big Bang Didn't Need God" Huffington Post, 17/4/2013

Reymond, Robert *A New Systematic Theology of the Christian Faith* Thomas Nelson, Nashville, 1998

Richardson, John "Anglican Update" in *Evangelicals Now* vol 26 #10, November 2013

Ryle, J C *Knots Untied* National Protestant Church Union, London, 1900 (1885)

Sailhamer, J "Genesis" in F E Gaebelein (Ed) *The Expositor's Bible Commentary Volume 2* Zondervan, Grand Rapids, 1990

——— *Genesis Unbound* Dawson Media, Colorado Springs, 2011

——— The Pentateuch as Narrative: a biblical-theological commentary Zondervan, Grand Rapids, 1992

Schaeffer, Francis A *How Should We Then Live* Crossway, Wheaton, 2005 (1976)

Sharp, Andrew *The World, the Flesh & the Devil* Auckland University Press, Auckland, 2016

Shead, A G "Sabbath" in Alexander *The New Dictionary of Biblical Theology* IVP, Leicester/Downers Grove, 2000

Sleeth, Nancey "Isn't It All Going to Burn Anyway?" in Trip York & Andy Alexis-Baker *A Faith Encompassing All Creation* Cascade, Eugene 2014

Smith, Claire *God's Good Design* Matthias Media, Kingsford, 2012

Smith, James K A *Whose Bible? Which Adam?* (Book Review of *The Evolution of Adam)* The Colossian Forum, Grand Rapids, 2012

Speiser, E. A. (James Pritchard ed) *Ancient Near Eastern Texts Relating to the Old Testament*, 3rd edition, Princeton, 1969

Spurgeon, C H "A Sermon and a Reminiscence" *Sword and Trowel,* March 1873,

Steinmann, Andrew "Lost World of Genesis One: John H. Walton, American Evangelicals and Creation" in *Lutheran Education Journal* 9 March 2012 (a review of Walton's *Lost World*)

——— " אחדas an Ordinal Number and the Meaning of Genesis 1:5" in the *Journal of the Evangelical Theological Society 45/4* Louisville, December, 2002

Stephens, Mark, *Annihilation or Renewal* Mohr Siebeck, Tubingen, 2011

Stewart, Angus "The Image of God in Man: A Reformed Reassessment" Covenant Protestant Reformed Church, Kells, Antrim, (Undated)

Tallman, Matthew "Pentecostal Ecology" in Amos Yong (Ed) *The Spirit Renews the Face of the Earth* Wipf and Stock, Eugene, 2009

Taylor, Justin Biblical Reasons to Doubt the Creation Days were 24-hour Periods The Gospel Coalition, 2015

Thistleton, Anthony C *Hermeneutics: An Introduction* Eerdmans, Cambridge, 2009

Thompson, Mark D *A Clear and Present Word: The Clarity of Scripture* (New Studies in Biblical Theology 21) Apollos, Nottingham, 2006

——— "Sola Scriptura" in Matthew Barrett (ed) *Reformation Theology: A Systematic Summary* Crossway, Wheaton, 2017

Toon, Peter *Our Triune God: A Biblical Portrayal of the Trinity* Bridge-Point, Wheaton, 1996

Dungen, Wim van den *Amun, the Great God :Hidden, One and Millions* v#5, Antwerp, 2015

——— On the Shabaka Stone, Antwerp, 2003,

Van Til, Cornelius *In Defense of the Faith Volume 3: Christian Theistic Ethics* P & R Phillipsburg, (undated)

Vanhoozer, Kevin J in Merrick & Garrett (Eds) *Five Views on Biblical Inerrancy* (Counter Points: Bible & Theology/Zondervan) Kindle, 2013

——— *Lost in Interpretation? Truth, Scripture and Hermeneutics* in the "Journal of the Evangelical Theological Society" (JETS), 48/1, Louisville, March, 2005

Vines, Matthew June 2015

Waltke, Bruce *Genesis, A Commentary*, Zondervan, Grand Rapids, 2001

Walton, John Ancient Near Eastern Thought and the Old Testament Baker Academic, Grand Rapids, 2006

——— *Genesis 1 As Ancient Cosmology* Eisenbrauns, Winona Lake, 2011

——— The Lost World of Genesis One: Ancient Cosmology and the Origins Debate IVP, Downers Grove, 2009

Walton, John and **Sandy,** Brent *The Lost World of Scripture: Ancient Literary Culture and Biblical Authority* IVP Academic, Downers Grove, 2013

Ware, Bruce "Eternal in Essence, Distinct in Roles *Journal for Biblical Manhood and Womanhood* Louisville, Fall 2008, Volume 13 #2 p43ff

——— The Man Christ Jesus: Theological Reflections on the Humanity of Christ Crossway, Wheaton, 2013

Warfield, B B The Biblical Idea of Inspiration Kindle Edition, 2013 [an extract from The Inspiration and Authority of the Bible 1948]

Weeks, Noel "Cosmology in Historical Context" *Westminster Theological Journal* WTJ68:2, Fall, 2006

——— "The Hermeneutical Problem of Genesis 1-11" *Themelios* 4.1, September, 1978

——— "Myth in the Ancient Near East" (undated paper supplied by Weeks)

——— *The Sufficiency of Scripture* Banner of Truth, Edinburgh, 1988

Wessel, "W W Blessing" in Douglas et al (Ed) *The New Bible Dictionary* IVP, London, 1962

White, Thomas I PhD *Whales, Dolphins and Ethics: A Primer* Whales and Dolphins Conservation

Williams, Michael *2 Peter 3 and the Destruction of the Earth* Third Millennium Ministries, (undated)

Wiseman, Donald *1 & 2 Kings: An Introductory Commentary* IVP, Nottingham, 1993

Young, E J *An Introduction to the Old Testament* Eerdmans, Grand Rapids, (Revised) 1960 (1949)

——— *An Introduction to the Old Testament* (revised) Tyndale Press, London, 1960 (1949)

——— In the Beginning: Genesis 1-3 and the Authority of Scripture The Banner of Truth Trust, Edinburgh 1984 (1976)

——— *Studies in Genesis 1* Presbyterian and Reformed, Nutlley (N.J.), 1957

——— *Thy Word is Truth* Banner of Truth, London, 1963

Zaspel, Fred "The Heavenly Temple" *Credo Magazine* 25 September 2013

Scripture Index

Index to Commentary on the Creation Week

Genesis

General Scripture Index

Genesis

Genesis continued

Exodus

General Index

Printed in Great Britain
by Amazon

65857569R00193